*Love*

OXFORD PHILOSOPHICAL CONCEPTS

OXFORD PHILOSOPHICAL CONCEPTS

Christia Mercer, Columbia University
*Series Editor*

PUBLISHED IN THE OXFORD PHILOSOPHICAL CONCEPTS SERIES

*Efficient Causation*
Edited by Tad Schmaltz

*Sympathy*
Edited by Eric Schliesser

*The Faculties*
Edited by Dominik Perler

*Memory*
Edited by Dmitri Nikulin

*Moral Motivation*
Edited by Iakovos Vasiliou

*Eternity*
Edited by Yitzhak Melamed

*Self-Knowledge*
Edited by Ursula Renz

*Embodiment*
Edited by Justin E. H. Smith

*Dignity*
Edited by Remy Debes

*Animals*
Edited by G. Fay Edwards and Peter Adamson

*Pleasure*
Edited by Lisa Shapiro

*Health*
Edited by Peter Adamson

*Evil*
Edited by Andrew Chignell

*Persons*
Edited by Antonia LoLordo

*Space*
Edited by Andrew Janiak

*Teleology*
Edited by Jeffrey K. McDonough

*The World Soul*
Edited by James Wilberding

*Powers*
Edited by Julia Jorati

*The Self*
Edited by Patricia Kitcher

*Human*
Edited by Karolina Hubner

*Modality*
Edited by Yitzhak Melamed and Samuel Newlands

*Love*
Edited by Ryan Patrick Hanley

FORTHCOMING IN THE OXFORD PHILOSOPHICAL CONCEPTS SERIES

*The Principle of Sufficient Reason*
Edited by Fatema Amijee and Michael Della Rocca

OXFORD PHILOSOPHICAL CONCEPTS

# Love

### A HISTORY

*Edited by Ryan Patrick Hanley*

OXFORD
UNIVERSITY PRESS

Oxford University Press is a department of the University of Oxford. It furthers
the University's objective of excellence in research, scholarship, and education
by publishing worldwide. Oxford is a registered trade mark of Oxford University
Press in the UK and certain other countries.

Published in the United States of America by Oxford University Press
198 Madison Avenue, New York, NY 10016, United States of America.

© Oxford University Press 2024

All rights reserved. No part of this publication may be reproduced, stored in
a retrieval system, or transmitted, in any form or by any means, without the
prior permission in writing of Oxford University Press, or as expressly permitted
by law, by license, or under terms agreed with the appropriate reproduction
rights organization. Inquiries concerning reproduction outside the scope of the
above should be sent to the Rights Department, Oxford University Press, at the
address above.

You must not circulate this work in any other form
and you must impose this same condition on any acquirer.

CIP data is on file at the Library of Congress

ISBN 978-0-19-753648-3 (pbk.)
ISBN 978-0-19-753647-6 (hbk.)

DOI: 10.1093/oso/9780197536476.001.0001

# Contents

SERIES EDITOR'S FOREWORD IX

LIST OF CONTRIBUTORS XI

Introduction: Love Transcendent and Immanent 1
RYAN PATRICK HANLEY

1. Love, Human and Divine in the Hebrew Bible and Judaic Tradition 16
LENN E. GOODMAN

2. Love in Plato and Aristotle 42
FRISBEE C. C. SHEFFIELD

*Reflection*: Platonic Love Poetry 66
ERIK GRAY

3. Love in the Christian Tradition 70
DAVID MCPHERSON

4. Love in Islamic Philosophy 94
WILLIAM C. CHITTICK

5. The Personal Experience of Transcendental Love: Mystics and Contemplatives in the Medieval Christian Tradition 126
CHRISTINA VAN DYKE

## CONTENTS

*Reflection*: Love That Moves: Dante, Petrarch, and Boccaccio 155
AKASH KUMAR

6. Turning toward the One / Good: Marsilio Ficino's Philosophy of Love 159
DENIS J.-J. ROBICHAUD

7. A Metaphysical Basis for Love? Descartes and Spinoza on the Metaphysics of Love 179
PATRICK R. FRIERSON

8. Anne Conway on the Love-Worthiness and Perfectibility of All Things 204
CHRISTIA MERCER

*Reflection*: Love, Sculpture, and Gian Lorenzo Bernini 226
INGRID ROWLAND

9. Love in Kant and the Enlightenment 235
MELISSA SEYMOUR FAHMY

10. Beyond the realms of dream that fleeting shade: Rousseau on Romantic Love 259
EVE GRACE

*Reflection*: Love in Jane Austen's Novels 282
ALBERT J. RIVERO

11. Kierkegaard's Theistic Conception of Love, Existentially Considered 287
SHARON KRISHEK

*Reflection*: The Concept of Love in Modern Psychology 311
ROBERT J. STERNBERG

12. Love and Desire in Nietzsche and Levinas 316
FIONA ELLIS

*Reflection*: Love as Social Force: Martin Luther King Jr. 339
ANDRE C. WILLIS

GENERAL BIBLIOGRAPHY 343

INDEX 369

# Series Editor's Foreword

Oxford Philosophical Concepts (OPC) offers an innovative approach to philosophy's past and its relation to other disciplines. As a series, it is unique in exploring the transformations of central philosophical concepts from their ancient sources to their modern use.

OPC has several goals: to make it easier for historians to contextualize key concepts in the history of philosophy, to render that history accessible to a wide audience, and to enliven contemporary discussions by displaying the rich and varied sources of philosophical concepts still in use today. The means to these goals are simple enough: eminent scholars come together to rethink a central concept in philosophy's past. The point of this rethinking is not to offer a broad overview, but to identify problems the concept was originally supposed to solve and investigate how approaches to them shifted over time, sometimes radically. Recent scholarship has made evident the benefits of reexamining the standard narratives about western philosophy. OPC's editors look beyond the canon and explore their concepts over a wide philosophical landscape. Each volume traces a notion from its inception as a solution to specific problems through its historical transformations to its modern use, all the while acknowledging its historical context. Each OPC volume is a history of its concept in that it tells a story about changing solutions to its well-defined problem. Many editors have found it appropriate to include long-ignored writings drawn from the

Islamic and Jewish traditions and the philosophical contributions of women. Volumes also explore ideas drawn from Buddhist, Chinese, Indian, and other philosophical cultures when doing so adds an especially helpful new perspective. By combining scholarly innovation with focused and astute analysis, OPC encourages a deeper understanding of our philosophical past and present.

One of the most innovative features of Oxford Philosophical Concepts is its recognition that philosophy bears a rich relation to art, music, literature, religion, science, and other cultural practices. The series speaks to the need for informed interdisciplinary exchanges. Its editors assume that the most difficult and profound philosophical ideas can be made comprehensible to a large audience and that materials not strictly philosophical often bear a significant relevance to philosophy. To this end, each OPC volume includes Reflections. These are short stand-alone essays written by specialists in art, music, literature, theology, science, or cultural studies that reflect on the concept from their own disciplinary perspectives. The goal of these essays is to enliven, enrich, and exemplify the volume's concept and reconsider the boundary between philosophical and extraphilosophical materials. OPC's Reflections display the benefits of using philosophical concepts and distinctions in areas that are not strictly philosophical, and encourage philosophers to move beyond the borders of their discipline as presently conceived.

The volumes of OPC arrive at an auspicious moment. Many philosophers are keen to invigorate the discipline. OPC aims to provoke philosophical imaginations by uncovering the brilliant twists and unforeseen turns of philosophy's past.

Christia Mercer<br>
Gustave M. Berne Professor of Philosophy<br>
Columbia University in the City of New York

# Contributors

WILLIAM C. CHITTICK is Distinguished Professor in the Department of Asian and Asian American Studies at Stony Brook University. Among his many books are *The Heart of Islamic Philosophy* (Oxford, 2001) and *Divine Love* (Yale, 2013).

FIONA ELLIS is Professor of Philosophy at the University of Nottingham. Her most recent monograph is *God, Value, and Nature* (OUP, 2014), and she has published on a variety of subjects including the philosophy of love and desire, the meaning of life, and the nature of religious understanding. She has recently been awarded a Visiting Fellowship at the University of Florida to work on a new monograph entitled *The End of Desire: Meaning, Nihilism, and God*.

MELISSA SEYMOUR FAHMY is Associate Professor at the University of Georgia. Her primary research interest is Kantian ethics, with particular focus on duties of love and respect, as well as the intersection of morality and happiness. Her work has appeared in *Kantian Review*, *Pacific Philosophical Quarterly*, and *The Journal of Value Inquiry*.

PATRICK R. FRIERSON is the Paul Piggott and William M. Allen Professor of Ethics and Philosophy at Whitman College. He writes extensively on modern philosophy, particularly Descartes, Adam Smith, Kant, and Maria Montessori. His publications include "Learning to Love: From Egoism to Generosity in Descartes" (*Journal of the History of Philosophy*, 2002), *What Is the Human Being?* (Routledge, 2013), and, most recently, *Maria Montessori's Moral Philosophy* (Bloomsbury, 2022).

LENN E. GOODMAN is Professor of Philosophy and Andrew W. Mellon Professor in the Humanities at Vanderbilt University. His books include *Judaism: A Contemporary Philosophical Investigation*; *On Justice*; *Creation and Evolution*; *In Defense of Truth*; *Religious Pluralism and Values in the Public Sphere*; *God of Abraham*; and his Gifford Lectures: *Love Thy Neighbor as Thyself*.

EVE GRACE teaches political philosophy at Colorado College. She is coeditor (with Christopher Kelly) of *Rousseau on Women, Love, and Family* (2009), *The Challenge of Rousseau* (2013), and most recently, *The Rousseauian Mind* (2019).

ERIK GRAY is Professor of English and Comparative Literature at Columbia University. He is the author, most recently, of *The Art of Love Poetry*, a transhistorical study of the relation between poetry and love in the Western tradition.

RYAN PATRICK HANLEY is Professor of Political Science at Boston College. A specialist in the moral and political philosophy of the Enlightenment, he is the author of *Adam Smith and the Character of Virtue*; *Love's Enlightenment: Rethinking Charity in Modernity*; and *Our Great Purpose: Adam Smith on Living a Better Life*. He is also the author of *The Political Philosophy of Fénelon* and translator of *Fénelon: Moral and Political Writings*, both recently published by Oxford.

SHARON KRISHEK is Associate Professor at the Philosophy Department at the Hebrew University of Jerusalem. She specializes in the philosophy of Kierkegaard and is the author of *Kierkegaard on Faith and Love* (Cambridge University Press, 2009), *Kierkegaard's Philosophy of Love* (in Hebrew, 2011), and *Lovers in Essence: A Kierkegaardian Defense of Romantic Love* (Oxford University Press, 2022).

AKASH KUMAR is an Assistant Professor of Italian Studies at UC Berkeley. His research primarily focuses on Dante and thirteenth-century Italian lyric through the lens of the history of science, Mediterranean and global exchange, and digital humanities. Recent work includes collaborating with Richard Lansing on the first complete English translation of the poetry of Giacomo da Lentini, contributions on Dante to Wiley-Blackwell's *Companion to World Literature*, the *Oxford Handbook of Dante*, and an essay on Dante and migration in the volume *Migrants Shaping Europe, Past and Present* (Manchester University Press, 2022).

He is currently finishing his first book, *Dante's Elements: Translation and Natural Philosophy from Giacomo da Lentini to the* Comedy.

DAVID MCPHERSON is Professor of Philosophy in the Hamilton Center for Classical and Civic Education at the University of Florida. He has previously held positions at Creighton University and the University of Colorado-Boulder. He works in the areas of ethics (especially virtue ethics), political philosophy, meaning in life, and philosophy of religion. He is the author of *The Virtues of Limits* (Oxford University Press, 2022), and *Virtue and Meaning: A Neo-Aristotelian Perspective* (Cambridge University Press, 2020), as well as the editor of *Spirituality and the Good Life: Philosophical Approaches* (Cambridge University Press, 2017). He is currently working on his third book monograph, *Spiritual Alienation and the Quest for God*.

CHRISTIA MERCER is the Gustave M. Berne Professor of Philosophy at Columbia University; general editor of *Oxford Philosophical Concepts*; coeditor of *Oxford New Histories of Philosophy*, a book series devoted to making philosophy more inclusive; and creator and director of the Center for New Narratives in Philosophy at Columbia. She also created and oversees Just Ideas, an educational program in Brooklyn's high-security Metropolitan Detention Center.

ALBERT J. RIVERO, Louise Edna Goeden Professor of English at Marquette University, has published widely on the literature of the British long eighteenth century. He has edited Samuel Richardson's *Pamela: or, Virtue Rewarded* and *Pamela in Her Exalted Condition*, published by Cambridge University Press, as well as Norton Critical Editions of Jonathan Swift's *Gulliver's Travels* and Daniel Defoe's *Moll Flanders*.

DENIS J.-J. ROBICHAUD is the John and Patrice Kelly Associate Professor in the Program of Liberal Studies, University of Notre Dame. He is the director of Physis: ND Laboratory for the Study of Nature in the Premodern World. He holds concurrent appointments in Philosophy, Medieval Institute, Italian Studies, and History and Philosophy of Science.

INGRID ROWLAND lives in Rome, where she is a Professor of History at the University of Notre Dame and writes on a variety of subjects for both general and scholarly readers. She won the Grace Dudley Prize for Arts Writing in 2022.

FRISBEE C. C. SHEFFIELD is an Associate Professor of Classics and a Fellow of Downing College, Cambridge. She works on ancient Greek philosophy, particularly ethics, moral psychology, aesthetics, and politics. She also works on the reception of ancient Greek philosophy in Hannah Arendt. She is the author of *Plato's Symposium: The Ethics of Desire* (2006) as well as coeditor of a collection of essays: *Plato's Symposium: Issues in Interpretation and Reception* (2006); coeditor of a new edition of Plato's *Symposium*, for the Cambridge Texts in the History of Philosophy series (2008); and coeditor of *The Routledge Companion to Ancient Philosophy* (2013).

ROBERT J. STERNBERG is Professor of Psychology at Cornell University and Honorary Professor of Psychology at the University of Heidelberg. His PhD is from Stanford, and he holds thirteen honorary doctorates. He has won the Grawemeyer Prize in Psychology as well as the William James and James McKeen Cattell Awards from the Association for Psychological Science. He is past president of the American Psychological Association.

CHRISTINA VAN DYKE is Term Professor of Philosophy at Barnard College of Columbia University, and Professor Emerita of Philosophy at Calvin University. Associate editor of the *Cambridge History of Medieval Philosophy*, Van Dyke is the author of *A Hidden Wisdom: Medieval Contemplatives on Self-Knowledge, Reason, Love, Persons, and Immortality* (Oxford University Press, 2023).

ANDRE C. WILLIS is Associate Professor of Religious Studies at Brown University. He is a philosopher of religion whose work focuses on Enlightenment reflections on religion, African American religious thought, critical theory, and democratic citizenship as it relates to "religious" notions of hope, recognition, and belonging. He is the author of *Towards a Humean True Religion* (2015).

# Introduction

LOVE TRANSCENDENT AND IMMANENT

*Ryan Patrick Hanley*

Can love be understood philosophically? Ask someone in love, and they're likely to say it can't be: love, every lover knows, is something we feel in our hearts, not something we think in our heads. Reasoning about love thus will strike some as missing the point, serving merely to blind us to the full range and extent of love's wonders. Even a philosopher might sometimes be sympathetic to this sort of skepticism; anyone who has been in love knows very well that love's vastness and intensity resist analysis.

And yet the truth is that the very vastness and intensity of love that render it so singular a phenomenon also make it impossible for us *not* to consider it philosophically. Love's vastness and intensity after all bring love into so many spheres of our lives: ethical, political, spiritual, and physical. Further, love's penetrability into so much of our lives renders considerations of what it means to love and to be loved, and what is worth loving and worth being, inextricable from our fundamental commitments in ethics, politics, religion, and metaphysics. Love then is impossible for philosophers to ignore—which explains, at least in part, why love has been a central concept of philosophical inquiry over the last several millennia, in the West and beyond.

The aim of this volume is to bring to the fore, and thereby tell the story, of some of the most significant moments in the history of how philosophers have thought about love over the course of this period. In keeping with the aims of the Oxford Philosophical Concepts series, it specifically aims to chronicle certain of the most significant events in this concept's long and complex evolutionary life. That said, it should be emphasized from the start that the story it traces is necessarily a selective one given the vastness of the terrain it aspires to examine. And with regard to the specific concept of love, this vastness makes itself felt in at least two different ways.

The first concerns the concept's substantive scope. The English word "love" famously encompasses a dizzying array of phenomena— phenomena whose relationships to each other are, at first glance, far from obvious. What, if anything, makes it possible for us to use the same word to describe our feelings toward such disparate entities as our pets, our friends, our children, our countries, our gods, our partners, our neighbors, our favorite flavors of ice cream? Substantively the concept of love is vast, and contains multitudes.

As if this weren't enough, the vastness of the concept of love also makes itself felt in a second and different way. This concerns the sheer range of thinkers and traditions that have set forth important reflections on the concept of love over the course of its history. Love simply has been and surely will continue to be a focal concept of inquiry for philosophers from a strikingly diverse range of orientations and specializations. This is especially evident today. Recent years have witnessed a resurgence of interest in the philosophy of love, with new studies examining it from a range of contemporary philosophical perspectives.[1] Even so—and perhaps of more direct relevance to this volume—love has a special place in the history of philosophy. Love was famously central to many ancient religions as well as to many classical philosophical traditions. Love remained a core concept of inquiry in the medieval period and the Renaissance, permeating not only philosophical discourse but also the preeminent theological, literary, poetic, and artistic contributions of these ages. And even amid the political and philosophical upheavals of the early modern period, love remained a key concept of philosophical inquiry throughout the long period extending from the revolutions of early modernity through Romanticism down to the more recent emergence of the natural and the social sciences.

All of which is to say that both the substantive range of and the history of reflection on the concept of love is strikingly—dauntingly—vast. Aspiring to tell the whole history of this concept in a single volume would be a fool's errand; even Irving Singer, in what remains the most comprehensive history of love available to us, took three thick volumes to tell his version of the story.[2] In light of this challenge, and in an effort not to duplicate the work of Singer and others whose books offer their own narrative histories, this volume aspires to fulfill two specific functions. First, its individual chapters aim to provide readers with introductions to what most would agree are some of the most significant moments in the history of philosophizing on love. Much of course is open to contention here, and many of us (myself

---

[1] Among many others, see, e.g., Harry Frankfurt, *The Reasons of Love* (Princeton, NJ: Princeton University Press, 2006); Luc Ferry, *On Love: A Philosophy for the Twenty-First Century*, trans. Andrew Brown (London: Polity, 2013); Berit Brogaard, *On Romantic Love: Simple Truths about a Complex Emotion* (New York: Oxford University Press, 2015); Carrie Jenkins, *What Love Is: And What It Could Be* (New York: Basic Books, 2017); and Patricia Mariano, *Philosophy of Sex and Love: An Opinionated Introduction* (London: Routledge, 2019).

[2] Irving Singer, *The Nature of Love*, 3 vols. (Chicago: University of Chicago Press, 1987–1994). See also Simon May, *Love: A History* (New Haven, CT: Yale University Press, 2011).

included) will have favorite thinkers not included here even as strong cases could be made for including them.³ But a single volume necessarily has limits, and thus the scope of this volume's coverage has been consciously restricted to interventions most would agree represent important, if not decisive, turning points in the evolution of the concept of love. Each chapter thus aspires to provide an introduction to one such turning point, and to do so in a way useful to nonspecialist readers yet also of interest to experts on these thinkers and periods.

But this volume also has another aim. Even as it presents itself as a collection of discrete chapters by individual contributors, the volume aspires to offer something more than just a mere recounting of a series of isolated highlights. It also aims to tell an interconnected story, such that those who read it cover to cover will glean a sense of the arc of the historical evolution of the concept of love. In this sense, the volume seeks not only to present a series of studies of crucial interventions in the history of thinking about love, but to bring these moments together in a way that encourages readers to speculate for themselves as to how these discrete moments might hang together in an intelligible way.

What then is the trajectory of this arc? At least a few key features demand notice at the outset. First and most importantly: a central idea behind the history of philosophical reflections on love traced in this volume is that the concept of love has not only experienced an evolution over time, but that this evolution has been decisively shaped by a particular revolution. Put most simply and briefly: this revolution consists in the way in which the concepts of love bequeathed to us by ancient philosophical and religious traditions were transformed by later philosophers who operated under very different conceptions of love's meaning and horizons. Specifically, where early religious and philosophical concepts of love tended to focus on love's relationship to the transcendent, more modern concepts of love have tended to

---

3 My own candidate: the seventeenth-century pure love debate and specifically the contributions of François Fénelon. See esp. Jacques Le Brun, *Le pur amour. De Platon à Lacan* (Paris: Seuil, 2002).

focus on love's relationship to the immanent. Thus, where ancient love concepts often emphasize the ways in which lovers are connected to phenomena that exist in a world beyond the self—phenomena such as the divine, or the good, or the beautiful—modern conceptions of love often emphasize the ways in which love connects lovers to other beings in this world, as well as the ways in which love is subjectively experienced by selves who exist in specific times and places, and which are determined by the conditions of their embodiment and their capacities for sensation.

Among the questions this transformation raises for a historian of philosophy is that of just how exactly this revolution came to be. How then did the ancient focus on the connection of the lover with the transcendent sphere come to give way to the focus on the experience of the lover's connection to other selves in this world characteristic of modern conceptions of love? How, that is, did the broad concepts of love familiar to us from various ancient traditions—*eros* and *agape*, among others—come to be supplanted by a concept of love that privileged the passionate love of one human being for and by another human being: what we today often think of as "romantic" love? Indeed for students of the history of the concept of love, this may well be the question that most demands attention: namely, how did romantic love come to be regarded as the quintessence of love, specifically at the expense of concepts grounded in the relationship of the human being to transcendent categories of the divine or the good or the beautiful?

With this question in mind, the chapters of this volume can be seen as organized into three rough groupings. The first group of chapters examines a set of ancient philosophical and religious ways of thinking about love, including those found in Judaic and Christian and Greek and Islamic religious and philosophical traditions. At least some of the love concepts that were central to these traditions are likely to be familiar even to nonspecialists, including, for example, the already-mentioned Greek concept of *eros*, and the biblical commands to love God above all else and to love one's neighbor as oneself. Different readers may be drawn to one or another of the chapters and concepts in this group, but one effect of reading the four chapters of this group together is that doing so can help us see the degree to which the discrete love concepts developed in the Judaic, Christian, Greek, and Islamic traditions are bound together by a common interest in the relationship of love to the transcendent. The second group of chapters examines the ways in which thinkers from the medieval period through the late Enlightenment conceived of love. This periodization may initially seem strange to those historians of philosophy accustomed to seeing early modernity in terms of a sharp break from the past. But an advantage of treating these eras together is that doing so helps bring into relief the ways in which a more immanent perspective on love began to emerge alongside a persistent interest in love's transcendent elements. The final section of the volume then examines the history of the concept of love from the beginning of the revolution inaugurated by Romanticism through the mid-twentieth century. The essays in this section call attention to the ways in which the concept of love came to be more explicitly and exclusively associated with sexual desire, and ever more distanced from certain more expansive traditional concepts.

Within each of the individual essays in these general sections, several specific claims are especially deserving of notice at the outset, as they can help bring into relief some of the ways in which each of the chapters contributes to the volume's larger arc. The volume begins with Lenn Goodman's study of human love and divine love in the Hebrew Bible and in the Judaic tradition. Goodman's point of departure is the twofold character of love in the Hebrew Bible: a love, as he says, that is "both natural and divine"—at once "a law of nature and a divine command." Love's transcendent dimension is thus on prominent display here and in what follows, as Goodman goes on to show the degree to which many of the Hebrew Bible's most familiar love stories—the first love of Adam and Eve, the marriage of Abraham and Sarah, the friendship of Jonathan and David—represent not simply human loves but ones that stand in accord with divine will and command. Even the love of the Song of Songs, amid all of its erotics, represents a manifestation, Goodman explains, of "the soul's link to God." Further, as the second half of Goodman's essay emphasizes, the connection of love to divinity is evident not only in the Hebrew Bible's portraits of marriage and friendship but also in later Judaic thinkers' reflections on other types of ethical love. These include the idea of *tzedakah*—the human being's practical emulation of God's acts of grace and justice—and the concept of *ḥesed*—the "loving kindness" that demands both grace and generosity. As Goodman compellingly shows, for Judaic philosophers such as Maimonides, these loves represent efforts of the human being to rise not just to "union" but to "communion" with the divine.

The volume's next essay turns to the ancient Greeks. In her study of Plato and Aristotle, Frisbee Sheffield makes clear that the divine is no less central to Greek concepts of love than it is to the Judaic and Christian love concepts profiled in the chapters preceding and following hers. Greek philosophical reflection on love, Sheffield notes, begins with Parmenides—for whom "the first god was Love"—and reaches its pinnacle in Platonic philosophy, here described as "the first stage of an enduring preoccupation in the Western tradition with the transformative potential of a love that can lead to the divine." This preoccupation is especially evident, Sheffield explains, in the famous account of the ascent of *eros* in Plato's *Symposium*, with its emphasis on the human being's love of the beautiful, and specifically the human desire for a "cognitive communion with a divine beauty" that "promises to deliver that 'god-like' state of stable and secure *eudaimonia*"—a view further developed in Erik Gray's reflection on Platonic love poetry, which shows how for Socrates, the "madness of love is a form of higher knowledge and insight." And noting that Plato was hardly the only Greek philosopher to examine the relationship of love to *eudaimonia*, Sheffield turns to Aristotle's concept of friendship-love, or *philia*. But one of the most welcome elements of the chapter is Sheffield's turn from the comparatively well-known ideas of Platonic *eros* and Aristotelian *philia* to the less well appreciated place of *eros* in

Aristotle and of *philia* in Plato, a turn likely to be of considerable interest to specialists, especially given the way in which Sheffield shows how these treatments can mitigate concerns that ancient ethics either privileges "egoism" or is "limited to self-interested concerns."

The volume's third chapter, by David McPherson, aims to survey the "main contours of Christian love," specifically as manifested in the New Testament, in Augustine and Aquinas, and in the work of Anders Nygren, the Swedish theologian famed for having set forth what many yet regard as the twentieth century's most influential theological treatment of Christian love. Calling attention to the undeniable "centrality" of love to Christian thought, McPherson begins with Jesus's two commandments to love God above all and to love one's neighbor as one's self—commandments that themselves of course restate the injunctions of the Hebrew Bible examined in Goodman's chapter. Here the transcendent dimension of love is especially evident. For not only is the Christian commanded to love the divine above all else, but the human being is, it is explained, on this basis called to a "demanding" and indeed "unconditional" love of neighbor that requires pursuit of an ideal perfection that may in fact be "humanly unattainable" and can at best be "approximated." The centrality of the transcendent within human love reappears in the treatment of Augustine and Aquinas, in which McPherson shows that for both thinkers, "rightly ordered love" requires above all else loving the right things in the right ways, specifically in such a way that God is recognized as the highest good, to be loved for Himself, with all else to be loved specifically for His sake. This emphasis reappears in the concluding treatment of Nygren's "caritas synthesis," which notes that human beings are fundamentally "beings made in the image of God who thus have intrinsic dignity and are loveworthy" and hence beings for whom the act of loving others requires a "self-transcendence" that alone enables us "to affirm the goodness of the beloved's existence."

The last chapter in this section of the volume is William Chittick's study of Islamic love poetry and philosophy. The texts on which

Chittick focuses may be less familiar to some readers than those examined in the previous three chapters, but the themes Chittick develops in his interpretations of these texts have evident connections to themes developed by Goodman, Sheffield, and McPherson. For here too the central category at issue is the relationship of love to divine perfection, a relationship especially evident in Chittick's account of the Sufi concept of love as representing at once "God's motive for creating the universe" as well as "the means whereby human beings can actualize their true humanity." As Chittick shows, the idea of divine love was seen by various Islamic thinkers as having crucial implications for the human being, for whom love was "an ontological reality, the divine force that brings possible things into existence with no external motivation." Chittick then turns to the way in which Islamic thinkers in their own modalities emphasized the necessity of the "return" to the divine, and, in particular, the significance of the human aim to realize perfection through "loving beauty and yearning for union with it"—an idea that resonates with Sheffield's examining of Greek *eros* as a longing for everlasting possession of the transcendent beautiful. Those interested in this concept of return will especially wish to attend to Chittick's treatment of Avicenna, who regards the rational soul as having "the potential to become a fully actualized intellect, unified with the Universal Intellect"—a being defined by the act of "seeking the good and the beautiful," whose "seeking is called 'love.'" From the texts of the Brethren to those of Avicenna to the observations of Mulla Sandra, foundational to Chittick's account of love is the core Islamic idea that "the human soul achieves perfection by way of love and yearning for the Necessary Existence."

It will be obvious, even from this brief overview, that all four traditions of thinking about love examined in the volume's opening section—Hebraic, Christian, Greek, Islamic—focus on the idea of the transcendent, and regard love within the context of the human being's longing to rejoin and reunify with the absolutely good and beautiful. But new understandings of love begin to emerge in the chapters that follow. One is the focus of Christina Van Dyke's chapter on love in medieval contemplative philosophy. Focusing on several thirteenth- and fourteenth-century mystical thinkers and their relationship to the courtly love, or *fin 'amor*, tradition, Van Dyke reveals the late medieval mystics' sensitivity to the "personal experience" of love. As Van Dyke shows, central to the thought of these mystics was their concern not only to define transcendental love but also to describe how it is practiced and experienced—a new stage of thinking about love in which to the traditional interest in the transcendent is joined a concern for and sensitivity to love's subjective experience, leading to a way of thinking about love that seeks to harmonize the "higher" and the "lower" faculties, and in so doing challenges the familiar distinction between "sacred love" and "secular love."

Denis Robichaud turns in the next chapter to the philosophy of love developed by the fifteenth-century Platonist Marsilio Ficino. As Robichaud shows, in his commentary on Plato's *Symposium*, Ficino developed a theory of love that was at once "henological" (that is, focused on the One) and "agathological" (that is, focused on the Good). Fundamental to this view was an "understanding of love as conversion or reversion to God," which the Platonist will identify with the One and the Good. In this, Ficino too draws on familiar traditional conceptions. But as Robichaud also shows—and indeed in ways that interestingly dovetail with the themes of the previous chapter—Ficino's philosophy of love is distinguished by its sensitivity to the place of desire, and especially the desire of the individual to return to the One. In so doing, Ficino too brings us to the intersection of traditional ideas of transcendent being and emerging ideas of the experience of desire, developing a concept of love as a "third term between lover and beloved" that "is itself the link that holds together the whole edifice within both hypercosmic and encosmic levels, and in turn also binds both levels together."

This emergent interest in the affective dimension of love chronicled in these chapters is continued in the reflections that follow. Akash

Kumar's reflection on Renaissance conceptions of love in the literary works of Dante and Petrarch and Boccaccio focuses on the relationships between human lovers rather than the relationship of human to divine—a turn to the immanent and affective that is also present in Ingrid Rowland's reflection on Bernini, which focuses on the sculptor's efforts to portray not only "spiritual ecstasy" but also "carnal love." And in Patrick Frierson's study of Descartes and Spinoza we begin to see the philosophical implications of this turn. Frierson's essay focuses on Descartes's efforts to articulate a concept of love "grounded in rationalist metaphysics." As Frierson shows, Descartes himself did not simply jettison altogether the older ways of thinking about love; even in Descartes, the idea that love represents a kind of "joining" remains central. But unlike Plato and Avicenna and other thinkers profiled in the first section of the volume, for Descartes the joining that matters is not the joining of the human to the divine but in fact the joining of self to other selves. Yet this raises challenges, Frierson shows, noting how in Descartes's case "the unity constitutive of love is inconsistent with core features of his metaphysics," and how in Spinoza's case the "love of God" is reduced to "pleasure in self-preservation." Frierson's chapter is followed by Christia Mercer's study of Anne Conway's theory of love, which forms another sort of bridge between traditional and more modern ways of thinking about love. The particular focus of Mercer's chapter is the "liminal space that Conway's philosophy occupies between transcendent and intimate kinds of love," and in delineating this space, Mercer specifically shows how Conway joins to a love of God and God's perfections a loving "bond among creatures" that is "one of passionate affection and devotion, resulting in an increasingly intimate relation between each creature and its beloved companions"—one that culminates in "a community of loving and love-worthy beings, intimately and sympathetically related."

The two essays that follow shift focus to the eighteenth century yet continue to probe the place of affect in love. The first of these is on Kant, a thinker not often considered as a theorist of love, thanks in large part to his famed critique of moral sentimentalism in the *Groundwork*. But as Melissa Fahmy makes clear, any caricatured view of Kant in which the *Groundwork* is taken to represent either the core or the whole of Kant's moral theory fails to do justice to Kant's belief that in fact "certain feelings are morally important." One key moral feeling Fahmy examines is the "aesthetic appreciation for beautiful inanimate nature"—a feeling Kant says helps to prepare human beings "for moral life." Drawing on and developing the focus on the role of sentiment in practical morality that has been of growing interest to recent Kant scholars, Fahmy casts helpful light on a side of Kant's moral theory that will be of interest both to specialists and students of the ancient traditions profiled in the first part of this volume—traditions that receive prominent echoes in Kant's emphasis on the "moral force" of love and the role of the beautiful in it, as well as Kant's explicit and sustained interest in Jesus's teachings on the two fundamental commands.

The second eighteenth-century thinker profiled is Rousseau. Placing Rousseau after Kant may seem anomalous given his influence on Kant. But in terms of the trajectory of the history of love, placing Rousseau after Kant makes sense insofar as it was Rousseau's and not Kant's ideas of love that would live on in the nineteenth century—a glimpse of which we are given in Albert Rivero's reflection on Jane Austen's views on romantic love and courtship and marriage, and in particular "the difficulty of governing the visceral demands of love." But beyond Austen, and as Eve Grace notes in her chapter on Rousseau, Rousseau's influence on the Romantics has been so often pointed out that it has become almost a "threadbare platitude." Even so, this influence is still worth mentioning given the pivotal role that his thoughts on love play in the wider history of the concept. As Grace also shows, for all the ways in which Rousseau's concept of love looks back to Socrates's—similarities especially evident in their shared emphasis on love's intensity and the way it inspires "enthusiasm"—ultimately Rousseau's theory of love trails in Descartes's wake and not Plato's. For not only does Rousseau feel compelled to grapple with the challenges of dualism, but he also works with a decidedly modern conception of the human person, one in which "human or rather animal life has no end or *telos*" and which is premised on the idea that "there is no good but pleasure." This turn not only distances Rousseau from earlier views of human nature but also leads Grace to speculate that "Rousseau's account of human beings and of love seems as relentlessly reductionist as any that he decries," and to suggest that his emphasis on metaphysical joining ultimately rests only on "an illusion," even as "it is only under the spell of illusion, paradoxically, that nature comes to fruition."

The volume's final essays bring us into the nineteenth and twentieth centuries. In her study of Kierkegaard, Sharon Krishek profiles one of modernity's preeminent theorists of love and in so doing takes up a question central to the trajectory of the volume. For Krishek, at the heart of Kierkegaard's theory of love is the question of the relationship between commanded Christian neighbor-love and spontaneous feelings of romantic love—on the one hand, a love that demands self-denial in the name of universalism, and on the other, a love that privileges not only feeling but also particularity and indeed the preferentiality of one individual over another. For students of Kierkegaard, this question in part gives rise to an interpretive question of how the theory of love developed in his *Fear and Trembling* comports with the theory of love advanced in his *Works of Love*. For students of love this raises the crucial question of how and whether the universality characteristic of Christian love can be reconciled with the particularity characteristic of erotic love—that is, in Krishek's words, how and whether it might be possible "to return to one's self while denying one's self."

The volume's final chapter, by Fiona Ellis, turns to Nietzsche and Levinas. It is of course with Nietzsche that the critique of transcendent love reaches its apex; as Ellis notes, Nietzsche's focus on what has been called "'an art of this-worldly love'" was deliberately framed by him as an alternative to various "otherworldly" concepts. But for all the vociferousness of his critique of Christianity, Nietzsche took very seriously indeed the question opened up by the alternative that he envisioned: namely "whether desire's transfigurative power can be accommodated in the absence of God." The question of desire so central to Nietzsche would in time come to animate much later social scientific research on love; indeed as Robert Sternberg's reflection on love and modern psychology shows, the concepts of desire and attachment forged in Nietzsche's wake by Freud have gone on to be extensively developed and challenged by later psychologists, including Sternberg's own accounts of intimacy, passion, and commitment. But with regard to desire Ellis's own focus is Levinas, one of whose chief concerns, Ellis shows, was to conceive of desire as a means by which we might "'express' the infinite"—a way by which individuals can develop a "picture of striving without the illusion of a lack to be filled." Levinas's is ultimately a view of desire that raises the question of whether indeed we can "accommodate the possibility of this insatiable power without reference to God."

Taken collectively, it is hoped that these essays will call attention not only to several of the most important moments in the evolution of the concept of love but also to the revolutionary shift that occurred in the long arc of the evolution of the concept itself, as more immanent concepts of love came first to supplement and later to supplant transcendent concepts. At the same time, it is crucial to note that this shift, fundamental and revolutionary as it may have been, was far from absolute. This is a point brought powerfully home in Andre Willis's concluding reflection on Martin Luther King Jr. As Willis shows, King's idea of love bears witness to the fact that even in the twentieth century some "jettisoned sentimental appeals to love and deemphasized its romantic qualities," and, in King's case, led him to reconceive love instead as a "social force" capable of inspiring political change. King himself, of course, drew on Christian ideas of love in developing this idea, and remembering this compels us to remind ourselves that the ways we think and talk about love today still retain certain resonances or vestiges of the language and ideas of transcendence. Put differently, love's revolution is yet incomplete; we may live in a modern and secular age, but the ancient and religious resonances of older love concepts remain with us today as part of the way we talk and think about love. The contributions of these traditions are thus not only integral parts of the evolutionary prehistory of our own concept of love, but in many ways their arguments and assumptions remain embedded in our concept. The result is that if we hope fully to understand what the concept of love might mean today, it will be helpful, if not necessary, for us to revisit the history of the concept and familiarize ourselves with the ways in which the specific stages in its evolution contributed to the particular concepts of love that have been bequeathed to us by this evolution—and which we, even today, are continuing to transform. Our concept of love and the history of our concept of love are then inextricable, and by chronicling this philosophical history this volume will, it is hoped, be useful both to historians of philosophy and readers seeking to better understand what exactly is encompassed by our concepts of love today.

CHAPTER 1

# Love, Human and Divine in the Hebrew Bible and Judaic Tradition

*Lenn E. Goodman*

Love in the Hebrew Bible is both natural and divine, at once a law of nature and a divine command. God shows His love in the act of creation and in the concern invested in that act, but also in revelation. God blesses His creatures but also speaks to them, at first informally, a familiar if somewhat overwhelming presence; later, more publicly, with an intricate body of law and precepts setting out a way of life. The recipients of that law are to love God with all their hearts and souls and might, but also to emulate the very holiness that seems to set God apart from them and their world, where life and joy and light itself are painted as the gifts of a love beyond desert.

Lenn E. Goodman, *Love, Human and Divine in the Hebrew Bible and Judaic Tradition*
In: *Love*. Edited by: Ryan Patrick Hanley, Oxford University Press. © Oxford University Press 2024.
DOI: 10.1093/oso/9780197536476.003.0002

## First Love

The Torah opens its story of humanity by telling of a first human couple, not master and slave but a woman and a man. Eve, Adam realizes on first beholding her, is the counterpart he has searched for among the creatures in God's garden (Genesis 2:20)—*bone of my bones and flesh of my flesh* (2:23). He and she, he sees, are not alien to one another. Both, in fact, are created in God's image (1:26–27)—not in bodily form. For bodily they differ. Yet they are counterparts (2:18). Torah speaks of God's fashioning Eve from Adam's rib (or side) to disclose his recognition of their deep affinity, firmly blocking the idea of an immemorial battle between the sexes. Men are not from Mars; women, not from Venus. Both are from God—and of the same earth (2:7, 3:19).

Genesis does not explore God's motives for creating. It does find God seeing the good in all His creations. Once tenanted with human beings, the world God sees is *very good* (1:31). God does state a reason for creating woman: *It is not good for a man to be alone* (2:18). From humanity's bearing God's image, Genesis draws an inference: The human person is sacred. All life must be respected. Hence the norms about the blood of animals (9:4) and against permitting suffering to a beast[1]—and protecting fruit trees even in wartime (Deuteronomy 20:19), leading to the rabbis' prohibiting any wanton destruction.[2] God cares about His creatures. But shedding human blood is a grave breach of God's trust, not commensurate with animal slaughter (Genesis 9:6).

Since men and women are of common bone and flesh, Genesis infers that the loyalty spouses owe each other runs deeper than even filial bonds. The Torah celebrates the primal union with a norm that is at once a social fact and a moral prescription: *Therefore does a man leave his father and his mother and cleave to his wife* (Genesis 2:24).

---

[1] The Babylonian Talmud [hereafter B.], Bava Metzia 32b, interpreting Exodus 23:5, Deuteronomy 22:4, 6.

[2] B. Shabbat 67b, Hullin 7b, Kiddushin 32a.

Adam and Eve, we read, were naked but unashamed (2:25). Their sin was not coitus but disobedience, prodded by appetite and passion—not just for a forbidden piece of fruit but a craving to be godlike (3:5). Their "fall," as Genesis describes it, is a portrait of human moral pride and willfulness, not a vicarious taint passed to their progeny.[3] There's trouble ahead for the couple, but God blesses their union. Eve acknowledges God's sponsorship of the first birth. That life will not remain idyllic is part of the narrative's point, contrasting the life we know with the virtuality Genesis pictures, the garden that might have been.

Genesis captures Adam's evasive answers to God's questioning and his readiness to blame Eve and even pass blame along to God, who gave him his bride. The Midrash makes amends, with its homiletic embroidery, having Adam choose mortality with Eve rather than deathlessness in the garden, but alone.

The first couple's trust in one another contrasts vividly with the machismo of the Torah's first polygamist (4:19). Lamech's two wives, Adah and Zillah—Dawn and Dusk, the Rabbis say—reflect pagan mores, adorning one wife with finery but plying her with contraceptive drugs while keeping the other in homely drudgery to bear the children.[4] Lamech boasts of the disproportion he holds in store for anyone who injures him (4:23–24), his grudge sharpened, ready for an affront. The Torah will denounce grudges (Leviticus 19:18) and insist that punishments fit the crime, not a victim and offender's standing.[5]

---

[3] See Lenn Goodman, "Is Maimonides a Moral Relativist?" in *Jewish Religious and Philosophical Ethics*, ed. Curtis Hutt et al. (New York: Routledge, 2018).

[4] Genesis Rabbah 23.4. The division the Rabbis cite is not fanciful. Demosthenes pled in court, "We have *hetairae* for our amusement, concubines for our daily bodily needs, and wives to bear us legitimate children and serve faithfully as guardians of our households" (*Orations* 59.122, *Against Neaera*). See Lenn Goodman, *Judaism: A Contemporary Philosophical Investigation* (New York: Routledge, 2017), 51n32.

[5] See Jeremiah Unterman, *Justice for All: How the Jewish Bible Revolutionized Ethics* (Lincoln: Jewish Publication Society and University of Nebraska Press, 2017).

Lamech's dual marriage mocks the partnership envisioned between Adam and Eve.[6]

Biblically there's cosmic significance in a couple's espousal to one another. They are not just two more animals charged to *be fruitful and multiply* (Genesis 1:22, 28, 9:1). Even for animals that command is at once a natural law and a divine blessing. For the emblematic first couple, companionship is critical to well-being. Beyond the Garden they will share their labors, triumphs, and frustrations. The love that grows between them is the fruit, which men and women must cultivate, of God's love in giving them to one another.

### Biblical Marriage

The Torah is rather matter-of-fact about the love between a woman and a man in its biological as well as social facets. Adults have spouses and raise children, as God intended. Emotional attachments were hardly foreign to men and women in ancient days. Polygamy and concubinage, practiced among the Patriarchs, are recognized but not celebrated. So Abraham's partners, including concubines, are acknowledged (25:1–5), as they must be if the biblical genealogy is to serve. Yet Genesis pulls no punches in portraying the rivalry of Rachel and Leah. Nor does it omit to mention their surrogates, Bilḥah and Zilpah, two more mothers of the tribes of Israel (29:29, 30:3, 9). Scripture does not soft-pedal the bitter rivalry of Samuel's mother, Hannah, and her co-wife Peninah (1 Samuel 1). The tale focuses on the gift of Samuel's birth—and Hannah's matching gift of her son to lifelong service as a man of God. But the story vividly renders the structural imbalance of polygamy, even when a husband like Hannah's loves his wives unstintingly (1:8). In time polygamy will be banned in Jewish law, as slavery

---

6 Eve is called *'ezer ke-negdo*, Adam's "helpmeet," in Tyndale's brilliant coinage—his counterpart and ally. Help, here, is not invidious or derogatory. God is frequently called a help. Glossing *'ezer ke-negdo*, literally, "a helper opposite him," the Midrash relates that a woman is an aid or an adversary depending on one's character.

was first mitigated radically, then abandoned, working out the dynamic of the Torah's moral themes.

Abraham shows the depths of his love not just when he pays the asking price for Sarah's gravesite in Hebron (Genesis 23) but also while she lives, when he hears God telling him, despite his own righteous dissent, that he must heed her cruel command to banish Hagar and Ishmael (21:8–21). God will look after them, but Sarah must be heeded. She holds the truest understanding of the line Abraham's progeny must take.

In Egypt and in the Negev, knowing Sarah's beauty, Abraham feigns she is his sister, lest he be slain for her by Pharaoh or Avimelekh (12:11–20, 20:2–18). Isaac will use the same ploy, equally foolishly, with the Philistines (26:6–11). All very primitive. But consider how Homer might have told such stories. One monarch would have taken and kept the lovely woman; the gods would take sides, and mortals marshaled for war. Biblically, the erring rulers relent, after some divine prompting. For there's just one God here. Even rulers, whom Abraham fears do not fear God, must acknowledge the justice that God stands for. The point, then: not that Abraham or Isaac was not above lying (or putting his wife at risk), but that there is no division in the heavens. Small éclat for the Patriarchs, but clarity for God—and love's sanctity.

Isaac's marriage was arranged for him, remotely—yet biblically seen as providential. Tellingly, the portents confirming its rightness—and God's *ḥesed*—His grace toward Abraham (24:12) centers on Rebecca's generous character (24:14–21), just as her acceptance of Isaac, sight unseen (24:58), shows her spunk. Her snap decision is confirmed when she first sees him and drops from her camel (24:64), not waiting for it to kneel. Isaac, for his part, falls in love with her, comforted for his mother's loss (24:67). She will bear Jacob and Esau, twins, rivals for the birthright that Jacob will buy from his famished brother for *a mess of pottage* (25:24–34)—rivals, too, for Isaac's blessing, which Rebecca will teach Jacob to win by a ruse, convincing his now-blind father that he is Esau and has brought him a dish of his favorite game (27:1–40).

The relations of couples have long varied, and the Torah reflects the changing mores of the ages. In every era and culture, women and men rub along and work things out against the backdrop of the norms they know, their relations no more uniform than their costumes. Some mores, like polygamy, are structurally unfair. But personal and interpersonal skills help men and women cope, more or less ably, thoughtfully, and considerately, even when the social deck is stacked. No biblical couple had a mid-Victorian lifestyle, with women at home and men off to the office. Deborah, a prophet and judge, handled cases under her palm tree (Judges 4:4–5). She was a wife and mother (5:7), but unafraid, when crisis called, to lead a volunteer force to war. And don't overlook the well-to-do Shunamite woman who would entertain Elisha as he made his rounds: *"Let's make a little room upstairs with a bed, table, chair, and lamp for him,"* she tells her husband. *"Then he can stay there when he comes through"* (2 Kings 4:10). She is no Deborah, but she has her home and family and is proud of her independence.

The ideal wife of the closing chapter of Proverbs (31:10–31), chanted at Sabbath eve tables in traditional Jewish homes each Friday night, is no sequestrated drudge. Trusted and resourceful, she manages her cottage industry that works with wool and flax; she oversees the family meals and the projects of her maids, invests in property and plants a vineyard with her profits. She keeps her light burning by night and stands behind the quality of the goods she sells. She's openhanded to the needy, her family warmly clothed in scarlet against the snow, her bed beautifully made up, her clothing of fine linen and rich purple fabric. Her husband is respected in the city gates, not least for her industry and charity. With plenty to sell traveling merchants, she need not fear the future. Her dignity, kindness, and intelligent conversation set the tone in her well-ordered home, winning respect from her children and plaudits from her mate. *Beauty is fleeting,* the poet concludes, *and grace deceptive. Piety deserves the praise. Give her credit for all she does. Her accomplishments sing her praises in the city gates.*

## A Surpassing Friendship

The Bible paints a special love between two human beings in portraying Jonathan and David. Jonathan broke with his father to defend David. Later, in a field, pretending to practice his bowmanship, he sealed his choice by warning David of Saul's murderous intent, for the king feared David as a potential usurper (1 Samuel 18:8–12). Taking in the full weight of Jonathan's choice, David threw himself to the ground before his friend. The men kissed and wept—David more strongly (20:41). He already knew that Jonathan loved him but only now saw that the prince would give up Israel's throne for his sake (20:30–34).

David is the figure most vividly portrayed in the Tanakh, seen through many eyes—not least, those of the women who celebrate his victories. But even before Saul gives him command in battle, we see him in Jonathan's eyes: *Jonathan's soul was bound up with David's, and Jonathan loved him as himself* (18:1). The two young men pledged their friendship on first meeting, and Jonathan gave the rustic lad the cloak he wore, his tunic, even his sword, bow, and belt (18:3–4), the spontaneous gesture of a young prince to the slender, roughly clad instant hero. Despite the prying fingers of later readers, Scripture sees no hint of eros here.

The Torah is not shy about the strengths and weaknesses of its dramatis personae, least of all the shepherd boy, poet, warrior, sometime fugitive, and future king. We learn of Moses's failings, like those of Adam, Noah, Abraham, Isaac, and Jacob—and of troubled, tragic figures like Samson and Saul. The steady focus is on God's covenant with Israel. In David's case, the narrative lenses are dynastic, moral, spiritual, military, and cultic, in kaleidoscopic play, as in real life. But, as in real life, the erotic is never far out of sight. We see the young king dancing in his ephod, *with all his might,* before the Lord's Ark. His elation, first plainly told, is seen again, through the disapproving eyes of Michal, his wife and Saul's daughter (2 Samuel 6). She too had saved his life from her father's jealous designs (1 Samuel 19:11–17). But David would never forgive her cutting remark about his self-display. She was condemned to childlessness, the biblical author believes, for her shattering comment, blunting David's moment of glory in his God and at his triumph, moving the Ark to his new capital (2 Samuel 6:23).

We see David on his rooftop, discovering Bathsheba bathing, and overhear his scheme to send her husband, Uriah the Hittite, a loyal officer, to die, exposed at the frontlines (2 Samuel 11). We even glimpse David's last days, an old man shivering in bed, with Avishag, a lovely Shunamite, recruited to keep him warm. The king slept with her literally, we're told; but, in the biblical sense, *he did not know her* (1 Kings 1:1–4). That last point matters. For Solomon's elder brother will persuade Bathsheba to beg Solomon to give him Avishag in marriage, to bolster his own royal pretensions—a fatal request, once Solomon learns of it (2:13–25).

The Torah does not seek to reduce its protagonists' human complexity to a single passion—nor to market their weaknesses. We watch David's eyes as he drinks in Bathsheba's beauty, but we're not invited to follow his gaze, as Rembrandt would do. The Torah can be graphic when need be—as in telling of Onan, or of Tamar and Amnon, or Judah and his daughter-in-law, or Ruth and Boaz. But turning the private public is not Scripture's purpose, serving prurient interests. I say this not in hopes of dissuading those who know there must be more to the love of David and Jonathan than meets the Torah's gaze, but because their story crystalizes one shining fragment of the complexity we call love. Had David and Jonathan indeed violated God's commandment, *Thou shalt not lie with a male as with a woman. It is an abomination!* (Leviticus 18:22), the prophet Nathan would not have kept silent about it, any more than he balked at confronting David with his wronging Uriah—and maneuvering the king, with a parable, to condemn his crime out of his own mouth (2 Samuel 11).

The sweet singer of Israel (2 Samuel 23:1) left no breathy Sapphics for Jonathan. But he did indite a threnody when Jonathan and Saul died in battle on Mount Gilboa:

> How have the mighty fallen!
> Tell it not in Gath....
> Heroes' shield begrimed,
> Saul's, not rubbed with oil...
> Jonathan's bow never gave way;
> Saul's sword, never unslaked.
> Saul and Jonathan,
> In life beloved and cherished,
> Not parted even in death!
> Swifter than eagles,
> Braver than lions.
> Weep for Saul, daughters of Israel,
> Who dressed you in finest crimson
> Who set gold jewels in your gowns.
> How have the mighty fallen
> In the thick of battle!
> Jonathan, slaughtered on thy heights!
> I grieve for thee, Jonathan, my brother,
> So dear to me,
> Your love, so wondrous to me—
> More than women's love!
> How have the mighty fallen,
> Perished those men, weapons of war! (2 Samuel 1:19–27)

David was no stranger to women's love. His warrior's hand served the eye and heart of a poet, his harp never far from his side (1 Samuel 19:9). David knows guile and has known fear. Never a simple shepherd, or a simple king, he has known love, a love not always marred by concupiscence.

### Biblical Passion

The Torah is not prudish about eros. But sex is not its cynosure. It celebrates *the way of a man with a maid* (Proverbs 30:19)—*too marvelous for me*, says the author, Solomon, by tradition, the wisest of men—wondrous as the eagle's flight, a snake's path on a rock, a ship cutting through the sea. Physics will explain how a ship stays upright and on course; physiology will disclose how an eagle flies and a snake makes its way on hard ground. None of these phenomena is unfathomable. But to the poet they are marvelous—like the phases of courtship that clinches the series. The marvel is no mystery but an intellectual and affective delight, acknowledging God's work in nature, and through it.

The Song of Songs celebrates human love in its concreteness. The somber, fraught dialogue of Job here gives way to lovers' voices in springtime. First heard, a young girl's solo voice, seeking her shepherd lover, complaining of her suntan and her brothers' setting her to watch the vineyards, taunted by her girlfriends, praising her beloved to them, fantasizing of a royal suitor, rejecting him for her real passion, whose voice invites her to a leafy bower, "*Our house, with beams of cedar, and cypresses for rafters.*" The two marvel at each other's beauty; she grows "*faint with love.*"

> *He's brought me to the wine shop,*
> *Pitched his love pennant above me . . .*
> *His left hand beneath my head,*
> *His right, caressing me . . .*[7]

She calls him a stag—

> *Leaping over mountains,*
> *Skipping over hills.*
> *He's a buck, my sweetheart,*
> *A young stag.*

---

[7] Verses from first two chapters of the Song, translation by Lenn Goodman and Saul Strosberg.

Then, in human form:

> *There he is, standing just outside our wall,*
> *Peeking through the window,*
> *Peering through the lattice!*
> *My love called! He told me,*
> *"Get up, darling, my beautiful,*
> *Come away.*
> *Winter is over.*
> *The rain is past and gone.*
> *Flowers are blooming in the country.*
> *It's time for singing.*
> *The turtledove's call sounds over our land.*
> *The fig tree, decked with little figs,*
> *The blossoming vines give up their scent."*

Passionate, loyal, she dreams of losing her beloved and seeking him through darkened streets, roughed up by the night watch, wishing he'd come, *to my mother's house, to the room where she conceived me.*

Knowing but awestruck, she tours his anatomy, and counsels her mocking friends against stirring up love before its time, urging them to await the real thing. Intensity lends color to readings of the Song as an allegory of Israel's or the soul's dalliance and disrupted romance with God. Some do battle to prove it a mere love song—or a pagan florilegium. What matters philosophically is not silly contests between sublimated and reductive readings but the recognition that it was love that homilists and poets chose to symbolize their quest and Israel's historic experience and longings.

Philo is sometimes berated for calling philosophy theology's handmaid. But beyond any worries over subordination, as if a philosophical handmaid would keep quiet long, what matters is that philosophy—not faith or feelings, or mystic experience, or drugs—was chosen. Similarly here: the truest symbol Jewish thinkers could find for Israel's or the soul's link to God was plangent, poignant love, with its impatient waiting, hopes and fears, moments of loneliness, loss, trust, and the abiding insistence that what's real outweighs any childish fantasy, infatuation, or stage-managed display.

### Laws of Love

"What's mine is mine, what's thine is thine," the Rabbis say, was the ethos of Sodom, forbidden by Jewish law.[8] The thought is a retort to the famous catchphrase of Justinian's code, *suum cuique dare*, "to give to each his own." The rabbinic prooftext naming Sodom's sinful ethos springs from Ezekiel's monitory words to his own countrymen: *Look! This was the sin of thy sister Sodom: arrogance! She had ample food, peace and plenty for her and her daughters, but she lent no hand to the poor and helpless!* (16:49). To love and serve God, the Rabbis argue, Israel must cultivate *middat ḥasidim*, a loving ethos.

*Ḥesed* in its simplest sense means favor. In the richer sense acquired from its assignment to God and its centrality in Jewish ethics, *ḥesed* means grace, generosity beyond desert. It's in that sense that 'grace' is a fitting translation for *ḥesed*, defining Jewish piety. For a *ḥasid*, a devotee of God, responds to God's *ḥesed*, His love of creation, not by seeking to repay it but by sharing it, emulating God's *middat ḥesed*, the attribute of love, by cultivating such an ethos.

*Ḥesed* is generosity beyond desert. Yet its exercise is not supererogatory. For *ḥesed* is a *mitzvah*, a commandment (Deuteronomy 6:18, 12:28; cf. Genesis 18:19, Micah 6:8), and keeping a commandment of God's is not just a duty but a blessing. Duties here are not seen as onerous, but as privileges; and privileges are not exemptions from the law but embrace of it, and by it.

---

8  B. Berakhot 29b, Eruvin 49a, Ketubot 103a, Bava Batra 12b, 59a, 168a.

The word *ḥesed* is often translated as 'loving kindness'. That tendency may reflect two concerns: first, perhaps, a need to skirt Christian debates over the rivalry of 'works' and 'grace' as avenues to salvation. Judaism does not regard this life as a place from which one needs rescue. Second, *ḥesed* is active not just attitudinal love. It is grace received and shared, giving works their content and demeanor. A life of *ḥesed* is the devotee's clearest way of living out God's love, fulfilling the commandment to walk in God's ways (Deuteronomy 5:30, 8:6, 10:12, 11:22, 13:5, 19:9, 26:17; cf. Psalms 119:1, B. Sotah 14a, Shabbat 133b) and pursue His transcendence: *Ye shall be holy, for I the Lord thy God am holy* (Leviticus 19:2).

Jewish tradition counts 613 commandments in the Mosaic Torah. Central among them is the call to love God with all one's heart and soul and might (Deuteronomy 6:5). That love does not compete with human kindness, for the same God commands us to love one another as we love ourselves (Leviticus 19:18).

The Torah situates that central commandment in a nest of *mitzvot* that puts flesh on its bones (Leviticus 19:9–19), giving palpable meaning to the bonds of fellowship that the Law seeks to build and build upon: Israelites must not reap their fields to the edges but must leave the corners and fallen sheaves for the landless poor and the stranger. We are not to lie or cheat or gossip. Nor may we retain a day worker's wage overnight but must pay him promptly day by day, as his needs require. When exercising judgment we must regard a person's acts, not his status, favoring neither the rich nor the poor. One may not take advantage of another's weaknesses—a broad obligation, biblically voiced in the imperative not to *curse the deaf or place a stumbling block before the blind.*

Glossing these paradigm cases, the Rabbis understand that one may not defame another behind his back, or tempt anyone, as by offering a drink to someone who should not drink, or selling a weapon to anyone unless for self-defense. Beyond not bearing a grudge, one may not take vengeance or harbor secret hatreds. Watching another do wrong without speaking to him (privately and tactfully, the Rabbis insist) would make one complicit. It's here that the obligation to love the other as oneself is invoked—warranting the duty of reproof: One must treat others as one would hope to be treated in like circumstances.

### Living and Learning

Bound textually to the commandment to love God are prescriptions to study God's laws and make the values they address salient in one's life—and to make them enduring by teaching them to one's children. The key word is *ve-shinantam* (Deuteronomy 6:6), usually translated, "teach them diligently." God's precepts are to be foregrounded in one's thinking and actions, public and private: *Speak of them at home and when going out, when lying down and getting up. Bind them as a sign on your hand, and make them frontlets between your eyes. Write them on the doorposts of your house and on your gates*—6:7–9).[9] Ritualized in the form of phylacteries and mezuzot, these meta-commandments mark the prominence God's laws are to have in one's actions and choices: Like a bowsight or a wristband, they are to be ever-present canons of God's guidance. Ḥesed is the clearest theme focusing God's charge, orienting the most ordinary actions, as well as the most critical, toward transcendence and God's call to holiness.[10]

That word *ve-shinantam* resonates in the title of the Mishnah, the earliest postbiblical Jewish law code, collating some five centuries of practice and prescription down to about 200 C.E. Pursuing the Torah's demands and exploring their meanings, the Mishnah itself became an object of intensive study. Expanded by the often digressive commentary of the Gemara, it anchored the Jerusalem and Babylonian

---

9 See Lenn Goodman, *The Holy One of Israel* (New York: Oxford University Press, 2019).
10 See Lenn Goodman, *Love Thy Neighbor as Thyself* (New York: Oxford University Press, 2008), 37–69.

Talmuds. A typical Mishnaic concern was the exercise of detailing the requirements of Torah law: How and how far may one move about on the Sabbath? How must witnesses be charged in a capital case, in due deference to the precious uniqueness of each human being? The Mishnah departs from its familiar concern with formalizing and calibrating biblical norms when it opens its discussion of the corner of the field reserved for the poor and the stranger:

> These things have no set measure: the corner of the field, the first fruit and pilgrimage offerings (Exodus 23:19, Deuteronomy 16:16–17), the practice of kindness (*gemilut ḥasadim*), and study of Torah. Of these one enjoys the fruits in this world, but the principle accrues in Eternity: honoring one's father and mother, practice of kindness, rising early to attend study sessions in the morning—and the evening—hospitality to strangers, visiting the sick, dowering the bride, due obsequies for the dead, devotion in prayer, and making peace between one person and another. And Torah study outshines them all. (Mishnah Peah 1.1)

Now, as to the corner of the field, there *is* a minimum—one sixtieth of the yield—but no outer limit. The Talmud (completed around 500 C.E.) explains that it makes no difference if strangers and the poor are provided for from the field's edge or from the center. But the Mishnah's open-ended obligations center on acts of *ḥesed*. Hospitality to strangers and visiting the sick exemplify "the practice of kindness" (B. Shabbat 127b). Indeed, hospitality takes precedence to diligent attendance at study sessions—and even to welcoming God's Presence. For the Torah suggests (the Sages propose, with typical playful creativity) that Abraham asked God Himself to wait while he hastened to welcome passing strangers (B. Shabbat 127a, citing Genesis 18:3).

Among the actions that bear a transtemporal reward, the Sages add giving others the benefit of the doubt. *Ḥesed* remains the orienting theme, as it is in dowering the bride. But even clearer is the commandment to raise up one's children in the study of Torah. Here one's loyalty confirms God's confidence that Abraham's house will preserve God's generous ways (Genesis 18:19).

Study of the Torah, the Sages' métier as well as their ideal, is understandably paramount in the Mishnah's listing. But, as the Rabbis explain, study anchors all the rest. For study of God's law, the Rabbis assume, must be committed and engaged. Torah students are expected to be ready and able to take to heart what they learn and let it guide their lives. Otherwise, such study is not merely empty but sacrilegious, its putative students discrediting the worth of their study.

The Law, then, is not to be held in a forceps as if it were some foreign object or ancient artifact. Its norms must be read as inspired expressions of God's expectations. Reading the ancient texts in that sense injects a dynamic into their interpretation that keeps the Law flexible and alive, ever responsive to the thrust of its most central, most humane themes.

Challenged to become *a kingdom of priests and a holy nation* (Exodus 19:6), Israel is to pursue God's holiness and share it with the nations of the world, fulfilling God's promise that Abraham's descendants and successors will be a blessing to every nation (Genesis 22:18; cf. 12:2, 18:18). They are to model the allegiance that gives substance to God's covenant and the active love of God it invites—not a turning away from life in the world but a turning toward it and toward others. That theme, reading piety as grace and generosity, persists. Thus Spinoza, to name a key philosophical instance, faithful to his heritage, defines *pietas* and *humanitas* in identical terms.[11]

Philosophers like Saadiah (882–942) and Maimonides (1138–1204) find the paradigm case of God's ḥesed in the act of creation, which addressed no prior desert.[12] But the Rabbis call it an act of *true ḥesed* to

---

[11] Spinoza, *Ethics* III, Proposition 29, Scholium, Definitions 43; V, Proposition 4, Scholium.

[12] See Saadiah's introduction to his commentary on Job, tr. Lenn Goodman as *The Book of Theodicy: Translation and Commentary on the Book of Job, by Saadiah Ben Joseph Al-Fayyumi* (New Haven, CT: Yale University Press, 1988), 123–24, glossing Psalm 89:3; Maimonides, *Dalālatu 'l-Ḥā'irīn*, ed. Salomon Munk (Paris: 1856–66; repr. Osnabrück: Zeller, 1964), 3 volumes. Cited

attend the dead to the grave. For here no requital is to be expected. We love and follow God by fulfilling His *mitzvot* (Leviticus 26:3), whose moral gravamen rests in God's love of humankind. So the attributes of grace and mercy are not left to God alone. When the Rabbis ask how flesh and blood can possibly walk in the pathways of a God who transcends all limitation, the answer comes without hesitation: As God clothed the naked, so should you clothe the naked; as He visited the sick, so should you visit the sick; as He comforted the bereaved, so should you comfort the bereaved; as He buried the dead, so should you bury the dead.[13] *Imitatio Dei* begins in acts of kindness.

## Intellectual Love

Encountering God at Sinai, Moses asks God to reveal His glory (Exodus 33:19). But God replies that His face cannot be seen (33:20)—God's ipseity, Maimonides explains, is beyond us, 'face' standing for God's true identity.[14] God promises to show Moses His "back"—or, more faithfully to the Hebrew, His "afterwards," the word being plural. This Maimonides takes to mean, what follows from God, His wake, as it were, His effects in nature. For Moses had asked after *God's ways* (33:13). Faced with the mission of governing a fractious people, who were worn down by slavery and oppression, he looked to God as the model of governance (33:12–13). So God showed him, Maimonides argues, the panoply of nature, in which he might discern the tenor of God's rule[15]—and then proclaimed the themes to be read in it. Ḥesed lies at the core of the epiphany (34:6).

---

below by part and chapter; here: *Guide* III 53; page references, by volume and page in Munk's edition, here: 3.131a. English is from the translation by Lenn Goodman and Phillip Lieberman, as *The Guide to the Perplexed* (Stanford, CA: Stanford University Press, 2024).

13 B. Sotah 14a; cf. Genesis Rabbah 8.13, Sifre to Deuteronomy 11:22, piska 49; Bava Batra 12b.
14 *Guide* I 54, 1.64b.
15 *Guide* I 54, 1.64b–65a.

God opens His Self-disclosure (33:14–15) by twice proclaiming the name He had revealed to Moses at the burning bush (3:2–15), where He called Himself *I AM THAT I AM*, declaring this to be the name by which He should ever be known: an existential Self-affirmation, encapsulated, Maimonides teaches, in the Tetragrammaton, signifying God's absoluteness.[16] To that name, now repeated, God adds epithets (thirteen "attributes" in all) stressing divine patience, mercy, and grace: *a God merciful and kind, long patient, and abundant in grace and truth, preserving grace thousandsfold, bearing with sin, misdeeds, and wrongdoing, but by no means effacing guilt* (34:6–7). Grace here is ḥesed; truth, here, means justice, as it often does in Hebrew, especially when paired with terms like ḥesed. Grace, patience, kindness, and mercy predominate among the traits Moses must cultivate—although God's Self-declaration does not omit what one can learn from the tenor of His governance in nature: that actions have consequences.

Wrongs are not always met with instant disaster, for God is patient. Evil does self-destruct, yet mercy outstrips severity thousandsfold: grace predominates, for being is a gift. The very idea of evil, as I've argued elsewhere, is parasitic on that of goodness, just as evil itself is parasitic on the good.[17] "We know with certainty," Maimonides writes, "that God cannot be called the proper cause of evil as a primary intention. That is unsound. All His acts are purely good. For He produces only being, and all being is good."[18] God's love, shown in the goodness of being, is emulated in human love—and, above all, in the special love persons merit. For, as Rabbi Akiva used to say, "Beloved is man, to

---

16  *Guide* I 63.
17  See Lenn Goodman, "Judaism and the Problem of Evil," in *The Cambridge Companion to the Problem of Evil*, ed. Chad Meister and Paul Moser (Cambridge: Cambridge University Press, 2017), 193–209.
18  *Guide* III 10, 3.17a.

be created in God's image—but even more beloved, in being given to know that he was created in God's image."[19]

Reason marks mankind's affinity to God, Maimonides argues. So our love of God has an intellectual as well as a moral dimension. We can see that clearly in the call to love God with all our hearts (Deuteronomy 6:5), for the Torah does not separate heart from mind. The moral virtues, Maimonides argues, prepare the soul to perfect the intellectual virtues, freeing the mind from the distractions and distortions arising from human appetites and passions. We love and emulate God by knowing Him, and the better we know God, purging every imperfection from our thought of God, the more closely, if asymptotically, we approach,[20] rising intellectually not toward union but communion, consummation symbolized by the kiss that Moses, Aaron, and Miriam experienced as they died, and alluded to when the Song of Songs makes erotic passion its symbol of the highest goal.[21]

"The most basic principle and foundation of all wisdom," Maimonides writes, "is to realize that there is a Prime Reality that gives being to all that is."[22] "How, then, can we love and reverence Him?" Clearly, by knowing: "When one contemplates His works, His great and wondrous creations, and sees the infinite, peerless wisdom in them, one will immediately love, laud, and glorify Him; and, seeing their beauty, will long intensely to know His great name—as David said, *My soul thirsts for God, for the living God* (Psalm 42:3)."[23] The intellectual love of God is our highest goal, attained not simply by mystical meditation but by serious study of nature.

---

19 Mishnah Avot 3.18, citing Genesis 9:6. Akiva, martyred by Rome in 135, named *Love thy neighbor as thyself* the Torah's cardinal precept.
20 *Guide* III 52–54.
21 *Guide* III 51, Munk 3.129a, citing Song of Songs 1:2, and B. Bava Batra 17a on Numbers 33:38 and Deuteronomy 34:5.
22 Maimonides, *Mishneh Torah* (Code of Jewish Law, below: *MT*), Book I, Laws of the Foundations of the Torah I 1, ed. Moses Hyamson, as *The Book of Knowledge* (New York: Feldheim, 1974), 34a.
23 *MT*, Book I, I 2.2, Hyamson, 35b.

It is the chance of success in this quest, Maimonides argues, that justifies human existence and renders intelligible even the suffering to which our embodiment makes us vulnerable.[24] Here, as in Plato's *Symposium*, every licit form of love is a rung on the ladder of love. For Maimonides that ladder and the imagery of the Divided Line in the *Republic* merge with the image of Jacob's Ladder (Genesis 28:11–14), anchored on earth but rising to the heavens, with God above its summit, and angels ascending and descending.

The angels, in Maimonides's exegesis, are human beings on their way to enlightenment—their ascent, followed by descent, to guide and teach those not yet enlightened. Just as those who have escaped the shadows of the Cave in the *Republic* may be called on to return, or as Bodhisattvas return with guidance for those left behind, the enlightened, Maimonides writes, feel powerfully compelled to share what they have learned. That is why they teach and write—even at risk to their own lives.

The moral and intellectual sides of love of God come together here, wedding an understanding, ultimately beatific, to the exercise of care for others. As in Aristotle, the intellectual holds pride of place. Our properly human goal is contemplation of ideas, "the highest and surest" being that of God. A human paragon will long "to master the world's mysteries and discover the causes of things, his thoughts turned ever upward"—toward the ultimate Cause: "His sole concern will be to know God, contemplate His works, and know what one should make of all this."[25]

The moral virtues lay the foundation. Passions like anger, grief, and lassitude can block or mar one's vision; the clamor of the appetites can distract one from the true goal. "Every passion is a bane and should be controlled as best one can."[26] The passion that truly matters is the

---

24 *Guide* III 12–24.
25 *Guide* II 36, 2.79a.
26 *Guide* I 54, 1.66a.

highest: to know God. But the road to fulfillment does not lie through the asperities of radical asceticism, as though God hated the body, Maimonides writes. It would be foolish to neglect the vehicle of our fulfillment. We must meet our bodily needs, as good health requires, and perfect our character, clearing the lens, as it were, through which enlightenment can shine through.[27] Focus on our most human and humanizing goal, knowledge of God, does demand one "drop a great many of his former doings and speak far less"—but not drop out of life. Indeed, Moses and Abraham, paragons of enlightenment, lived in the world without losing their focus on the Highest, since all that they did was for the sake of God.[28]

> One who is focused on this goal will not be keen to decorate his walls with gold or have gold borders on his clothing—unless, good Lord, to raise his spirits and preserve his psychic health, his soul kept fit and free of illness, polished and pure, receptive to the light of knowledge—as the Sages said, "A nice house, an attractive wife, a comfortable bed for the scholar. These enlarge the mind" (B. Shabbat 25b). For souls may weary of dwelling constantly on knotty problems. Just as the body tires from hard work and needs rest and relaxation to restore its vigor, so does a soul need to re-create and refresh itself by contemplating works of art and other lovely things, to ease its fatigue. So when the Rabbis tired, they say, they would speak in a lighter vein (B. Shabbat 30b). Used in this way, it's doubtful that paintings and decorative work on buildings, salons, and clothing should be deemed frivolous or untoward.[29]

---

27 See "Eight Chapters," 8, in *Hakdamot ha-Rambam la-Mishnah*, ed. Isaac Shailat (Jerusalem: Ma'aliyot, 1995), 44–55.
28 *Guide* III 51, 3.127a.
29 "Eight Chapters," 5; cf. *Guide* III 25.

Prophets and other seekers have isolated themselves, fearing distractions in a corrupt society or seeking to purge its influences. But those who ape such extremes, Maimonides argues, are as foolish as those who suppose that if strong medicines help the ill they'll be even better for the well. A Nazirite[30] who completes his ascetic vow, Maimonides reminds readers, must bring a sin offering. Against whom did he sin, the Sages ask. Against his soul, by denying himself.[31]

The moral virtues, for Maimonides, are instrumental in their role and social in their setting. They are not our highest goal but are critical means toward it. Yet they are also intrinsic goods. And, although our highest goal is to know God and His ways—His *ḥesed*—even this highest good serves instrumentally. For it fosters better character and helps one guide others toward the ways of love and peace. Enlightenment, indeed, can help one build practices and foster institutions that promote character growth in others as well as in oneself—and such growth is critical to higher reflection. Indeed, it also aids in establishing the material conditions without which no spiritual quest is possible: "For one cannot think a thought, even if it's explained to him (let alone discover it for himself) when in pain, or famished, or parched, or extremely hot or cold. Only after bodily well-being is secured can one reach that doubtlessly higher sort of perfection, the sole avenue to everlasting life."[32]

One's "truly human attainment," Maimonides writes, as he concludes his philosophical masterpiece, *The Guide to the Perplexed*, is to win the rational virtues and gain the spiritual heights, a goal truly one's own. But such higher thoughts redound to the good of others morally as well as intellectually, as better moral and material conditions are laid down and strengthened.

---

30 Numbers 6.
31 Maimonides, "Eight Chapters," 4, citing B. Ta'anit 11a.
32 *Guide* III 27, Munk 3.60a; "Eight Chapters," 7.

Setting Jeremiah's counsels alongside the summum bonum of Aristotle and the Platonists, Maimonides writes,[33]

> Our prophets taught us the same ideas, laid out just as the Philosophers did, declaring wealth, health, and character not what one should boast of or yearn for. The attainment we should covet and take pride in is knowledge of God—real knowledge. As Jeremiah says, naming these four attainments: *So saith the* LORD, *"Let not the wise man glory in his wisdom, nor the hero glory in his might, nor the rich man glory in his wealth, but let him who would glory glory in this: that he understandeth and knoweth Me—[that I am the* LORD, *who worketh grace, justice, and righteousness on earth—for in these do I delight," saith the* LORD.] (Jeremiah 9:22-23). Note how he ranks them as the vulgar do: to them, the highest attainment is the rich man's wealth, then the strong man's power, then the wise man's wisdom, meaning moral virtue, for the virtuous are esteemed by the masses, whom the prophet addresses here. Hence the sequence. The Sages read the verse just as I have in this chapter: Wisdom unqualified, named our ultimate goal in every context, is knowledge of God. But the goods vied for and cherished as real attainments are nothing of the sort. Likewise all those biblical practices—the acts of piety and morality so beneficial in our human interactions—hold not a candle to this ultimate goal; they only pave the way to it.

But then comes the keystone linking the moral to the intellectual:

> Having cited this verse and all its wonderful implications, and having cited the Sages' glosses, I should turn to what it says at the end. For Jeremiah does not stop at naming our highest goal, knowledge of God. Were that his intent he'd have said, *but let him who would glory*

---

[33] *Guide* III 54.

*glory in this: that he understandeth and knoweth Me*, and stopped there—or "understandeth and knoweth Me, that I am One"—or "have no shape," or "that there is none like Me," or the like. But what he said one should be proud of is awareness *of Me*—knowledge of God's attributes, meaning His actions, as I've explained in regard to the words, *show me, pray, Thy ways* (Exodus 33:13).[34] The verse specifies the actions we must know and emulate: grace, justice, and righteousness (*ḥesed, mishpat, tzedakah*).

The divine attributes one must emulate are those we know as human virtues. *Ḥesed* is chief among them. And justice (*mishpat*) finds its proper place among them only alongside righteousness, *tzedakah*, which Maimonides explains means much more biblically than "giving each his own." For, as he writes, preparing the ground for his summing up:

> The word *tzedakah* derives from *tzedek*, justice, which means giving everyone his due and treating all beings as they deserve. But fulfilling your obligations to others in the first of these two senses is not what Scripture calls *tzedakah*. It's not called *tzedakah* to pay someone his wages or repay a debt. *Tzedakah* is what virtue demands in your treatment of others—like healing the hurts of all who are broken. Thus, of returning the pledge of the poor by nightfall,[35] it says, *this will be righteousness* (tzedakah) *on thy part* (Deuteronomy 24:13). For a life of moral virtue gives your rational soul its due; you have done right by it. Every moral virtue is called righteousness. So it says of Abraham, *He trusted in the* LORD, *and this was counted*

---

34 Maimonides recalls his exposition of Moses's epiphany at *Guide* I 54.
35 The pledge is a pawn. One might think oneself entitled to keep it until it is redeemed. But the Torah demands a poor debtor's pledge not be held overnight, *that he may sleep in his garment and bless thee, and it shall be* tzedakah *on thy part* (Deuteronomy 24:13); cf. Exodus 22:25: *If thou dost ever take thy neighbor's garment in pledge, thou shalt return it to him by sundown. It is his only clothing, the covering of his flesh. What shall he lie down with. Should he cry out to me, I shall hear him, for I am caring* (Exodus 22:25–26).

*righteousness in him* (Genesis 15:6)—referring, I take it, to his virtue of loyalty.[36]

Still looking to his text from Jeremiah, Maimonides writes,

> He adds a final subtlety by saying, *on earth*. This is the Torah's polestar. Contrary to what the rash pretend, who suppose God's care halts at the sphere of the moon and slights the earth and all that is in it—that *the* LORD *hath forsaken the earth* (Ezekiel 9:9)—the master of all who know told us plainly, *the earth is the* LORD*'s* (Exodus 9:29). Providence, Jeremiah is saying, cares for the earth too, as befits it, just as it cares for the heavens as befits them. That is why he says, *"that I am the* LORD *who worketh grace, justice, and righteousness on earth"*—and completes the thought by saying, *"for in these do I delight," saith the* LORD—meaning, "My intent is that you show grace, justice, and righteousness on earth"—as I explained regarding the thirteen attributes (I 54): The point is to emulate those attributes and pattern of our lives on them.

What the verse means, then, is that the human attainment one may rightly glory in is, clearly, to reach, so far as one can, an awareness of God and of His care for His creatures, giving them being and looking after them as He does. The life of one who wins such awareness will show constant grace, justice, and righteousness, emulating God's acts.

In Freud's eyes all motives point to love. One might say the same of Plato. But does talk of sublimation turn all higher aspirations to false consciousness and all caring to ersatz eros? In Plato's case we see not reduction but elevation. In Maimonides, thoughts of love begin with a comparison, phrased in the biblical manner as an imperative: our calling is to love God passionately, as a man would love a woman.[37]

---

[36] *Guide* III 53, 3.131ab.
[37] *Guide* III 51, 3.124b–125a.

Hence the power of the kiss and the symbolism laid upon the Song of Songs. The commandment to love each other as we love ourselves would have little purchase if not grounded in a healthy love of self, and even the love of self is found to have little staying power without its higher goal. The idea of loving God as a man might love a woman, with a passion not all-consuming but all-fulfilling, is energized, not etiolated, by the recognition that love of humanity does not rival the love of God but reflects its source—and the love between a woman and a man is not displaced by love of God but is the worthy emblem of that higher love.

CHAPTER 2

# Love in Plato and Aristotle

*Frisbee C. C. Sheffield*

Ancient Greek philosophers put love on the philosophical agenda. Parmenides claimed that the first god was Love, and Empedocles posited love and strife as rival cosmic powers. Plato wrote two dialogues exploring *erōs*, passionate desire, or love (*Phaedrus* and *Symposium*), and characterized the philosopher in terms of *erōs* in several works. He was also concerned with *philia* (*Lysis*, *Phaedrus*, *Laws*), which most centrally refers to love between family and friends, and binds together the city in his political works (*Republic*, *Statesman*, *Laws*). Though Aristotle gave a marginal role to *erōs* in his ethical writings, *philia* occupies two books of the *Nicomachean Ethics*[1] and fosters community in the *Politics*. Appreciating why love, in its various forms, mattered to Plato and Aristotle emphasizes their focus on a question

---

[1] And Book VII of the *Eudemian Ethics*.

with a practical orientation: how ought we to live? This concern was seen not just to involve attempts to provide a rational basis for how we should conduct our lives; the aim was to develop a character that is orientated toward certain values as objects of desire and love, and toward certain persons seen as worthy of goodwill and concern.[2] What we love reflects what matters to us and shapes our attitude toward those things and pursuits, by ensuring that we pursue them willingly, reliably, and wholeheartedly. The question of how we ought to live, then, inevitably involves reflection on what it is good for us to desire and love.[3] The same holds true for their political works; both Plato and Aristotle suppose that it is not enough to reflect on laws and regulations without also thinking about how citizens are disposed toward one another such that they are capable of living together in a political community. This is why friendship is of greater concern to the legislator than justice (Aristotle, *Nicomachean Ethics* 1155a22; cf. Plato, *Laws* 743c5–6).

The importance of love speaks to another aspect of their work. It is often held that ancient ethics is egoistic, in the sense that achievement of the agent's own flourishing (*eudaimonia*) is the central goal of action. Though the "eudaemonist axiom" is clearly important in a number of ancient texts,[4] the importance of *philia* for both Plato and Aristotle shows that their ethics is not limited to self-interested concerns. Reflection on the value of *philia* is one way to recognize the claims of others, who deserve to be treated as worthy of care and concern; love mitigates egoism in their ethics.

Such reflection is possible, in part, because of how *erōs* and *philia* are conceived: not primarily as emotions upon which we cannot exercise

---

[2] This is related to a focus on the character of the virtuous agent, and not just on rules for good action; see Julia Annas, *The Morality of Happiness* (Oxford: Oxford University Press, 1993).

[3] Compare Frankfurt: "The totality of the various things that a person cares about—together with his ordering of how important to him they are—effectively specifies his answer to the question of how to live" (Harry Frankfurt, *The Reasons of Love* [Princeton, NJ: Princeton University Press, 2004], 23).

[4] The opening lines of Aristotle's *Nicomachean Ethics*; Plato: *Gorgias* 466a, 468e; *Meno* 77a–b; *Euthydemus* 278e–282c, 288c–292e.

control and agency, but as phenomena that involve affective appraisal of their objects, a cognitive component that is deeply implicated in our perception of value.[5] Love is a practice whose ideal mode of expression requires work; indeed, for Socrates, there was an *art* of love, something to which he laid claim despite his characteristic disavowal of knowledge (*Symposium* 177d8–9; *Phaedrus* 277c, 257b). To perceive value keenly, and to attend to that value in the proper way, is the basis of this art, and it requires substantial and transformative work by its practitioners. Partly in virtue of this fact, love and friendship are ethical notions: they are best expressed by, and between, persons who are good, and certain of its forms are "a virtue, or involve virtue."[6]

## *Erōs*: Plato

Plato's philosophy represents the first stage of an enduring preoccupation with the transformative potential of a love that can lead to the divine. The *locus classicus* for this view is the *Symposium*'s account of *erōs*:

> This is what it is to approach love matters, or to be led by someone else in them, in the correct way: beginning from these beautiful things here, one must always move upwards for the sake of that beauty I speak of, using other things as steps from one to two and from two to all beautiful bodies, from beautiful bodies to beautiful activities, from activities to beautiful branches of knowledge, and finally from these to *that* knowledge, which is knowledge of nothing

---

[5] The phrase "affective appraisal" is taken from Jennifer Robinson (see her *Deeper Than Reason: Emotion and Its Role in Literature, Music, and Art* [Oxford: Oxford University Press, 2005]) and is designed, in part, to leave open the extent to which emotions have simple, or complex, cognitive content. A noncognitive view of the emotions is a relatively modern idea that fails to do justice to ancient thinking on the emotions. For the view that emotions have evaluative and cognitive content, see Martha Nussbaum, *Upheavals of Thought: The Intelligence of Emotions* (New York: Cambridge University Press, 2001), and Anthony Price, "Emotions in Plato and Aristotle," in *The Oxford Handbook of Philosophy of Emotion*, ed. Peter Goldie (Oxford: Oxford University Press, 2009), 122–141.

[6] Aristotle on *philia* (*N.E.* 1155a).

other than beauty itself, in order that one may finally know what beauty is... the uniformity of divine beauty itself. (*Symposium* 211c1–e4; trans. Rowe, with modifications)

This ascent of *erōs* from bodily beauty to knowledge of a divine object, the intelligible form of beauty, leads the agent in question to become dear to the gods (212a6). This is the correct practice of love, for Plato. The transformation of *erōs*, from a phenomenon often, though by no means exclusively, associated with sexual desire, to love of a divine and intelligible object is not without controversy. Critics have bemoaned the fact that "personal affection ranks low on Plato's *scala amoris*," an observation that has led to the charge of "spiritualized egocentrism."[7] Diffusing this charge requires a clearer sense of both the Greek and the Platonic senses of *erōs*.

Long before Plato's transformation of the term, there is evidence in Greek literature that *erōs* referred to the experiences of a desiring agent aroused by the stimulus of beauty.[8] Many features we think of as central to love—such as disinterested concern for the well-being of another, reciprocity of affection, and such like—would be more suited to discussion of *philia* and are not on the agenda in a discussion of *erōs*.[9] Even if interpersonal love is dethroned in favor of a focus on the lover's

---

7  Gregory Vlastos, "The Individual as an Object of Love in Plato," in *Plato: II, Ethics, Politics, Religion and the Soul*, ed. Gail Fine (Oxford: Oxford University Press, 1999), at 161 and 160 for the phrase "spiritualized egocentrism." For arguments against this charge, see Frisbee C. C. Sheffield, "The *Symposium* and Platonic Ethics: Plato, Vlastos and a Misguided Debate," *Phronesis* 57 (2012): 117–141.

8  David Konstan has argued that "the classical Greek notion of beauty is closely related to *erōs*, that is, passionate desire. Indeed, I would say that the fundamental response that was excited by beauty in ancient Greece was understood to be precisely desire" (*Beauty: The Fortunes of an Ancient Greek Idea* [Oxford: Oxford University Press, 2014], 62). Also relevant here are texts where *erōs* stands for desire, e.g., for food, drink, or sex in Homer's *Iliad* (3.442); see also Aeschylus, *Eumenides* (865); Herodotus, *Histories* (V. 32).

9  See David M. Halperin, "Plato and Erotic Reciprocity," *Classical Antiquity* 5 (1986): 60–80; G.R.F. Ferrari, "Platonic Love," in *The Cambridge Companion to Plato*, ed. Richard Kraut (Cambridge: Cambridge University Press, 1992), 248–277; and Charles Kahn, *Plato and the Socratic Dialogue: The Philosophical Use of a Literary Form* (Cambridge: Cambridge University Press, 1996), 261. Kahn argues, "In such a theory the object of desire is only initially or instrumentally a person. Reciprocal relations between persons would have to be treated in an account of

experience of beauty, *erōs* would never have delivered what we call for in an account of love. What is central to the Greek conception of *erōs* is that it is a form of passionate love or desire, which is responsive to beauty (*to kalon*); this is also a key feature of Plato's accounts of *erōs* (*Symposium* 204b–c; *Republic* III 402d; *Timaeus* 87d7–8; *Phaedrus* 250e1).[10] Though *to kalon* is a difficult phrase to translate, both 'the beautiful' and 'the fine' capture much of its sense, especially where the range is broader than the superficial appearance of a thing.[11] To call something *kalon* was to appraise the object, and to suggest that it had a relationship with the good (*to agathon*).[12] This relationship between *erōs* and goodness is a crucial part of the Platonic practice. If *erōs* involves the perception of value in what the agent loves and that moves the lover to love it (*Symposium* 201a8–10, b6–7, c4–5, 202d1–3, 203d4), this allows for reflection on that value, which would not be possible if this were not a cognition involving desire. Further, given the range of phenomena designated *kalon*—bodies, souls, cultural practices, and so on—there will be a range of objects to which *erōs* can respond. Many dialogues associate the highest objects of wisdom with beauty.[13] Given that *erōs* is, for Plato, a desire for beauty, and given that the objects of wisdom are among the most beautiful things (*Symposium* 204b), we can appreciate why one can have *erōs* for an intelligible beauty. That the kind of philosophical practice we see in the "ascent" is *erōtikos* (*Phaedo* 66e2–4, 67e5–68a2, 68a7–b6; *Symposium*

---

*philia* which Plato did not develop" (*Plato and the Socratic Dialogue*, 261). I disagree that Plato did not develop an account of *philia*, however; on which, see below.

10 See also *Charmides* 167e, where *epithumia* has pleasure as its proper object, while *erōs* is directed toward the *kalon*.

11 See Rachel Barney, "Note on Plato on the *Kalon* and the Good," *Classical Philology* 105 (2010): 363–377; and Aryeh Kosman, "Beauty and the Good: Situating the *Kalon*," *Classical Philology* 105 (2010): 341–357.

12 Since the *kalon* had a connection with the appearance of a thing, and the good of a thing, one way to capture this connection is to say, with Kosman, that "it is the mode of the good that shows forth; it is the splendour of the appearance of the good" (Kosman, "Beauty and the Good," 355).

13 See, e.g., *Cratylus* 439c; *Euthydemus* 301a; *Laws* 655c; *Phaedo* 65d, 75d, 100b; *Phaedrus* 254b; *Parmenides* 130b; *Philebus* 15a; *Republic* V 476b, 493e, 507b.

204b–c; *Republic* 485b, 490b, 501d2; *Phaedrus* 252c–253b) is no metaphor. Though philosophical *erōs* is not sexual in any sense, it is truly *erōtikos*—for the fundamental experience of *erōs* is a desire for beauty (*Symposium* 206e), the most basic expression of which is sexual *erōs* for embodied beauty, though this is simply one of its common forms.

Such observations speak to the possibilities for the practices advocated in Plato's ascent; we have yet to explain why they lead to such heights. To answer that question we need to turn to Plato's account of the nature and the aims of *erōs*. *Erōs* is a specific kind of desire, for something the agent perceives to be valuable (201a8–10, b6–7, c4–5, 202d1–3, 203d4) and wants on that basis, and this is something she lacks (either now or in the future: 200e3–5). What the desiring agent hopes to achieve is the possession of some good thing thought to deliver happiness (*eudaimonia*, 205a2–3); *erōs* is, specifically, the name of that desire for good things and happiness. *Eudaimonia* is the ultimate aim of *erōs* because, unlike other desirable objects, no one would ask why someone desires *that*. The desire for happiness is essentially a desire to possess good things for oneself "always" (206a11–12), exposed as an aspiration toward the immortal and happy state of the gods, who possess good and beautiful things forever (202c6–7). This is not an alternative to the idea that we desire *eudaimonia*; the immortal gods are the ideals toward which we aspire in our attempt to secure *eudaimonia*.[14] This aim begins to clarify the status of persons in the Platonic account: for, if what we desire, ultimately, is some good thought to satisfy the desire for a divine state of *eudaimonia*, this will be a heavy burden for any individual person to carry.

We have not yet explained how the pursuit of beauty is related to this aim. According to the *Symposium*'s account, when something is pursued with *erōs*, it is valued as supremely beautiful and perfect, and,

---

14 See Long: "In order to understand ancient philosophical usage of *eudaimonia* we need to attend to the word's etymology and its implicit reference to goodness conjoined with divinity or *daimōn*" (A.A. Long, "Eudaimonism, Divinity and Rationality in Greek Ethics," *Proceedings of the Boston Area Colloquium in Ancient Philosophy* 19 (2004): 126).

as such, standing in some relationship to the divine (204c4, *teleon kai makariston*). In the presence of such a beautiful person or thing, we become aware of how far we fall short of its divine perfection, which awakens resourceful attempts to overcome our mortal deficiencies as we aspire toward a divine state of happiness. A beautiful person, or thing, may be misleading in this role, but when it is such as to arouse *erōs*, its manifest value is held to be capable of helping us to achieve a divine state of *eudaimonia*. This explains why objects of *erōs* are pursued with such obsessional devotion; they are valued as that which, above all else, make life worth living.[15] Since *erōs* involves this specific valuation, it also has a specific mode of activity. Someone with *erōs* does not just want to gaze at the value of the beautiful desired object, nor come to possess it in the sense in which one wants to get a piece of property. Nor does one desire to care for the object in such a way that the object is benefitted; *it* is seen as perfect and blessed (204c4–5). Rather, the desiring agent wants to act for the sake of this end in such a way that the value of the beautiful thing is embodied in their *own* character and life, and captured in a way that brings their own life closer to that of the blessed gods, who possess all good and beautiful things (202c5–7). Since we have a mortal nature, which cannot possess anything—even our own bodily or psychic states—in any straightforward way, we have to be productive to secure what we value (207c5–208b5). Productive, or creative, activity in beauty (however specified) is the way in which mortal creatures like ourselves try "to have a share in" the divine (208b5). Against this backdrop, then, we can appreciate that *erōs* is not straightforwardly

---

15 See Ludwig: "Erōs occurs in cases in which the desire, whether sexual or not, becomes obsessional and the subject of desire becomes willing to devote nearly all his or her life, time, or resources to achieving the goal. Erōs tends to engage the whole self or to throw every other concern into the shade" (Paul Ludwig, *Eros and Polis: Desire and Community in Greek Political Theory* [Cambridge: Cambridge University Press, 2002], 13). Compare Suzanne Obdrzalek, "Why *Erōs*?," in *The Cambridge Companion to Plato*, 2nd ed., ed. David Ebrey and Richard Kraut (Cambridge University Press, 2022), 205.

*possessive*: the desire to possess good things for oneself for all time requires *creative* expression.[16]

Plato develops this point through the curious images of pregnancy and procreation (206c): all human beings are pregnant in body and soul, and the experience of beauty calls forth an act of replication, or reproduction, as we try to transform ourselves in its presence and thereby hope to secure *eudaimonia*. Different kinds of beauty are pursued by different kinds of desiring agents because they are appropriate to their conception of *eudaimonia*: *erōs* for bodily beauty manifests itself in the attempt to capture that value by the production of physical offspring, thought to provide "memory and happiness for all time to come" (208e4–5); *erōs* for a beautiful city, or soul, issues in attempts to capture that value by the production of fine laws, poems, or speeches, thereby securing an honorable life as a poet, or educator, for their producers (208c3, 209b). *Erōs* for beauty is a desire to give some kind of creative expression to ourselves, to reproduce the value we see in the world and capture it in a life of our own, as parents, poets, legislators, or philosophers.[17]

If we turn to the famous "ladder of love" in the *Symposium* with these ideas in mind, we can appreciate the nature of this pursuit. If the aim of *erōs* is a state of stable and secure *eudaimonia*, achieved by our creative endeavors, then the beautiful objects that inspire this transformative work must be capable of delivering that end. Creative endeavor is not just inspired, but also *informed*, by its creative environment: "grasping an image one gives birth to an image" (212a–b). Here Plato's metaphysical views take center stage: while sensible particular beautiful things

---

16 Though *erōs* is not straightforwardly possessive, it would be too hasty to infer from this that *erōs* is not egocentric. The goal remains the production of good things for the agent herself, though this may (or may not) involve other-directed activity, depending on the nature of the production. See further below.

17 See David Halperin: *erōs* is "the desire to realize an objective potential in the self" (Halperin, "Platonic *Erōs* and What Men Call Love," *Ancient Philosophy* 5 (1985):161–204 at 182).

are subject to change and decay, are beautiful at one time, or to one person and not to another, the intelligible idea, or form, of beauty is beautiful at all times, to all capable perceivers, changeless and divine (211b). Such beauty does not appear as the beauty of a body or a soul, with all the limitations on its appearance this manifestation would entail, but on its own, "pure, unmixed." There is no crude dualism here, though: it is because the form of beauty appears to us in sensible things, like bodies and souls, albeit dimly, or partially, that someone with *erōs* can be responsive to the idea that articulates and determines that experience of beauty. And since the aim is to pursue what is genuinely beautiful ("not an image, but the truth," 212a4–5) in order to produce something of genuine and lasting value, one must grasp beauty as it is, freed from the trappings of perspective and context. That grasp will not be a bodily one but an intellectual one, since beauty itself is intelligible; this is why the climax of *erōs* resides in the contemplation of an intelligible and divine form of beauty. This promises to deliver that 'god-like' state of stable and secure *eudaimonia*.

The divine heights toward which Platonic *erōs* leads, then, are largely due to two features. Its responsiveness to beauty shines a light on value in the world (however conceived): *erōs* plays a crucial role in making us cognizant of this evaluative property, and responsive to attempts to broaden our evaluative perspective. We are not just cognizant of value in the experience of *erōs*, though: the obsessional devotion and intensity of its pursuit of beauty reveals what is most important to us in our conception of a worthwhile and happy life, and inspires creative efforts to elicit whatever we consider to be best in ourselves as we struggle to find our own place in that evaluative landscape. Whether we accept the metaphysical premises that lead to the claim that only a divine and intelligible object can satisfy these demands, the metaphysical determination eventually given to beauty floats free of the call to broaden our horizons beyond any one individual. In this way, Plato urges us to liberate ourselves from that Aristophanic comic fantasy that supposes that another individual can make us complete and whole (*Symposium*

189–191c). That is too limited a view of the rich possibilities for human aspiration.

The range of beautiful objects to which *erōs* can be responsive explains why Plato can deploy *erōs* to characterize the philosopher's desire for wisdom (*Phaedo* 66e2–4, 67e5–68a2, 68a7–b6; *Republic* VI. 485b, 490b, 501d2; *Phaedrus* 252c–253b)—and even the citizens' relationship to the ideals of the city in the later *Laws*.[18] This does not yet explain *why* Plato promotes an *erōtikos* orientation to the beauty of such ideals, rather than restricting himself to arguments that claim they are the highest good. Much here concerns Plato's account of virtue, which emphasizes that it is not enough to do the right thing, or to follow the laws: one must do so with an orientation that ensures they will be pursued willingly, reliably, and with a harmony between desire and reason.[19] Specific features of *erōs* assist this enterprise, if rightly directed. Having *erōs* for wisdom, for example, is a mark of one who is orientated toward this value as something that, *above all else*, makes life worth living; this is precisely how it *ought* to be valued, for Plato (*Apology* 29d–e; *Euthydemus* 281e2–282a6). The accompanying dispositional features of this desire—its characteristic intensity and devotion—ensure that one is bound to this value, since it entails a strength of focus that ensures the wholehearted pursuit of the desired object, as well as a degree of commitment to, and identification with, that object, as one tries to capture its value through one's own creative

---

18 The lawgiver should turn his attention to *erōs* (III. 688b1–4) and cultivate an *erōs* for the ideal of perfect citizenship (I. 643c8–d3, I. 643e4–5). Children are led in play to desire passionately what they are to become when they grow up: through a variety of educational practices where beauty is central (II. 668b9–669b4), they will "fall in love with" the ideal of perfect citizenship (I. 643c8–d3). Lucia Prauscello, *Performing Citizenship in Plato's Laws* (Cambridge: Cambridge University Press, 2014), is an exception to those who argue that *erōs* has a marginal role in Plato's later works (e.g., Mark Munn, "*Erōs* and the Laws in Historical Context," in *Plato's Laws: Force and Truth in Politics*, ed. Gregory Recco and Eric Sanday (Bloomington: Indiana University Press, 2013), 31–47; and Mitchell Miller, "Reading the Laws as a Whole: Horizon, Vision, and Structure," in *Plato's Laws: Force and Truth in Politics*, ed. Gregory Recco and Eric Sanday (Bloomington: Indiana University Press, 2013), 11–30, at 12.

19 On which, see *Republic* IV. 443d and *Laws* III. 688b with Julia Annas, *The Morality of Happiness* (Oxford: Oxford University Press, 1993).

efforts.[20] Plato's continued deployment of *erōs* tells us something about the kind of value wisdom is, and the role it should play in our lives. The pursuit of wisdom is not just an inclination toward truth, but a desire to reproduce, or re-create, ourselves in its image; *erōs* powers that process.

## *Erōs*: Aristotle

If *erōs* is such a pervasive feature of Plato's thought, one might wonder why Aristotle, otherwise a keen commentator on many aspects of Plato's thought, "tacitly disowns Plato's divine *erōs*."[21] Although a work titled *Eroticus* (now lost) is listed by Diogenes Laertius, *erōs* makes a meager appearance in Aristotle's ethics and is described in rather disparaging terms.[22] Though he agrees with Plato that having the right desires is important for the virtuous agent, Aristotle does not discuss these under the auspices of *erōs*.[23]

One answer is suggested by attention to the cultural context of Plato's *Symposium*. At the end of the ascent of love, Socrates claims that it provides an account of how one should go about loving boys in the correct way (211b5), a remark that locates the discussion within the context of pederastic relationships. There may be reasons why Aristotle rejects this context. Plato grounds his account of human aspiration in relationships of that kind because such practices were, ideally, a context for the education of the young in the era in which his works were set. These relationships were prominent in the archaic and early

---

20 See *Republic* VI. 485d–e: if desires incline strongly in one direction, then like a stream that is not diverted, the strength of the flow will be strong and steady, weakening the force of other inclinations. Cf. *Phaedrus* (252a).
21 Richard Walzer, "Platonism in Islamic Philosophy," in *Greek into Arabic: Essays on Islamic Philosophy* (Oxford: Bruno Cassirer, 1962), 241; quoted in Anthony Price, *Love and Friendship in Plato and Aristotle* (Oxford: Clarendon Press, 1989), 236.
22 Aristotle mentions it to clarify the different relationship of friendship: *NE* VIII.4, IX.1.
23 When Aristotle argues that each man is active in relation to that he loves most, he uses *agape*; *orexis* also occurs twice in this passage (*N.E.* 1175a10–20).

classical periods and had aristocratic and military overtones. Since the origins of pederasty were thought to be Dorian, such practices had a strong Spartan association. Plato's work harks back to an earlier age where such institutions were still part of the education of the Athenian elite; but these came to be regarded with suspicion, as elitist, and the *symposion* was seen as a breeding ground for subversive activity.[24] Aristotle's neglect of such practices could be a sign that they were declining institutions, and that *erōs* was too specifically contextualized to serve as the driving force of human aspiration. Further, one of the ways in which Plato employs *erōs* is in converting young men to philosophy, particularly via an attachment to Socrates.[25] A private, individual attachment, away from the city, is a fitting medium for moral education for those who hold the political and cultural scene with suspicion; not so, for Aristotle, for whom moral development begins with exposure to the habits and practices of one's city and wider culture. The lack of attention to the propaideutic function of *erōs* in Aristotle's ethics can be explained further, perhaps, by thinking about the kind of audience Aristotle has in mind in the *Ethics*: it is designed to engage those who already aspire to the good life, not those who need seducing into it (1095b4–6).

Most significant, though, is surely the following. Aristotle held that erotic pederastic relationships provided an unstable framework for the more enduring relationships of friendship that Aristotle privileges, characterized as they are by excess (1164a2–13) and asymmetry (1157a3–12; 1159b12–19; 1163b32–1164a2).[26] This is responsible for the greater emphasis in his work on *philia* than on *erōs*. For Aristotle, *erōs*

---

24 See, e.g., Aristophanes's *Wasps* where he refers to pederasty as a pastime for "nobles and Laconizers," with Oswyn Murray (*Sympotika: A Symposium on the Symposion* (Oxford: Clarendon Press, 1995), 141–161.

25 See Elizabeth Belfiore, *Socrates' Daimonic Art: Love for Wisdom in Four Platonic Dialogues* (Cambridge: Cambridge University Press, 2012).

26 Though Aristotle agrees with Plato that such relationships can provide an opportunity for grounding *philia* relationships (1157a3–12), these are associated with a lesser form of friendship of utility between contraries: "for what a man actually lacks, he aims at," and this is why lovers

is an *excess* of friendship (*N.E.* 1171a10–13; cf. Plato, *Laws* VIII. 836a6–9), which sits uncomfortably in his ethical world. Virtuous behavior is a mean between two extreme states, at one end of which is excess; the other, deficiency (1106a26–b28). As an extreme form of love, *erōs* is part of the problem for Aristotle, rather than part of the solution: an extreme, rather than a mean, state. As such, it offers him little of value in his overall account of the nature and supporting conditions for the *eudaimōn* life.[27]

*Erōs* makes an appearance in a rather different context in Aristotle's works, attention to which suggests he saw a distinctive feature of significance for Plato. In *Metaphysics Lambda*, where the most beautiful and divine object is under consideration, Aristotle considers how unmoved movers move. For Aristotle, that which has the power to move things, without itself being moved, is an object of desire or thought (1072a26–7). In such a case, the beautiful object moves the faculty of desire, which moves the agent to action, without itself changing in any way (1072a27–8). So, if there is some supremely beautiful object that the first heaven desires, this could be an unchanging cause of the motion of the heavens. In light of these considerations, Aristotle claims that the Prime Mover moves the heavenly bodies as an object of love moves (*kinei dē hōs erōmenon*, 1072b3).[28] The specific use of *erōs* here seems to characterize a distinctive way of acting for the sake of an end, which is uniquely suited to capturing a relationship with a divine object. As Plato's analysis suggested, *erōs* is an asymmetrical relation, in which the object is seen as supremely beautiful and in need of nothing; as a result, it is a relationship in which one seeks to effect a change *in*

---

sometimes seem ridiculous, when they "demand to be loved as they love" (1159b12–19). See Price, *Love and Friendship in Plato and Aristotle*, 246–249.

27 Thanks to James Lesher for discussion of this paragraph.

28 One need not suppose that the Prime Mover actually is an object of *erōs*, though; the phrase captures the kind of movement characteristic of an object of *erōs*.

*oneself* and not in the object for whose sake one acts.[29] The characteristic action of *erōs* is to want "to have a share in," to change in accordance with the perceived value in the object, to "approximate" the object of its attention. This feature of *erōs* was appreciated by later Platonists too: Plotinus and Proclus made *erōs* central to their accounts of the movement of all things toward the One, where each entity becomes the best image of its progenitor.[30] The hallmarks of *erōs* are uniquely suited to action for a divine end, a feature that had a lasting impact on the erotic-mystical tradition from third-century Platonism, through certain branches of Christianity, nineteenth-century Romanticism, and beyond.[31]

## *Philia*: Plato

The interpersonal aspect of love is developed by Plato and Aristotle in their accounts of *philia*, the paradigmatic forms of which are love between family and friends.[32] It has been argued that Plato did not develop such an account beyond the seemingly aporetic *Lysis*, and this has

---

29 See Richardson Lear: "Perhaps Aristotle wants to indicate with his use of the word *erōmenon* that the first heavenly bodies are related to the unmoved mover as lovers are related to the Forms of the Good and Beautiful in Plato's *Symposium* and *Phaedrus*," (Richardson Lear, *Happy Lives and the Highest Good: An Essay in Aristotle's Nicomachean Ethics* [Princeton, NJ: Princeton University Press, 2004], 79), where "the urge to approximate" (72), i.e., to capture their value in some productive activity, is central.

30 On which, see Arthur Hilary Armstrong, "Platonic *Erōs* and Christian *Agape*," *Downside Review* 3 (1961): 105–121; and Werner Beierwaltes, "The Love of Beauty and the Love of God," in *Classical Mediterranean Spirituality: Egyptian, Greek, Roman*, ed. Armstrong (London: Routledge, 1986), 189–205. Plotinus associates *erōs* with the notion of *homoiōsis*, 'becoming like' (VI. 7, 31, 10). Cf. Proclus (*In Alc*. 61.3–5): all that exists is moved toward the One by *erōs*. He also discusses "assimilation to the origin." On Proclus's use of *erōs*, see Gilles Quispel, "God Is Erōs," in *Early Christian Literature and the Classical Tradition: In Honorem Robert M. Grant*, ed. W. R. Schoedel and R. L. Wilken (Paris: Beauchesne, 1979), 189–205.

31 On which, see Simon May, *Love: A History* (New Haven, CT: Yale University Press, 2011).

32 The semantic range of *philia* is broader than friendship. Konstan argues that "the form *philia* does in fact cover relationships far wider than friendship, including the love between kin, and the affection or solidarity between relatively distant associates such as members of the same fraternity or city" (*Friendship in the Classical World* [Cambridge: Cambridge University Press, 1997], 9).

seemed inadequate.[33] It raises puzzles about friendship: who is friend to whom is one of the central difficulties. Those who are good seem not to need friends; for "if one were in want of nothing one would feel no affection, and he who felt no affection would not love" (215a6–c2), a remark that suggests that friendship is analyzed in terms of the use, or benefit, provided by friends to each other, as if we are incapable of loving others for their own sake. It may well be fair to say that Plato entertained quite seriously the thought that most of us *are* incapable of loving others for their own sake, but this is not to say that Plato ignored this ideal; rather, it is presented as a form of love, that requires work and which is possible only for persons of a certain kind.

This helps to explain why Plato developed a positive account of *philia* within an account of *erōs*, as he did in the *Phaedrus*.[34] A relationship between a lover and a beloved is not the only context in which *philia* might arise, of course (*Phaedrus* 233b6–d4); such relationships could obtain between family members, or citizens, as is the case in the *Laws*. Nonetheless, the value of exploring *philia* within an account of *erōs* is that it emphasizes that an agent's broader evaluative commitments, expressed in their *erōs*, inform the kind of friendship sought and the nature of the attachment. In both the *Phaedrus* and the *Laws* (VIII. 836e5–837d8), Plato operates with a threefold account of friendship, and in the *Phaedrus*, each type is distinguished by a love (*erōs*) that informs the friendship. The desire for pleasure, the desire for some kind of advantage or honor, and the desire for wisdom and virtue, determines the location of interest in each case and affects whether the features characteristic of friendship are expressed freely

---

33 Gregory Vlastos, "The Individual as an Object of Love in Plato," is the classic statement of this problem; cf. Kahn, *Plato and the Socratic Dialogue*, 261. For a positive account of the *Lysis*, see Terry Penner and Christopher Rowe, *Plato's Lysis* (Cambridge: Cambridge University Press, 2005). Compare Dimitri El Murr, "*Philia* in Plato," in *Ancient and Modern Conceptions of Friendship*, ed. Suzanne. Stern Gillet and Gary. M. Gurtler (Albany, NY: SUNY Press, 2014), 3–34.

34 The *Phaedrus* is concerned with whether *erōs* is compatible with *philia* and to what extent (231b7–c7; 232d1–4; 232d7–e2; 233a1–4; 237c6–8; 253c5; 255b5–7), to show how others are benefited by loving relationships.

or inhibited. Those who seek pleasure use others to serve their own ends ("for the purpose of filling up," *Phaedrus* 241d1; *Laws* VIII. 837c2) and the goodwill (*eunoia*) characteristic of friendship is stunted by the subject's desire for their own gain (*Phaedrus* 232c5–e2). Goodwill is shown only insofar as the other provides pleasure, and the other's good is not valued if it is inconsistent with that (230e–240a; 241c6–d1). Once sated, this person is "compelled to default," so the association will be fleeting (232e6). This is an unequal, nonreciprocal relationship, based on one party needing something from the other.[35] A second kind holds between those who love honor and whose relationship is based on an exchange of pledges (*Phaedrus* 256c–d), which suggests some advantage for both.[36] Such types do not have characters free of conflict, which makes them susceptible to the limitations of the first kind of friendship; their *philia* is not as great as it could be (256b7–d3).[37]

A third kind of friendship holds between those who are alike and both of a good, wisdom-loving character (*Phaedrus* 252e3, 255b; *Laws* VIII. 837c2). In this case, the other is loved not for some pleasure or advantage for the one loving, but for their good nature (*Phaedrus* 252e–253b; *Laws* VIII. 837a4–b3, c2). Parties who share such a nature are capable of appreciating the value of those qualities (such as wisdom and virtue) constitutive of the soul's beauty; the other is treated with "reverence and awe" (*Phaedrus* 255a; *Laws* VIII. 837c), as if "equal to the gods" (*Phaedrus* 255a2), which are clear indications that they are an end of care and concern. The reverential appreciation of the value of another allows each party to see their nature and value more clearly, and this attentive concern provides inspiration and support for their

---

35 Compare *Laws* (VIII. 837b–c).
36 In the *Symposium*, the advantage for the beloved is education, while the lover receives honor from his edifying speeches (209b7–8 with 208c3).
37 Compare *Laws* (VIII. 837c) on the mixed friendship: the agent is interested in soul (and self-control and intelligence) but also desires "to be filled" (c1). There is clearly something the other wants from the other, which, at times, eclipses the all-important consideration—the other's character (VIII. 837c2).

development; it fosters appreciation of their shared good nature "mirrored" in each other (*Phaedrus* 255d). As similar types, they each care about what the other values and express that together in mutually benefiting activities, which foster their commitment to a shared evaluative orientation.[38] So begins a partnership, characterized by philosophical discussion (*Phaedrus* 256b1, c1), in which there is much goodwill (255b4, 256a3) and no envy (253b7), because neither sees the other as a possession to be had, but as a nature to be celebrated. Since this friendship is not grounded in contingent, marginal, and changeable features of the other, but in their good nature, it is more stable than the other kinds (256b1).

Here, we come as close as anything in the dialogues to the privileged notion of love for another "for their own sake," the value of which lies in the thought that others are to be treated as genuine ends of care and concern, a view from which much moral philosophy takes its lead.[39] This feature is not without difficulty for those who argue that the properties that ground such treatment are too generic to capture the particularity and uniqueness of the beloved; they provide equal reason to love and befriend similar others.[40] This need not be overplayed: the object of *philia* is, and remains, a person with whom a lifelong—if not exclusive—relationship is forged. A good and beautiful character may well be held by similar others; there may be only contingent reasons why one appears more lovable than another. The fact that all similar others are equally worthy of love is not a problem for Plato, though, but an opportunity. He is less concerned with how to justify particular

---

38 On the relationship between caring about others and caring about what they value, see Bennett W. Helm, *Love, Friendship and the Self* (Oxford: Oxford University Press, 2010), 41 and 86.
39 See Gregory Vlastos, "Justice and Equality," in *Social Justice*, ed. Richard Brandt (Englewood Cliffs, NJ: Prentice Hall, 1962), 31–72 at 48–49, with Vlastos, "The Individual as an Object of Love in Plato," 143n24, who attributes such a thought to Aristotle, but not to Plato: "Aristotle's wishing another good for his sake, not yours, though still far from the Kantian conception of treating persons as ends in themselves, is the closest any philosopher comes to it in antiquity."
40 Vlastos, "The Individual as an Object of Love in Plato," 161, who writes of Platonic love that "the individual, in the uniqueness and integrity of his or her individuality, will never be the object of our love."

intimate friendships, and more concerned to explore the development of a character and orientation that fosters beneficial relationships with others—the more the better—who are seen as worthy of care and concern. Indeed, this broad basis for *philia* is precisely what enables it to play a broader role in structuring political communities in the *Republic*, *Statesman*, and the *Laws*. For once the grounds for this relationship are so conceived, *philia* can generate an extended partiality toward all members of one's community, insofar as each is acknowledged as willing supporters of the common goals and projects that constitute their virtuous community (even if the intimacy and individual affection that characterizes more personal friendships is diminished in such contexts).[41] As the Athenian puts it in the *Laws*, "What the would-be great man should be in love with is not himself or his own possessions, but what is just, whether this in fact manifests itself in his own actions, or in somebody else's" (*Laws* 731d6–732a3).[42] *Philia* can be employed to forge bonds of connectedness in the city because the nature of its grounds enable its operation as both partial and (in a virtuous community) broadly egalitarian. As such, it can provide a basis for what we might recognize as a moral concern.[43] And yet, given these grounds and what they require—namely, promoting the good of

---

[41] In the *Republic*, the Noble Lie teaches citizens to treat each other as *philoi*; cf. *Republic* IX. 590c–d, where the citizens are described as "alike and *philoi* as far as possible, all governed by the same principle," where this is characteristic of a virtuous community united in promotion of shared aims. See Murr, "*Philia* in Plato." In the *Laws*, friendship is specified as one of three goals that should guide legislation (I. 639b–e). It is paired with key political ideals, such as rule "for the sake of the ruled" (III. 697d2–3), community (III. 697c8), freedom (III. 694a6, III. 701d7–9), equality (VI. 757b–d), and happiness (V. 743c5–6), which friendship helps to foster. See M. Schofield, "Friendship and Justice in the *Laws*," in *The Platonic Art of Philosophy*, ed. G. Boys-Stones, D. El Murr, and C. Gill (Cambridge: Cambridge University Press, 2016), 293–297, and F. C. C. Sheffield, "Love and the City: *Erōs* and *Philia* in Plato's *Laws*," in *Emotions in Plato*, ed. Laura. Candiotto and Olivier. Renaut (Leiden: Brill, 2020), 330–372.

[42] Compare *Symposium* 205e, where Socrates explains that since we are willing to cut off our own arms and legs if we are diseased, it is not what is akin to ourselves that we love, but what is good.

[43] Friendship plays a more negligible role in more recent discussions of ethics and politics, in large part because it is seen as too partial and preferential to ground the kinds of universalizing claims of ethics, or to provide any basis for legislation. On whether Plato's account of friendship deals with such problems, see Frisbee C. C. Sheffield, "Moral Motivation in Plato's *Republic*? *Philia* and Return to the Cave," *Oxford Studies in Ancient Philosophy* 59 (2021): 79–131.

others in a shared life—those outside of the circle of *philia* will have no moral claim on us.[44]

## *Philia*: Aristotle

Though the *Phaedrus* and the *Laws* provide evidence that Plato had a positive account of *philia*, the account lacks the robust conceptual analysis provided by Aristotle, who evidently drew inspiration from Plato's threefold analysis. In the *Nicomachean Ethics*, Aristotle begins by exploring what is found lovable (*to philēton*, VIII. 1155b18–19, 1156a6–8) and finds there are three such objects: what is pleasant, what is useful, and what is good (1155b18–19). Friendship is ranked in accordance with these values, and "complete friendship is the friendship of good people similar in virtue" (1156b7–8). Central here is why and how the other is valued.[45] When we love another insofar as they are pleasant or useful to us, we are responding to some incidental feature of the other (*kata sumbebēkos*, 1156a16–17), which is to say we love the other for what they have, or can give to us, rather than for what they are (1164a9–11). When others are loved because of their good character, by contrast, they are loved for themselves (*kath' hautous*, 1156b9), that is, "for being persons of a certain sort" (1156a10–16). This seems to determine how the hallmarks of friendship are expressed. Though friendship is mutually reciprocated and acknowledged goodwill (*eunoia*, 1155b33–1156a6), ideally, at least, for the other person's own sake (1155b31), the

---

44 See Terence Irwin, *Plato's Ethics* (Oxford: Oxford University Press, 1995), 316.
45 The details of which depend on how the claim that friendship is "on account of" (*dia*) pleasure, utility, or goodness (1236a23–32) is construed. Some take this to specify what *causes* the friendship (see, e.g., John M. Cooper, "Aristotle on the Forms of Friendship," *Review of Metaphysics* 30 (1977): 619–648), which need not determine how they are valued; others take this as an end in view in the friendship, which specifies what they hope to be *produced* (see, e.g., Kenneth D. Alpern, "Aristotle on the Friendships of Utility and Pleasure," *Journal of the History of Philosophy Quarterly* 21 (1983): 303–315; and David K. O'Connor, "Two Ideals of Friendship," *History of Philosophy Quarterly* 7 (1990): 109–122; or both (see, e.g., Terence Irwin, *Nicomachean Ethics: Aristotle* (Indianapolis: Hackett Press, 1999), in which case it will play a formative role in how others are valued.

extent to which this is the case is dependent upon what each finds lovable in the other, for "people who love one another wish good things to one another in that respect in which they love" (1156a9–10).[46] The reciprocal goodwill characteristic of friendship (1155b33, 1156a3–5) is informed by these grounds, and since friends do not only wish good things for each other, but do them as well (1157b8–9), this also determines the kind of activities the friends engage in together—for friendship requires shared activity (IX. 1172a3–8). For those who are good, such pursuits will not be restricted to drinking, or playing dice together, but will involve supporting their good character, central to which is rational activity, hence the importance of "sharing in discussion and thought" (*koinōnein logōn kai dianoias*, 1170b10–12).[47] Such friendship lasts as long as they are good (1165b23–5), "and excellence is an enduring thing" (1156b12).

Here we come upon an issue raised by Plato (*Lysis* 215a–b) and addressed explicitly by Aristotle.[48]

> People say that those who are blessed and self-sufficient have no need of friends, since they already have the things that are good, and, being self-sufficient, need nothing further. But a friend, since he is another self, provides what a person cannot provide by himself. (IX. 9. 1169b; trans. Crisp)[49]

The reason people hold this mistaken view, according to Aristotle, is that they suppose that the blessed person will have no need of friends

---

46 See Kenneth Alpern, "Aristotle on the Friendships of Utility and Pleasure," *Journal of the History of Philosophy* 21 (1983): 303–315.

47 "Each person would seem to be the intellectual part—*nous*, or primarily this" (1166a23).

48 On which, see Jennifer E. Whiting, "The Nicomachean Account of *Philia*," in *The Blackwell Guide to Aristotle's Nicomachean Ethics*, ed. Richard Kraut (Hoboken, NJ: John Wiley & Sons, 2006), 279; and Zena Hitz, "Aristotle on Self-Knowledge and Friendship," *Philosophers' Imprint* 11 (2011): 4–5).

49 I am using Roger Crisp's translation as it appears in Aristotle, *Nicomachean Ethics*, ed. Crisp (Cambridge: Cambridge University Press, 2014).

who are useful, or of friends for pleasure, "since he already has what is good"; but this does not exhaust the possibilities. In the striking claim that the friend is "another self," Aristotle begins his alternative account, which is explored in the following:

> If being happy consists in living and engaging in activity, and the activity of the good person is good and pleasant in itself, as we have said at the beginning; and if what is our own is pleasant; and if we are better able to contemplate our neighbours than ourselves, and their actions than our own; and if the good person finds pleasure in the actions of good people who are his friends, (since they have both the qualities that are pleasant by nature); then the blessed person will need friends like this, since he rationally chooses to contemplate actions that are good and his own, and the actions of a good person who is his friend are like this. (1169b30–1170a4; trans. Crisp)

The claim that the friend is "another self" (1168b7; 1170b6) relies, in part, on the importance of action and activity to living (1170a16–19). Human beings realize their being in activity, and since the activities that constitute one's life will also be those that characterize the life one has with the virtuous friend (1172a1–3), collaborating together in these activities helps to constitute the being of each. Being human, it seems, is a team sport. This is both because it is easier to be continuously active with friends (1170a5–6), sharing in discussion and thought (1170b11–14), and because "we are better able to contemplate our neighbors than ourselves," and so to appreciate more clearly the value of realizing a good character.[50]

There is no crude narcissism involved in the claim that the friend is another self: one values one's friend's good activity, because it is good

---

[50] John Cooper ("Aristotle on the Forms of Friendship," *Review of Metaphysics* 30 (1977): 619–648) with *Magna Moralia* 1213a20–4: "Just as when we wish to see our own face we do so by looking in the mirror, in the same way when we wish to know ourselves we can obtain that knowledge by looking at our friend. For the friend is, as we assert, a second self."

and such is pleasant in itself (1169b32), *and* "the actions of good people are the same or similar in kind" to our own (1156b15–17). The attitudes that the *eudaimôn* agent has for their friend are related to those they have for themselves (1170b5–8), in the sense that they are both are grounded in the value of virtue, which is good in itself (1170b5).[51] Nonetheless, the idea that these are other selves who "share the activities that constitute what we are and help us with them"[52] requires careful specification. For if the activities of friendship promote the agent's own *eudaimonia,* on the grounds that it is easier to be continually active with friends (1170a5–6) and good friends provide practice in goodness (1170a11–13), then this may threaten the crucial notion of wishing well to another *for the other's sake.* The best form of friendship is distinguished by *not* being grounded in some good or pleasure for the one loving (1156a10–14).[53]

Aristotle's question is why one should want friends when one is *eudaimôn* already, and not whether friends are needed to make one *eudaimôn* in the first place. One may suppose that a *eudaimôn* agent able to enjoy what is "good and pleasant in itself" (such as the activities of the good other) will have friends because the mutually

---

51 Whiting argues that "I can value my friend's good and the activities in which *it* consists in the same way that I value my own *without* having to regard them as *mine*" ("Impersonal Friends," *Monist* 74 [1991]: 10). For passages that support this view, see *N.E.* 1117b8–10: "Someone's own being is choice-worthy because he perceives that he is good and this sort of perception is pleasant in itself." See also *Magna Moralia*: "The good man is a lover of good, not a lover of self; for he loves himself only, if at all, because he is good" (II.14. 1212b18–20; cf. *N.E.* 1166b11–13) with Plato's *Symposium*: we are willing to cut off our own arms and legs if they are diseased (205e), so it is not the *oikeion* as such that is desired, but the good. Compare Plato, *Laws* V. 731d6–732a3 with Aristotle, *N.E.* IX.8. 1168b29–30; 1168b35–6.

52 Hitz, "Aristotle on Self-Knowledge and Friendship," 17.

53 Michael Pakaluk (*Aristotle: Nicomachean Ethics Books VIII and IX* [Cambridge: Cambridge University Press, 1998], 187) asks "how love for a friend on account of his being one's own activity would be compatible with loving him 'in his own right' and 'on account of himself'' (as in VIII. 3)." David Brink ("Rational Egoism, Self and Others," in *Identity, Character, Morality: Essays in Moral Psychology*, ed. Owen Flanagan and Amelie Rorty (Cambridge, MA: MIT Press, 1990), 339–378) argues that the friend is an extension of one's own activity, and Cooper argues that friendship is a mode of self-realization. See the arguments against these views in Whiting, "Impersonal Friends"; and Whiting, "The Nicomachean Account of *Philia*," in *Blackwell Guide to Aristotle's Nicomachean Ethics*, ed. Kraut, 276–304.

acknowledged and reciprocated goodwill characteristic of friendship is the appropriate response to such value in another.[54] One might be concerned that this downplays the role that friendship plays in making the *eudaimôn* agent's own life better. There is humility in the acknowledgment that even for the *eudaimôn* agent, there are things he "cannot provide by himself" (1169b); even the most blessed life is nevertheless a human life, and "a human is a social being and his nature is to live in the company of others" (1169b17–18).[55] Loving the friend for their own sake—enjoying and promoting their worth and value—is not incompatible with loving them *also* for the sake of their contribution to our own flourishing; the virtuous agent would love such a person even if they made no such contribution, but a human life is better with friends.[56]

The fact that we are social animals finds its richest expression in Aristotle's *Politics*, where he argued (with Plato) that friendship, albeit of a different kind, binds together communities, the most important of which is the city-state, or *polis* (*Politics* 1252a1–7); the city is a community of friends who decide to live together for the sake of living well (*Politics* 1.2. 1253a15–8). This allows us to appreciate that *philia* is not, fundamentally or exclusively, a private phenomenon, whose intimacy threatens the public sphere, but a partnership (*koinōnia*) in pursuit of some common (*koinon*) good, variously specified (*N.E.* 1159b5–32), which carries with it a degree of reciprocal goodwill and mutual concern to function as such.[57] Though Aristotle does not explicitly specify how political friendship relates to the three forms of friendship outlined in the *Nicomachean Ethics*, he appears to regard it as a form of

---

54 See Whiting ("The Nicomachean Account of *Philia*," 297): friendship "is an *appropriate* response to ways the world is."

55 Compare *Politics* 1253a28–9: "He who is unable to live in society, or who has no need because he is sufficient for himself, must be either a beast or a god."

56 *N.E.* 1.7 suggests that choosing something for its own sake is not incompatible with also choosing it for the sake of something else.

57 What distinguishes political animals is not just living together, but working together for common goals (*H.A.* 1.1. 487b33–488a14), as is characteristic of friends.

advantage friendship (*N.E.* 1160a11–14; *E.E.* 1242a6–13), achieved without recourse to ties of family, or ethnicity, but born of the acknowledgment that one's own way of life is dependent on others, with whom one is bound, to secure mutual help and assistance, in a common mode of living based on agreement on practical ends of importance (*homonoia*, 1167b2–4). Like all such love, it is based on a sense of the value of others, as co-contributors to the community, and it is a response to the worth of others as partners in that shared enterprise. This generates a degree of reciprocal goodwill and mutual concern, such that one treats others fairly and does not begrudge them goods and opportunity. This is why, as Aristotle puts it, "*philia* seems to hold cities together, and lawmakers seem to take it more seriously than justice" (*N.E.* 1155a23). Friendship, for both Plato and Aristotle, is the engine of ethical and political ideals. It is how we acknowledge the worth and value of each other, and our dependence on those others in cultivating worthwhile lives and communities. It may also provide the basis for ideals beyond the confines of particular communities. As Aristotle notes, "We praise those who are lovers of humankind (*philanthrōpous*); for one might see in travelling widely that every human is akin (*oikeion*) to every other and likewise lovable (*philon*)" (*N.E.* 1155a14–22).

# *Reflection*

## PLATONIC LOVE POETRY

*Erik Gray*

If we really want to understand how the ancient Greek and Roman worlds conceptualized love, we must look to the poets. In other areas, too, classical philosophy goes hand in hand with poetry, often citing poems as evidence or even being written in verse. But nowhere else is the relation between philosophy and poetry quite so intimate. Classical thought about love takes its cue from poetry, and love in classical poetry is in large part a matter of thought.

    Classical love poetry can be seen as being bracketed by two titanic figures: Sappho and Ovid. They don't actually stand at the chronological extremes: others were already singing of love in the centuries before Sappho, and after the death of Ovid Latin love poetry persisted. But it is convenient nevertheless to think of them as bookends, because—aside from the shared circumstance of their both being exiles—they seem to be such perfect opposites. The opposition extends to the form in which their poetry has been passed down to us as much as to its content. Sappho is a poet of fragments, of broken speech, of love as ineffable passion—wild, overwhelming, irresistible. Ovid is a poet of polished, self-contained couplets, which present love as a wry, recognizable, self-conscious affair. Yet both are equally essential to the classical conception of *eros*.

If we consider Plato's *Phaedrus*, one of his two great dialogues (along with the *Symposium*) devoted to the subject of love, it seems at first glance far more Sapphic than Ovidian. The dialogue begins with Phaedrus reading out a speech that sounds like it could have been written by the Ovid of *The Art of Love*, arguing that a lover whose attachment is coolly considered and rational is preferable to one who is swept away by passion. But Socrates, claiming to be inspired by "the lovely Sappho," responds by completely dismissing Phaedrus's speech.[1] He offers instead his own account of the highest and most desirable love, describing its symptoms in terms strongly reminiscent of those used by Sappho in fragment 31, one of her few poems to have survived nearly intact. Sappho's speaker says that the man sitting beside her beloved "seems to me equal to gods," and that the mere sight of them "puts the heart in my chest on wings . . . fire is racing under skin . . . and cold sweat holds me."[2] Socrates similarly says that the lover, beholding the beauty of the beloved, "gazes at him with the reverence due to a god"; then "his chill gives way to sweating and high fever, because the stream of beauty that pours into him . . . waters the growth of his wings" (251a). This is the "god-sent madness" of love, which Socrates directly compares to poetic inspiration, "the Muses' madness" (245a–b).

But that is not the whole story of the *Phaedrus*—or for that matter of Ovid and Sappho. It is true that Socrates claims that love is madness, but there is madness and there is madness. Love-madness is not the raving of mere insanity that sees things as they are not. To the contrary, Socrates claims that the madness of love is a form of higher knowledge and insight. The lover's

---

[1] Plato, *Phaedrus* 235c; all quotations refer to the translation by Alexander Nehamas and Paul Woodruff in *Plato on Love*, ed. C. D. C. Reeve (Indianapolis: Hackett, 2006).
[2] Sappho 31, lines 1, 6, 10, 13; in *If Not, Winter: Fragments of Sappho*, trans. Anne Carson (New York: Vintage, 2003).

frenzy at beholding the beloved's beauty springs from a sudden understanding, a recognition of the true, absolute Beauty that the soul once knew in heaven. Love is thus a form of self-possession and mental clarity, even as it involves a partial disordering of the senses.[3] And this complexity is reflected in the form of Socrates's long speech on the subject (244a–257b), which is in equal parts impassioned and detached: although clearly meant to be taken as communicating his true thoughts, it is presented epideictically—simply as a model, that is, of something one might say.[4] Socrates's speech is at once more heartfelt than the one Phaedrus reads out at the beginning of the dialogue and more self-consciously contrived.

It is tempting to call this duality Ovidian: Ovid's love poetry, from the *Amores* onward, is distinguished by its mingling of genuine sentiment with artistic wit and self-display. But in fact such a mixture, in varying proportions, is characteristic of all classical love poetry, including Sappho's. In the late twentieth century, critics began to suggest that much of Sappho's poetry, which had always been read as the direct expression of personal feeling, was actually, in its original context, dramatic or choric, a form of public performance rather than private effusion.[5] Such a reading does not disenchant Sappho, as it might seem to do; rather it restores to her poems a crucial dimension that earlier readings had obscured. Classical love, in all its discursive manifestations, is vibrantly

---

[3] Socrates goes on to illustrate the double effect of love by comparing the soul to a chariot with two horses: at the sight of the beloved, one horse goes wild with desire while the other keeps its head (253d–254d).

[4] Part way through, Socrates interrupts himself to remind us that his whole discourse is fictional: "This is the experience we humans call love, you beautiful boy (I mean the one to whom I am making this speech)" (252b).

[5] See, for instance, *Reading Sappho: Contemporary Approaches*, ed. Ellen Greene (Berkeley: University of California Press, 1996).

paradoxical, a matter of simultaneous madness and self-possession, confusion and recognition, impulse and forethought. The simultaneity of these experiences is what gives love its characteristic thrill.

Hence the paradigmatic love scene in classical literature—which also happens to be one of the earliest—is the reunion of Odysseus and Penelope in book 23 of Homer's *Odyssey*. Here the affective climax coincides, as Plato would lead us to expect, with a moment of conscious recognition.[6] After twenty years of separation and mutual longing, husband and wife do not fly immediately into each other's arms when they meet; instead, they continue to think as deeply as they feel. Penelope secretly puts Odysseus to the test, craftily performing in a way that he alone would be able to detect.[7] Penelope's plan succeeds in allowing the lovers to know each other all over again: she recognizes the wily Odysseus in his answering of her "riddle"; he recognizes the faithful Penelope in the very fact of her having proposed it. Only then does their passion overcome them: Penelope's knees give way, as she and Odysseus both dissolve in tears and cling to each other as if they could never let go. The whole of Plato's philosophy of love, as well as the whole subsequent tradition of classical love poetry, could be seen as a series of footnotes to this scene, in which the deliberation, recognition, and ecstasy of love all combine.

---

[6] Compare Aristotle's account of the crucial role of recognition (*anagnorisis*) in tragedy, particularly when it coincides with the moment of *peripeteia* or reversal (*Poetics*, ch. 11).

[7] Penelope orders a servant to move the couple's bed out of their room; Odysseus alone can understand this to be impossible, since he built the bed and knows it to be rooted to the ground.

CHAPTER 3

# Love in the Christian Tradition

*David McPherson*

No understanding of love has had more influence on Western culture than that which emerges from the Christian tradition.[1] This essay traces some of the main contours of Christian love and examines key issues pertaining to it. The first section explores the picture of love that arises from the New Testament. The second section considers Augustine's and Aquinas's accounts of the "order of love," which address tensions inherent to the New Testament teachings on love, especially regarding (1) love for the Creator and created things and (2) universal and particular love. It will be shown that Christian ethics is above all concerned with *rightly ordered love*. The third section examines the relationship

---

[1] See, e.g., Raimond Gaita, "Goodness beyond Virtue," in *A Common Humanity: Thinking about Love and Truth and Justice* (New York: Routledge, 1998); Charles Taylor, *Sources of the Self: The Making of the Modern Identity* (Cambridge, MA: Harvard University Press, 1989), esp. the conclusion; Simon May, *Love: A History* (New Haven, CT: Yale University Press, 2011), esp. chs. 1, 6–7, 17.

between two conceptions of love, *agape* and *eros*, especially in light of Anders Nygren's work, which criticizes the way of thinking about love that is exemplified in the work of Augustine and Aquinas. Against Nygren, it will be argued that Christian *agape* should be regarded as involving appraisal love that is both conditional and unconditional, in different respects, and as connected to *eros* in meeting our desire for fulfillment.

## Love in the New Testament

A comprehensive account of love in the New Testament is of course not possible here, and so we focus on some of the most important features of the New Testament picture of love. To begin with, we should be impressed by the *centrality* of love to the Christian message, where it is regarded as having *supreme value*. When a lawyer questioned Jesus about which commandment of the law is the greatest, the Gospel of Matthew says that he replied, "'You shall love the Lord your God with all your heart, and with all your soul, and with all your mind.' This is the greatest and first commandment. And a second is like it: 'You shall love your neighbor as yourself.' On these two commandments hang all the law and the prophets" (Matthew 22:37–40; see also Mark 12:28–34; Luke 10:25–28).[2] We might wonder here how exactly the second commandment "is like" the first. One plausible interpretation is offered by John Cottingham: "Since [we are] made in the image of God (Genesis 1:27), each human being has a special dignity and worth, and is owed something of the respect and love that is due to God. So failure to love our neighbour is, in a certain way, a failure to love and respect God."[3] We later consider another way that love of God and

---

[2] All Scripture references are from the New Revised Standard Version; see *The New Oxford Annotated Bible: New Revised Standard Version with the Apocrypha*, 3rd ed. (Oxford: Oxford University Press, 2001).

[3] John Cottingham, "Love and Religion," in *The Oxford Handbook of Philosophy of Love*, ed. Christopher Grau and Aaron Smuts (Oxford: Oxford University Press, 2024), 562. I am indebted

neighbor are connected, but for now we should note that this twofold love commandment combines two separate passages from the Torah: Deuteronomy 6:5 ("You shall love the LORD your God with all your heart, and with all your soul, and with all your might") and Leviticus 19:18 ("You shall love your neighbor as yourself").[4] We get a sense of just how important Jesus believes these two love commandments are when he says that all the teachings of the law and the prophets "hang" on them.

It is not difficult to see how following the twofold love commandment fulfills the Ten Commandments (Exodus 20:1–21; Deuteronomy 5:1–21). As Paul writes, "[One] who loves another has fulfilled the law. The commandments, 'You shall not commit adultery; You shall not murder; You shall not steal; You shall not covet'; and any other commandment [pertaining to one's neighbor], are summed up in this word, 'Love your neighbor as yourself.' Love does no wrong to a neighbor; therefore, love is the fulfilling of the law" (Romans 13:8–10). The commandment to love God with one's whole heart, soul, and mind can also be seen as fulfilling the commandments "You shall have no other gods before me," "You shall not make for yourself an idol," "You shall not make wrongful use of the name of the LORD your God," and "Remember the sabbath day, and keep it holy" (Exodus 20:3–11).

The centrality of love in Christianity is expressed on several other notable occasions in the New Testament. In one of the greatest encomiums on love ever written, Paul remarks, "If I speak in the tongues of mortals and of angels, but do not have love, I am a noisy gong or a clanging cymbal. And if I have prophetic powers, and understand all mysteries and all knowledge, and if I have all faith, so as to remove

---

to Cottingham's essay and May's *Love: A History* for how I structure this section, though my discussion differs in many respects.

4 See Lenn Goodman's Chapter 1 in this volume for more on love in the Hebrew Bible and the Jewish tradition.

mountains, but do not have love, I am nothing. If I give away all my possessions, and if I hand over my body so that I may boast, but do not have love, I gain nothing" (1 Corinthians 13:1–3). In other words, love is what gives worth to all of our activities and abilities, and without it, they are worthless. Paul goes on to describe some features of this love: "Love is patient; love is kind; love is not envious or boastful or arrogant or rude. It does not insist on its own way; it is not irritable or resentful; it does not rejoice in wrongdoing, but rejoices in the truth. It bears all things, believes all things, hopes all things, endures all things. Love never ends" (1 Corinthians 13:4–8). He concludes by saying, "Faith, hope, and love abide, these three; and the greatest of these is love" (1 Corinthians 13:13).

In the fourth chapter of the First Letter of John we find the centrality of love expressed in a more "mystical" key:

> Beloved, let us love one another, because love is from God; everyone who loves is born of God and knows God.... God is love, and those who abide in love abide in God, and God abides in them.... We love because he first loved us. Those who say, "I love God," and hate their brothers or sisters, are liars; for those who do not love a brother or sister whom they have seen, cannot love God whom they have not seen. The commandment we have from him is this: those who love God must love their brothers and sisters also. (1 John 4:7–21)

Several noteworthy things here: First, we have an identification of love as a defining feature of God ("God is love"). We have a statement that love comes to us from God, and "We love because he first loved us." And when we love in this way, we are said—and this especially is the "mystical" part—to participate in God's love ("those who abide in love abide in God, and God abides in them"). Here we also see another reason for why the second love commandment (to love our neighbor) is like the first (to love God): if we love God, we must also love our neighbor (or "brothers and sisters"), because loving God means participating in God's love. Since God graciously first loved us, we should extend the same love to our neighbor.

A second important feature of the New Testament picture of love is that, as we have seen, love for God and neighbor is *commanded*. This stands in contrast to Kant, who writes, "Love as an inclination cannot be commanded: but beneficence from duty, when no inclination impels us and even when a natural and unconquerable aversion opposes such beneficence, is practical, and not pathological, love. Such love resides in the will and not in the propensities of feeling, in principles of action and not in tender sympathy; and only this practical love can be commanded."[5] But the New Testament clearly commands not only "practical love" (i.e., good deeds) but also "pathological love" or love from the "heart" (indeed, love without feeling does not seem to be love at all, so this is hardly surprising). And we saw that good deeds have worth only insofar as they are motivated by such love ("If I give away all my possessions, and if I hand over my body so that I may boast, but do not have love, I gain nothing"). We are called to *metanoia* (Matthew 3:2, 4:17; Luke 5:32; Acts 11:18; 2 Peter 3:9; Romans 12:2), that is, to conversion or repentance, which involves not just a change of mind but also a *change of heart* (i.e., affectivity) so as to become more fully aligned with the good. Indeed, we are called to a life conversion that is so radical as to be described as "rebirth" (John 3:3–7). Such conversion is often the work of a lifetime in cooperation with God's grace.[6] What it ultimately enables is the "abundant life" for which we long

---

5 Immanuel Kant, *Grounding for the Metaphysics of Morals* [1785], trans. James W. Ellington, 3rd ed. (Indianapolis, IN: Hackett, 1993), 12. Cottingham also discusses this passage in "Love and Religion," 561. On Kant's theory of love, see also Melissa Seymour Fahmy's chapter in this volume.

6 Pope Benedict XVI writes, "The love-story between God and man consists in the very fact that this communion of will increases in a communion of thought and sentiment, and thus our will and God's will increasingly coincide: God's will is no longer for me an alien will, something imposed on me from without by the commandments, but it is now my own will, based on the realization that God is in fact more deeply present to me than I am to myself" (*God Is Love* [San Francisco: Ignatius Press, 2006], 44; see also 8, 38).

(John 10:10). As Jesus says in the Gospel of John, "If you keep my commandments, you will abide in my love, just as I have kept my Father's commandments and abide in his love. I have said these things to you so that my joy may be in you, and that your joy may be complete" (John 15:10–11).

The call to *metanoia* is also connected to a third important feature of the New Testament picture of love: its demanding nature. We have already seen that Christian love should be unconditional ("It bears all things, . . . endures all things"): that is, it is not undermined by what someone makes (or does not make) of his or her life. However, it is not unconditional in the sense that there is no *basis* for this love: its fundamental basis is the love-worthiness of human beings as made in the image of God. Besides being unconditional, Christian love can also require great sacrifice. As Jesus teaches (and exemplifies), "Greater love has no one than this—to lay down his life for his friends" (John 15:13). But it is not just our friends—in the ordinary sense of the term—that we are to love. In the Sermon on the Plain in the Gospel of Luke, Jesus teaches us to love those who are especially difficult to love:

> Love your enemies, do good to those who hate you, bless those who curse you, pray for those who abuse you. If anyone strikes you on the cheek, offer the other also; and from anyone who takes away your coat do not withhold even your shirt. Give to everyone who begs from you; and if anyone takes away your goods, do not ask for them again. Do to others as you would have them do to you. . . . Be merciful, just as your Father is merciful. (Luke 6:27–36; see also Matthew 5:38–48)

These are hard teachings: it is not clear that anyone besides God could fully live up to them. Nevertheless, we are implored to imitate God's love and mercy. As the Gospel of Matthew puts it, "Be perfect, therefore, as your heavenly Father is perfect" (5:48). What is operative here is something other than a Kantian conception of duty where "ought implies can." We are commanded to strive for an ideal that is humanly unattainable; at best it can be approximated.

Later in the Gospel of Luke, Jesus is questioned about his understanding of the commandment to love one's neighbor as oneself. A lawyer (seemingly the same one mentioned earlier from Matthew 22:34–40), who is said to be wanting to justify himself, asks, "Who is my neighbor?" Jesus replies with the parable of the Good Samaritan:

> "A man was going down from Jerusalem to Jericho, and fell into the hands of robbers, who stripped him, beat him, and went away, leaving him half dead. Now by chance a priest was going down that road; and when he saw him, he passed by on the other side. So likewise a Levite, when he came to the place and saw him, passed by on the other side. But a Samaritan while traveling came near him; and when he saw him, he was moved with pity. He went to him and bandaged his wounds, having poured oil and wine on them. Then he put him on his own animal, brought him to an inn, and took care of him. The next day he took out two denarii, gave them to the innkeeper, and said, 'Take care of him; and when I come back, I will repay you whatever more you spend.' Which of these three, do you think, was a neighbor to the man who fell into the hands of the robbers?" He said, "The one who showed him mercy." Jesus said to him, "Go and do likewise." (Luke 10:30–37)

Notably, in this parable Jesus turns the question on the lawyer, changing it from "Who is my neighbor?" to "Who was a neighbor to the man in need?" Here the concept of "neighbor" is *moralized*. Rather than identifying those who live nearby, it embodies a normative ideal: *we* ought to be a "neighbor" to everyone, including strangers, whom we come across. In other words, we should be ready to act with solidarity for any human being in need. We also see here that this moralization is the basis for the widely recognized universalization of the concept of "neighbor" in the parable: it is not to be limited to members of one's own political, ethnic, or religious community. As we see, it is the Samaritan, an "outsider," who responds correctly. However, the proximity or tangible nearness of the person in need—"when [the Samaritan] saw him, he was moved with pity"—also seems to matter here, as the concept of "neighbor" suggests. We return to this point later.

The parable of the Good Samaritan also highlights (as does the preceding passage from the Gospel of Luke) that not only do we have negative duties to others (such as those specified in the Decalogue: don't murder, don't steal, don't commit adultery, etc.) but we also have positive duties, including duties of beneficence that at least in some dire need cases we are strictly obligated to fulfill (see also Matthew 25:31–46; Luke 18:18–25).[7] Thus, we have a view of love that is very demanding: it is unconditional (i.e., not based on what one makes of his or her life), it is universal in scope (extending even to enemies and strangers), and it involves positive duties of assistance. However, we are still left with some issues to be resolved: How should we understand the relationship between the love that is due to our Creator, which is supposed to be with one's *whole* heart, and love for created things? How should we balance the demands of love for all human beings with the demands of particular love for family, friends, fellow citizens, coreligionists, and so on, which the New Testament authors also affirm?[8] These questions are left to subsequent Christian thinkers to work out through seeking to clarify the proper "order of love." We now turn to consider on this front the efforts of two of the most important thinkers in the Christian tradition: Augustine and Aquinas.

---

7 Cf. Kant, who regards duties of beneficence as "imperfect duties," i.e., encouraged but not strictly required.
8 See Matthew 15:4; John 11:33–36, 15:12–17, 19:25–27; Galatians 6:10; Ephesians 5:21–6:4; 1 Timothy 5:8.

## The Order of Love: Augustine and Aquinas

According to Augustine, "A brief and true definition of virtue is 'rightly ordered love.'"[9] Aquinas maintains something similar when he writes that "charity" (*caritas*)—which encompasses love of God and neighbor—is "the form of the virtues," that is, it orders all the virtues toward our ultimate end of friendship with God.[10] In both cases we can see how central the idea of rightly ordered love is to Christian ethics.[11]

Augustine works out his account of rightly ordered love in book 1 of *On Christian Teaching*. He begins by distinguishing "enjoyment" (*frui*) and "use" (*uti*): "There are some things which are to be enjoyed, some which are to be used, and some whose function is both to enjoy and use."[12] The main difference between what is to be enjoyed and what is to be used is that the former "make us happy," while the latter "assist us and give us a boost . . . as we press on towards our happiness, so that we may reach and hold fast to the things which make us happy" (1.2–4). These two categories relate to love in that to "enjoy something is to hold fast to it in love for its own sake," whereas to "use something is to apply whatever it may be to the purpose of obtaining what you love" (1.2–4). In short, we can love something for its own sake and enjoy it, and we can "love" something as a means to what is loved for its own sake.

The problem, according to Augustine, is that we often love things in a way that they ought not to be loved: namely, when we enjoy things

---

9 Augustine, *The City of God* [426], trans. Henry Bettenson (New York: Penguin, 2003), bk. 15, ch. 22.

10 Thomas Aquinas, *Summa Theologiae* [1266–1273], II-II, q. 23, a. 8, in *Summa Theologica*, 5 vols., trans. Fathers of the English Dominican Province (Notre Dame, IN: Ave Maria Press, 1948). Other references henceforth appear in the text with the abbreviation "ST."

11 On the continued importance of an ethic of rightly ordered love, see Stephen J. Pope, *The Evolution of Altruism & the Ordering of Love* (Washington, DC: Georgetown University Press, 1994); Pope, "The Order of Love and Recent Catholic Ethics: A Constructive Proposal," *Theological Studies* 52 (1991): 255–288.

12 Augustine, *On Christian Teaching* [397], trans. R. P. H. Green (New York: Oxford University Press, 1997), 1.2–4. Other references henceforth appear in the text.

that instead should be used. The result is that we are "impeded" or "diverted" from advancing to our goal of true happiness (1.2–4). To illustrate this point, Augustine asks us to imagine that we are travelers who are only able to live happily in our homeland, and in order to return home we have to use certain means of transportation. However, if we become overly enthralled with the journey itself, enjoying things that ought only to be used, we might be reluctant to finish the journey promptly and thereby become "ensnared in the wrong kind of pleasure and estranged from the homeland whose pleasures could make us happy" (1.4). Augustine remarks, "So in this mortal life we are like travelers away from our Lord: if we wish to return to the homeland where we can be happy we must use this world, not enjoy it" (1.4). Here we have an account of the proper relationship between the love that is due to our Creator and love for created things. As he later puts it, "It is only the eternal and unchangeable things [namely, the persons of the Trinitarian God: Father, Son, and Holy Spirit] . . . that are to be enjoyed; other things are to be used so that we attain the full enjoyment of those things" (1.18–22). For Augustine, it is only what is eternal, unchanging, and excellent in every way that can be the source of complete happiness. By placing our hopes in such a Being we can rest assured that we never have to fear losing the object of our enjoyment or happiness. As Augustine prays to God in his *Confessions*: "[You] have made us for yourself, and our heart is restless until it rests in you."[13]

In *On the Trinity*, Augustine writes, "Nothing but wrong use or wrong enjoyment constitutes the faultiness or blameworthiness of human life."[14] This can happen either because of ignorance or "covetousness." In contrast to "charity"—that is, love of God and love of creatures insofar as such love is directed toward love of God—"covetousness"

---

13 Augustine, *Confessions* [397–400], trans. Henry Chadwick (Oxford: Oxford University Press, 1991), 1.1.

14 Augustine, *On the Trinity* [ca. 400], trans. John Burnaby, *Augustine: Later Works* (Philadelphia: Westminster Press, 1955), 10.10. Cf. Aquinas: "[Every] sinful act proceeds from inordinate desire for some temporal good" (ST I-II, q. 77, a. 4).

is when "the creature is loved for its own sake," which "serves not to aid our use but to corrupt our enjoyment."[15] But is it really true that all enjoyment of created things and love of them for their own sake is covetous and fails to love properly our highest good, that is, God? Augustine, it must be said, has a strange view of enjoyment in taking it to mean that which we regard as our highest good or ultimate end. This is too constricted. We can enjoy something as intrinsically good (e.g., a human being, a beautiful sunset, etc.) and love it for its own sake *without* seeing it as our highest good. Aquinas writes, "The first change wrought in the appetite by the appetible object [i.e., the perceived good] is called *love*, and is nothing else than complacency in that object; and from this complacency results a movement towards that same object, and this movement is *desire*; and lastly, there is rest which is *joy*" (ST I-II, q. 26, a. 2). This suggests that anything *not* loved for its own sake and experienced as a source of joy is in fact not loved at all. Moreover, a biblical worldview affirms that the created world is lovable for its own sake and is a source of enjoyment. We see this in the creation story in Genesis where God creates the world and declares it "very good" (Genesis 1:31) and then rests to enjoy his creation.[16] In keeping the Sabbath, we imitate God by adopting an affirmative stance of restful enjoyment of the goodness of the world. Of course, we should also see the world's goodness as having its source in God's goodness. Augustine does say that we should "derive eternal and spiritual value from corporeal and temporal things" (1.4–6), but for him this is a matter of proper *use*. No doubt there is always a possibility of idolatry in love for created things. But there is no reason why we cannot delight in created things and love them for their own sake, while also seeing them as having their source in God, who is to be loved and enjoyed above all and with our whole heart.

---

15 *On the Trinity* 9.7.

16 The inherent goodness of the created world is also affirmed in Aquinas's claim that being and goodness are "convertible" (see ST I, q. 5, a. 1).

Augustine's view that we should use rather than enjoy created things is especially problematic when it comes to our fellow human beings. He realizes that he is confronted with a dilemma: we as human beings, who enjoy and use things, are ourselves a "major kind of thing, being made 'in the image and likeness of God' . . . by virtue of having a rational soul" (1.22). The question then is "whether humans should enjoy one another or use one another, or both." Since we are commanded to love our neighbors as ourselves, Augustine also frames the question as whether human beings should be loved on their "own account or for some other reason." He answers, "If something is loved on its own account, it is made to constitute the happy life," therefore human beings "should be loved for another reason," namely, that they come to love God with all their hearts. In other words, we love them *for God's sake*, who does constitute the happy life: "So a person who loves his neighbour properly should, in concert with him, aim to love God with all his heart, all his soul, and all his mind. In this way, loving him as he would himself, he relates his love of himself and his neighbor entirely to the love of God, which allows not the slightest trickle to flow away from it and thereby diminish it" (1.22). Augustine concludes, "The person who lives a just and holy life is . . . a person who has ordered his love, so that he does not love what it is wrong to love, or fail to love what should be loved, or love too much what should be loved less (or love too little what should be loved more)" (1.26–27).

For Augustine, rightly ordered love is where God is regarded as the highest good and "loved for himself" and where all other things are loved for God's sake, since he is the proper object of enjoyment. Human beings are to be loved more than other created things, since we are made in the image of God and can share in fellowship with God; however, human beings (including ourselves) are to be loved on account of God and not for their own sake. Augustine does acknowledge that there is a sense in which we can enjoy other human beings "in God," but in such cases he thinks you are still really "enjoying God rather than that human being," since you refer this love for others to the love of God, who is the source of complete happiness. Moreover, Augustine says that the notion of enjoying others in God is still very similar to the idea of "using someone or something together in love," since you go beyond the enjoyment of a human relationship and "relate it to your permanent goal," and thus are using it, or enjoying it "not in a literal sense, but in a transferred sense" (1.33). Genuine enjoyment, for Augustine, is thus still only possible in relation to God. But again there is no need for such a constricted sense of enjoyment, as we see with Aquinas's position: we can and should love human beings for their own sake and find joy in doing so while still affirming that the order of love requires that God be loved above all and that loving our neighbor means willing his or her greatest good, which is sharing in friendship with God (see ST I-II, qq. 26–28; ST II-II, qq. 25–26). Indeed, regarding charity, Aquinas says, "The aspect under which our neighbor is to be loved, is God, since what we ought to love in our neighbor is that he may be in God" (II-II, q. 25, a. 1).

However, in addition to what we might call the *forward-looking* accounts of Augustine and Aquinas of how we should order our love of neighbor toward the love of God through willing that our neighbor come to share in the fullness of friendship with God, we should also recognize a *backward-looking* account. This applies not just to our fellow human beings but to all creatures, since all creatures have their ultimate creative source in God and can be seen as gifts from God. On this account when we love creatures properly we also love God as the ultimate source of the given good of each creature. In this way we can and should love our neighbor and other creatures "in God," that is, *as creations of God*. In both ways we can love God above all and with our whole hearts and our neighbor as ourselves.

Let us now consider the second issue identified at the end of the previous section: how should we balance the demands of love for all human beings with the demands of particular love for family, friends, fellow citizens, coreligionists, and so on? In *On Christian Teaching* Augustine writes, "You cannot do good to all people equally, so you should take particular thought for those who, as if by lot, happen to be particularly close to you in terms of place, time, or any other circumstances" (1.26–29). In addressing this issue, Aquinas cites this passage from Augustine and goes on to remark,

> Grace and virtue imitate the order of nature, which is established by Divine wisdom. Now the order of nature is such that every natural agent pours forth its activity first and most of all on the things which are nearest to it.... Therefore we ought to be most beneficent towards those who are most closely connected with us. Now one man's connection with another may be measured in reference to the various matters in which men are engaged; (thus the intercourse of kinsmen is in natural matters, that of fellow-citizens is in civil matters, that of the faithful in spiritual matters, and so forth): and various benefits should be conferred in various ways according to these various connections, because we ought in preference to bestow on each one such benefits as pertain to the matter in which, speaking simply, he is most clearly connected with us. And yet this may vary according to the various requirements of time, place, or matter in hand because in certain cases one ought, for instance, to succor a stranger, in extreme necessity, rather than one's own father, if he is not in such urgent need. (ST II-II, q. 31, a. 3; see also q. 26, aa. 6–8)

For Aquinas, then, in our beneficence we should generally give preference to family, friends, fellow citizens, and coreligionists over strangers, given the greater connectedness. Yet in some cases—namely, encounters with human beings in dire need—we can be strictly obligated to help a stranger, to be a "neighbor" to him or her.

However, as suggested earlier, proximity seems to matter here: while we can be strictly obligated to help in Good Samaritan–type cases where we confront dire need face-to-face, we do not seem to be similarly obligated to help everyone in dire need around the world. That would be impossibly demanding, and attempting to help everyone would also be self-alienating (or self-mutilating) because of undermining the particular relationships and projects that give meaning to our lives.[17] Aquinas writes, "Absolutely speaking it is impossible to do good to every single one: yet it is true of each individual that one may be bound to do good to him in some particular case. Hence charity binds us, though not actually doing good to someone, to be prepared in mind to do good to anyone if we have time to spare" (ST II-II, q. 31, a. 2, ad. 1).[18] This suggests that though there are cases of strict obligation, other cases will be matters of discretion, where it is good to help if we can, but we need to weigh this against other considerations (see ST II-II, q. 31, a. 3, ad. 1).

But does "discretion" mean that in regard to dire need around the world one can do nothing, where he or she can do *something*, and be blameless? Not necessarily according to a Christian viewpoint: we will be judged on what we have done with what we have (see Matthew 25:14–46; see also 26:6–13; Mark 14:3–9). So discretion should be understood in terms of figuring out what is *required* of us in the course of our lives, given our circumstances and all the different considerations that need to be weighed against each other. But there are cases where having the virtue of neighbor-love will mean that we recognize a kind of *moral necessity* to render aid when we encounter someone in dire need. In his reflections on the parable of the Good Samaritan, Peter Winch remarks that the Samaritan responds compassionately to "what he sees as a *necessity* generated by the presence of the injured man." In other words, he experiences—in a way that the priest and Levite who passed by on the other side evidently do not—a kind of impossibility

---

17 See Bernard Williams, "A Critique of Utilitarianism," in *Utilitarianism: For and Against,* coauthored with J. J. C. Smart (Cambridge: Cambridge University Press, 1973), esp. at 95–118; Williams, "Persons, Character and Morality," in *Moral Luck* (Cambridge: Cambridge University Press, 1981), 1–19; John Cottingham, "Impartiality and Ethical Formation," in *Partiality and Impartiality: Morality, Special Relationships and the Wider World,* ed. Brian Feltham and John Cottingham (Oxford: Oxford University Press, 2010), 65–83.

18 Aquinas continues the passage, "There is however a good that we can do to all, if not to each individual, at least to all in general, as when we pray for all, for unbelievers as well as for the faithful."

that is expressed in the thought "I can't just leave him here to die."[19] It is of course possible that one might also properly recognize a kind of moral necessity with regard to some cases of more distant need, but face-to-face encounters with dire need are the most obvious cases where such moral necessity properly arises. In any case, it is clear that Christian love at least requires that we be disposed to be a "neighbor" to everyone, seeing every human being as made in the image of God and so as being worthy of our concern.[20]

## *Agape* and *Eros*

Let us turn now to consider an influential critique of the way of thinking about love that is exemplified in the work of Augustine and Aquinas, namely, the critique by the twentieth-century Swedish Protestant theologian Anders Nygren of what he calls the "caritas synthesis," which he claims brings together two incongruous conceptions of love: Platonic *eros* and Christian *agape*.[21] In making this turn we are regrettably skipping over centuries of valuable reflections on Christian love after Aquinas (e.g., in the writings of Julian of Norwich, Luther, Calvin, Teresa of Ávila, John of the Cross, De Sales, etc.); likewise, by focusing on Augustine and Aquinas we also regrettably skipped over many valuable reflections on Christian love during Late Antiquity and

---

19 Peter Winch, "Who Is My Neighbour?," in *Trying to Make Sense* (Oxford: Blackwell, 1987), 157.
20 For a similar account, see David Oderberg, "Self-Love, Love of Neighbour, and Impartiality," in *The Moral Life*, ed. Nafsika Athanassoulis and Samantha Vice (New York: Palgrave Macmillan, 2008), 58–84, esp. at 63–66. Oderberg writes, "It is simply in virtue of sharing a common human nature that every one of us is bound to love every other; in theological terms, we are all made in the image of God. Yet this is only the starting point for moral reflection, not the terminus" (63). He sums up his view as follows: "The closer the relationship and the more severe the need, the greater the obligation of charity" (64). I have explored these issues further in David McPherson, *Virtue and Meaning: A Neo-Aristotelian Perspective* (Cambridge: Cambridge University Press, 2020), 104–114, and McPherson, *The Virtues of Limits* (Oxford: Oxford University Press, 2022), 71–83.
21 *Eros* and *agape*, along with *philia*, are transliterated Greek words for love. *Agape* is one of the common words used for love in the original Greek of the New Testament, and it is used by those who translated the Torah into Greek in what is known as the "Septuagint" (see May, *Love: History*, 21–22).

the Middle Ages (e.g., in the writings of Gregory of Nyssa, Basil the Great, Maximus the Confessor, Bernard of Clairvaux, and others). Since it is not possible to cover every significant reflection on Christian love in this essay, some selectivity is required. The justification for focusing on Augustine and Aquinas is obvious enough, but why focus on Nygren? First, because, as mentioned, he provides an influential critique of the way of thinking about love that is exemplified in the work of Augustine and Aquinas. Second, no one else has provoked more discussion about the nature of Christian love in the last hundred years. Third, Nygren's work raises a key issue that should be addressed in an essay exploring love in the Christian tradition: namely, the relationship between *agape* and *eros*.

In his book *Agape and Eros*, Nygren contends that these two conceptions of love are fundamentally opposed and originally had nothing to do with one another.[22] The essential difference between them, according to Nygren, is that Platonic *eros* starts from an *egocentric* perspective, where one desires to become happy and seeks to discover and obtain whatever will make him or her happy; Christian *agape* is *theocentric* in that it concerns God's absolute goodness, particularly as expressed in God's offer of fellowship with us (44–45). As he later puts it, "Eros-love ascends and seeks the satisfaction of its needs; Agape-love descends in order to help and to give" (469).[23] Nygren sees Augustine (and others who endorse a similar way of thinking about love, such as Aquinas) as making all love "acquisitive love" (476). The "caritas synthesis" accepts the aim of classical Greek and Roman ethics of pursuing happiness, but, unlike them, it maintains that accepting and participating in God's *agape* is necessary for attaining this happiness (470–475).

---

22 Anders Nygren, *Agape and Eros*, trans. Philip S. Watson (Philadelphia: Westminster Press, 1953 [1930/1936]), 30–31. Other references are henceforth provided in text.

23 Cf. C. S. Lewis's distinction between "gift-love" and "need-love" in *The Four Loves* (Orlando, FL: Harcourt, 1960). Lewis also has the category of "appreciative love," and he writes, "In actual life, thank God, the three elements of love mix and succeed one another, moment by moment" (17). I suggest that it is in fact appreciative love that is fundamental in the discussion below.

In this synthesis of *agape* and *eros*, Nygren thinks that *agape* loses out because it serves as a means for attaining the aim of *eros*, and thus it is not really *agape* at all (55–56, 503). So how then should Christian *agape* be understood?

Nygren identifies four main features. First, *agape* is "unmotivated" (75). There are no "extrinsic grounds" for God's love, but rather such love is spontaneous and receives its "motivation" from God's very nature, since "God is *Agape*," and through first loving us he summons us to respond in kind in love for one another and so become a "channel" of God's love (see 91–102, 733–737). Second, *agape* is "indifferent to value" (77). This is a further specification on the first point. In contrast to *eros*, where a person must first be motivated to love by the perceived value of some object, with *agape* the initiating Divine love is not motivated by the value or lack of value of the object: "*any thought of valuation whatsoever* is out of place" (77). Nygren sees evidence for this claim in God's love for sinners. Third, *agape* is creative (78). This can also be seen as further specifying the previous points: "Agape has nothing to do with the kind of love that depends on the recognition of a valuable quality in its object; Agape does not recognize value, but creates it. Agape loves, and imparts value in loving" (78). In other words, *agape* is a form of "bestowal love" rather than "appraisal love."[24] Finally, God's *agape* is "the initiator of fellowship with God" (81), or as 1 John 4 puts it, "We love because he first loved us." Nygren presents this overall picture of *agape* as a revolutionary understanding of love, and thus it is unsurprising that he thinks *agape* loses its character when combined with *eros*.

There is reason, however, to take issue with Nygren's first three points (which, as indicated, are all related): that is, that *agape* is "unmotivated," "indifferent to value," and "does not recognize value, but creates it." Part of why it is desirable to be loved is that we believe that

---

24 Irving Singer makes this distinction in *The Nature of Love* (Chicago: University of Chicago Press, 1966).

love is responsive to and affirmative of some perceived lovableness or love-worthiness in ourselves. A love that is not responsive to who we are seems depersonalizing and therefore repugnant. Moreover, to say that *agape* is completely indifferent to value seems to make such love arbitrary: the lover could just as well have loved a rock as a human being in this way. The idea that love can create value in someone is also unconvincing: while we can create things (e.g., works of art, relationships, and so on) that *have* value, value itself is not something that can be created or "bestowed." It is either something objective or else it is merely subjective (i.e., value refers not to anything about the object but only to the subject's caring about something).[25] If the latter account of value were the case, its acknowledgment would have a deflationary effect since it denies the ordinary human experience of love as responsive to something about the loved one being love-worthy. In fact, it is not clear that it even makes sense to say that love is not responsive to some perceived value. A love that is not responsive to perceived value seems *unintelligible*. All love, it would appear, has to be appraisal love rather than bestowal love.

One concern with appraisal love is that if love is based on perceived valuable features, then this could make the loved one replaceable by someone who had similar features, and perhaps in greater quantity or with other valuable features. Additionally, there is a concern that appraisal love makes it too easy for love to cease when the beloved loses valuable qualities.[26] This can connect up with a concern to affirm an "unconditional" form of love. Indeed, one might think that something like Nygren's account of *agape* as "indifferent to value" is what is needed for love to be "unconditional." Nygren seems to have this in mind when he appeals to God's love of sinners. But this overlooks

---

25 For the latter view, see Harry Frankfurt, *The Reasons of Love* (Princeton, NJ: Princeton University Press, 2004).

26 See Eleonore Stump, *Wandering in Darkness: Narrative and the Problem of Suffering* (Oxford: Oxford University Press, 2010), 85–90.

the different ways that someone or something can have value, and therefore the different ways that love can be "conditional" or "unconditional." As suggested earlier, a view of *agape* involving appraisal love can be regarded as "unconditional" in that it does not depend upon what the beloved makes (or does not make) of his or her life. In this way we can certainly love the sinner. But this does not mean that such love is completely unconditional: while it does not depend on what we *do* (or fail to do), it is based on what we fundamentally *are*, namely, beings made in the image of God who thus have intrinsic dignity and are love-worthy. In this regard, the saint and the sinner are both equally loved through *agape*. In short, there is a fundamental conditionality (our intrinsic love-worthiness as human beings) at the heart of the unconditionality of *agape* (it is not based on what we do).[27]

Therefore, *agape*, so understood, entails that we won't stop loving other human beings (our "neighbors") if they lose some of their valuable qualities, since it involves the appraisal that there is a valuable quality that they cannot lose (it is "inalienable"): namely, their intrinsic love-worthiness as beings made in the image of God. Moreover, each human being is *uniquely* made in the image of God and is someone with whom we can form a distinct relationship, and thus they cannot be regarded as replaceable.

There is, however, a final concern regarding appraisal love as the basis of *agape* to which we need to respond: Nygren's claim that appraisal love is connected to *eros* and so is *egocentric* by virtue of seeking after one's fulfillment. A proper response should affirm this connection with *eros*, but deny that it must be egocentric. It is helpful here to consider Josef Pieper's defense of the Augustinian-Thomistic tradition against Nygren.[28] Pieper—who is a Catholic philosopher—endorses

---

[27] Cf. May, *Love: A History*, 236–237, which critiques unconditionality but assumes a Nygren-like view of it.
[28] Two other well-known responses are John Burnaby, *Amor Dei* (London: Canterbury Press, 1938), and Martin C. D'Arcy, SJ, *The Mind and Heart of Love* (New York: Meridian Books, 1947).

an appraisal account of love and regards the basic act of love to be the affirmation of the goodness of the beloved's existence (this is what C. S. Lewis calls "appreciative love"), which seems the opposite of egocentric. Pieper writes,

> In every conceivable case love signifies much the same as approval.... It is a way of turning to [someone or something] and saying: "It's good that you exist; it's good that you are in this world!" ... The approval I am speaking of is ... an expression of the *will*. ... It testifies to being in agreement, assenting, consenting, applauding, affirming, praising, glorifying and hailing.... We have been taught to restrict the concept of willing to the idea of willing to do.... [But] there is a form of willing that does not aim at doing something still undone and thus acting in the future to change the present state of affairs. Rather, in addition to willing-to-do, there is also a purely affirmative assent to what already is.... To confirm and affirm something already accomplished—that is precisely what is meant by "to love." ... [Love] is the primal act of willing that permeates all willing-to-do from its very source.... Whether for good or evil, each man lives by his love. It is love and it alone that must be "in order" for the person as a whole to be "right" and good.... "Virtus est ordo amoris [Virtue is rightly ordered love]."[29]

Pieper goes on to say, "It is God who in the act of creation anticipated all conceivable human love and said: I will you to be; it is good, 'very good' (Gen. 1:31), that you exist" (171).

---

29 Josef Pieper, "On Love" [1972], in *Faith, Hope, Love* (San Francisco: Ignatius Press, 1997), 163–167. Other references are henceforth provided in the text. The following is the clearest indication of Pieper's endorsement of an appraisal account of love: "[Our] love ... never creates 'values' or makes anything or anyone lovable.... What comes first is the actual existence of lovability, independently presented to us. Then this existence must enter into our experience. And only then, hence anything but 'unmotivatedly' and 'without reason', do we say in confirming love, 'It's good that this exists!'" (220–221).

In light of this affirmation of the goodness of the beloved's existence, there follows, according to Pieper (and Aquinas), two desires: (1) good for the beloved and (2) union with the beloved (194–197).[30] In fact, these are related, as Aquinas writes: "When a man loves another with the love of friendship, he wills good to him, just as he wills good to himself: whereof he apprehends him as his other self, in so far, to wit, as he wills good to him as to himself" (ST I-II, q. 28, a. 1). There is a "union of affection" here in which we affectively identify with the beloved and regard the beloved's good as our own such that we desire good for the beloved for his or her own sake and for our own.[31] When such love is reciprocated there is then a "mutual indwelling" where each person desires good for the other and regards it as his or her own good (ST I-II, q. 28, a. 2). But the fact that we regard the beloved's good as our own is by no means egocentric. Rather, it precisely involves self-transcendence to affirm the goodness of the beloved's existence and to identify with the beloved and his or her good. As Aquinas says, love involves "ecstasy": "a man's affection goes out from itself . . . ; because he wishes and does good to his friend . . . for his sake" (ST I-II, q. 28, a. 3).

We can see then two ways that love for another is connected to our own happiness or fulfillment. First, affirming the goodness of the beloved's existence involves a rejoicing or delighting in the beloved. Second, through the union of affections we regard the beloved's happiness as our own. Is it problematic that love should be connected to our desire for our own happiness or fulfillment? The fundamental

---

30 See Eleonore Stump's discussion of Aquinas's account of love in *Wandering in Darkness*, ch. 5, where she mentions these two features of love. My language here is closer to Stump's than Pieper's, but they put forward the same idea, which is unsurprising given that both are indebted to Aquinas. See ST, I-II, qq. 27–28; II-II, q. 27. a. 2.

31 On affective identification, see Jules Toner, SJ, "The Experience of Love" [1968], in *Love and Friendship* (Milwaukee: Marquette University Press, 2003), 117–124.

disagreement that Pieper has with Nygren here is over the relationship between nature and grace, and in particular over whether grace in the form of God's *agape* and our sharing in it is something opposed to natural desire (as Nygren suggests), which would seem to eliminate human agency in cooperating with grace (we become a mere "channel"), or whether it perfects our nature (as Pieper, following Aquinas, maintains) and is something with which we actively cooperate.

If *eros* is understood as "the quintessence of all desire for fullness of being, for quenching of the thirst for happiness, for satiation by the good things of life, which include not only closeness and community with our fellowmen but also participation in the life of God himself," then, Pieper contends, it "must be regarded as an impulse inherent in our natures, arising directly out of finite man's existence as a created being, out of his creatureliness" (222–223). It is not a "persisting human weakness," but rather "the indispensable beginning of all perfection in love": "All love has joy as its natural fruit. What is more, all human happiness . . . is fundamentally *the happiness of love*, whether its name is eros or *caritas* or agape and whether it is directed toward a friend, a sweetheart, a son, a neighbor or God himself" (223–224). "Our whole being," Pieper further maintains, "is so set that it wants to be able to say with reason, 'How good that this exists; how wonderful that you are here!'" (226). We are primarily focused here on the goodness of the beloved's existence, and yet "our desire for happiness can be satisfied precisely by such affirmation directed toward another, that is, by 'unselfish' love," as we delight in the beloved (241). In light of this, Pieper draws the following lesson:

> The indispensable goods of life can be acquired only by their being "given" to us; they are not accorded to us when we directly aim for them. . . . That love, insofar as it is real love, does not seek its own remains an inviolable truth. But the lover, assuming that he is . . . not calculating, does after all attain his own, the reward of love. And this

reward, in its turn and in view of human nature, cannot be a matter of indifference to him. (244–245)

Here we see the meeting ground for *eros* and *agape*: God's *agape* comes to us as a gift that meets our deepest human longings for fulfillment, or "abundant life," that our "joy may be complete." In short, grace perfects nature.[32]

---

32 I would like to acknowledge with gratitude my debt to my spouse, Kirstin (a fellow philosopher), for numerous conversations that helped to shape my thinking in this essay. I would also like to thank Ryan Patrick Hanley for helpful comments on an earlier draft of this essay. Finally, I would like to express my gratitude to my former teacher Roland J. Teske, SJ. It was in his course on Augustine (fall 2005) that I began thinking extensively about the order of love.

CHAPTER 4

# Love in Islamic Philosophy
*William C. Chittick*

By the third century of Islam—the ninth Christian century—Muslims were producing literature in many fields of learning. Scholars who occupied themselves with jurisprudence (*fiqh*) kept themselves busy codifying the Shariah, the body of law set down by the Qur'an and the Prophet; they had no reason to talk of love other than to formulate rules for its physical enactment. Early experts in Kalam (scholastic theology) investigated the right way to understand God as revealed in the Qur'an; they seemed to have considered love of little relevance to their abstruse discussions of divine attributes.[1] Many sorts of scholars composed poetry in which love played a prominent role, and some wrote anthologies of poetry with anecdotes about lovers, leading historians

---

[1] From about the sixth/twelfth century, some scholars of Kalam began to discuss it in detail. See Joseph Norment Bell, *Love Theory in Later Hanbalite Islam* (Albany: State University of New York Press, 1979).

to speak of a genre of "profane love" in Arabic literature.[2] Teachers of Sufism, a word I use to designate the living spirituality of the tradition, typically paid more attention to love than scholars in any other field, for they understood it both as God's motive for creating the universe and as the means whereby human beings can actualize their true humanity.

As for experts in philosophy per se—Arabic *falsafa*—their earliest independent treatise on love was written by the anonymous ninth- to tenth-century philosophical fraternity, the Brethren of Purity (Ikhwān al-Ṣafāʾ). Avicenna (d. 1037), the most famous of the philosophers, wrote an influential treatise on the topic. Suhrawardī (d. 1191), the founder of the Illuminationist school of philosophy, paid special attention to love in his Persian visionary treatises. Ibn ʿArabī (d. 1240), typically classified as a Sufi in the secondary literature, integrated Avicenna's metaphysics, cosmology, and psychology into the Qurʾanic worldview and wrote extensively about the interplay of divine and human love. Mullā Ṣadrā (d. 1640) revisited earlier theories of love and brought them together in his "transcendent wisdom" (*al-ḥikmat al-mutaʿāliya*), a school of philosophy that has flourished into modern times.[3]

Numerous words were used to designate love, especially by poets. Scholarly analyses focused on *ḥubb*, an important Qurʾanic term, and *ʿishq*, which is not used in the revealed book. Early literary and Sufi writings took *ḥubb* as the generic word and held that *ʿishq* designates intense or erotic love. Philosophers generally preferred *ʿishq* as the

---

2 See Lois Anita Giffen, *Theory of Profane Love among the Arabs: The Development of the Genre* (New York: New York University Press, 1971).

3 A number of scholars made important contributions to love theory combining Sufi and philosophical perspectives, such as al-Daylamī (d. ca. 1000) and al-Dabbāgh (d. 1296); see Abuʾl-Ḥasan al-Daylamī, *Kitāb ʿaṭf al-alif al-maʾlūf ʿalāʾl-lām al-maʿṭūf*, trans. Joseph Norment Bell and Hasan Mahmood; Abdul Latif Al Shafie, *A Treatise on Mystical Love* (Edinburgh: Edinburgh University Press, 2006); Binyamin Abrahamov, *Divine Love in Islamic Mysticism: The Teachings of Al-Ghazâlî and Al-Dabbâgh* (London: Routledge, 2003).

generic word, but from about the sixth/twelfth century onward, the two terms were often used interchangeably.

Discussions of love invariably connected it with beauty, *jamāl* and *ḥusn*. The most significant scriptural use of *jamāl* comes in a saying of Muhammad: "God is beautiful, and He loves beauty." Philosophers and Sufis argued that all love is directed at beauty. According to Avicenna, "Every perceived beauty, agreeableness, and good is the object of love and affection."[4] As Ibn 'Arabī put it, "The cause of love is beauty, for beauty is loved by its very essence."[5]

The Qur'an uses *ḥusn* and its derivatives in almost two hundred verses. Four of these say that God possesses the names that are "the most beautiful" (*ḥusnā*). Echoing the Hebrew Bible, the Prophet said, "God created Adam in His own form (*ṣūra*)." The Qur'an calls God the "Form-Giver" (*al-muṣawwir*, 59:24) and tells us that God "formed you and made your forms beautiful" (40:64). All beauty, then, is divine or divinely rooted, so "Anything beautiful that comes to you is from God, and anything ugly that comes to you is from yourself" (4:79). When speaking of the afterlife the Qur'an turns the adjective "the most beautiful," which it applies to the divine names, into a substantive: "Those who do what is beautiful will have the most beautiful and an increase" (10:26). Commentators suggest that this "increase" will be a vision of God Himself, beyond any delineation by names and attributes.

Another word that needs to be highlighted in discussion of love is *raḥma*, which is usually translated as mercy or compassion. Derived from the concrete noun *raḥim*, "womb," it suggests the loving qualities of a mother.[6] Almost every chapter of the Qur'an begins with a

---

4 Ibn Sīnā, *al-Mabda' wa'l-ma'ād*, ed. 'Abdullāh Nūrānī (Tehran: McGill Institute of Islamic Studies, 1984), 17.
5 Ibn al-'Arabī, Muḥyī al-Dīn, *al-Futūḥāt al-makkiyya* (Cairo: 1911) vol. 2, p. 326, line 24.
6 Among Ibn 'Arabī's followers, this etymology gave rise to discussions of the cosmos as "the womb of the All-Merciful." See Sachiko Murata, *The Tao of Islam: A Sourcebook on Gender Relationships in Islamic Thought* (Albany: State University of New York Press, 1992), ch. 7.

formula using two derivatives from the root: "In the name of God, the All-Merciful (*raḥmān*), the Ever-Merciful (*raḥīm*)." Sufis generally understood mercy as God's unqualified love for His creation. When God says in the Qur'an, "My mercy embraces everything" (7:156), scholars like Ibn ʿArabī understood this to mean that mercy is the Qur'anic equivalent of the philosophical term *wujūd*, existence or being, which alone comprehends all of reality. Mercy was considered distinct from love because it is unidirectional, which is to say that God has mercy on creation, but creatures cannot have mercy on God. Love is bidirectional, for both God and man are lover and beloved of each other.

Early philosophers generally avoided the word *raḥma*. Avicenna explains that the word implies affectivity (*infiʿāl*), but this "is not correct for God, for He acts [*fiʿl*] upon all things with firm wisdom [*ḥikma*], and affectivity has no entrance into wisdom."[7] He and other philosophers did not ignore God's concern for creation, but they preferred the non-Qur'anic word *ʿināya*, solicitude or providence. As Avicenna writes, "Everything that comes into existence enters under the First Solicitude. . . . Sufficient solicitude toward the things is that they have existence from [the Necessary Existence]."[8] Ibn ʿArabī makes the same point when he says, "The abode of mercy is the abode of existence."[9]

## Origin and Return

Kalam experts classified the articles of faith under three headings: the assertion of divine unity (*tawḥīd*), prophecy (*nubuwwa*), and eschatology (*maʿād*). The literal meaning of this last word is "return" or

---

[7] Ibn Sīnā, *al-Taʿlīqāt*, ed. ʿAbd al-Raḥmān Badaw (Cairo: al-Hayʾat al-Miṣriyya al-ʿĀmma liʾl-Kitāb, 1973), 117–118.
[8] Ibn Sīnā, *Sharḥ kitāb Uthūlūjiyya*, ed. ʿAbd al-Raḥmān Badawī, *Arisṭū ʿind al-ʿarab* (Kuwait: Wikālat al-Maṭbūʿāt, 1978), 73.
[9] Ibn al-ʿArabī, *Futūḥāt* 4:4.32.

"place of return." In discussing it, theologians analyzed the extensive Qur'anic descriptions of the Resurrection and its aftermath with a view toward human accountability. Philosophers were no less interested in the afterlife, but they came at it from a different angle. While acknowledging that God provides a prescriptive command (*amr taklīfī*) addressed at human free will, they preferred to focus on the existentiating command (*amr takwīnī*), mentioned in the verse "His only command to a thing, when He desires it, is to say to it 'Be!,' and it comes to be" (36:82). This Qur'anic *fiat lux* is supplemented by numerous verses that speak about stages of creation and orders of being and becoming. Several of these mention that all things "return" to God just as they "originated" from God. Philosophers used the same two words when discussing the coming and going of all possible things. Both Avicenna and Mullā Ṣadrā wrote books called "Origin and Return" (*al-mabda' wa'l-ma'ād*, Latin *exitus et reditus*).

In the introduction to his book by this title, Avicenna says that his goal is to explain the fruit reaped by the Peripatetics from two great sciences: metaphysics (*mā ba'd al-ṭabī'a*) and physics (*ṭabī'iyyāt*, "the natural things"). The fruit of the first is knowledge of the Divinity and the manner in which all existent things are tied back to God. The fruit of the second is knowledge of the manner in which souls return to their origin.[10] He summarizes the overall picture like this:

> The beginning order in the arrangement of the origins goes from the First Origin down to the elements, and the returning order in their arrangement goes from the elements up to man. At man the return is complete, for he has the real return and gains similarity with the intellective origins. So it is as if these [origins] circle back upon themselves, for he was an intellect [*'aql*], then a soul [*nafs*], then a

---

10 Ibn Sīnā, *Mabda'* 1.

bodily thing, then a soul, then an intellect that returns to the level of the origins.[11]

As a general rule, Kalam experts concerned themselves primarily with the prescriptive command, which is to say that they tried to understand and interpret the instructions for right activity found in Scripture. Philosophers in contrast devoted most of their attention to the existentiating command, so they looked for normative guidelines in the nature of things. The differing standpoints of the two approaches to knowledge are reflected in the respective stress they placed on the two most commonly cited verses on love in the Qur'an. Theologians emphasized the first verse, which makes divine love conditional on praxis: "Say [O Muhammad!]: 'If you love God, follow me, and God will love you'" (3:31), so God's love can only be actualized by following revealed guidance. Philosophers were more likely to focus on the second verse: "He loves them, and they love Him" (5:54), which was understood to mean that God loves human beings eternally, and man loves God innately.

In sum, philosophers discussed love as an ontological reality, the divine force that brings possible things into existence with no external motivation. As Avicenna put it, "Since He is lover of His essence, and since the things emerge from an essence that has this attribute—that is, beloved—what emerges from Him must be the object of solicitude, for love is His essence and He desires the good for what emerges."[12] This same force then permeates creation and, as a human attribute, motivates people to return to their Origin. Discussion of these two

---

11  Ibn Sīnā, *Mabda'* 91. Mullā Ṣadrā provides an expanded depiction of the circle of existence in his book by the same title: *al-Mabda' wa'l-ma'ād*, ed. Muḥammad Dhabīḥī and Ja'far Shāh-Naẓarī (Tehran: Bunyād-i Ḥikmat-i Islāmī-yi Ṣadrā, 1381/2002), 336–338.
12  Ibn Sīnā, *Ta'līqāt* 157.

interwoven loves—God's creative love and man's consummating love—are omnipresent in the literature, not least in the poetry of the various Islamic languages.

### Early Philosophy

In their treatise on love, the Brethren of Purity begin by reviewing various definitions of love provided by Greek and Islamic sources, suggesting that the most adequate definition is "intense yearning for unification" (*shiddat al-shawq ila'l-ittiḥād*). They explain that this yearning increases at each ascending level of soul—vegetal, animal, and human. The vast differences in the objects of human love have to do with the sort of soul that dominates in the makeup of each individual. If the vegetal soul dominates, people will love gratification of the senses; if the animal soul, then power and control; if the human soul, rationality. The Brethren then turn to describing the various sorts of love, "whose number cannot be counted by anyone but God." These include the love of animals for pairing, the love of parents for children, the love of leaders for leadership, the love of artisans for artifacts, the love of traders for trade, the love of scholars for knowledge, and the love of lovers for thoughts, cares, sorrows, and joys. "If people did not love," they conclude, "all their virtues would stay hidden, and none of their vices would be recognized."

As for the reason that God placed love in human souls, this was to provide a means of refining the soul and focusing all of its attention on that which is good and beautiful in essence, not just in appearance.

> The final goal of love's existence is to awaken souls from the sleep of heedlessness and the slumber of ignorance. It disciplines them, making them ascend and advance away from sensory, corporeal things toward soulish, intelligible things, and away from the bodily level toward spiritual beauties. It guides them to recognize their own substance, the eminence of their own element, the

beautiful qualities of their world, and the wholesomeness of their Return.[13]

In the last chapter of their treatise the Brethren explain that human souls reach perfection by loving beauty and yearning for union with it. The common people are attracted to outward beauty, but sages are attracted to the beauty of the wise Artisan who created all beautiful things. They strive to attain similarity with the Universal Soul in their activities, character traits, and knowledge, ascending at last to the true Beloved. Finally the Brethren remind their readers that all objects of love come from the same single origin:

> All these beautiful qualities, virtues, and good things come from God's effusion and the shining of His light upon the Universal Intellect; from the Universal Intellect they fall on the Universal Soul, and from the Universal Soul on hyle. These are the forms seen by the particular souls in the world of bodies on the outsides of the individuals and bodily things.... Thus it is clear from what we mentioned that God is the first object of love, that existent things yearn for Him and aim for Him, "and to Him the affair is returned, all of it" [Qur'an 11:123], for in Him they have existence, abidance, subsistence, continuity, and perfection. This is because He is the Sheer Existent [*al-mawjūd al-maḥḍ*], and He has everlasting subsistence and continuity and never-ending completion and perfection.[14]

Avicenna's *Treatise on Love*, like his *Origin and Return*, summarizes his metaphysics and psychology but in terms of love. In brief, the love of the Necessary Existence brings forth all things and steers them from potentiality to actuality, deficiency to perfection, and dispersion to

---

13  Ikhwān al-Ṣafāʾ, *Rasāʾil Ikhwān al-Ṣafāʾ* (Beirut: Dār Ṣādir, 1957), 3:282.
14  Ikhwān al-Ṣafāʾ, *Rasāʾil* 3:286.

unity. Avicenna sets down one of his theses in the first sentence of the introduction: "Each of the governing ipseities inclines by nature toward its own perfection." By ipseity (*huwiyya*) he means the individual being, while governing (*tadbīr*) refers to the relationship between a being and what it controls, whether the being be God in relation to the universe or, as here, spirits and souls in relation to bodies. Avicenna is articulating a theme that runs throughout Islamic philosophy and Sufism: the divine mercy and solicitude bestow on each thing an inclination, desire, and love for its own perfection. All beings strive by nature to become what they have the potential (*quwwa*) to be. At each ascending level of their return to their Origin, they achieve a perfection vaster and more inclusive. On the highest level of the hierarchy of souls—the human state—there is no essential limit to what can be reached, for the rational soul has the potential to become a fully actualized intellect, unified with the Universal Intellect or, in Sufi texts, in union with the First Lover, who is also the Supreme Beloved.

Ibn ʿArabī describes this ultimate state of human perfection as "the station of no station" (*maqām lā maqām*), for it is the actuality of all actualities, the total realization of every perfection prefigured by the creation of man in the divine form.[15] The philosophers often referred to it as *taʾalluh* (deiformity) or *al-tashabbuh biʾl-ilāh* (similarity to God). Theologians frequently called it *al-takhalluq bi akhlāq Allāh* (becoming characterized by the character traits of God). In his books on metaphysics, Avicenna provides a capsule description. Though he does not mention love, he refers both to its object and to its goal—beauty and unification:

> The perfection specific to the rational soul is for it to become an intellective world within which is represented the form of the all, the arrangement intelligible in the all, and the good that is effused upon

---

15 See William C. Chittick, *The Sufi Path of Knowledge: Ibn Al-ʿArabī's Metaphysics of Imagination* (Albany: State University of New York Press, 1989), ch. 20.

the all, beginning from the Origin ... until it fully achieves in itself the guise of all of existence. It turns into an intelligible world, parallel with all the existent world, and witnesses absolute comeliness, absolute good, and real, absolute beauty while being unified with it, imprinted with its likeness and guise, strung upon its thread, and coming to be of its substance.[16]

It should be kept in mind that Avicenna and other philosophers treated love as a relatively minor topic. When they did talk about human love, they understood it in terms of the soul's deiformity, which can only be actualized if the soul becomes attuned to the normative hierarchy of the cosmos, in which the intellect (*'aql*) is a transcendent power located at the coincidence of the Origin and the Return. This originating and culminating intelligence appears in the outside world as prophetic revelation and in the inside world as the rational soul. In elaborating upon his just-quoted depiction of the soul's intellective goal, Avicenna reminds us that love will not be actualized unless the soul becomes firmly grounded in moral and spiritual qualities, what he calls "the habitude of the mean" (*malakat al-tawassuṭ*). Not least among these qualities is dominance over the animal soul, which is attracted by nature to visible appearances. As Avicenna puts it, "What is meant by 'the habitude of the mean' is for the rational soul to transcend states of yielding [to the world of the senses] and to keep itself in its own innate disposition while gaining ascendancy and transcendence."[17]

The several chapters of Avicenna's *Treatise on Love* recapitulate the ascending stages of the soul as described in his major works. He explains the manner in which love appears successively, first in Prime Matter and inanimate things, then in plants, animals, young men, and

---

16 Ibn Sīnā, *al-Ilāhiyyāt min al-shifāʾ/The Metaphysics of the Healing*, ed. Michael E. Marmura (Provo: Brigham Young University Press, 2005), 350; Ibn Sīnā, *al-Najāt*, ed. Mājid Fakhrī (Beirut: Dār al-Āfāq al-Jadīda, 1982), 328.

17 Ibn Sīnā, *Ilāhiyyāt* 354; Ibn Sīnā, *Najāt* 332.

finally "divine souls," by which he means those who have actualized the fullness of the intellect. In each case, all things are seeking the good and the beautiful, and their seeking is called "love." In something like a definition, he writes, "In reality love is to deem the beautiful and the agreeable exceedingly beautiful. This love is the origin of inclination toward the beautiful when it is absent—if it be something that may be apart—and of unification with it when it is found. Every existent thing deems beautiful what it finds agreeable and inclines toward it when it does not have it."[18]

In *al-Ishārāt wa'l-tanbīhāt* ("Allusions and Admonitions"), Avicenna offers a more precise analysis by distinguishing between love and yearning, perhaps with a view toward the Brethren of Purity's definition of love as "intense yearning for unification." He wants to explain how the Necessary Existence can be qualified by love even though It already possesses all objects of love, for all possible things are present within It. He says, "Real love is delight [*ibtihāj*] in being in-formed by the presence of some essence." The word "being in-formed" (*taṣawwur*) is usually translated as "conceptualizing," but this translation obscures the fact that the word is derived from form (*ṣūra*) and means to perceive or actualize a form within oneself. The "form" of a thing is its intelligible reality, disengaged (*mujarrad*) from the matter (*mādda*) that allows for its appearance. In philosophical terms the Necessary Existence is "the Bestower of Forms" (*wāhib al-ṣuwar*), though Sufi teachers preferred the Qur'anic divine name, "the Form-giver." Avicenna is saying that when we assert that the Necessary Existence loves, we are acknowledging that It perceives the intelligible forms of all possible things within Itself and delights in their presence.

By describing love as "delight in being in-formed," Avicenna is able to show that love can be found at every level of "perception" (*idrāk*),

---

18 *Risāla fī'l-'ishq*, ed. Ḥusayn al-Ṣiddiq and Rāwiyya Jāmūs (Damascus, Dār al-Fikr, 2005), 52–53.

a word that applies to God's awareness of things as well as to the activities of four basic levels of cognition: sensation, imagination, sense-intuition (or estimation), and intellection. Having explained that this delight appears in everything that perceives—every governing ipseity—he goes on to differentiate love from yearning. The latter, he says, is "the movement toward completing this delight once the form has assumed an image in some way," that is, in some mode of perception, "but has not assumed an image in some other way." He gives the example of imagining the form of someone while yearning to perceive that person with the senses. "Thus," he says, "every yearner has attained something and lacks something."

Avicenna continues this passage by employing the distinction between love and yearning to differentiate between divine and created love in the various levels of being. At the highest level, God loves because He delights in the presence of the forms, but He never yearns, for He lacks nothing. On the second level, the highest angels—who are intellects disengaged from any sort of matter—also lack nothing, for they contemplate God while loving Him. At lower levels of existence, everything that loves also yearns, because everything perceives beautiful forms while lacking them in some way, so they yearn to complete their perception. Avicenna also points out that the distinction between love and yearning helps differentiate between souls that are present in this life and those that have gone on to paradise. "When human souls attain the highest bliss in their life in this world, their greatest state is for them to be lovers who yearn. They will not be delivered from their connection to yearning except in the hereafter."[19]

---

19 Ibn Sīnā, *al-Ishārāt wa'l-tanbīhāt*, ed. Sulaymān Dunyā. (Cairo: Muṣṭafā al-Bābī al-Ḥalabī, 1947), 4:41–45; trans. Shams Inati, *Ibn Sīnā and Mysticism: Remarks and Admonitions: Part Four* (London: Kegan Paul International, 1996), 78–79.

## God's Love for Himself

Given that love implies a duality of lover and beloved, and given that Islamic thought is built on asserting unity, philosophers and Sufis often set out to explain how the One God can be an eternal lover of created things without duality. Their basic answer is that by loving Himself, God loves everything that arises from Himself, which is all that exists. This answer is implicit in the Hadith "God is beautiful, and He loves beauty." Since He is beautiful, He loves Himself. Since "He created all things beautifully" (Qur'an 32:7), He loves creation. As Avicenna explains, "All these existent things emerge from His essence and are required by His essence, so they do not contradict Him. He loves His essence, so all these things are desired for the sake of His essence."[20] Or again, "He loves His essence, and His essence is the origin of the entire order of the good. So the order of the good is beloved to Him by the secondary aim."[21]

That God loves His own essence was taken for granted by the philosophers. Al-Fārābī (d. 950), the greatest philosopher before Avicenna, explains why this should be so in *Mabādi' ārā' ahl al-madīnat al-fāḍila* (*Origins of the Views of the Folk of the Virtuous City*). In the passage he uses both words for love, *ḥubb* and *'ishq*, translated here as love and affection:

> In the First Cause, the lover is the same as the beloved, the admiring the same as the admired, and the one with affection the same as the object of affection. This is the opposite of what we find in ourselves, for in us the beloved is virtue and beauty, but the lover is not beauty and virtue.... So the First Cause is the first beloved and the first

---

20 Ibn Sīnā, *Taʿlīqāt* 16.
21 Ibn Sīnā, *Taʿlīqāt* 72.

object of affection, whether or not anyone else loves It and whether or not anyone else has affection for It.[22]

In the introductory chapter of *Treatise on Love*, Avicenna explains that God in His unity is love, lover, and beloved.

The Good loves the Good because of Its access to attaining and perceiving It. The First Good perceives Its essence in actuality endlessly throughout the ages, so It loves Itself with the most perfect and fullest love. Given that the divine attributes in the Good's essence have no distinction by essence among themselves, it follows that love is the same as the Essence and the Existence—I mean the Sheer Good.[23]

In his *Metaphysics*, Avicenna explains in more detail why the Necessary Existence loves Itself:

The Necessary Existence has sheer beauty and splendor, and It is the origin of the beauty and splendor of all things. . . . Every perceived beauty, agreeableness, and good is the object of affection and love. The origin of all of this is perceiving it—whether by sensation, imagination, sense-intuition, supposition, or intellect. The more intensely perception penetrates and the more intensely it realizes, the more perfect and more eminent will be the essence of the perceived thing, so the perceiving faculty's love for it and joy in it will be more. Hence the Necessary Existence has the utmost perfection, beauty, and splendor. It intellects Its essence in the utmost limit of splendor and beauty with a complete intellection, an intellection in which the intellecter and the intellected are one in reality. So by essence

---

22 Abū Naṣr al-Fārābī, *Mabādi' ārā' ahl al-madīnat al-fāḍila/On the Perfect State*, ed. Richard Walzer (Chicago: Kazi Publications, 1998), 86–88.
23 Ibn Sīnā, *Risāla* 54.

Its essence is the greatest lover and beloved and the greatest enjoyer and thing enjoyed.[24]

The famous theologian al-Ghazālī (d. 1111) was critical of many conclusions of the Peripatetic philosophers, but he had great respect for rational thought and the goal of the philosophical quest. He devoted one of the forty volumes of his magnum opus, *Iḥyā' 'ulūm al-dīn* ("Giving Life to the Sciences of the Religion"), to love and yearning. Among the many issues he mentions is that God's love for creation derives from His love for Himself. He largely agrees with Avicenna, but he brings the terminology more into line with the current theological discourse. To help make his point, he cites a saying of a famous Sufi teacher, Abū Sa'īd ibn Abi'l-Khayr (d. 1049), whom Avicenna is reported to have met:

> All perfection, beauty, splendor, and majesty that are possible on the part of the Divinity are present, attained, and possessed necessarily without end and without beginning; renewal and disappearance are inconceivable. Hence He does not gaze on other than Himself inasmuch as it is "other." Rather, He gazes only on His own essence and acts, and there is nothing in existence other than His own essence and acts. This is why, when God's words "He loves them and they love Him" [Qur'an 5:54] were recited before Shaykh Abū Sa'īd, he said, "He loves them truly, for He loves only Himself." He meant to say that He is the all, and there is nothing other than He in existence. When someone loves only himself, his own acts, and his own compositions, his love does not transgress his essence and the concomitants of his essence inasmuch as they are connected to his essence, so he loves only himself.[25]

---

24 Ibn Sīnā, *Ilāhiyyāt* 297; Ibn Sīnā, *Najāt* 281–282.

25 Muḥammad al-Ghazālī, *Iḥyā' 'ulūm al-dīn* (Beirut: Dār al-Hādī, 1993) 4:328; see *Love, Longing, Intimacy and Contentment*, trans. Eric Ormsby (Cambridge: Islamic Texts Society, 2011), 101–102.

In *Origin and Return*, Mullā Ṣadrā quotes this passage from al-Ghazālī approvingly after pointing out that God does not love all things equally, for He created the universe in a wise arrangement on the two arcs of origin and return and distributes His love according to the capacity of the possible things to receive it. This means that those whom He loves most are those who are nearest to Him:

> Once it has been established that God loves His essence and that this love is identical with the fact that He knows that His essence comprehends the attributes of perfection and the descriptions of beauty, it is also established that He loves His requisites and traces, which are the existent things of the cosmos in their totality.... But the layers of the existence of the creatures in relation to the Highest Origin are disparate in terms of proximity and distance, eminence and meanness, and perfection and deficiency. Hence the most worthy of creatures for the love of the Real is the most eminent of the possible things and the nearest of them to Him in the two chains of originating and returning, hereafter and here-below.[26]

Also in *Origin and Return*, Mullā Ṣadrā describes God's self-love while explaining the seven essential attributes of the Necessary Existence. He asserts, in keeping with the view of many theologians and philosophers, that these attributes are knowledge, power, desire, life, hearing, seeing, and speech. In explaining desire (*irāda*)—which the Qur'an mentions as the source of the existentiating command—Mullā Ṣadrā insists that God's desire for creation does not imply duality, for it is nothing but His love for Himself.

Even though the Necessary loves and desires Its act because the act is one of the traces of Its essence and one of the overflows of Its

---

26 Mullā Ṣadrā, *Mabda'* 251.

effusion, this does not require that the act be a delight and a good for It. Rather the delight of the Necessary lies only in that which is Its beloved by essence, and that is Its own transcendent essence, for every perfection and every beauty is an overflow and effusion from Its beauty and perfection. Hence Its love and desire for the act do not require that It be seeking perfection outside of Itself, for in reality that which is beloved and desired is Its very essence by Its essence. In the same way, when you love a person, you love her traces, though in reality your beloved is that person. Thus it has been said,

> I walk the land—the land of Salma—
> kissing this wall, kissing that wall.
> It is not love for the land that impassions my heart
> but love for her who dwells within it.[27]

In his magnum opus, *al-Ḥikmat al-mutaʿāliya* (The transcendent wisdom, better known as *The four journeys*), Mullā Ṣadrā provides a long disquisition on love, again in the context of the seven essential attributes of the Necessary Existence. Here, however, instead of "desire" he calls the relevant attribute "solicitude and mercy," thus making explicit that the philosophical term "solicitude" and the Qurʾanic term "mercy" are synonyms. Most of the first fourteen chapters of this section deal with theodicy, explaining why both good and evil pertain to the divine mercy. The last eight chapters explain, in a structure based on Avicenna's *Treatise on Love*, how love pervades the entire universe, driving all things on the ascending ladder of the return to God.

## Universal Love for God

If philosophers understand the Qurʾanic statement "He loves them" to mean that God's love for human beings is a necessary concomitant of

---

27 Mullā Ṣadrā, *Mabdaʾ* 215.

God's love for Himself, it should not be surprising that they read the second half of the verse, "They love Him," as an ontological imperative, not as a prescriptive command. Human beings and all creatures cannot not love God, which is to say that they love God by their very natures, and God responds to their love in the measure of their capacity to receive Him. Avicenna makes this the thesis of the concluding chapter of his *Treatise on Love*. Interestingly, he uses the term "self-disclosure" (*tajallī*) several times to designate the Sheer Good's manifestation of Itself to all things, though he does not use this word in his major works. It is derived from a pregnant Qur'anic verse about Moses at Mt. Sinai and becomes one of the most common expressions in Sufi literature both for the all-encompassing theophany that is the universe and for the specific theophany that is God's unveiling (*kashf*) of His mysteries to His friends (*awliyā'*). Avicenna writes,

> In this chapter we desire to elucidate that each of the existent things loves the Absolute Good with an innate love, and that the Absolute Good discloses Itself to Its lover. Their receptions of Its self-disclosure and their conjunctions with It, however, are disparate. The furthest limit of proximity to It is the reception of Its self-disclosure in reality, I mean, as perfectly as possible. This is the meaning that the Sufis name "unification." In Its munificence, the Good loves that Its self-disclosure be received, and things come to exist by means of Its self-disclosure.[28]

Avicenna sums up his argument by explaining that the perfection of God's love is attained only by "deiform souls" (*al-nufūs al-muta'alliha*), that is, those who have fully actualized their intellects.

The love of the Most Excellent for Its own excellence is the most excellent love, so Its true beloved is that Its self-disclosure be attained.

---

28  Ibn Sīnā, *Risāla* 82.

This is the reality of Its attainment by deiform souls. This is why it may be said that they are Its beloveds. To this refers to what has been related in the reports where God says, "When the servant is such and such, he loves Me, and I love him."[29]

In one of his Persian philosophical tales, *Fī ḥaqīqat al-'ishq* ("On the reality of love"), Suhrawardī tells the story of the three sons of the First Intellect: beauty (*ḥusn*), love (*'ishq*), and sorrow (*ḥuzn*). Toward the end of the tale he sums up their role in bringing about the soul's perfection:

> One of the names of beauty is *jamāl* and another is *kamāl* [perfection].... All existent things, whether spiritual or corporeal, are seeking perfection.... All are seeking beauty and trying to reach beauty. Reaching the beauty sought by all, however, is difficult, for arrival at beauty is impossible except by means of love, and love does not give itself to just anyone.... If on occasion it finds someone worthy of this felicity, it sends sorrow, which is its doorkeeper. Sorrow purifies the house and lets no one inside. It reports that the Solomon of love will be entering, and it gives out this call: "O ants, enter your houses, lest Solomon and his armies trample you" [Qur'an 27:18]. Then each of the ants—the outward and inward senses—will settle down in its own place and remain safe from the blows of the army of love, and no defect will find its way to the brain. Love will then wander around the house and look at everything. It will come into the room of the heart, destroying some of it and repairing some of it. It will restore the heart's work to its first manner, staying busy with this for several days. Then it will set out for the threshold of beauty.[30]

---

29 Ibn Sīnā, *Risāla* 87–88.
30 Shihāb al-Dīn Yaḥyā Suhrawardī, *Fī ḥaqīqat al-'ishq*, ed. Seyyed Hossein Nasr, *Majmū'a-yi Muṣannafāt-i Shaykh-i Ishrāq* (Tehran: Académie Impériale Iranienne de Philosophie, 1977), 284–285.

Sufi teachers often speak of God as the beloved of all, even though people imagine that they love this or that. Ibn ʿArabī describes the situation:

> None but God is loved in the existent things. In every beloved it is He who is manifest to the eye of every lover—and there is nothing that is not a lover. So the universe is all lover and beloved, and all of it goes back to Him.... No one loves any but his own Creator, but he is veiled from Him by his love for Zaynab, Suʿad, Hind, Layla, this world, money, position, and everything loved in the world. Poets exhaust their words writing about all these existent things without knowing, but the true knowers never hear a verse, a riddle, a panegyric, or a love poem that is not about Him, hidden behind the veil of forms.[31]

The poetry and prose of Rūmī (d. 1274) provide many descriptions of the divine love that permeates the universe. In a typical passage, he explains how love acts through the existentiating command, and then has God Himself explain the wisdom in love's work:

> Love makes the ocean boil like a pot,
>     love grinds mountains down to sand.
> Love splits heaven into a hundred pieces,
>     love shakes earth with a mighty shaking. . . .
> "If not for pure love,
>     why would I give existence to the spheres?
> "I raised the celestial wheel on high
>     so that you would understand love's elevation."[32]

---

[31] Ibn al-ʿArabī, *Futūḥāt* 2:326.18.
[32] Rūmī, *Mathnawī*, ed. R. A. Nicholson (London: Luzac, 1925-40), 5:2735-2740; William C. Chittick, *The Sufi Path of Love: The Spiritual Teachings of Rumi* (Albany: State University of New York Press, 1983), 198.

Mullā Ṣadrā also reminds us that everything is sustained by the divine solicitude and permeated by love and yearning for God. The reason for this, he says, is that the final goal of all is the everlasting existence of the Necessary, which is the sheer and absolute good from which no good is excluded. In one passage he explains this while repeating Avicenna's distinction between love and yearning:

> God has established for each of the existent things—whether intellective, soulish, sensory, or natural—a perfection, and He has planted in its nature a love and yearning for that perfection and a movement toward its completion.... Everything loves existence, seeks the perfection of existence, and shuns nonexistence and deficiency.... Hence love is constantly present in the thing, whether in the state of the existence of its perfection or the state of the lack of its perfection. As for yearning and inclination, these are present in the thing only when it lacks the perfection. Hence love pervades all existent things, but yearning does not pervade all. Rather, it pertains specifically to those who lack something of which they are in-formed.[33]

Mullā Ṣadrā devotes a good deal of space to differentiating among the objects of creaturely love and describing where they are situated on the ascending and descending arcs of existence. He demonstrates that "every love for the low will be led and directed to a love for the high in the most complete and perfect manner. This will continue until love for the Necessary Existence is reached."[34] In continuing this passage he explains the natural hierarchy of love for the high:

> Given that the body becomes complete through nature, it loves that which completes it, which is nature. Nature becomes complete

---

33 Mullā Ṣadrā, *Ḥikma* 7:148–150.
34 Mullā Ṣadrā, *Ḥikma* 7:157.

through the soul that governs it, so it loves it. The soul becomes complete through the intellect, so it loves it. The intellect, or rather, all things, become complete through the Necessary, so the intellect loves It and all things become complete through It. Or rather, It is the all in oneness. It delights in Its essence, not in anything else, for there is nothing else . . . for It is the returning place of all and the final goal of all.[35]

In short, the human soul achieves perfection by way of love and yearning for the Necessary Existence. Each lower level of the soul, and indeed, each faculty of the soul, has an appropriate love, but none of love's lower objects is a worthy object for the rational soul. Its true beloved can only be the First Intellect, which is the form of its matter, or God Himself, in whose form man was created. All objects of love other than the Real can be nothing but bridges leading in the direction of the true Beloved. Here Sufi texts like to quote a dictum well-known to literary theorists: "The metaphor [*majāz*] is the bridge to the reality [*ḥaqīqa*]." Mullā Ṣadrā stands in a long line of Sufi theorists when he says, "Human love is divided into real and metaphorical. Real love is love for God, His attributes, and His acts inasmuch as they are His acts. Metaphorical love is divided into soulish and animal."

By soulish love Ṣadrā means the love of one human soul for another, and by animal love he means love driven by the natural appetite of the animal soul. In soulish love the rational soul rules over the animal soul and thus, for example, observes the moral and legal strictures surrounding love. In animal love, the animal soul rules over the rational soul and leads to illicit forms of love. Concerning the soul's metaphorical love for another soul he writes,

---

[35] Mullā Ṣadrā, *Ḥikma* 7:157.

It softens the soul and brings about yearning, ardor, sorrow, weeping, and tenderness of heart and thought. It is as if the soul is seeking something inward and hidden from the senses. So the soul cuts itself off from its this-worldly occupations, turns away from everything but its beloved, and makes all its concerns one concern. This is why turning toward the real Beloved is easier for such a person than for others, for he does not need to cut himself off from many things. Rather, he turns his longing for one person toward the One.[36]

As for real love, it occurs when the soul actualizes its intellective nature and is no longer attracted to traces and metaphors. As Ṣadrā writes,

> Once the soul has reached perfection through the divine sciences and become an actual intellect, encompassing the universal sciences and possessing the habitude of conjunction with the world of holiness, it must no longer busy itself with love for these beautified, fleshly forms and subtle, human traits, for its station has gone beyond this station. This is why it is said, "The metaphor is the bridge to the Reality." Once someone has crossed the bridge to the World of the Reality, returning once more to that from which he has crossed would be ugly and counted as a vice.[37]

Among Sufi poets, Rūmī has frequent recourse to the distinction between real and metaphorical love. The beauty of beloveds in this world is simply gold plating, he tells us, so we should travel back to the mine.

---

36 Mullā Ṣadrā, *Ḥikma* 7:174–175.
37 Mullā Ṣadrā, *Ḥikma* 7:175.

> Love is an attribute of God, who has no needs—
> love for anything else is a metaphor.
> The beauty of the others is gold-plated:
> outwardly light, inwardly smoke.
> When the light goes and the smoke appears,
> metaphorical love turns to ice....
> When gold jumps from the face of counterfeit coin,
> it returns to sit in its own mine....
> Those with eyes turn their love to the mine of gold,
> each day their love increasing.[38]

Despite his frequent criticisms of metaphorical love, Rūmī also celebrates love in all its forms, for love is accompanied by the sorrow and pain of separation, and the awareness of this pain is the beginning of wisdom. As Suhrawardī pointed out, sorrow is inseparable from its brothers, love and beauty. It is no accident that Rūmī begins his monumental epic of love, the *Mathnawī*, with this line: "Listen to this flute as it complains, telling tales of separation." The pain and sorrow of separation light up the fire of love. Rūmī sums up the positive role played by metaphorical love with these lines addressed to disappointed lovers:

> Consider it His solicitude that you have lost in the lane of love.
> Put aside metaphorical love, for the end is love for the Real.
> The soldier gives his son a wooden sword
> for him to become a master and take a sword into battle.
> Love for a human being is that wooden sword.
> Once the trial ends, the love will be for the All-Merciful.[39]

---

38 Rūmī, *Mathnawī* 6:971–980; Chittick, *Sufi Path of Love*, 202–203.
39 Rūmī, *Kulliyyāt-i Shams yā dīwān-i kabīr*, ed. B. Furūzānfar (Tehran: Dānishgāh, 1336-46/1957-67), vv. 336–338.

## All-Pervading Mercy

In his vast corpus of prose and poetry Ibn ʿArabī discusses love in far more detail than any of the official philosophers. Like Avicenna and Mullā Ṣadrā he builds his vision on the concept and reality of *wujūd*, existence or being. Unlike them, however, he does not look at the human soul simply as a potential intellect that needs to be actualized. As important as intelligence and rationality are to the definition of what it means to be human, the true defining characteristic of man is that he was created in the form of the Necessary Existence, thereby receiving the potential to actualize all forms in the divine knowledge and to reach the Station of No Station. These forms are not limited to the intelligible realities, but also include the images and symbols that appear as nature and Scripture. For the soul to realize its full potential it must actualize along with intellect a complementary power of equal importance, namely *khayāl*, imagination.

The philosophers understood imagination as an internal sense of the animal soul, more to be overcome than to be actualized. They described it as the faculty that perceives sense objects without the intermediary of the five outward senses, as in memory or dreaming. In some lesser-known works, especially the symbolic tales of Avicenna and Ibn Ṭufayl (d. 1185), philosophers acknowledged the important role of imagination in the perception of metaphysical realities. Aaron Hughes has argued that such treatises were written as practical aids in the development of the fullness of human understanding. As he put it, "These tales focus poetically on this world and attempt to show how the beauty within it relates to the divine world.... Imagination becomes crucial to the philosophical enterprise, since the imagination is the faculty that is ultimately responsible for bridging the gap between the phenomenal and the transcendental."[40]

---

40 Aaron W. Hughes, *The Texture of the Divine: Imagination in Medieval Islamic and Jewish Thought* (Bloomington: Indiana University Press, 2004), 171. For a broad-ranging investigation of this issue in philosophy and Sufism, see Cyrus Ali Zargar, *The Polished Mirror: Storytelling and the*

Whether Ibn ʿArabī was aware of these symbolic tales or not, he objected to the widely accepted notion of imagination as a mere faculty of the soul. To some extent he was motivated by an attempt to integrate the received philosophical wisdom into the symbolic and imagistic language of the Qurʾan and the Hadith. This is to say that he explained the Origin and Return not only in terms of the existentiating command—as was the wont of the early philosophers—but also in terms of the prescriptive command, claiming that the imagistic and symbolic depictions of the soul's becoming, linked by Scripture to commands and prohibitions, provide a far more accurate portrayal of the soul's reality than the abstruse analyses of the philosophers. In one of many passages where he critiques the approach of mere rationality, he offers a visionary tale of his own. Perhaps he is responding to Ibn Ṭufayl's well-known philosophical novel, *Ḥayy ibn Yaqẓān*, in which an autodidact philosopher attains the same level of understanding as a prophet.[41] In Ibn ʿArabī's tale, a philosopher and a follower of Muhammad ascend together through the heavenly spheres in the direction of God. At each level of ascent, the follower is given a plethora of richly imagistic lore by the prophet who rules over the sphere in question—Moses, Abraham, Jesus, and so on—but the philosopher perceives only the qualities and characteristics of the relevant planet.[42] In effect, the Prophet's follower reaps the fruit of the promise made in the verse of conditional love: "Follow me, and God will love you." It is this path of following that Ibn ʿArabī calls "the religion of love" in a famous poem referring to the Station of No Station, even if most

---

*Pursuit of Virtue in Islamic Philosophy and Sufism* (London: Oneworld, 2017). See also Kazuyo Murata, *Beauty in Sufism: The Teachings of Rūzbihān Baqlī* (Albany: State University of New York Press, 2017).

41 See Ibn Ṭufayl, *Hayy ibn Yaqzan: A Philosophical Tale*, trans. Lenn E. Goodman (Chicago: University of Chicago Press, 2009).

42 For a translation, see Stephen Hirtenstein, trans., *The Alchemy of Human Happiness. Chapter 167 of Ibn ʿArabi's Meccan Illuminations* (Oxford: Anqa, 2017).

Western observers have ignored his commentary on the line and read it instead as an ecumenism before its time.

> My heart has become the receptacle for every form,
>   a pasture for gazelles, a monastery for monks,
> A house of idols, a Kaaba for the circumambulator,
>   tablets for the Torah, a volume for the Qur'an.
> I practice the religion of love wherever its camels turn their faces.
>   This religion is my religion and my faith.[43]

In any case, imagination played a far more central role in Ibn 'Arabī's worldview than it did in the vision of the philosophers, but to see the importance he gave to it, we need to understand that he added new dimensions to the word's meaning. In Arabic, *khayāl* means both imagination and image, which is to say that it designates both the mind's power of picturing things and images independent of the mind. Ibn 'Arabī insists that the word simultaneously affirms and denies what it signifies. Thus, images we see in mirrors or in our own thoughts are and are not what they appear to be. The key to the meaning of imagination lies in its ambiguity, which Ibn 'Arabī finds in three primary sorts of intermediacy. In the broadest sense, *khayāl* designates the universe in its entirety, for every possible thing dwells in an ambiguous realm between the Necessary Existence and absolute nonexistence, so it is an image of both being and nonbeing, belonging in truth to neither side. In a second broad sense, imagination designates one of the three hierarchically ordered worlds of the cosmos, namely the world of images, which is located above the world of bodies (what we call "the physical world") and beneath the world of spirits and intellects. In a third sense, imagination designates the human soul as a totality, for the soul is an

---

[43] William C. Chittick, "The Religion of Love Revisited," *Journal of the Muhyiddin ibn 'Arabi Society* 54 (2013): 37–59.

image of both spirit and body; in itself it is neither spiritual nor bodily, or it is both spiritual and bodily at the same time.

Ibn 'Arabī held that Aristotelian logic, with its insistence on either/or, fails to grasp the nature of things, for it wants to strip the images found in and by the soul from their specific designations and turn them back into abstract, intelligible realities dwelling above and beyond. But the images in their particularity and exactitude, on whatever level of existence they may appear, convey the immanent presence of the Necessary Existence while simultaneously affirming nonexistence. Each thing in the universe dwells in the ambiguity of imagination; it is both there and not there. We perceive the things, but they have no independent existence. All perceived reality is in fact a *barzakh*, an "isthmus" between existence and nonexistence, displaying the properties of both sides without being reducible to one or the other.[44]

The great virtue of intellect lies in its ability to perceive universals and disengage forms from their matters, allowing it to set up distinctions, differences, and classifications. Only intellective discernment, Ibn 'Arabī insists, can provide an adequate understanding of God's utter transcendence, which is the nakedness of the Necessary Existence, bereft of anything other than Itself. In contrast, the great virtue of imagination is the ability to perceive the presence of some things in other things. Actualized properly, imagination witnesses the omnipresence of the Necessary Existence in the possible things. The quest for human perfection, then, demands a balanced vision of transcendence and immanence, which can only be actualized by seeing simultaneously with "the two eyes of the heart," intellect and imagination.

For Ibn 'Arabī and others, the urgency of developing imagination derives from the fact that the only way to achieve the soul's perfection is to actively engage in the return to the One, and the only power

---

[44] On some of the philosophical implications of this notion of intermediacy, see Salman H. Bashier, *Ibn 'Arabi's Barzakh: The Concept of the Limit and the Relationship between God and the World* (Albany: State University of New York Press, 2004).

that can actualize this return is love. As Suhrawardī said in the passage quoted earlier from *Fī ḥaqīqat al-ʿishq*, "Arrival at beauty is impossible except by means of love." The motivation for love comes not from abstract concepts and demonstrative proofs but from concrete visions of beauty, that is, the immanent presence of the Good and the Beautiful in the created realm. As Ibn ʿArabī remarks in one of his critiques of intellect's limitations, "If we had remained with our rational proofs ... no created thing would ever have loved God."[45] The proper role of love, as Rūmī tells us, is to be a fire that, "when it blazes up, burns away everything except the everlasting Beloved."[46]

In one of the many ways in which Ibn ʿArabī adds an imaginal dimension to the philosophical positions, he describes the relationship between the Necessary Existence and the possible things in terms of love. Though he talks about Avicenna's "love that pervades all things," he typically uses more concrete language, speaking, for example, of "the marriage act that pervades all atoms." All possible things, in other words, are pervaded by a sexual intercourse that can be perceived on every level of existence. The first of these existentiating marriages takes place between God's essence and His infinite knowledge and brings about God's delight (*ibtihāj*) in the presence of the things.

> That which is desired from marriage may be reproduction—I mean the birth of offspring—or it may simply be enjoyment. The Divine Marriage is the attentiveness of the Real toward the possible thing in the presence of possibility through the desire of love, so that there may be delight along with desire. When the Real turns His attentiveness toward the possible thing as mentioned, He makes manifest the existentiation of this possible thing. Hence, that which is born from this union is the existence of the possible thing. ... This

---

45 William C. Chittick, *Divine Love: Islamic Literature and the Path to God* (New Haven, CT: Yale University Press, 2013), 4.
46 Rūmī, *Mathnawī* 5:588.

marriage is constant and continuous in existence. There can be no cessation or divorce in this marital contract.[47]

One of Ibn ʿArabī's better-known technical terms is "fixed entity" (ʿayn thābita), which he employs in place of the philosophers' "quiddity" (māhiyya). He points out that the fixed entities are the possible things known to the Necessary Existence for all eternity. The entities can never have existence of their own, since real existence pertains exclusively to the Necessary. When It sees that the moment for a possible thing's existence has arrived, It issues the existentiating command and brings the thing into relative existence, though the thing remains forever nonexistent in itself. Why then does God bother saying, "Be," to nonexistent things, giving them a whiff of existence in the cosmos? He does so because of love and mercy, or in philosophical terms, because of solicitude.

In discussing human love, Avicenna maintains a relatively detached stance, describing it as an ontological attribute coursing through all things. Ibn ʿArabī and other Sufi teachers give equal or greater weight to the need for right thought and right practice in order to participate in God's conditional love. They insist that the human existential plight derives from inherent love and yearning for union. Unless people understand that they are in fact lovers of God, they will not step into the path of following the guidance that brings down God's conditional love. They should strive to become aware of their innate love and intensify it through praxis. Sufi poets aim to stir up this love by highlighting beauty. As Rūmī put it, "What is Love? Perfect thirst. // So let me explain the Water of Life."[48]

Thirst is the pain of separation, driving lovers to seek the water of union. Avicenna states that the Necessary Existence lacks nothing, so it has no such yearning. Ibn ʿArabī takes a somewhat different

---

47 Ibn al-ʿArabī, Futūḥāt 3:516.3. On "macrocosmic marriage," see Murata, Tao, ch. 5.
48 Rūmī, Kulliyyāt, v. 17361.

standpoint, arguing that every beloved is nonexistent in relation to the lover. All things other than the Necessary Existence, the Supreme Lover, are nonexistent by definition, so all are objects of His love. "The created thing," he writes, "is nonexistent, so it is the object of God's love constantly and forever. . . . As long as there is love, one cannot conceive of the existence of the created thing along with it, so the created thing never comes into existence."[49] God loves the possible thing eternally, so it can never truly appear in the realm of being. At the moment it makes an appearance, God ceases loving it, loving instead the next moment of its appearance. This is one of his arguments to prove his well-known doctrine of "the renewal of creation at each instant" (*tajdīd al-khalq maʿaʾl-ānāt*).

Given that possible things never truly come into existence, they are in fact images of existence, not real existence. Ibn ʿArabī explains this imaginal existence in many ways, such as having recourse to "the Breath of the All-Merciful" (*nafas al-raḥmān*). Drawing from Qurʾanic references to the universe as the words of God, he devotes a book-length chapter of his *Futūḥāt al-makkiyya* (The Meccan openings) to a description of the circle of Origin and Return in terms of the All-Merciful's articulation of twenty-eight successive letters corresponding to the Arabic alphabet. The first and second letters designate the First Intellect and the Universal Soul. The intermediate letters represent the descending and ascending stages of the universe. The penultimate letter designates the human being, and the final letter represents the ascending degrees of human perfection in the climb to the intellect and beyond.[50]

In explaining how all possible things are embedded in the All-Merciful Breath, Ibn ʿArabī says that things have the same status

---

49 Ibn ʿArabī, *Futūḥāt* 2:113.29. For more on Ibn ʿArabī's views on love, see William C. Chittick, *Self-Disclosure of God: Principles of Ibn al-ʿArabī's Cosmology* (Albany: State University of New York Press, 1998), chs. 2–3; Zargar, *Sufi Aesthetics*.

50 See Chittick, *Self-Disclosure of God*, xxviii–xxxii.

in relation to the divine breath as our words have in relation to our breath. We bring words into existence because of our desire and love to put them there, though they disappear instantly. So, also, God's eternal speech brings the possible things into existence at each instant, but once they exist, they immediately disappear. God's existentiating command then articulates the next moment of their existence, and so on without end.

God's words appearing in His All-Merciful Breath are images of Himself, just as our words appearing in our breath are images of us. They are the same as ourselves, yet different. In this extended meditation on the divine and human form, which he develops in many directions, Ibn ʿArabī tells us that what we call "existence" is nothing but the divine mercy that permeates all things. "The cosmos is identical with mercy, nothing else."[51] Existent things can only be understood as the self-disclosures of a loving, merciful, and compassionate God, a God who has given us to ourselves so that we may benefit, who has articulated His Breath as existentiated words for the sake of the ultimate happiness of all beings. More than any other Muslim theologian and philosopher, Ibn ʿArabī insists that all shall be well. In a typical passage he puts it this way: "The final issue will be at mercy, for the actual situation inscribes a circle. The end of the circle curves back to its beginning and joins with it. The end has the property of the beginning, and that is nothing but existence."[52]

---

51 Ibn al-ʿArabī, *Futūḥāt* 2:437.24.
52 Ibn al-ʿArabī, *Futūḥāt* 4:405.7. See William C. Chittick, "The Hermeneutics of Mercy," in *Ibn ʿArabi: Heir to the Prophets* (Oxford: Oneworld, 2005), ch. 9.

CHAPTER 5

# The Personal Experience of Transcendental Love

MYSTICS AND CONTEMPLATIVES IN THE MEDIEVAL CHRISTIAN TRADITION

*Christina Van Dyke*

Although the debate over the supremacy of intellect versus will continues in scholastic circles throughout the thirteenth and fourteenth centuries, by the late thirteenth century it was generally agreed in broader cultural and contemplative Christian circles that love reigns supreme. The main discussions in contemplative circles center around the practice of love (what sorts of activities and disciplines develop and increase love) and the nature and experience of love (what love is, and what the right sort of love "feels like"). As I discuss in the first section, imaginative meditation develops as a spiritual discipline aimed at teaching the practitioner how to love via engagement of the senses and imagination. This leaves open the question of what love is, though; in the second section, I address the multilayered nature of love. Today, a distinction is often drawn between sacred love (charity or *caritas*) and secular love (*amor*). In the Rome-based Christian contemplative tradition of the later Middle Ages, however, not only were these terms used more or less interchangeably, but the tropes and images associated with the terms overlapped extensively as well, so that transcendent love for God is described using all available means. In fact, as we see in the final section, first-person reports of what this love feels like in this period often use the language of "courtly love" or *fin'amor* to depict religious experiences, including the search for and the culmination of love's union with God.

## The Practice of Love: Kindling the Fire of Love via Meditations on the Life of Christ

Most people today are unaware of the existence of medieval meditations as a genre of devotional literature, or the fact that meditation was one of the most widely practiced spiritual exercises of the later Middle Ages, and yet the significance of this practice and its impact on religious life and art in the mid-thirteenth through sixteenth centuries would be hard to overstate.[1] Originally developed in the twelfth century by Guigio II as a contemplative practice for cloistered monks, by the beginning of the fourteenth century brief and lively meditations on the life of Christ had become extremely popular for layfolk as well as religious, and guided meditation a discipline recommended

---

1 For more on the history and impact of meditation as a medieval Christian devotional practice, see Thomas Bestul, "*Meditatio*/Meditation," in *Cambridge Companion to Christian Mysticism*, ed. Amy Hollywood and Patricia Z. Beckman (Cambridge: Cambridge University Press, 2012), 157–166; Holly Flora, *The Devout Belief of the Imagination: The Paris Meditationes Vitae Christi and Female Franciscan Spirituality in Trecento Italy*, Disciplina Monastica 6 (Turnhout: Brepols, 2009); Christina Van Dyke, "From Meditation to Contemplation: Broadening the Boundaries of Philosophy in the Thirteenth to Fifteenth Centuries," in *Pluralizing Philosophy's Past—New Reflections in the History of Philosophy*, ed. Amber L. Griffioen and Marius Backmann (Cham, Switzerland: Palgrave Macmillan, 2023), 213–229.

to everyone who desired a deeper and more personal relationship with God.[2] The central appeal of meditation as a spiritual exercise was that it was explicitly designed to engage and train the "lower" faculties of human beings (e.g., sense perception, sense appetite, and imagination) to work with rather than against the "higher" faculties (e.g., intellect and will) in their search for fulfillment in God. From at least the time of Plato, the senses, faculties, and imagination were notorious for their ability to distract human beings from higher pursuits, as when a mathematician's rumbling stomach leads them to start wondering what's for lunch instead of focusing on their complicated proof. The medieval practice of meditation seeks to use those same sensations and imaginings to further higher pursuits—asking us, for instance, to channel our own hunger into more vividly imagining Christ's hunger when he fasted for forty days in the desert. At its heart, meditation was intended to encourage a visceral sense of connection to and personal love for the incarnate Christ, kindling a fire of affection that can then be fanned into a burning love leading to still greater love, knowledge, and virtue.

Before looking more closely at the discipline of meditation in the later Middle Ages, it's important to note that it was widely understood—and practiced—as the second of four linked spiritual exercises. The first of these four practices is "*lectio divina*": reading holy texts slowly and carefully; imaginative meditation (*meditatio* in Latin) then brings the content of those texts to life to cultivate a personal connection to God. The third practice, contemplative prayer (*oratio*), draws on this connection to align one's will more closely with God's. The fourth discipline, contemplation (*contemplatio*), is the apex of the religious

---

[2] Guigio II, a Carthusian monk, originally outlines the practice and purpose of meditation in his *Ladder of Monks and Twelve Meditations*. Carthusians took strict vows of silence, emphasizing the importance of the written word, and this emphasis on texts carries over when the practice becomes more widespread. In fact, it is almost certainly one of the factors in reading becoming a sign of religious devotion in women in the later Middle Ages. (For more on this development, see *Medieval Holy Women in the Christian Tradition c. 1100–c. 1500*, ed. A. Minnis and R. Voaden [Turnhout: Brepols, 2010].)

and moral life.³ Often identified as the final end for human beings, the culmination of contemplation—union with God—is something for which human beings can only seek to prepare themselves via the previous exercises; it is a gift of grace, not something we can make happen.

In the context of these four linked disciplines, imaginative meditation's practice of turning our 'lower' powers toward God was seen as an important move toward our ultimate end.⁴ More particularly, it was where the revealed truths of Scripture take on personal significance. To use an analogy that goes back to Guigio II, if the act of reading (*lectio divina*) is putting spiritual food in one's mouth, then meditation is chewing that food. As the widely read late-thirteenth-century *Meditations on the Life of Christ* puts it after musing about how difficult it must have been for Joseph to realize that Mary was pregnant with a child that wasn't his, and how much patience the newly incarnate Christ must have needed to remain in Mary's womb for nine months: "You see how appetizing the spiritual food courses are that have been served here for you; if you wish to taste their sweetness, mentally chew them, thoroughly and often."⁵

We earthbound creatures have a hard time loving things we can't see or otherwise experience with our senses. This is also why the subject of

---

3   For chapter-length discussions of each of these practices, see the *Cambridge Companion to Christian Mysticism*, ed. Amy Hollywood and Patricia Z. Beckman (Cambridge: Cambridge University Press, 2012): respectively, E. Ann Matter, "*Lectio Divina*" (147–156); Thomas Bestul, "*Meditatio*/Meditation" (157–166); Rachel Fulton Brown, "*Oratio*/Prayer" (167–177); and Charlotte Radler, "*Actio et Contemplatio* / Action and Contemplation" (211–224); as well as Bernard McGinn, "*Unio Mystica* / Mystical Union" (200–210).

4   For more on this, see Michelle Karnes, *Imagination, Meditation, and Cognition in the Middle Ages* (Chicago: University of Chicago Press, 2011); Sarah McNamer's *Affective Meditation and the Invention of Medieval Compassion* (Philadelphia: University of Pennsylvania Press, 2009) discussion of the practice of meditation is also worth reading, although the central thesis of the book has been extensively critiqued (by Karnes, among others).

5   Chapter 6 of John of Caulibus (?)'s *Meditations on the Life of Christ*, trans. and ed. F. Taney, A. Miller, and C. M. Stallings-Taney (Asheville, NC: Pegasus Press, 2000), 23. The *Meditations* was translated into a number of vernaculars, including Nicholas Love's influential Middle English *Mirror of the Blessed Life of Jesus Christ*. It was also deeply influential on later devotional texts, such as Thomas à Kempis's early-fifteenth-century *The Imitation of Christ*. For the definitive Latin edition, see *Meditationes Vitae Christi*, ed. Mary Stallings-Taney, *Corpus Christianorum Continuatio Mediaevalis*, CCCM 153 (Turnhout: Brepols, 1997).

these meditations is so often the life of Christ: by taking on human nature, the Second Person of the Trinity becomes God-with-Us in a way that human beings can finally grasp. Bonaventure (who wrote scholastic treatises in his capacity as chair of theology at the University of Paris and a number of influential contemplative works and sermons in his capacity as friar in the Franciscan Order) is a strong proponent of this account of the Incarnation. In *The Mystical Vine*, for instance, Bonaventure explains this from Christ's viewpoint: "In forming you, I conformed you to the likeness of my divinity; to re-form you [after the Fall], I conformed myself to the likeness of your humanity. . . . I became human and visible so that you might see me and thus love me, since, unseen and invisible in my divinity, I had not been properly loved."[6] Christ's human life both provides a model for our own lives and presents a God we can relate to on a personal level.

When the late-thirteenth-century Carthusian Marguerite d'Oingt asks in her *Page of Meditations*, "What shall I do, when I still do not know how to love you?"[7] the answer is provided by the meditation itself, which dwells on Christ's life of love from its humble beginnings to its agonizing end. "Oh God, how marvelous were the things that love did!" Marguerite cries. "Love led him who was so big that the whole world was not able to hold him, and who held the whole world in his fist, to enter the body of a young girl; and so from he who was himself true God, [love] made a mortal human being. And he who was the king of kings and lord of lords and who created the heavens and all

---

[6] *Works of Bonaventure: Journey of the Mind into God—The Triple Way, or Love Enkindled—The Tree of Life—The Mystical Vine—On the Perfection of Life, Addressed to Sisters*, trans. José DeVinck (Mansfield Centre, CT: Martino Publishing, 2016), 204. See also ch. 1 of *On the Incarnation of the Word*, where Bonaventure explains that Christ took on human nature because after the Fall, human beings—"carnal, animal, and sensual"—could not "know, or love, or follow anything that was not proportional and like it (*consimilia*)." Thus, the Word was made flesh so that human beings could "know and love and imitate him" and in this way humanity "could be healed of the disease of sin." *Brevilioquium*, part 4, *On the Incarnation of the Word*, ch. 1.3, in S. *Bonaventurae Opera Theologica Selecta*, vol. 5 (Firenze: Quaracchi, 1964), my translation.

[7] *Page of Meditations*, 13, in *Oeuvres de Marguerite D'Oyngt Prieure de Poleteins*, ed. E. Philipon (Lyon: N. Sheuring, 1877), 1–33. Translations are mine, from a reproduction of the text accessed December 29, 2022, from Wikisource, la bibliothèque libre: https://fr.wikisource.org/wiki/Page%3AOingt_-_Oeuvres_de_Marguerite_d_Oyngt.pdf/54.

creatures who exist in order to serve him—this love, I say, led him to serve human beings."[8] Love is the agent here—a motivating force so powerful that it can subvert the natural order of the cosmos.

To help fan the flame of this love, medieval meditations typically describe events in Christ's life in vivid detail and ask their readers to engage imaginatively with those scenes. The *Meditations on the Life of Christ* counsels the meditator to "place yourself in the presence of whatever is related as having been said or done by the Lord Jesus, as if you were hearing it with your own ears and seeing it with your own eyes, giving it your total mental response."[9] The purpose of this, as mentioned earlier, is to harness the powers of sensation (*sensualitas*) and imagination to assist the will and the intellect in preparing for contemplation. According to commonly accepted theories of human nature at this time, sensation's telos is to help the will desire the good by acquainting us with "all of physical creation, both pleasant and unpleasant" and helping us focus on the right objects.[10] The balance of this relationship was disrupted by the Fall, however, so that sensation now often fights or distracts the will instead of assisting it. In the same way, imagination—"the power that helps us form mental images of anything present or absent"—is *supposed* to assist the intellect in the discovery of the truth, both by calling up sense impressions from our memory so that the intellect can consider them in its search for Truth and by working with the intellect to isolate various features of past sensory experiences and/or combine them in new and interesting ways.[11] This relationship was also disrupted by the Fall; we now use the imagination in any number of ways that don't lead us closer to truth or goodness.

---

8 *Page of Meditations*, 6, accessed December 29, 2022. https://fr.wikisource.org/wiki/Page%3AOingt_-_Oeuvres_de_Marguerite_d_Oyngt.pdf/47 .
9 John of Caulibus (?), "Prologue," in *Meditations* 4.
10 The *Cloud of Unknowing* describes 'sensualitas' as "the power that affects and controls our body's perceptions," which allow us to "know and experience all of physical creation, both pleasant and unpleasant." *The Cloud of Unknowing: With the Book of Privy Counselling*, trans. Carmen Acevedo Butcher (Boulder, CO: Shambhala, 2009), ch. 66, p. 147.
11 *Cloud of Unknowing*, ch. 65, p. 145.

The discipline of meditation attempts to restore the original purposes of sensation and imagination. As *Meditations on the Life of Christ* explains, "You will find no place else where you can become so schooled against vain and passing enticements, trials, and adversities ... as in the life of the Lord Jesus, a life that was absolutely perfect and without any defect. For as a result of frequent and habitual meditation on his life, the soul is influenced toward a certain familiarity with it, confidence in it, and love for it, so that the soul despises and holds in contempt all else."[12] To develop this love and confidence, the reader is encouraged not just to dwell on the events described in Scripture but also to imaginatively explore and engage events in Christ's life that aren't recorded in Scripture. "You should not think that all his words and deeds that we can meditate on were actually written down," states the author of the *Meditations*: "I will tell you about these unwritten things just as if they had actually happened ... doing this in accord with certain imaginary scenarios. For we can meditate on divine Scripture, explain it, and understand it in multifarious ways, insofar as we believe it useful, provided it not be contrary to the truth about his life, or justice, or doctrine."[13]

The author then immediately puts this into practice by opening with three extrascriptural meditations (on the angels' plea for God to redeem humanity, on a debate between Mercy and Peace over the redemption of humanity, and on Mary's life prior to the Annunciation) before turning to events described in the Gospels. The *Meditations* continues to muse on imagined scenes throughout. When discussing the Holy Family's poverty in Egypt, for instance, Mary is described as taking in mending to make money ("Did not she herself go about through the neighboring homes seeking garments and other articles on which she could work?"), with the young Jesus helping her ("But also, when the boy Jesus was about five years old, did he not consider

---

12  John of Caulibus (?), "Prologue," in *Meditations*, 1.
13  John of Caulibus (?), "Prologue," in *Meditations*, 4.

himself his mother's agent, by seeking work for her? She had no other helper. Did he not also return the finished work, asking for payment for his mother?").[14]

The *Meditations* also repeatedly counsels its readers to actively place themselves at these scenes and to interact with the biblical figures. The author breaks from imagining Jesus's life of poverty in Egypt, for instance, to instruct the reader, "Meditate on these and similar thoughts about the boy Jesus: I have given you the setting. Enlarge on it and proceed as it seems fit, and be a little girl with the child Jesus, and disdain neither such humble activities nor meditating on what seems childish."[15] After Jesus's crucifixion, the *Meditations* first describes the Apostle John taking Mary to his own home and attempting to console her in her grief, and then it directly addresses the reader again: "If you would like to know how to console and comfort her, busy yourself in preparing and serving them something to eat. Encourage her to take some nourishment soon, and see to it that the others take something to eat, because they were hungry by now."[16] The reason for engaging in this sort of exercise is "to produce devotion, increase love, enkindle fervor, and induce compassion"—in short, to build good affective habits.

Visual images were also often used to aid meditation: not only did these images further engage the senses and the imagination, but they also made the practice more accessible to those who lacked access or the ability to read the relevant texts. Portrayals of Mary and the baby Jesus in this period, for instance, emphasize activity and human relatability over the serenity and divinity that characterize earlier medieval depictions (see Figure 5.1 vs. Figure 5.2). Scenes depicting Christ's passion also become much more expressive, showing the pain of both

---

14 John of Caulibus (?), *Meditations*, ch. 12, pp. 44 and 45, respectively.
15 The passage continues to list a number of other benefits: "bestow purity and simplicity, add to the strength of your humility and poverty; preserve intimacy, and produce unanimity, as well as raise your hope" (John of Caulibus (?), *Meditations*, 45).
16 John of Caulibus (?), *Meditations*, ch. 80, p. 265.

FIGURE 5.1 Madonna and Child Enthroned, unknown Italian artist, c. 1200–1250, Detroit Museum of Art.

PERSONAL EXPERIENCE OF TRANSCENDENTAL LOVE 135

FIGURE 5.2 Madonna of the Magnificat, Giovanni di Turino, c. 1420, Sant'Agostino, Siena.

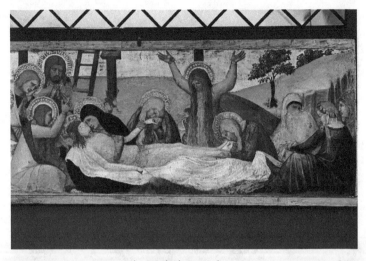

FIGURE 5.3 Lamentation over the Dead Christ, Ambrogio Lorenzetti c. 1342–4, Siena Pinacoteca.

Christ and of the witnesses (see Figure 5.3). Contemporary meditators were sometimes added to these scenes as well. Although the text itself says that Mary had no one to assist her in Egypt but Jesus, for instance, an extensively illustrated fourteenth-century Italian text of the *Meditations on the Life of Christ* depicts two women working alongside her (see Figure 5.4). The art historian Holly Flora has observed that the scribe's instructions for the illustrator (which remain visible in this manuscript) specify the inclusion of these two women, who she believes represent Franciscan nuns (for whom this text was produced)—thus making it easier for the people who would be using this text to imaginatively engage with it.[17] Similarly, the lamentation over Christ's body in Figure 5.3 (by Ambrogio Lorenzetti, most famous for his *Allegory of Good and Bad Government* in Siena's Palazzo Pubblico) includes not just figures mentioned in Scripture—whose names are inscribed in their halos and who occupy the places of importance at

---

17 Flora, *Devout Belief of the Imagination*.

# PERSONAL EXPERIENCE OF TRANSCENDENTAL LOVE 137

FIGURE 5.4 Detail of Meditationes vitae Christi, Fourteenth Century, ms. Ital. 115, Bibliothèque nationale de France.

Jesus's head and torso—but also four unidentified women mourning at his feet, thought to represent nuns from the convent for which the painting was created.

When it came to kindling and fanning the fire of love for God, no practice was more widely recommended in the later Middle Ages than meditating on the life of Christ. As we see in the next section, the first-person experience of love for God was also a central topic of interest for medieval contemplatives and mystics. Love in this tradition is not just *caritas* but also *amor*—not just a warm glow of benevolence but also an all-consuming passion. Where this passion leads is the subject of the final section.

## The Nature of Love: *Caritas*, *Amor*, and *Fin'Amor*

The triumph of love over knowledge in the later Middle Ages is epitomized by the fourteenth-century English *Cloud of Unknowing*, which at one point states, "Only love—not knowledge—can help us reach

God."[18] The *Book of Privy Counseling* (anonymous but likely written by the same author as the *Cloud*) expands on this thought, using the Old Testament story of Rachel, who dies giving birth to her son Benjamin, to emphasize the importance of contemplative love over human rational powers: "As soon as seekers of God are touched by genuine contemplation, they work to make themselves nothing and God everything, and in this high, noble decision, it's as if their reason dies.... Benjamin is a symbol of all contemplatives who experience the ecstasy of love that takes them beyond the powers of the mind."[19] As we saw earlier in the chapter, the practice of imaginative meditation was designed to help us attain the heights of contemplation, this "ecstasy of love."

But what *is* love? At its most basic, love in this period is understood as movement of the will toward an object perceived as good. The will's proper object is the good, and the Highest Good is God (in the same way that the intellect's proper object is the true, and the Ultimate Truth is God). Thus, the will's most proper object is God, and the movement of the will toward God—that is, love for God—is love in its highest form. That said, the nature and experience of love is anything but basic, and medieval understandings of love are correspondingly complex. Is the love for the Highest Good affective and compelling, burning and fierce, or is it a quiet security and peace that passes understanding? Medieval contemplatives answer "yes" to all of those questions; contemplative texts from the mid-thirteenth to early fifteenth centuries merge metaphors, embrace paradoxes, and combine conceptions that seem contradictory in an effort to capture love's multifaceted nature.

Contrary to modern philosophical and theological discussions of love influenced by C. S. Lewis's *Four Loves*, in fact, which distinguish love-as-affection (*storge*), love-as-friendship (*philia*), and romantic love (*eros*) from unconditional-"God"-love (charity or *agape*), in medieval

---

18 *Cloud of Unknowing*, ch. 8, pp. 28–29.
19 *Cloud of Unknowing*, 193.

contemplative literature, distinctions between kinds of love (even "sacred" vs. "secular" love) are often blurred and sometimes denied altogether.[20] All love is a movement of the will toward something perceived as good: the relevant difference between loves is not so much whether the will is moved toward a "holy" object versus a "worldly" object but whether the will is "rightly ordered" in its desires—that is, whether things are loved in the correct proportion and order relative to other things.[21] A knight's love for his horse, for instance, is appropriate and good when it is stronger than his love for his hunting dog and less strong than his love for his Beloved or king; the same love would be disordered if the knight's love for his steed were stronger than the knight's love for his Beloved or king and thus led the knight to avoid battle for fear of the horse's injury or death.[22]

This conception of love as a unified (and unifying) force lies at the heart of medieval contemplative literature: love is what unites us with God, our neighbors, and ourselves. As the late-thirteenth-century Flemish beguine Hadewijch writes, "If two things are to become one, nothing may be between them except the glue wherewith they are united together. That bond of glue is Love."[23] The idea of love as essentially connective is also integral to the motivation of meditation as an embodied practice: the discipline of using the senses and imagination to vicariously experience events in Christ's life helps us feel so powerfully connected to God that we are able to reorder our loves for the

---

20 C. S. Lewis's *The Four Loves* (New York: Harcourt Brace, 1960) develops some of the ideas from his earlier study of love in the Middle Ages: *The Allegory of Love: A Study in Medieval Tradition* (Oxford: Clarendon Press, 1936). For a book-length argument that demonstrates the permeability of medieval conceptions of the sacred and secular, see Barbara Newman's *Medieval Crossover: Reading the Secular against the Sacred*, Conway Lectures in Medieval Studies (Notre Dame: University of Notre Dame Press, 2013).

21 This is the main lesson of Augustine's *On Free Choice of the Will*, bk. 1, for instance, which defines "evildoing" as "inordinate love."

22 For more on the relationship between knights and their steeds, see "Animals and Thirteenth Century Chivalric Identity," in Nigel Harris, *The Thirteenth Century Animal Turn: Medieval and Twenty-First-Century Perspectives* (Cham: Palgrave Macmillan, 2020), 63–86.

23 *Hadewijch: The Complete Works*, ed. and trans. Mother Columba Hart (Mahwah, NJ: Paulist Press, 1980), Letter 16, 80.

better. For medieval contemplatives, love's unitive nature transcends hard-and-fast distinctions in a way that allows love for God to be discussed using the same terms as love for one's human paramour.

A look at two of the central terms used in contemplative discussions for love—*caritas* and *amor*—demonstrates this point.[24] Today, *caritas* is often translated as "charity," which in modern English primarily connotes concrete acts of benevolence or love for one's neighbor. In the later Middle Ages, though, the term applies more broadly to the sort of love involved in *both* of the Great Commandments (love God above all else and love your neighbor as yourself). In fact, the word *caritas* is used regularly to refer to the purest and highest form of love—love for and from God. (Because of this, I continue to use the Latin word *caritas* here rather than the English "charity.") *Caritas* is identified not just as a virtue but as the highest of the "theological" virtues: faith, hope, and *caritas*. All three virtues involve being rightly oriented toward God, but while faith and hope involve things unseen and desire unsatisfied, *caritas* involves a connection to God that is already present and yet always promising more.[25] Because rightly oriented love involves the will being in an ideal relationship with intellect and reason, *caritas* is also associated with both theoretical and practical wisdom. As Catherine of Siena puts it, in the flourishing tree of self, "discernment and charity are engrafted together" and grow as one.[26] The inner expression of *caritas* was seen as including joy (over one's union with God), peace (the experience of the harmonious self), and mercy (toward others); its external expression includes beneficence (general benevolence toward others), almsgiving (material expression of neighbor love), and

---

[24] A third word for love, *delictio*, also appears regularly in these texts, but it doesn't carry forward in the way that *caritas* and *amor* do, and so I do not discuss it in any detail here.

[25] The "cardinal" virtues—wisdom, courage, moderation, and justice—are seen as subordinate to the theological virtues. For a classic discussion of all seven virtues and their relation to each other, see Thomas Aquinas, *Summa theologiae* I-II, qq. 55–67, particularly qq. 61–62.

[26] *Catherine of Siena: The Dialogue*, trans. Suzanne Noffke (Mahwah, NJ: Paulist Press, 1980), ch. 9, p. 41.

fraternal correction (practical expression of neighbor love in situations where something has gone wrong).[27] Although the earlier iconography of *caritas* portrayed a woman (the personification of Caritas) giving clothes to someone in need, in this period Caritas is more often shown breastfeeding a child.[28]

At the same time, the iconography of *caritas* increasingly features Caritas holding a heart on fire or wearing a fiery crown (or both), and the word associated with this sort of fiery love—*amor*—appears in discussions of *caritas* not as a contrast term but as a synonym. We can literally see this in personifications of *caritas* that combine both benevolence (in the form of the breastfeeding mother) and passion (in the form of the heart on fire and/or fiery crown) (see Figure 5.5).

Although *caritas* is today sometimes distinguished from *amor* as a way of contrasting "sacred" and "secular" love, from the time of Augustine on, the two words are used more or less interchangeably in philosophical and theological contexts. A number of the passages cited in the first section, for instance, use *amor* to pick the highest sort of love in the same way as *caritas*. In the prologue to *Meditations on the Life of Christ*—where the positive effects of meditation are described as "familiarity, confidence in, and love for it [the life of Christ], so that the soul despises and holds in contempt all else"—for instance, the word for "love" is *amor*.[29] In Marguerite d'Oingt's *Page of Meditations*, the word for the love that characterizes God's actions and drives Christ to become Incarnate is also *amor*, while in Marguerite Porete's *Mirror of Simple Souls*, the love that identifies itself with God is *amor*. We

---

27 See, e.g., Aquinas's *Summa theologiae* II-II, q. 23 and *Disputed Questions on Caritas*.

28 For more on this and the development of this iconography, see R. Freyhan, "The Evolution of the Caritas Figure in the Thirteenth and Fourteenth Centuries," *Journal of the Warburg and Courtauld Institutes* 2 (1948): 68–86. Sometimes the woman who personifies *Caritas* is portrayed as breastfeeding an old man—this image is sometimes called "Roman Charity" because of its roots in a Roman legend of a loyal daughter who visits her father who is being starved in prison to breastfeed him.

29 Latin text of the *Meditations*: "Ex frequenti enim et assueta meditacione iute ipsiu adducitur anima in quondam familiaritatem, confidenciam, et amorem ipsius, eta quod alia uilipendit et contemnit" (John de Caulibus [?], *Meditationes*, p. 7, ll. 18–20).

142 LOVE

FIGURE 5.5  Carità, Piero del Pollaiolo, 1469, Uffizi Gallery Museum.

FIGURE 5.6 Casket with Scenes of Romances, Paris c. 1310–1330, Met Cloisters Museum.

find this same fluidity in vernacular contemplative writings of the period. In her late-fourteenth-century Italian *Dialogue*, for instance, Catherine of Siena moves between *amor* and *caritas* when discussing the love that God has for us (as well as the love we should have for God and others).[30] Works in Middle English—such as *Cloud of Unknowing*, the *Book of Privy Counselling*, Richard Rolle's *The Form of Living*, and Julian of Norwich's *Showings*—also regularly alternate between talking about "love" (the Middle English translation of *amor*) and "charite," making no hard-and-fast distinction between the terms.[31]

The fluidity of terms for love also lends itself to an additional layer of complexity in medieval contemplative literature, in its extensive

---

30 As Suzanne Noffke comments in her translation of the *Dialogue*, "In Catherine's writings, *carità* and *amore* are often used quite interchangeably" (*Catherine of Siena: The Dialogue*, 26n4).

31 For numerous examples, see the original texts in *English Mystics of the Middle Ages*, ed. Barry Windeatt (New York: Cambridge University Press, 1994), which include selections from Richard Rolle, Walter Hilton, the anonymous *Cloud of Unknowing* and the *Book of Privy Counseling*, Julian of Norwich, Margery Kempe, and an unattributed Middle English translation of Margeurite Porete's *Mirror of Simple Souls* (with commentary by the translator).

use of imagery and tropes from the *fin'amor* (courtly love) tradition.[32] Popularized by troubadours (most famously Chrétien de Troyes), *trouvère*, and *minnesänger* in the twelfth century, love in the *fin'amor* tradition is highly stylized.[33] It is not a quiet affection; it is a scorching fire that defies the status quo and causes the fall of the wise and mighty. In contrast to the portrayal of *caritas* as peaceful, just, and wise, the love associated with *fin'amor* is often tumultuous and unfair, and makes fools of its practitioners. In one legend that appears frequently in panels depicting famous stories of love's supremacy, Aristotle burns so hotly for his student Alexander's wife Phyllis that he allows her to saddle and ride him.[34] (See Figure 5.6, in which Aristotle appears in the first panel as an authority figure, instructing Alexander the Great, and in the second as love's fool, subordinated to a woman while Alexander looks on and laughs. The two panels on the right portray the story of Thisbe and Pyramus, whose star-crossed love ends in their dual suicide.) The power of love in this tradition is ultimate: the medieval sagas of both Tristan and Iseult and Lancelot and Guinevere, for instance, contain sections in which their love-frustrated heroes go mad and live like animals in the forest for a time, and Elaine, "the Fair Maid of Astolat," eventually dies from her unrequited love for Lancelot.

At the same time, love in the *fin'amor* tradition is inherently ennobling: its all-consuming passion pulls the lover away from mundane matters and inspires increasingly heroic feats. In this world of up-ended priorities, the lover will sacrifice everything for love's sake—wealth,

---

[32] Because the term "courtly love" doesn't appear until the nineteenth century and was applied only retroactively, its use has become controversial in academic circles; *fin'amor*—an Occitan phrase that appears already in the twelfth century—is increasingly preferred as more accurate, so I use it here.

[33] See *The Complete Romances of Chrétien de Troyes*, trans. David Staines (Bloomington: Indiana University Press, 1990).

[34] These stories are frequently depicted on ivory caskets whose covers show images of the allegorical "Attack on the Castle of Love"—sieges in which flowers are used as ballistics and the only arrows are shot by the god of love. For further discussion of the connections between the siege on the soul and the siege on love, see "Allegorical Sieges" in Malcolm Hebron, *The Medieval Siege: Theme and Image in Middle English Romance* (Oxford: Oxford University Press, 1997), 136–165.

reputation, family, sanity, even life itself. Gaining love's favor and becoming worthy of the Beloved motivates the lover's every action, and this single-minded quest is portrayed as the highest goal of existence. Given this framing, it's not difficult to see why medieval mystics and contemplatives would use the tropes of *fin'amor* in an effort to communicate what it's like to be in a love relationship with God. The *fin'amor* tradition itself drew on erotic metaphors in the monotheistic religious traditions, particularly from the Song of Songs, for in the Rome-based Christian tradition, a rich tradition had developed of reading the song of Songs as a love song between Christ and the Church (often described in the Christian Bible as Christ's bride).[35] This fluid interplay of "sacred" and "secular" metaphor, analogy, and allegory allows medieval mystics and contemplatives to combine tropes associated with *caritas*, *amor*, and *fin'amor*.

Marguerite Porete, for instance, extensively employs metaphors from the *fin'amor* tradition in her *Mirror of Simple Souls* to express the experience of the loving soul.[36] (*Fin'Amor* even appears as a character who calls the others to action.[37]) The entire treatise is cast in terms of the nobility of love's quest. In the *Mirror*'s prologue, for example, Porete relates the popular romance of Candace and Alexander the Great, in which Candace, "a maiden, daughter of a king, of great heart and nobility and also of noble character," hears of the "great gentle courtesy and nobility of the king, Alexander" and falls deeply in love with this far-off figure. She becomes inconsolable—"for no love except this one would be sufficient for her"—and orders a painting "which would represent the semblance of the king she loved," so that

---

[35] See Anne Astell, *The Song of Songs in the Middle Ages* (Ithaca, NY: Cornell University Press, 1990).
[36] For a wonderful discussion of how love plays a starring role in the *Mirror* in a myriad of ways, see Suzanne Kocher, *Allegories of Love in Marguerite Porete's Mirror of Simple Souls* (Turnhout: Brepols, 2009).
[37] See "Mirror of Simple Souls," in *English Mystics of the Middle Ages*, 87. As Ellen Babinsky comments in her translation note 6, for Porete, *fin'amor* "is divine, perfect love" (223).

she could dream of him.[38] This painting, Porete explains, represents her *Mirror*, which was written by Love so that its hearers might be "more worthy of the perfection of life and the being of peace to which the creature is able to arrive through the virtue of perfect charity." The rest of the book is a lively dialogue between Lady Soul, Lady Love, and Lady Reason, with a number of other abstract entities (such as Truth, Holy Church, and the Courtesy of the Goodness of Love) making cameos. The worthiness of the soul is expressed in language used to describe high-born ladies, as when the soul who has reached the fourth stage of the journey toward God is described as "so impenetrable, noble, and delicate that she cannot suffer any kind of touch except the touch of the pure delight of love, by which she is singularly joyful and charmed."[39]

Although her works are not permeated with the tropes of *fin'amor* in the same way as those by Hadewijch, Mechthild of Magdeburg, or Marguerite Porete (as we see in the next section), Catherine of Siena describes Christ as held on the cross "by nails of love", and urges "those who would be true knights" to fight against temptations, armed in their love for virtue, which "is a suit of armor that keeps blows from piercing them through."[40] She is also associated with the tradition via an episode described by Raymond of Capua in his *Legenda major*, in which Catherine is reported as first giving Christ her heart and then receiving his heart in exchange.[41] A popular theme in *fin'amor*, the exchange of hearts symbolizes undying devotion (see Figure 5.7, where Minne shoots arrows of love into a suitor, who then gives her his heart with the arrows still protruding); images of Catherine offering her

---

38 "Mirror of Simple Souls," in *English Mystics of the Middle Ages*, 80.
39 "Mirror of Simple Souls," in *English Mystics of the Middle Ages*, 190. For more on Porete's use of this tradition, see Joanne Robinson, *Nobility and Annihilation in Marguerite Porete's Mirror of Simple Souls* (Albany: State University of New York Press, 2001).
40 *Catherine of Siena: The Dialogue*, ch. 77, p. 143.
41 I use the passive voice here to signal the sometimes conflicting aims of Catherine herself and Raymond, her confessor. For more on this with respect specifically to this episode, see Heather Webb, "Catherine of Siena's Heart," *Speculum* 80 (2005): 802–817.

FIGURE 5.7 Coffret (Minnekästchen), German, Upper Rhineland, c. 1325–50, Met Cloisters Museum.

heart to Christ (see Figure 5.8) and receiving his in turn symbolize her mystic experiences and her spiritual espousal to Christ.[42]

### First-Person Experience(s) of Transcendent Love

It might perhaps seem surprising that religious figures dedicated to a life of chastity would feel free to use such erotic metaphors and to write so passionately about God. Yet the way in which medieval Christian mystics and contemplatives use metaphors of sexual intercourse (a physical experience they have chosen to forswear for God's sake) to express how love for and experience of God overwhelms them bears strong parallels to the way in which medieval Islamic mystics and contemplatives use metaphors of drunkenness (a physical experience they have chosen to forswear for Allah's sake) to express how

---

42 It's important not to associate the romantic image of the contemplative as "the bride of Christ" just with religious women. Any number of male mystics and contemplatives employ and develop this trope as well, including John van Ruysbroeck, who writes *The Spiritual Espousals* as instructions and encouragement for all, and Henry Suso, who relates his own mystical marriage to Christ in the extremely popular devotional *Horologium Sapientiae*.

FIGURE 5.8 St. Catherine of Siena exchanging her heart for that of Jesus, Guidoccio Cozzarelli, c. 1475–1517, Siena Pinacoteca.

love for and experience of Allah overwhelms them.[43] In both cases, the choice of language acknowledges the transcendent nature of the experience: mystical experience of union with the Divine goes beyond human capacity to understand or express, and these metaphors capture a sense of the blurring of personal boundaries and altered states of being. In general, medieval Christian contemplatives purposefully juxtapose various tropes associated with love to give voice to the unspeakable experience of union with God, providing complicated and contradictory expressions of their own experiences in ways meant to instruct others aimed at the same goal.

Hadewijch, for instance, uses the tropes popularized by French troubadours and *trouvère* and exemplified in the *minnesang* (love song) of her own region to create a new genre: *minnemystik*.[44] In this genre, the questing knight becomes the soul, and the Beloved for whom the knight pines becomes God, who is also at times identified with Love itself. Importantly, the true nature of love is mysterious, revealing itself at its own pace, much to the frustration of the searching soul. As Hadewijch writes in one poem,

> Love is so sweet in her nature
> That she conquers every other power.
> He who serves Love has a hard adventure
> Before he knows Love's mode of action,
> > Before he is fully loved by her.
> > He tastes her as bitter and sour;
> > He cannot rest for an instant,
> > So long as Love does not fetter him completely in love
> > And bring him into the union of fruition.[45]

---

43 See, for instance, *The Wine of Love and Life: Ibn al-Farid's al-Khamriyah and al-Qaysari's Quest for Meaning*, ed. and trans. Emil Homerin (Chicago: Middle East Documentation Center on Behalf of the Center for Middle Eastern Studies, University of Chicago, 2005).

44 See Barbara Newman, "*La mystique coutoise*: Thirteenth-Century Beguines and the Art of Love," in *From Virile Woman to WomanChrist: Studies in Medieval Religion and Literature* (Philadelphia: University of Pennsylvania Press, 1995), 137–167.

45 *Hadewijch*, poem 2: "Triumph Hard-Won," stanza 4, 131.

The pain and frustration of the loving soul is a theme that runs throughout Hadewijch's writings, which also include letters and visionary literature, but the subject is most clearly expressed in her poetry. The "union of fruition" that the soul searches for is often elusive; at the same time, it is the only truly worthwhile goal, and anyone who has loved at all is familiar with the restlessness of love unsatisfied. (Hadewijch is thoroughly Augustinian in her theology here as elsewhere.)

In the chapter's first section, we saw Marguerite d'Oingt describe love as a force that drove God to become human; in another of her poems, Hadewijch stresses love's power by noting that even God sacrificed all for Love's sake—and that this is the way to experience Love's goodness fully:

> Now pay heed, all you wise ones,
> And learn how great is Love's power:
>    She wields the almighty scepter
>    Over all that God created;
> She brought Him Himself to death!
>    Against Love, there is no defense.
> He who serves in the fidelity of Love becomes her partner,
>    And tastes to the full her noble goodness.[46]

The paradox of God being subject to Love while simultaneously being Love itself also underscores the unity of love discussed in the second section. Any experience of love gives us a taste of Love, so that no matter where we start, the possibility of transcendent love is open to us.

Perhaps the most comprehensive and concise description in Hadewijch of the tension between the promise of fulfilled union with Love and the tension of our current searching state is contained in the following stanzas:

---

46 *Hadewijch*, poem 13: "Seeming and Truth" stanza 8, 161–162.

For Holy Church proclaims to us—
Her lofty, her lowly, her priests, her scholars—
That Love is of the highest works
> And the noblest by nature:
Even though she conquers us, she conquers all strength,
> And her power shall last.

When all things have passed away,
Noble Love shall remain
And reveal her whole clarity,
> When you, in a new beginning,
Shall contemplate Love with love:
> "Behold, this is what I am!"

When Love thus draws the soul in resemblance to her,
And the loving soul shows love to Love,
I know not how, for it remains unspoken
> And also past understanding;
For no comparison is adequate for this—
> How Love can embrace the loving soul.

All who love must be moved to pity
That Love lets me moan thus
And cry so often: "Woe is me!"
> In what season and when
Will Love reach out to me
> And say: "Let your grief cease"?
I will cherish you;
I am what I was in times past,
Now fall into my arms,
And taste my rich teaching![47]

---

47 *Hadewijch*, poem 20: "Love's Sublimity," stanzas 9–12, 182–183.

The idea that the fruition of love cannot be expressed in words even by people who have experienced it is a constant in this tradition. In book 1 of Mechthild of Magdeburg's *Flowing Light of the Godhead*, for instance, Lady Soul goes to meet her "Fairest of lovers" in a secret room and finds a bed prepared. "Take off your clothes," the Lord tells her. "What will happen to me then?" asks Lady Soul. The following exchange is heated, but at the crucial moment, a veil is drawn across the scene:

> "Lady Soul, you are so utterly formed to my nature
> That not the slightest thing can be between you and me.
>
> And so you must cast off from you
> Both fear and shame and all external virtues.
> Rather, those alone that you carry within yourself
> Shall you foster forever.
> These are your noble longing
> And your boundless desire.
> These I shall fulfill forever
> With my limitless lavishness."
>
> "Lord, now I am a naked soul
> And you in yourself are a well-adorned God.
> Our shared lot is eternal life without death."
> "Then a blessed stillness
> That both desire comes over them.
> He surrenders himself to her,
> And she surrenders herself to him.
> What happens to her then—she knows.
> And that is fine with me."[48]

---

[48] Mechthild of Magdeburg, *The Flowing Light of the Godhead*, trans. Frank Tobin (Mahwah, NJ: Paulist Press, 1998), book 1, p. 62.

Here the experience of Love is one in which the soul is stripped of everything but the "noble longing" and "boundless desire" familiar from the *fin'amor* tradition, and in which the culmination of Love involves the "blessed stillness" that characterizes *caritas*. Our ultimate end is a transcendent union in which like recognizes like—what Hadewijch calls the "fruition of love," in which we can "be God with God."[49]

## Conclusion

The supremacy of love in the contemplative Christian tradition of the later Middle Ages is uncontestable: it is identified as the primary activity of our final end, its culmination our ultimate goal. This gives immense significance to practices that develop and increase the right sort of love. As we saw in the first section, the discipline of meditation—imaginatively engaging with key moments in the life of Christ—becomes the most popular devotional practice of the fourteenth through sixteenth centuries because it harnesses the power of the senses and imagination and turns them toward kindling and stoking love for God. The love that meditation encourages, however, is no simple thing. Medieval contemplatives layer contradictory descriptions on top of each other (love as peace, love as a burning fire; the lover as noble, the lover as fool, etc.), combining tropes associated with *caritas*, *amor*, and *fin'amor*. Descriptions of transcendent love from the first-person perspective display the same sort of fluidity, often employing language used for erotic encounters to signify the ineffable experience of becoming one with God.

Not surprisingly, given the variety of philosophical and theological conceptions of human nature developed in the thirteenth century and beyond, the general agreement over love being the supreme activity by which we are joined to God does not equate to general agreement over

---

[49] *Hadewijch*, 280.

the exact nature of the ultimate culmination of this love. In particular, there is a question as to how distinct the human participant in this union remains. Do we dissolve into God like a drop of wine into water, or do we retain a sense of individuality? I have addressed this question elsewhere, so I have not hashed it out here.[50] Suffice it to say that what I have discussed in this chapter is only the tip of the glorious iceberg that is medieval contemplative views of love, and that my hope is that I have said enough to motivate readers to explore further.

---

50 See, in particular, the chapters "Love" and "Immortality" in Christina Van Dyke, *A Hidden Wisdom: Medieval Contemplatives on Self-Knowledge, Reason, Love, Persons, and Immortality* (Oxford: Oxford University Press, 2022).

# Reflection

LOVE THAT MOVES: DANTE, PETRARCH, AND BOCCACCIO

*Akash Kumar*

The deployment of love as a philosophical concept pervades the literary culture of fourteenth-century Italy, as seen in its most prominent exponents, the authors who became known as the three crowns (*tre corone*) of Italian literature: Dante Alighieri, Francesco Petrarca, and Giovanni Boccaccio. From the early moments of vernacular love poetry that emerged in the thirteenth-century court of Frederick II, high philosophy in the form of Aristotelian concepts and Scholastic argumentation was infused with a newly forming literary language to speak of the thing called love. In the period of transition between the medieval era and the Renaissance, this trend manifests itself in remarkable ways in the poetry and prose of the canonical founding fathers of Italian letters. This brief reflection on love as a philosophical concept in their work is by no means all-encompassing; many books have been written on the subject, and many more will be written still.[1] Rather, this is a

---

[1] The bibliography is indeed immense, but I signal some recent and select work: Christopher Celenza, *The Intellectual World of the Italian Renaissance: Language, Philosophy, and the Search for Meaning* (New York: Cambridge University Press, 2018); Filippo Andrei, *Boccaccio the Philosopher: An Epistemology of the Decameron* (Cham: Palgrave Macmillan, 2017); and the section "A Philosophy of Desire" in Teodolinda Barolini, *Dante and the Origins of Italian Literary Culture* (New York: Fordham University Press, 2006), 23–102.

snapshot of these writers and some of the philosophical inflections of their works, as they look to forge a new path for Italian literature.

The first instance of the word "love" in Dante's *Divine Comedy* makes it out to be a force of creation. As Dante describes the dawn hour in which he finds himself beset by beasts in *Inferno* 1, he writes, "The time was the beginning of morning; / the sun was now rising in fellowship / with the same stars that had escorted it, / when Divine Love first moved those things of beauty" (*Inferno* 1.37–40). This understanding of love as a motive, creative force informs the poem from first to last, as the *Comedy* ends with the magnificent verse "the Love that moves the sun and the other stars" (*Paradiso* 33.145).[2]

But the celestial hits far closer to home in the intense personal drama that we are introduced to in *Inferno* 2, when Beatrice makes her first appearance in Virgil's recounting of their meeting and his mission to save Dante for her sake. Beatrice's charge to Virgil picks up on the same language of love as motive force and introduces the vital element of speech and language creation to the dynamic as well: "For I am Beatrice who send you on; / I come from where I most long to return; / Love prompted me, that Love which makes me speak" (*Inferno* 2.70–72). In crafting the engine of the *Comedy*'s motion, from the journey to be reunited with Beatrice atop the mountain of Purgatory to the ascent through Paradise by way of Beatrice's guidance, Dante departs from the paradigm of lyric poetry before him. No longer are the secular and sacred opposed, since love for Beatrice, a human woman existing in time, becomes a way to reach the Divine. And she is not the silent object of desire as seen in the tradition of courtly love poetry, but a speaking subject who is moved to act and moves others with her words.

---

[2] I cite from the Mandelbaum translation of the *Commedia*, retrieved from Digital Dante, Columbia University Libraries, New York, 2018, https://digitaldante.columbia.edu/dante/divine-comedy/inferno/inferno-2/.

Petrarch's collection of lyric poetry, the *Rerum vulgarium fragmenta* (*Fragments of vernacular things*; Rvf), revives anew the tension between the erotic and the spiritual that was harmonized in Dante's Beatrice. In addition to mixing the register of love poetry with the political and the spiritual, Petrarch's desire for Laura in life and death is animated by a metaphysical approach to time and language. From the very first sonnet of the 366-poem collection (most of which are sonnets, though Petrarch's use of the sestina form also plays into his metaphysical concerns with time, motion, and fixity), we see the essence of Petrarch's torment and tension in the characterizing of his love as a "youthful error" (*giovenile errore* [Rvf 1.3]) that has him asking for pity and forgiveness. It also provokes intense personal reflection that takes the form of highly reflexive language, as in the verse "I am often ashamed of myself within" (*di me medesmo meco mi vergogno* [Rvf 1.11]). Even at the level of sound, we can hear the repeated m's of self-reproach that feed into the bleak yet strangely hopeful understanding of the world as "but a brief dream" (Rvf 1.14).[3]

Perhaps the most synthetic way to capture how Petrarch modifies Dante is his redeployment of Beatrice's words of *Inferno* 2 in the final poem of his collection, a hymn to the Virgin Mary in which he writes, "love drives me to speak words of you" (Rvf 366.4). Petrarch vacillates between desire for Laura and the Augustinian realization that this love of his is a "beautiful mortal thing [that] passes and does not endure" (Rvf 248.8). This tension persists, even the wake of Laura's early death, as we can see in the end of sonnet 280: "The waters speak of love and the breeze and the branches and the little birds and the fish and the flowers and the grass, all together begging me always to love. But you, born in a happy hour, who call me from Heaven: by the memory of your untimely death you beg me

---

[3] Citations of Petrarch are from *Petrarch's Lyric Poems: The* Rime Sparse *and Other Lyrics*, ed. and trans. Robert M. Durling (Cambridge, MA: Harvard University Press, 1999).

to scorn the world and its sweet hooks" (Rvf 280.9–14). Petrarch may view love as a force of nature, as Dante did, but he frames it in opposition to the celestial perspective.

Boccaccio's *Decameron* is replete with tales of desire and despair that ground the amorous idealism and philosophical abstraction of Dante and Petrarch in a lived social reality. Where Petrarch anguishes over unrequited desire, spiritual conflict, and the mortal condition, Boccaccio will have an old lady advise an unsatisfied wife in *Decameron* 5.10 not to waste her youth and say in unrepentantly sexualized terms, "You must help yourself to whatever you can in this world, especially if you're a woman" (*Decameron* 5.10, 435).[4] Perhaps the clearest articulation of this socially inflected philosophy of love is in *Decameron* 4.1, a story of a widow who returns to her father's home, takes a lover, and is found out to tragic results. When confronted by her father, Tancredi, the heroine Ghismonda reasons philosophically and takes up the Dantean mantle of social revolution through love by arguing that nobility is not related to birth but to inborn worth: "hence any man whose conduct is virtuous proclaims himself a noble, and those who call him by any other name are in error" (*Decameron* 4.1, 297). She thus justifies to her overly possessive father her choice of a lover of low class. But she also follows through to the extreme ends of courtly love, making literal the figurative language of consuming the beloved's heart that we can find throughout the tradition of courtly love poetry as well as in the first visionary sonnet of Dante's *Vita Nuova*. Ghismonda ends her life by consuming a poison-filled chalice with the preserved heart of her beloved and so provides a startling way for Boccaccio to represent the clash of abstract ideals about love and their real-world implications.

---

4 Citations of Boccaccio are from Giovanni Boccaccio, *The Decameron*, trans. G. H. McWilliam (New York: Penguin, 2003).

CHAPTER 6

# Turning toward the One / Good

MARSILIO FICINO'S PHILOSOPHY OF LOVE

*Denis J.-J. Robichaud*

Marsilio Ficino's (1433–1499) dialogic commentary on Plato's *Symposium*—the *De amore*, completed by 1469—was a Renaissance best-seller in both its original Latin text and in Ficino's own self-translated Tuscan version.[1] Ficino, however, is neither the first nor certainly the last Renaissance thinker to theorize about love's power to unite lover and beloved. But what is strikingly new for the fifteenth century about Ficino's *De amore* (and a source of inspiration for later

---

[1] I cite from Ficino's *Commentarium in Convivium platonis* as the *De amore*, which is Ficino's title. There are two principal editions of Ficino's *De amore*, an earlier one by Marcel and an updated and revised edition by Laurens: Marsile Ficin, *Commentaire sur le Banquet de Platon*, ed. Raymond Marcel (Paris: Les Belles Lettres, 1956); Marsile Ficin, *Commentaire sur le Banquet de Platon, De l'Amour. Commentarium in convivium platonic, De amore*, ed. Pierre Laurens (Paris: Les Belles Lettres, 2002). Ficino's Tuscan translation has been edited by Sandra Niccoli: *Marsilio Ficino, El Libro dell'Amore* (Florence: Olschki, 1987). All translations are my own unless otherwise indicated. I also only provide the original language of translated texts in footnotes when I provide my own translation. I would like to dedicate this chapter to the memory of Michael J. B. Allen.

Denis J.-J. Robichaud, *Turning toward the One / Good* In: *Love*. Edited by: Ryan Patrick Hanley, Oxford University Press. © Oxford University Press 2024. DOI: 10.1093/oso/9780197536476.003.0009

Renaissance philosophers of love) is that it provides a philosophical system that is both henological (i.e., a philosophical system derived from the One qua first principle) and agathological (i.e., a philosophical system derived from the Good qua first principle).[2] Ficino's metaphysics of love provides a causal framework to underpin all facets of his thinking on love, whether ethical, epistemological, aesthetic, cosmological, or medicinal. The whole is governed by the principle that all beings proceed from the Good, which is itself beyond being, in an act of providential love, and all beings desire to return to the Good in an act of conversive love. In the first oration of the *De amore*, which is Ficino's interpretation of Phaedrus's speech from Plato's *Symposium*, Ficino's interlocutor Giovanni Cavalcanti puts forward the governing metaphysical understanding of love as conversion or reversion to God, which Ficino, in Platonic fashion, also designates as the One/Good. The birth of love, Ficino explicates, occurs when Intellect is formed below the One:

> In the beginning God created the substance of this Intellect, which we also call its essence. In that first moment of its creation, it is formless and obscure. But since it is born from God, it is converted to God by a certain inborn desire. Having converted to God, it is illuminated by his ray. Through the radiance of that ray its desire is inflamed. Inflamed, its desire completely adheres to God. And in its adhering, it is formed. For God, who has power over all, fashions in the Intellect that adheres to him the natures for the creation of things. In it, therefore, are painted, so to speak, in a certain spiritual manner, everything that we perceive in these bodies. It is there that are born the spheres of the heavens and elements, the stars, the

---

2  The term "agathological" is suggested to me by Stephen Gersh. I have not read the manuscript of his forthcoming book, but Stephen Gersh informs me that it too discusses the question of agathology in Ficino's philosophy: Stephen Gersh, *Marsilio Ficino as Reader of Plotinus: The "Enneads" Commentary* (Leiden: Brill, forthcoming). I am very confident that Gersh's book will be an important contribution to the discussion.

nature of vapors, as well as the forms of stones, metals, plants, and animals.[3]

Love and desire unfold in this passage into the Platonic triad of remaining (*monē*, sometimes rendered as "rest"), proceeding (*proodos*, sometimes interpreted as "emanating" or "producing"), and reverting (*epistrophē*, sometimes translated as "conversion"). Ficino explains that love is born when Intellect, the first radiance proceeding from God, reverts or converts, as Ficino's Latin suggests, to its original source. This self-reversion forms the Intellect into its own substance, the site of intelligible beauty itself. This metaphysical function of proceeding from and returning toward a higher principle beyond being establishes itself as the pattern forming all subsequent substances, painted, as Ficino phrases it, spiritually within the Intellect as paradigms for all things, including souls and beings in the material cosmos. Ficino describes this order as both hypercosmic and cosmic births resulting from an effect's desired union with its cause. Underpinning this causal order is the birth of love itself at the 'moment' when Intellect first turns to God qua One/Good.

Ficino's comments outline a henological order. The One is posited as beyond being, and in turn each being is made one by turning itself toward the One. Ficino interprets Phaedrus's claim in the *Symposium* that love is the oldest god to mean that love is the first being (i.e., the formation of Intellect when the One's reflected splendor turns back to its origins), but that the One is even prior to this oldest god.[4]

---

[3] "Principio deus mentis illius creat substantiam, quam etiam essentiam nominamus. Hec in primo illo creationis sue momento informis est et obscura. Quoniam uero a deo nata est, ad deum sui principium ingenito quodam appetitu conuertitur. Conuersa in deum, ipsius radio illustratur. Radii illius fulgore ille suus appetitus accenditur. Accensus appetitus deo totus inheret. Inherendo formatur. Nam deus, qui potest omnia, in mente sibi inherente creandarum rerum naturas effingit. In ea igitur spiritali quodam modo pinguntur, ut ita loquar, omnia que in corporibus istis sentimus. Illic celorum elementorumque globi, sidera, uaporum nature, lapidum metallorum, plantarum, animalium forme gignuntur." Ficino, *De amore* 1.3 (Laurens, 11; Marcel, 139).

[4] Plotinus's philosophy of love, especially *Enneads* 3.5, *On Love*, is a source of inspiration for Ficino. For a discussion of Ficino's Platonic sources for his philosophy of love in the *De amore*,

In other words, Ficino understands the chronological priority of gods in Phaedrus's appeal to Hesiod's theogony as metaphysical priority. Moreover, insofar as the first principle is also identified as the Good, it also expresses an agathology wherein love and desire are akin to the movements from a first and toward final cause. Procession is thus explicated as the Good's overflowing goodness by which all things proceed providentially from the first principle, and in turn, reversion is understood as the principle that all things possess a natural desire to return to their source in the Good, which always remains transcendent. Cause and effect are therefore intimately and dynamically connected in a hierarchy. Beauty, for Ficino, is thus the splendor of the Good and the first instantiation of being that entices or rather calls lovers to turn toward their beloved—as Ficino says following Plato's etymological play in the *Cratylus* on the Greek words *kallos* and *kaleō*.[5] Love, as the third term between lover and beloved, is itself the link that holds together the whole edifice within both hypercosmic and encosmic levels, and in turn also binds both levels together.

Much has been made of Ficino's supposed Christianization of Plato in the *De amore*. This is often at the expense of recognizing either his Platonizing of Christianity or even his Platonism tout court

---

see Maria-Christine Leitgeb, *Liebe und Magie. Die Geburt des Eros und Ficinos De amore* (Maria Enzersdorf: Roesner, 2004), a new edition of which has been published in Italian as Maria-Christine Leitgeb, *Amore e Magia: La Nasciata di Eros e il De amore di Ficino*, trans. Nicola Gragnani and Sebastiano Panteghini, rev. Paola Megna and Stéphane Toussaint, in *Cahiers Accademia* 5 (2006); Plotinus, *Traité 50 (III, 5)*, ed. and trans. Pierre Hadot (Paris: Éditions du Cerf, 1990); Pierre Hadot, "'L'amour magicien,' Aux origines de la notion de *magia naturalis*: Platon, Plotin, Marsile Ficin," in Marsile Ficin, *Commentaires sur le Traité de l'amour ou le Festin de Platon*, ed. Sylvain Matton (Paris: SÉHA, 2001), 69–81; Stéphane Toussaint, "Les formes de l'invisible," in Giovanni Pico della Mirandola, *Commento*, trans. Stéphane Toussaint (Lausanne: Éditions l'Age d'Homme, 1989), 9–69; and my discussion of Plotinian and Proclean dimensions of Ficino's understanding of Socrates and *eros* in Denis J.-J. Robichaud, *Plato's Persona: Marsilio Ficino, Renaissance Humanism, and Platonic Traditions* (Philadelphia: University of Pennsylvania Press, 2018), 111–148. For the most recent overview of the long history of Platonic love, see *Platonic Love from Antiquity to the Renaissance*, ed. Carl Séan O'Brien and John Dillon (Cambridge: Cambridge University Press, 2022), including Paul Richard Blum's article in this collection: "Human and Divine Love in Marsilio Ficino," 201–210.

5 Plato, *Cra.* 416a–e.

(i.e., an interpretation of the Platonic corpus that does not clothe it in Christian vestments). Scholars have overlooked the fact that Ficino wrote his *De amore* in a thoroughly Platonic or even quasi-pagan authorial persona. This is not to say that Ficino is a pagan, anti-Christian, or anything of the sort, but rather that Ficino composes the *De amore* in a dialogic manner that permits him to express his theory of love in a certain un-Christian ironic voice and to examine and even perform Platonism on its own terms, at least as he conceives it and to the degree that he is able (which, of course, is still inevitably situated within the historical and Christian hermeneutical horizons of Ficino's times).[6] There are, of course, many *implicit* Christian allusions in the *De amore* but there are very few *explicit* references to Christian authors. To be precise, except for a couple of occasions when Ficino speaks generally of "nostri" or "nonnulli Christiani," Ficino only makes a single and rather trivial reference to Augustine in passing (to say that the bishop agrees with pagan theologians on the topic of veiled language) and only mentions the *Corpus Dionysiacum* in five chapters.[7] Ficino thus situates Augustine and Pseudo-Dionysius in Platonic traditions, and cites no other Christian authors explicitly in the *De amore*. Ficino's point is not to make Platonic love separate from or incommensurable to Christian love—as many have argued about the supposed incommensurability of Platonic *erōs* and Christian *agapē*. Rather, Ficino wishes to argue for a unity of love—including Christian love—from a Platonic perspective.[8]

---

[6] Ficino's philosophical innovations were not lost on his contemporaries, some of whom thought that Ficino was playing a dangerous game with pagan philosophers. See Robichaud, *Plato's Persona*, 111–148.

[7] Ficino's mention of Augustine: Ficino, *De amore* 4.2 (Laurens, 67; Marcel, 168–69). Ficino mentions the *Corpus Dionysiacum* in the following chapters of the *De amore*: 2.2 (Laurens, 25; Marcel, 146), 3.1 (Laurens, 53–55; Marcel, 161), 3.2 (Laurens, 55; Marcel, 161), 6.3 (Laurens, 133–135; Marcel, 203), 6.15 (Laurens, 189; Marcel, 232).

[8] The work of Anders Nygren has influenced many to adopt a version of this claim: Anders Nygren, *Agape and Eros*, trans. Philip S. Watson (Chicago: University of Chicago Press, 1982).

Much has also been made of Ficino's so-called theory of 'two loves', so much so that scholars have missed how Ficino's interpretations of Plato's 'two loves' seeks to unite them into one. The most glaring section of Plato's *Symposium* that could lead to a radical doctrine of two incommensurable loves is of course when Pausanias distinguishes between the celestial Aphrodite (*Ourania*) and the popular Aphrodite (*Pandēmos*), which correspond to Aphrodite's two genealogies: Hesiod reports that she is born without a mother from Ouranos following his castration by Kronos, and Homer recounts that she is the daughter of Zeus and Dione. Each Aphrodite, Pausanias relates, is accompanied by a respective Eros (Cupid).[9] As Ficino stipulates, commenting on this passage, "It is deemed necessary that there are just as many desires [*cupidines*] as there are Aphrodites."[10] Ficino's interpretation of Pausanias's speech is indebted to Plotinus and Proclus insofar as he reconciles the two genealogies as something like a division of labor shared by twin Aphrodites (or Venuses) and twin Erotes (or loves), but he does not conceive of this differentiation as a radical dualism of two incommensurable loves:

> The Platonists therefore call the highest God Ouranos (*Celus*), because just as heaven (*celus*), that sublime body, contains and rules over all bodies, so too that highest God oversees all spirits. But the Platonists give Intellect many names, for they sometimes call it Kronos (*Saturnus*), sometimes Zeus (*Iovis*), and sometimes Aphrodite (*Venus*). For truly that Intellect exists, lives, and intelligizes. And the Platonists became accustomed to designating its essence as Kronos, its life as Zeus, and its intelligizing as Aphrodite. Moreover, we similarly call the world soul (*anima mundi*) Kronos, Zeus, and Aphrodite. Insofar as it intelligizes higher things it is

---

9 Plato, *Symp*, 180d–182a.
10 "Totidemque esse cupidines quot sint et ueneres necessarium arbitrator." Ficino, *De amore* 2.7 (Laurens, 39; Marcel, 153–154).

named Kronos, insofar as it moves the heavens, Zeus, and insofar as it generates inferiors, Aphrodite.[11]

Ficino is here identifying the divine names of the Hellenistic gods with the Platonic principles being, life, and intellect. What is more, Ficino correlates these three principles with the Platonic triad of remaining (being), proceeding (living), and reverting (intelligizing), all three of which first occur in the Intellect. He thus identifies the celestial Aphrodite as Intellect as it adheres in intellection, reverting (*epistrophē*) upward, and being fulfilled by the beauty of God. He further identifies popular Aphrodite with the power of procreation of the *anima mundi*, that is, nature processing and projecting (*proodos*) beauty downward to inferior beings as it generates living beings.[12] Ficino is careful, however, not to create an ontological dichotomy of opposing deities and opposing loves. Both Aphrodites share a common connective bond in that they participate and ensure the unbroken transmission of divine noetic beauty: "The first Aphrodite embraces the first radiance of divinity, and then projects it onto this second Aphrodite. She emanates the sparks of that radiance into the matter of the cosmos. And by

---

11 "Celum Platonici summum deum ideo uocant, quia sicut celum istud sublime corpus omnia corpora regit et continet, sic summus ille deus omnes spiritus supereminet. Mentem uero pluribus nominibus nuncupant. Saturnum enim modo, modo Iouem, modo Venerem uocant. Est namque mens illa, uiuit, intelligit. Essentiam suam Saturnum, uitam, Iouem, intlligentiam Venerem apellare consueuerunt. Animam preterea mundi Saturnum similiter et Iouem uocamus et Venerem. Prout superna intelligit, Saturnum; prout celestia mouet, Iouem; ut inferiora generat, Venerem." Ficino, *De amore* 2.7 (Laurens, 39; Marcel, 154).

12 Allen broke ground on the study of Ficino's multiplication of gods and principles in Michael J. B. Allen, *The Platonism of Marsilio Ficino: A Study of His Phaedrus Commentary, Its Sources and Genesis* (Berkeley: University of California Press, 1984), 113–143. Now see also Denis J.-J. Robichaud, "Ficino and the *Nodus Divinus*: Timaean and Iamblichean Mean Terms and the Soul in *Platonic Theology* 1–4," *Bruniana & Campanelliana* 26, no. 2 (2020): 379–401; Robichaud, "The Twelve Gods of Plato's *Phaedrus*: Mathematical Theology, Polytheistic Myths, and Divine Names in Marsilio Ficino," in *Plato's Phaedrus: Proceedings of the 5th Platonic Summer Seminar / Letnie Seminarium Platońskie, Instytut Filozofii i socjologii, Uniwersytet Pedagogiczny im. KEN w. Krakowie and KRONOS: metafizyka, kultura, religia, Lanckorona, Poland*, ed. Andrzej Serafin (Leiden: Brill, 2023) (forthcoming); and Maria Vittoria Comacchio, "Yehudah Abarbanel's Astromythology: In the Footsteps of Marsilio Ficino's Prisca theologia," *Bruniana & Campanelliana* 26, no. 2 (2021): 437–452.

means of the presence of these sparks every single body in the cosmos appears beautiful [*spetiosa*] to the degree that it is capable by nature."[13] Because this procession communicates divine beauty to each being in the world, Ficino understands that there cannot be only two manifestations of Aphrodite with Eros; they are manifest wherever there is beauty and desire in nature (qua lower activity of soul). In the words of Plotinus, the divine presence of Aphrodite and Eros multiplies itself into a plurality of Aphrodites and Erotes across the spectrum of being:

> But one must think that there are many Aphrodites in the All, which have come into being in it as spirits along with Love, flowing from an universal Aphrodite, many partial ones depending from that universal one, with their own particular loves—if one assumes, that is, that soul is the mother of love, and Aphrodite is soul, and love is the activity of soul reaching out after good. So this love here leads each individual soul to the Good, and the love which belongs to the higher soul is a good, who always keeps the soul joined to the Good, but the love of the mixed soul is a spirit.[14]

Even as it expresses a desire for a particular good, each particular love is a manifestation of the desire for the Good. As Ficino explains, the celestial Aphrodite does not simply revert upward to divine beauty: she also turns downward in what one could call an act of providential love toward the beings of the world. Similarly, the popular Aphrodite, that is, *anima mundi,* does not simply propagate herself downward in the natural procreation of beings in the cosmos. By communicating divine beauty and goodness to the furthest reaches of being, she also ensures

---

13 "Illa diuinitatis fulgorem in se primum complectitur; deinde hunc in Venerem secundam traducit. Hec fulgoris illius scintillas in materiam mundi transfundit. Scintillarum huiusmodi presentia singula mundi corpora, pro captu nature, spetiosa uidentur." Ficino, *De amore* 2.7 (Laurens, 41; Marcel, 154).

14 Plotinus, *Enneads*, 7 vols., trans. A. H. Armstrong (Cambridge, MA: Harvard University Press, 1969–1988), 3:5.4.

that every single being is accompanied by the presence of an Eros causing a desire to revert upwards to the Good. The far reach of popular Aphrodite guarantees that whatever nature touches, wherever existence extends itself, is boniform (*agathoeides*). Love is thus a unified and singular bond unfolding itself into a multiplicity and reverting back into simplicity. It is a metaphysical movement from the Good to the Good, as Ficino phrases it in a philosophical epigram that decorated the walls of his study.[15] We could describe Ficino's interpretation of the *Symposium* as charitable insofar as, like love itself, it unites both loves, and indeed all loves, as lovers of the Good.

Returning to the question of the explicit Christian references in the *De amore*, we should now also note that in each of the instances where Ficino refers to the *Corpus Dionysiacum* in the *De amore* he confirms the Platonic nature of Pseudo-Dionysius's theory of love, especially as it is expressed in the *De divinis nominibus*. To take one example, when Ficino discusses how Diotima in Plato's *Symposium* characterizes love as a great spirit or demon, Ficino compares Platonic demonology to Dionysian angelology and concludes, "For this reason, the difference between Plato and Dionysius is one of words rather than meaning."[16] For Ficino, there is no daylight between Plato's demonic *erōs* and Dionysius's angelic *agapē*. And indeed, Pseudo-Dionysius himself employs Plato's words from the *Phaedrus* to convey the same point,

---

15  Marsilio Ficino, *Lettere*, ed. Sebastiano Gentile, 2 vols. (Florence: Olschki, 1990–2010), 1:92–93 (*Epist.* 1.47). Gentile dates the letter after January 6, 1475, in Ficino, *Lettere* 1.261. I am preparing a detailed study of this epigram in another publication.

16  "Quare inter Platonem et Dionysium uerborum potius est quam sententie discrepatio." Ficino, *De amore* 6.3 (Laurens, 135; Marcel, 203). On Ficino and angelology, see Robichaud, "The Afterlife of Chaldean Angels in Iamblichus, Proclus, Psellos, Pletho, and Ficino," *Travaux et Mémoires* of the Centre d'études sur l'Histoire et la Civilisation de Byzance du Collège de France, Paris, special issue: *Inventer les anges de l'Antiquité à Byzance* 25, no. 2 (2022): 763–808, and literature cited therein. On the comparison of Dionysius with Plato in the Renaissance, see Robichaud, "Cardinal Bessarion and the *Corpus Dionysiacum*: Platonic Love between East and West," in *Byzantine Platonists (284–1453)*, ed. Frederick Lauritzen and Sarah Klitenic Wear (Steubenville, OH: Franciscan University Press, 2021), 231–253, and Stéphane Toussaint, "L'Influence de Ficin à Paris et le Pseudo-Denys des humanistes: Traversari, Cusain, Lefèvre d'Étaples. Suivi d'un passage inédit de Marsile Ficin." *Bruniana & Campanelliana* 5, no. 2 (1999): 381–414.

writing: "Let us not be afraid of this word '*erōs*,' nor should any discourse fearing it disturb us. For, it seems to me that theologians hold that the words '*agapē*' and '*erōs*' share a common meaning, and that they would rather attribute 'real *erōs*' (*ontōs erōta*) to things divine because of a strange prejudice that some men have about it."[17] To take another example, in his interpretation of Eryximachus's speech, Ficino analyzes the nature of final causality to argue that love is present in all things. He posits that there are three levels in causality—superiors, inferiors, and equals—and then explains the vertical hierarchy of causality. Superiors are the causes of inferiors, and inferiors are the effects of superiors. This vertical model of causality constructs a metaphysical theory of participation and a providential theory of love: "But causes love their effects as their own parts and images, and indeed effects also desire their conservators."[18] This system of causes also provides a framework for understanding how the providential order of God proceeds hierarchically through angels, souls, and bodies, and how in turn these manifestations of love also return back up the chain to the higher terms from which they proceeded: bodies do not wish to be separated from souls; souls desire the happiness of celestial spirits; and celestial spirits happily venerate the majesty of the supernal divinity.

---

17  "Ὥστε τοῦτο δὴ τὸ τοῦ ἔρωτος ὄνομα μὴ φοβηθῶμεν μηδέ τις ἡμᾶς θορυβείτω λόγος περὶ τούτου δεδιττόμενος. Ἐμοὶ γὰρ δοκοῦσιν οἱ θεολόγοι κοινὸν μὲν ἡγεῖσθαι τὸ τῆς ἀγάπης καὶ τοῦ ἔρωτος ὄνομα, διὰ τοῦτο δὲ τοῖς θεόις μᾶλλον ἀναθεῖναι τὸν ὄντως ἔρωτα διὰ τὴν ἄτοπον τῶν τοιούτων ἀνδρῶν πρόληψιν. Θεοπρεπῶς γὰρ τοῦ ὄντως ἔρωτος οὐχ ὑφ' ἡμῶν μόνον, ἀλλὰ καὶ πρὸς τῶν λογίων αὐτῶν ὑμνουμένου τὰ πλήθη μὴ χωρήσαντα τὸ ἑνοειδὲς τῆς ἐρωτικῆς θεωνυμίας οἰκείως ἑαυτοῖς ἐπὶ τὸν μεριστὸν καὶ σωματοπρεπῆ καὶ διῃρημένον ἐξωλίσθησαν, ὃς οὐκ ἔστιν ἀληθὴς ἔρως, ἀλλ' εἴδωλον ἢ μᾶλλον ἔκπτωσις τοῦ ὄντως ἔρωτος. Ἀχώρητον γάρ ἐστι τῷ πλήθει τὸ ἑνιαῖον τοῦ θείου καὶ ἑνὸς ἔρωτος. Διὸ καὶ ὡς δυσχερέστερον ὄνομα τοῖς πολλοῖς δοκοῦν ἐπὶ τῆς θείας σοφίας τάττεται πρὸς ἀναγωγὴν αὐτῶν καὶ ἀνάτασιν εἰς τὴν τοῦ ὄντως ἔρωτος γνῶσιν καὶ ὥστε ἀπολυθῆναι τῆς ἐπ' αὐτῷ δυσχερείας." *Corpus Dionysiacum*, vol. 1, *De divinis nominibus*, ed. Beate Regina Suchla (Berlin: Walter de Gruyter, 1990), 709b; cf. Plato, *Phaedrus*, ed. and trans., Harold North Fowler (Cambridge, MA: Harvard University Press, 2005), 245b–c: "Ὥστε τοῦτό γε αὐτὸ μὴ φοβώμεθα, μηδέ τις ἡμᾶς λόγος θορυβείτω δεδιττόμενος." Editors and translators of the the *Corpus Dionysiacum* often ignore that Pseudo-Dionysius is partially quoting from Plato's *Phaedrus* in this passage but Suchla's excellent edition responsibly flags this passage as a citation of Plato in her notes.

18  "Cause uero opera sua tamquam sui partes et imagines diligent. Opera quin etiam causas tamquam sui conseruatrices expetunt." Ficino, *De amore* 3.1 (Laurens, 53; Marcel, 160).

Love's hierarchical order, according to Ficino, also intersects with its power to form horizontal bonds: "But those who are located on the same order are affected in turn by a mutual love for one another as though they are members of one and the same body."[19] Ficino offers examples. Elements in nature—fire, earth, water, and air—bind themselves in mutual accord, and animals of the same species unite themselves mutually in intercourse. "It is here," Ficino adds, "that the love of equals and similars is observed." He concludes by drawing on the *Hymn to Love* (*Eros*) in the *De divinis nominibus*:

> Who, therefore, could doubt that love is inborn in all and for all? And it is this that Dionysius the Areopagite in his book *De divinis nominibus* meant when he quoted these words from the mind of Hierotheus: "Whether we speak of divine love, angelic love, spiritual love, animal love, or natural love, we understand a certain grafting and uniting power, which indeed moves superiors toward the providence of inferiors, and unites equals again in a social communion for one another, and finally admonishes the inferiors to convert to the more superior and more sublime."[20]

Ficino here cites the opening lines of Pseudo-Hierotheus's *Hymn to Love* (*Eros*) in *De divinis nominibus* (712a–b) in the Latin version of

---

19 "Que autem in eodem ordine locata sunt, ad se se inuicem quasi unius et eiusdem similia membra mutua caritate afficiuntur." Ficino, *De amore* 3.1 (Laurens, 53; Marcel, 160).

20 "Ubi amor ad equalia similiaque conspicitur. Cui nam igitur dubium erit, quin amor omnibus ad omnia sit ingenitus? Atque id est quod Dionysius Areopagita in libro *De divinis nominibus* ex Hierothei mente his uerbis significauit. Amorem siue diuinum siue Angelicum sive spiritalem siue animalem siue naturalem dixerimus, insitiuam quamdam intelligamus commiscentemque uirtutem, que superiora quidem ad inferiorum prouidentiam mouet, equalia rursus ad socialem sui inuicem communionem conciliat, ac postremo inferiora queque ammonet, ut ad potiora sublimioraque conuertantur." Ficino, *De amore* 3.1 (Laurens, 53–55; Marcel, 161). Ficino was already working with this Dionysian structure in one of his earliest writings, the vernacular tract titled *Epistola ad Fratres Vulgaris*, which is edited in Kristeller, *Supplementum ficinianum*, 2 vols. (Florence: Olschki, 1937–1945), 2:109–128.

Ambrosio Traversari.[21] Like Ficino, Pseudo-Dionysius posits a threefold order of causality:

1. When love causes a higher lover to turn toward a lower beloved, it is called providential love (*erōs pronoētikos*).
2. When love causes a lover to turn toward an equal beloved, it is called a common love (*erōs koinōnikos*).
3. When love causes a lower lover to turn toward a higher beloved, this love is called a conversive love (*erōs epistreptikos*).

Elsewhere Pseudo-Dionysius gives a fourth name to love, a binding love (*erōs synektikos*), to denote the binding power of love when it causes the lover to turn toward himself (qua beloved) in an act of self-preservation or self-knowledge. On occasion Pseudo-Dionysius also employs a binary schema of causes consisting only of providential love (*erōs pronoētikos*) and conversive love (*erōs epistreptikos*)—and as I mentioned at times he adds common love (*erōs koinōnikos*) to make it a triadic order.[22] The point of differentiating between twofold, threefold, and fourfold orders of love is not to divide love into separate kinds of love. On the contrary, Ficino and Pseudo-Dionysius both believe not only that love is a unifying power but also that it is itself a unified power because it is a unified form (*henoeidēs*). This single unified and unifying love moves, Pseudo-Dionysius writes, in a circle, in a straight

---

21 There are minor variants between the Latin cited by Ficino in the *De amore*, as reported in the editions of Marcel and Laurens, and the text of Traversari, as edited by Philippe Chevalier in *Dionysiaca. Recueil donnant l'ensemble des traductions latines des ouvrages attribués au Denys de L'Aréopage*, 2 vols. (Bruges: Desclée de Brouwer, 1937–1950), 1:225–226: "Amorem sive divinum sive Angelicum sive spiritualem sive animalem sive naturalem dixerimus, conjunctivam quadam intelligamus commiscentemque virtutem, superiora quidem moventem ad inferiorum providentiam, aequalia vero rursus ad socialem sui invicem communionem, ac postremo loco inferiora ut ad potiora et sublimiora convertantur adigentem."
22 For example, one finds the triadic order at *Corpus Dionysiacum*, vol. 1, *De divinis nominibus*, 713a–b.

line, and even in a spiral, the latter of which connects the two circular and linear movements of conversion and providence.[23]

Ficino completed his *De amore* around the same time that his older colleague Cardinal Bessarion published his *In Calumniatorem platonis* (which Bessarion seems to have completed by 1459). In this work, Bessarion too finds the sources of Pseudo-Dionysius's philosophy of love in Plato. But both Bessarion and Ficino also came to realize that in his commentary on Plato's *First Alcibiades*, Proclus puts forward a schematic order for love's different names, directional movements, and causal operations that closely resembles the outline in the *Corpus Dionysiacum*.[24] Ficino partially translated and paraphrased Proclus's *Commentary on the First Alcibiades*, which he only published in 1497. And at the outset of this fragmentary translation Ficino signals to his readers that what is most noteworthy in this work is that according to Proclus, *eros* is a threefold principle of conversion: "There are three forms of conversion, for whatever is converted either turns toward something that is inferior to it, during which it lapses from its perfection, or it rises to something superior on account of the natural vigor and activity of its life, or it is reflected onto itself, on account of the knowledge that is coordinated with it on its same order and the mediating form of motion."[25] Proclus's theory of love must have inspired Pseudo-Dionysius's because they share so many similarities. Proclus's three names for love also designate a threefold order of causes that ultimately accounts for three moments in a unified and unifying love that revolves from the Good to the Good. And although Ficino still holds

---

23 *Corpus Dionysiacum*, vol. 1, *De divinis nominibus*, 704d–705b.
24 Cf. Proclus, *Sur le premier Alcibiade de Platon*, ed. Alain-Philippe Segonds, 2 vols. (Paris: Les Belles Lettres, 2003), 20.1–21.9; 30.7–8; 31.9–14; 53.1–17; 55.13–56.5; 56.2; 63.12; 64.11; 140.19–141.11; 328.14; 336.5. See my examination of the question in Robichaud, "Cardinal Bessarion and the *Corpus Dionysiacum*."
25 "Tres sunt conversionis species quicquid enim conuertitur, uel ad aliquid uertitur se deterius, dum a perfectione propria labitur, uel consurgit ad melius propter cognitionem sibi consortem mediamque speciem motionis." *Excerpta Marsilii Ficini ex graecis procli commentariis in Alcibiadem Platonis primum* (Venice: Aldus Manutius, 1497), folio i$^v$. Cf. Proclus, *In Alc.* 21.

to the belief that the author of the *Corpus Dionysiacum* was Paul of Tarsus's convert on the Areopagus, Ficino argues in his later commentaries on Pseudo-Dionysius that the author of the *Corpus Dionysiacum* is at heart a Platonist.[26] To make his case, it is remarkable—but not altogether surprising given Ficino's close study not just of Plato and the *Corpus Dionysiacum* but also of later Platonists like Plotinus, Porphyry, Iamblichus, and Proclus—to see Ficino breaking new ground in Dionysian studies by deploying his unparalleled command over the Platonic tradition in his commentary.

Ficino is thus a major protagonist in the long story of Plato's philosophy of love. He argues clearly and strongly that love is constitutive in the most fundamental way of all levels of reality. Love is a process of actualization. As a point of comparison, Aristotle writes in the *De anima* about two grades of actuality (*entelecheia*) and compares these grades to the soul's states and activities.[27] That is, as everyone recalls, Aristotle advances that soul is the first grade of actualization of a body capable of life, but that a living soul (qua first grade of actualization) is different from the soul's activities, habits, and states (qua second grades of actualization). Aristotle further differentiates grades in these activities—for example, possessing knowledge from exercising knowledge.[28] A pianist, for example, is still a pianist while not playing the piano, and a geometer is still a geometer while ceasing to think about mathematics in his sleep. That is, one may actually possess knowledge without exercising it. But we are neither born pianists nor geometers. We need to learn these forms of knowledge, and it is in practicing these

---

26 Ficino's remarks about the *Corpus Dionysiacum*'s Platonism in his opening comments to the *De divinis nominibus* are especially noteworthy: Marsilio Ficino, *On Dionysius the Areopagite*, ed. and trans. Michael J. B. Allen, 2 vols. (Cambridge, MA: Harvard University Press, 2015), 1:90–92 (I). I quote from Allen's edition and translation of Ficino's *On Dionysius the Areopagite*, but I wish to signal to the reader the existence of Pietro Podolak's edition: *Dionysii Areopagitae. De mystica theologia, De divinis nominibus, interprete Marsilio Ficino*, ed. Pietro Podolak (Napoli: M. D'Auria Editore, 2011), 1.1.

27 Aristotle, *De an.* 2.1; cf. Aristotle, *Metaph.* 9.

28 Myles F. Burnyeat has characterized this as Aristotle's "triple scheme" in Burnyeat, "*De anima* II 5," *Phronesis* 47, no. 1 (2002): 28–90.

forms of knowledge that we actualize them in us, that is, that we come to acquire them. Love, for Ficino, is somewhat different. In his commentary on the *De divinis nominibus*, Ficino explains how we do not learn to love in the same way that we learn a discipline:

> We perceive matters divine in three ways; either actively, or in a passive way, or in a motion that is as it were mixed. We perceive actively mainly when we come to these discoveries ourselves, not when we have been informed by others, but by using the discursiveness proper to our reason and in the light of nature. We perceive in passivity when we perceive we are divinely inspired. Finally, we perceive with a mixed motion, that is, partly by being acted upon and partly by acting, when we are taught by a teacher or by words or by letters. For at that point, to the extent we are being moved from another direction, we are in a way being acted upon, but to the extent we bring our own judgment and scrutiny to bear, we seem to be acting too. Moreover, both external teaching and our own discovery of matters divine must be directed as to a sign only to this goal: namely that we should be utterly open to God who is continually inspiring us. But we perfect this in the love of him alone. For this only we direct all things to God, and we submit to God who is secretly inspiring us. With Him inspiring and moving us as it were and acting upon us, suddenly we are moved by, and submit to, and are filled with the Spirit. But such an affective state is called passion or passivity, (1) because it is an amatory feeling (but love, in transferring the lover into the beloved, compels the lover to become passive), and (2) because, now that our own proper actions are empty of reason and understanding, we are formed by the divine light, formed, that is passively. Let us prepare for this light only with the most fervent love. For just as a fierce heat often purges or attenuates opaque materials, those impervious to light, and makes them pervious to light, so our amatory fervor for God, in purging the rational soul as it were from the perturbations and storm clouds of the body, makes it, so to speak,

serene again and prepared for the divine light. With this light we finally attain both a union closer than understanding and a faith more certain than human knowledge. We arrive at this state, as Plato too says, neither by way of doctrine, nor by way of our own finding out, nor in turn can we express this state or teach [it] to others. But to love the Good itself we must be not so much persuaded as taught. For with nature constantly prompting us, in loving individual goods we must as a consequence love the Good itself. We must garner up this love that has been misdirected toward various goods and focus it only on the Good itself, whereby all things are good and worthy to be loved by us.[29]

One might thus begin to characterize Ficino's philosophy of love as an affective theory, as Ficino initially seems to suggest in the passage quoted before clarifying his position. But one should be careful in doing so insofar as love, according to Ficino, is not like other transient appetites and contingent bodily passions. Love is not, for example, like fear, anger, and other short-lived emotions. Love is always present, even if we are not consciously aware of its presence, because love constitutes our being. Reframed in Aristotelian terms, love is present at our first grade of actualization. As Ficino conceives it, love working through nature is responsible for the actualization of our substantial form. Unlike pianists and geometers, we are born lovers. Since, moreover, we are all born from love, we are loved from birth. But, according to Ficino, love is not just constitutive of *our* being (*our* first grade of actualization, as it were), it is constitutive of being as a whole (the first grade of actualization of being per se). Particular beings and being as a whole are thus all boniform (*agathoeides*) and unified (*henoeidēs*). This unity of being and love first occurs at the level of Intellect, and this unity proceeds in nature's generation of beings throughout the

---

[29] Ficino, *On Dionysius the Areopagite* 1:235–239 (LIX) (Podolak, 2.29).

cosmos. It seems that for this reason Ficino ultimately says that nature teaches us to love the Good (our second grade of actualization, to continue with Aristotelian terminology) by loving particular goods. Love is pre-intellectual for Ficino, but it is constitutive of Intellect per se, and therefore coincides with the first existential act of Intellect. Love and Intellect are thus in unity in the divine nature of the first being, but in desiring the Good, love ultimately carries the Intellect beyond itself and beyond being.

Ficino is being somewhat cryptic in these comments on the *De divinis nominibus*. He appeals to the *Seventh Epistle* of the *Corpus Platonicum* to propose that we neither arrive at this state by learning nor by self-discovery, nor again can we express or teach it. We are presumably left to conclude that one arrives at the love of the Good simply through an affective state (which seems to be the only remaining option out of the three that Ficino posits), but Ficino quickly seems to shelve that option too when he says that nature teaches us to love the Good. Two points should help us understand what Ficino is getting at. First, in stating that we purge ourselves in preparation for a higher unity with the Good, Ficino is deploying the triadic structure of purgation-illumination-perfection found in the *Corpus Dionysiacum* but also evident in the earlier writings of Iamblichus and Proclus. Second, in saying that we are taught to love the Good, Ficino suggests that it is nature that does the teaching by instigating us to love particular goods (our natural appetites), which in turn teaches us to love the Good itself.[30] This is a position not far removed from what Proclus articulates in proposition 31 of the *Elements of Theology*, for example. But in his formulation, Ficino emphasizes nature's role. I might attempt to fill in Ficino's silences in his commentary on the *De divinis nominibus* with what we already heard him say in the *De amore*, namely that nature herself is the loving activity of the propagation of the *anima*

---

30 On Ficino's theory of natural appetites, see Paul O. Kristeller, *Il Pensiero filosofico di Marsilio Ficino* (Firenze: Le Lettere, 2005), 180–212.

*mundi*—that is, of the popular Aphrodite and her Eros—or rather the many Aphrodites and Erotes that populate the cosmos. Moreover, just as Plotinus argues in *Enneads* 3.8, nature, for Ficino, communicates a noetic activity, spreading her forming principles (*logoi* or *rationes seminales*), which are themselves derived from the Intellect. The book of nature, according to Ficino, also turns out to be a book of love poetry. Ultimately then, in Ficino's statement on how we learn to love, we find something like a coincidence of opposites between intellectualist and affective approaches at three stages: at the highest level of Intellect, at the lowest level of nature, and in between in the rational soul.

That love is part of learning should come as no surprise to any philosopher, much less a Platonist. Take as an example what Plotinus says in *Ennead* 5.5.12:

> And we must consider that men have forgotten that which from the beginning until now they want and long for. For all things reach out to that and long for it by necessity of nature, as if divining by instinct that they cannot exist without it. The grasp of the beautiful and the wonder and the waking of love for it come to those who, in a way, already know it and are awake to it. But the Good, since it was there long before to arouse an innate desire, is present even to those asleep and does not astonish those who at any time see it, because it is always there and there is never recollection of it; but people do not see it, because it is present to them in their sleep. But the passionate love of beauty, when it comes, causes pain, because one must have seen it to desire it. Beauty is shown to be secondary because this passionate love for it is secondary and is felt by those who are already conscious. But the more ancient, unperceived desire of the Good proclaims that the Good itself is more ancient and prior to beauty.[31]

---

31 Plotinus, *Enneads* 5.5.12.

While a Dionysian strain of philosophy of love is certainly present in Ficino's *De amore*, so too is the Plotinian.[32] The same could be said about Ficino's commentaries on the *Corpus Dionysiacum*. In fact, in his commentary on the *De divinis nominibus*, Ficino demonstrates how Plotinus and Pseudo-Dionysius agree with each other and with Plato's philosophy of love:

> The light with which the sun lights itself within and shines without, and, in shining without, illuminates all, is seen to be the same light. Again, the light with which all these illuminated things shine in themselves—with the transverse striking of their rays reflecting light on others, and with a straight reflection shining back toward the sun—this light is seen to be the same light. Here Plotinus thinks that the sun's light itself perpetually depends on the sun, and everywhere accompanies the sun, and from all sides reflects itself back toward the sun. Similarly, because God is everywhere, the love whereby God loves himself and other things is also everywhere. But in loving Himself and other things, He ignites the love in all wherein they love themselves, love God, and love other things. And He ignites this love in all things even at the outermost levels of the universe, since He Himself is equally everywhere and loves all. But the love of each single thing, as by a necessary reason, depends on the first [love] inasmuch as it arises from it, preserves itself, and is moved, so that there seems to be one unique amatory force flourishing everywhere, a force dependent on the prime Good indeed and residing in itself, just as light exists everywhere in its unmingled purity. And like light this force is turned back finally to the first Good, inasmuch as all things, in loving a particular good, choose as a consequence the Good of all goods. But just as the sun's ray, with its power waxing everywhere, does not shine in order that all things

---

32 On the Plotinian (and Proclean) aspects of Ficino's philosophy of love in the *De amore*, see the works cited in n. 4 above.

may shine everywhere, but rather that all things may heat up so to speak, and that the many may live by being heated rather than by being lit, so it does not follow with regard to the good present everywhere that single things are capable of knowing, but rather that they are capable of loving. For all things always love the Good itself; yet they barely know in the end even the lowliest things. So loving to have the Good and to imbibe life from that Good is far more necessary than having knowledge of it. Hence that "chain" of rays introduced earlier, which, being once grasped, draws the supplicant toward the Good, and is the love rather than the investigation of matters divine.[33]

In this quotation—as well as in his *De amore*—Ficino is clear that loving the Good brings us in closer unity with it than knowing the Good, even though we need to learn from nature how to love the Good itself through our love of particular goods. In his many writings on the philosophy of love, Ficino seeks to help our nature rekindle and awaken a love that was always present in us but might sometimes be dormant. And if a sleeping geometer occasionally while dreaming uncovers a mathematical truth of which he was not aware while he was awake, this truth remains true even in a dream. So too, Ficino contends, even if we ignore our desire for the Good itself while desiring our particular goods, we remain lovers of the Good. For this reason, Ficino believes, even those of us who are snoozing on the love of the Good will on occasion inevitably feel the bittersweet pangs and pleasures of this truth in the experience of nature and beauty.

---

33 Ficino, *On Dionysius the Areopagite* 1:420–422 (CXXX) (Podolak, 4.52).

CHAPTER 7

# A Metaphysical Basis for Love?

DESCARTES AND SPINOZA ON THE METAPHYSICS

OF LOVE

*Patrick R. Frierson*

This chapter investigates how two prominent early modern philosophers seek to metaphysically ground the value of love for other beings, and especially for other human beings. Descartes—the first of these philosophers—famously compared all of philosophy to a "tree," where "the roots are metaphysics, the trunk is physics, and the branches emerging from the trunk are all the other sciences," including "morals" (P IXB:14–15).[1] While I argue here that Descartes is ultimately

---

[1] Throughout, references to Descartes's works are to the volume and page number in *Oeuvres de Descartes*, edited by Charles Adam and Paul Tannery (rev. ed.: Paris: Vrin/C.N.R.S., 1964–1976). Individual titles take the following abbreviations: C = Correspondence; D = Discourse on the Method; M = Meditations; P = Principles of Philosophy; PS = Passions of the Soul. References to Spinoza are to Part and Proposition in the *Ethics*, unless otherwise noted. While I have updated some secondary literature, other secondary literature that has appeared since this paper was originally commissioned is not discussed, and I particularly regret not being able to engage with Denis Kambouchner, "Spinoza and the Cartesian Definition of Love," in *Mind, Nature and Morality,*

unsuccessful in providing a metaphysical defense of interpersonal love, his account of love exemplifies a broader trend among some early modern philosophers of seeking to ground discussions of the emotions in general and love in particular in metaphysical realities. Descartes offers resources that seemingly provide a metaphysical basis for love as the passion by which one willingly joins oneself with another "in such a way that we imagine a whole of which we think ourselves to be only one part and the thing loved another" (XI:387). The second philosopher I discuss here—Baruch Spinoza—seems to provide a metaphysics in which each of us really is, in a metaphysical sense, a part of a greater whole that includes all others. In fact, however, once Spinoza develops his account of the individuation of particular ethical agents, he ends up with an even more deeply egoistic account of love than Descartes, albeit one that hints at a new way of thinking about how one might be united with others by virtue of shared humanity.

From the outset, I should note that this chapter will predominately *not* focus on the love of God, which was a particularly important sort of love for many early modern philosophers, including Descartes and Spinoza. Others have written about the love of God in Descartes[2] and Spinoza,[3] and even comparatively about the love of God in both Descartes and Spinoza.[4] For both thinkers, the love of God is an important feature of their overall ethical theories. Descartes describes the

---

*A Volume Honoring Lilli Alanen,* ed. F. Svensson and M. Reuter (Abingdon: Routledge, 2019), which I discovered only as I was doing the final edits on this chapter.

2 Alberto Frigo, "A Very Obscure Definition: Descartes's Account of Love in the *Passions of the Soul* and Its Scholastic Background," *British Journal for the History of Philosophy* 24 (2016): 1097–1116.

3 Clare Carlisle, "The Intellectual Love of God," in *A Companion to Spinoza,* ed. Yitzhak Melamed (Oxford: Blackwell, 2021); Yitzhak Melamed, "The Enigma of Spinoza's Amor Dei Intellectualis," in *Freedom, Action and Motivation in Spinoza's Ethics,* ed. N. Naaman-Zauderer and N. Naaman (London: Routledge, 2019); Steven Nadler, *Spinoza's Ethics: An Introduction* (Cambridge: Cambridge University Press, 2002); Amélie Rorty, "Spinoza on the Pathos of Idolatrous Love and the Hilarity of True Love," in *Feminist Interpretations of Baruch Spinoza,* ed. M. Gatens (University Park: Pennsylvania State University Press, 2009).

4 Lilli Alanen, "Descartes and Spinoza on the Love of God." In *DE NATURA RERUM: Scripta in honorem professoris Olli Koistinen sexagesimum annum complentis,* ed. Hemmo Laiho and Arto Repo (Turku: University of Turku, 2016).

"love [of] God" as "the most delightful and useful passion possible" (D VI:608). And Spinoza's whole *Ethics* culminates in the claim that "blessedness consists in love towards God" (V.P42), such that some have claimed that for Spinoza, "there does not seem to be any proper, reliable object of love other than God."[5] While early modern accounts of the love of God are interesting and important, however, this chapter discusses the love of God only insofar as it is relevant to better understanding the sorts of love that one might justifiably have toward other particular things (especially other human beings). Both Descartes and Spinoza seemingly offer metaphysical justifications for this interpersonal love, though—as we will see—neither offers an account free of problems.

## René Descartes: A Metaphysical Basis for Love?

For Descartes, love consists of an "assent by which we consider ourselves . . . as joined with what we love in such a manner that we imagine a whole of which we take ourselves to be only one part and the thing loved to be the other" (XI:387; see too C IV:601), to the extent that one who loves "often puts their [the beloved's] interests before his own and is not afraid of sacrificing himself in order to save them" (XI:389). Elsewhere, I've argued that the best way to integrate this seemingly altruist account of love with Descartes's egoist account of the passions—all of which serve "to move the soul to consent and contribute to actions which may serve to preserve the body or render it more perfect" (PS XI.429)—hinges on a "practical" rather than a metaphysical argument, according to which "it makes sense from the agent's own point of view . . . to progress . . . [from] an egoist love . . . into a morally rich, self-sacrificial love."[6] While I've argued that Descartes's

---

5 Alanen, "Descartes and Spinoza on the Love of God," 91.
6 Patrick Frierson, "Learning to Love: From Egoism to Generosity in Descartes," *Journal of the History of Philosophy* 40 (2002): 314. Recent work on Descartes's ethics includes Frigo, "A

metaphysical defense of love depends not on the *truth* of lovers' consideration of themselves as parts of wholes, but on the *practical value* of such considerations, in this chapter I reflect in more detail on what a fully metaphysical defense of the value of love would look like for Descartes, and what the limits of such an account would be. This sets the stage for thinking about Spinoza's quite different defense and articulation of love.[7]

Descartes articulates love's holist nature and ethical importance in correspondence and his *Passions of the Soul*. In a 1645 letter to Elizabeth, he insists that "one must . . . think that one . . . is, in effect, one part of the universe and, more particularly even, one part of this earth, one part of this state, and this society and this family" (C IV:291–293). His next letter to Elizabeth identifies this attitude with "the Christian virtue we call charity [*charité*]" (C IV:309). In a letter to Chanut, he slightly revises this into what becomes his standard definition of love:

---

Very Obscure Definition"; Donald Rutherford, "Descartes's Ethics," in *Stanford Encyclopedia of Philosophy*, ed. Edward N. Zalta, 2013 edition, http://plato.stanford.edu/archives/spr2013/entries/descartes-ethics/; Lisa Shapiro, "Descartes on Human Nature and the Human Good," in *The Rationalists*, ed. Justin Smith and Carlos Fraenkel (New York: Springer/Synthese, 2011); Shapiro, "Descartes's Ethics," in *Blackwell Companion to Descartes*, ed. Janet Broughton and John Carriero (Oxford: Blackwell, 2007); Shapiro, "Cartesian Generosity," in *Norms and Modes of Thinking in Descartes*, ed. Tuomo Aho and Mikko Yrjönsuuri, *Acta Philosophica Fennica* 64 (1999): 249–75; Frans Svensson, "The Role of Virtue in Descartes' Ethical Theory, Or, Was Descartes a Virtue Ethicist?," *History of Philosophy Quarterly* 27 (2010): 215–236; Svensson, "Non-Eudaimonism, the Sufficiency of Virtue for Happiness, and Two Senses of the Highest Good in Descartes's Ethics," *British Journal of the History of Philosophy* 23 (2015): 277–96; and Cecelia Wee (Lim), "Self, Other and Community in Cartesian Ethics," *History of Philosophy Quarterly* 19 (2002): 255–273. On the *Passions* more generally, see Amelie Rorty, "Descartes on Thinking with the Body," in *The Cambridge Companion to Descartes*, ed. John Cottingham (Cambridge: Cambridge University Press, 1992); and Rorty, "The Functional Logic of Cartesian Passions," in *Emotional Minds: The Passions and the Limits of Pure Inquiry in Early Modern Philosophy*, ed. S. Ebbersmeyer (Berlin: de Gruyter, 2012). However, Frigo rightly notes ("A Very Obscure Definition," 109919) that the only recent detailed discussions of love in Descartes are Frierson, "Learning to Love," and the editorial material in Kambouchner's edition of Descartes and Chanut's correspondence (*Lettres sur l'amour* [Paris: Mille et une nuits, 2013]), to which we can now add Alanen, "Descartes and Spinoza on the Love of God," and Kambouchner, "Spinoza and the Cartesian Definition of Love."

7 The initial impetus for this investigation was to set the stage for Anne Conway's more successful metaphysical approach, which is not included in the present contribution.

It is the nature of love [*l'amour*] to make one consider oneself and the object loved as a single whole of which one is but a part; and to transfer the care one previously took of oneself to the preservation of the whole. (C IV:611; cf. C IV:308; XI:387)

Descartes connects this love to ethics, introducing it to Elizabeth as a "truth" "most useful" "to discern the best course in all actions of life" (C IV:291).

Beyond holism and ethical relevance, the final component of Cartesian love is metaphysical grounding. Descartes's approach to love initially seems promising in this regard. He claims that both his moral theory in general (P IXB:14–15) and his theory of love in particular (C IV:612–613) are grounded in his metaphysics. He describes his explanations of love as "metaphysical thoughts" (C IV:613), and his description of "useful" truths starts with core claims of his metaphysics—God's existence and the soul's nature (C IV:490; cf. M VII:1–2)—before turning to his claim about love. *Passions*, in which he finally defines love, proceeds from a metaphysics of mind and body through a physiological treatment of passions to a description of their nature, and Descartes explicitly describes the work as that of "a natural philosopher" (XI:326). Cartesian love *seems* solidly grounded in Descartes's metaphysics.

Despite this appearance, however, the metaphysical basis of love in Descartes is elusive. For Descartes, each individual is a unity of mind and body. One's mind is an independent thinking substance that can persist without the body; "my essence consists solely in the fact that I am a thinking thing. . . . I am really distinct from my body and can exist without it" (M VII:78). The argument for the essential independence of mind from body is based on the broader premise that "everything I clearly and distinctly understand is capable of being created . . . so as to correspond with my understanding of it" (M VII:78). Given this premise, the second Meditation—in which one can think of one's own existence without the existence of any other thing—implies the metaphysical distinctness of one's thinking soul from every other thing.

Later in Meditation VI, however, Descartes argues for a metaphysical union of mind and body, such that an individual human's mind and body are "substantially united" and "form a unit" (M VII:228, 81). Without getting into the details of that argument—as they are unpacked over a series of letters with Elizabeth and ultimately in his *Passions*—the gist of Descartes's argument is that our "sensations of pain, hunger, thirst and so on" teach "that I am not merely present in my body as a sailor is present in a ship, but that I am . . . intermingled with it" to form a "union . . . . of the mind with the body" (XI:81). While the soul *could* exist without the body, it *does not* exist without the body, so "I" am a whole consisting of soul and body. And for that reason, my passions properly direct me toward what is good for my body, because what is good for my body is good for me. The metaphysical union of mind and body justifies an *embodied* self-love.

Interpersonal love is harder to ground than the love of myself for my body because I am not metaphysically united with other persons into a single whole, as I am with my body. That said, one might draw on several metaphysical resources in Descartes to try justifying Cartesian love for others. One approach would emphasize the metaphysical unity among material things. While each *soul* is a separate substance from every other soul, the *material* universe is a single interconnected whole. As a matter of basic (Cartesian) physics, my body is in fact a part of a greater whole, namely extended substance as such. Because my mind is substantially united to my body, there could be some sort of transitive metaphysical unity between myself and all other things. This approach, unfortunately, suffers from several problems. First, it fails to take seriously the ethical priority of soul over body. For Descartes, it is "useful . . . to know . . . the nature of our mind, insofar as it subsists without the body and is much more noble than it and capable of enjoying . . . contentments not found in this life," because this truth "detaches our affection from things of the world" (C IV:292).

Despite mind-body unity, Descartes emphasizes, even for discerning "the best course in all actions of life," the soul's priority over body. The metaphysical unity among bodies would connect the human person at most with the least important dimension of other persons. Second, even for bodily passions, Descartes identifies both the origin and purpose of the passions with the preservation of the specific body to which one's individual soul is united: "the function of the ... passions" is "to move the soul to consent and contribute to actions which may serve to preserve the body or render it more perfect" (PS XI.430). While the body might be metaphysically united with the rest of the physical world, passions (including love) aim to preserve the integrity of the particular part of the world to which one's soul is united. Metaphysical unity among physical bodies provides insufficient basis for a Cartesian passion of interpersonal love.

A second metaphysical approach to defending Cartesian love would be through the consideration that "whenever we are inquiring whether the works of God are perfect, we ought to look at the whole universe, not just at one created thing" (M VII:55–56).[8] Here the "universe" refers to all created things, not merely extended substance(s). In its context—the fourth Meditation—Descartes uses this claim to defend God's goodness in the light of the fact that human minds are susceptible to cognitive error. While God could have made us "more perfect" and even such that we never erred,

> There may in some way be more perfection in the universe as a whole because some of its parts are not immune from error.... And I have no right to complain that the role God wished me to undertake in the world is not the principal one. (M VII:61)

---

8 Frigo hints at this passage as an answer to Frierson, "Learning to Love" (see Frigo, "A Very Obscure Definition," 1109n29). Unfortunately, Frigo doesn't fully develop his provocative suggestion to "compare the letters of Elizabeth and some expressions of the *Fourth Meditation*" (ibid.).

Just as I can reconcile the goodness of God with my capacity for sin and error because my imperfections may contribute to perfection in the whole, so, too, one might hope to justify love on the grounds of promoting "perfection in the universe as a whole." That is, since I literally am just a part of the universe, to love another thing—that is, to see myself and that other thing as two parts of a whole—merely brings my affections in line with God's created reality. To care more about the whole than my own part is merely to bring my will in line with God's own.

However, Descartes's account of individual agents' motivational psychology distinguishes between the "goodness of each thing... in itself" and "goodness . . . in relation to ourselves," where Descartes argues, "We should not consider anything as good, in relation to ourselves, unless we either possess it or have the power to acquire it" (C V:82). Even if, in the abstract, one can recognize goodness in the universe as a whole (M VII:55–56, 61; C IV:291–292, 609), this recognition provides no metaphysical basis for considering such universal goodness to "relate to oneself." Despite his exhortation to *consider* oneself part of a whole, in fact "each of us is a person distinct from others" (C IV:293), and the goods relevant to *my* perfection do not as such include the good of the universe as a whole.

One might try to enhance the motivational force of considering the universe as a whole through love of God. As Descartes explains in a letter to Chanut, "We [can] love God and *through him* unite ourselves willingly to all the things he has created" (V.56, emphasis added). Carole Wee, drawing on the aforementioned passages from the fourth Meditation, argues,

> The Cartesian ethical agent sees the agent as embodying a God-enacted order. Far from being alienated from the universe, she recognizes herself to be a part of this wider order, fulfilling a specific function within the overall whole.[9]

---

9 Wee, "Self, Other and Community in Cartesian Ethics," 262–63.

For Wee, the Cartesian agent who understands the universe as God's creation "accepts that the good of the larger whole must take precedence over his own good."[10] Likewise, I've argued that once "Descartes...establish[es] that a rational individual will love God, he has an independent basis for loving others" because "abandoning himself altogether to God's will, [the rational individual] strips himself of his own interests and has no other passion than to do what he thinks pleasing to God."[11]

This otherwise promising metaphysical route to Cartesian love suffers from two weaknesses. First, it requires metaphysically justifying the love of God. In an early letter to Elizabeth, Descartes suggests that God's perfection justifies such love: "Since the true object of love is perfection, when we elevate our minds to considering God as He is, we will find ourselves naturally...inclined to love him" (C IV:291–292). However, God is not the only thing with some degree of perfection. Every finite thing has some perfection, so if the perfection of a thing were sufficient to justify love of it, then Descartes could directly argue for love of finite things based on the perfection of those finite things. However, Descartes's distinction between what is good in itself and what is good in relation to oneself undermines this quick argument from perfection to love-worthiness—not only for finite things, but also for God. God is perfect, to be sure, but God is also distinct from me, so treating myself and God as two parts of a whole cannot be justified by the mere fact of God's perfection. In fact, love of God actually seems *harder* to justify than love for other things, for a reason that Descartes himself highlights as a "strong reason for doubting that one can love God by the power of the natural light alone" —namely that God's attributes are "so high above us that we do not see at all how they can be fitting for us and so we do not join ourselves to them willingly" (C IV:607).[12] Whereas other creatures might legitimately be considered

---

10 Wee, "Self, Other and Community in Cartesian Ethics, 264.
11 Frierson, "Learning to Love," 336; C IV:294; cf. C V:56.
12 Descartes's other problem, that "nothing about God can be visualized by the imagination," problematizes only "sensuous love" (C IV:607), so I don't discuss it here.

part of a metaphysical whole that shares the status of having been created and governed by God, God is so metaphysically greater than us that we cannot coherently think of ourselves alongside God as parts of a single whole. Descartes does think there is a "way to reach the love of God," but his argument requires that we "consider... that our soul's nature resembles his sufficiently for us to believe that it is an emanation of his supreme intelligence, a 'breath of divine spirit'" (C IV:608); this metaphysical similarity makes it possible to consider ourselves parts of a whole with God. But Descartes's resort to poetic language is informative here, as is the language of "emanation," which he never uses in his metaphysics and even expressly rejects in an early letter to Mersenne (see C I:152). According to the metaphysics laid out in his *Discourse*, *Meditations*, and *Principles*, human beings are thinking substances, created by and dependent upon but essentially distinct from God. There is no metaphysical basis for a *Cartesian* love of God.

Finally, even if one could justify love of God, such love provides at best an *indirect* metaphysical basis for love of other people and things. I would treat myself and another thing as parts of a common whole, not from recognition that we *are* parts of a common whole, but from the desire to please God. Only "through him" would we "unite ourselves willingly to all the things he has created" (C V:56). The metaphysical unity we'd *posit* would be illusory, a voluntary adoption of a stance toward others justified not as metaphysically true but only indirectly, as a way of loving God.

Ultimately, the best defense of Cartesian love within Descartes's metaphysics is, like this unsuccessful theistic approach, indirect. While Wee, and at times Descartes himself, argue indirectly for a love of others via the necessity of loving God, Descartes also offers a defense of love in terms of the structure of human passions and the best hope for experiencing joy and happiness in life:

> If we think only of ourselves alone, we can enjoy only those goods that are particular to us. On the other hand, if we consider ourselves

as part of some other body, we participate as well in the goods held in common, without being deprived of those that are proper to ourselves. It is not the same with the evils. For according to philosophy, evil is nothing real but only a privation. (C IV:308)

This argument rests on one important metaphysical claim: evil is mere privation, a claim to which Descartes *is* committed in his broader metaphysics (especially M VII:54–55). The argument is also based, indirectly, on claims about the nature of human enjoyment defended in Descartes's *Passions*, where he argues that "joy" involves any "consideration of a present good ... when the good ... is one that we regard as belonging to us" (P IXB:376). If joy arises whenever we consider a good as belonging to oneself, one should want to consider oneself joined with more goods in order to experience more joy.[13] This does not, of course, show that one is *in fact* part of a greater whole, nor does it show how (psychologically) one could come to consider oneself part of such a whole. But it does provide motivation for wanting to love others. While grounded in Descartes's account of human passions and motivation, this justification is fundamentally a practical argument for love, one at best indirectly metaphysical.

The practical argument for Cartesian love gives agents reasons to consider themselves parts of a whole without providing any metaphysical justification for claiming they *are* parts of a whole. While not complete abdication of his metaphysical project, these arguments involve a sort of noble lie. Cartesian love adopts attitudes toward the world that are at odds with how that world really is; we treat ourselves as united with others, when in fact we are distinct substances. This prompts the question of whether a different metaphysical approach to love might

---

13 See too Frigo, "A Very Obscure Definition." Frigo's discussion of how Descartes reappropriates Scholastic notions of the "presence" of the thing loved helps support this overall account while situating it in a broader late medieval and early modern context.

not do better. Could metaphysics more *directly* support Cartesian love, not only justify *considering* ourselves united with others, but show this consideration to be *true*?

### Baruch Spinoza: Monism, Individuation, Love?

Early in his philosophical life, Spinoza was considered "someone who excelled in Cartesian philosophy,"[14] and in 1663, while "by no means an uncritical disciple of Descartes,"[15] he nonetheless published his own reconstruction of Descartes's philosophy, which he called the *Principia Philosophia*. With respect to love in particular, in his *Short Treatise on God, Man, and His Well-Being*, Spinoza adopts Descartes's description of love as "a union with the object . . . whereby both the lover and what is loved . . . together constitute one whole,"[16] but even in that work, Spinoza already departs substantially from Cartesian metaphysics, and the echoes of a Cartesian concept of love are used to argue for something more like the intellectual love of God that Spinoza emphasizes in his later *Ethics*. In his *Ethics* (started as early as 1661 but not finished until 1675), Spinoza largely leaves behind Descartes's conception of love. Spinoza explicitly criticizes as "very obscure" "the definition given by those writers"—including Descartes and also his own earlier *Short Treatise*—"who define love as the lover's wish to be united with the object of his love" (III, Def of Emotions 6, Explanation).[17] Moreover, to a much greater extent than Descartes, Spinoza focuses on the love of God, particularly within his *Ethics*. Nonetheless, as I show here, Spinoza recognizes the importance of an interpersonal and even seemingly altruistic love for other persons, particularly in his discussions of friendship, in both his *Ethics* and his *Political Treatise*.

---

14 Quoted in Nadler, *Spinoza's Ethics*, 198.
15 Nadler, *Spinoza's Ethics*, 244.
16 *Spinoza's Short Treatise on God, Man, and His Well-Being*, trans. A. Wolf (London: Adam and Charles Black, 1910), 79.
17 References to Spinoza's *Ethics* are to the Part number and the relevant section under that part.

Moreover, despite his eventual eschewal of Descartes on love, Spinoza's metaphysics actually seems particularly well-suited, at least prima facie, for defending a broadly Cartesian conception of love. Whereas, for Descartes, each of us is a distinct substance from every other, Spinoza affirms that there is only one single substance: "There can be, or be conceived, no other substance but God [or Nature]"[18] (I, P14). All "things that are finite and have a determinate existence" are merely *modes* or affections of the single substance of the universe (II, Def 7). Such modes are of some "attribute" of substance, where an attribute is "that which the intellect perceives of a substance as constituting its essence" (I, Def 4). In keeping with Cartesianism, the only attributes humans know are "thought" and "extension" (II, PP1, 2). Reality exists as a physical universe that takes up space (extension) and as a realm of thought, something like a space of reasons consisting solely of ideas. Individual things are not "substances," but rather each individual is a specific *way* that extension or thought is. The universal law of gravitation is an infinite mode of extension, an unchanging and general way the physical universe is. A specific rock is a determinate finite mode of extension, a way that extension is in a particular time and place. A human body, like a rock, is a determinate finite mode of extension. And the human mind, for Spinoza, "is basically nothing else but the idea of an individual actually existing thing" (II, P11); in particular, the human mind is the mode of thought that represents the specific mode of extension that is the human body. As a mind, I am just one idea in a network of ideas that constitutes the single substance of the universe. As a body, I am just one mode of spatial extension in a network of spatial extension that constitutes the single substance of the universe. Holist metaphysics is true. As Amelie Rorty has put it, "The world is composed wholly and entirely of particular individuals so interrelated that they form a complex individual, a unified system."[19]

---

18 For the phrase "God, or Nature," see I, 29 Scholium, p. 52.
19 Rorty, "Spinoza on the Pathos of Idolatrous Love and the Hilarity of True Love," 66.

To go back to our definition of Cartesian love, I literally *am* "only one part" of that complex individual, where "the thing loved [is] another" (XI:387).

This metaphysics seemingly provides a direct route to interpersonal love, where as I better understand the truth, I become more loving. If love consists in considering myself part of a greater whole, the fact that I *am* part of a greater whole suggests that metaphysical knowledge should increase love. Arne Naess's bold appropriation of Spinoza for his holist environmental ethics takes this route.[20] Spinoza partly endorses this short argument for love, pointing out that "love arises from the third kind of knowledge," where knowledge "of the third kind" is rationally intuited understanding of necessary features of the universe (V, 42 Proof; II, 40–44; V, 24). Strikingly, however, the "love" *Spinoza* emphasizes is love *of God*, not of other individuals—and this love turns out to be a form of self-love that does not extend to loving particular others as fellow parts of the divine whole.

To see why the direct Spinozist argument for a Cartesian notion of love fails, we must consider in more detail the nature of the individual loving agent. From the perspective of the universe, individual humans are merely finite modes of a single substance, but this isn't how each individual considers *herself*. While all individuals are merely modes of a single substance, they are individuated as distinct things with distinct essences, ends, and motivations. Human individuation is based on the individuation of physical human bodies: "In order to determine the difference between the human mind and others . . . , we have to know the nature of its object . . . , that is, the nature of the human body" (II, 13, Sch, p. 72). For Spinoza, "Bodies are individual things which are distinguished from one another in respect of motion and rest" (II, 13, Lemma 3 Proof, p. 73). The simplest bodies—"atoms" in the classical sense—are distinguished simply by persisting relative motion. An

---

20 Arne Naess, "Spinoza and Ecology," *Philosophia* 7 (1977): 45–54.

extended region within which no part moves relative to another is an individual atom. For more complex composite things, what matters is that the "bodies composing an individual thing... keep the same mutual relation" in a more general sense (II, 13 Lemma 6, p. 75). Spinoza's account is imprecise, but persistent "motion and rest" for complex things like human bodies means something like the enduring patterns or structures of a thing. Phenomena such as replacement of parts (II, 13, Lemma 4, p. 74), growth or diminution (Lemma 5, p. 75), and movement relative to other complex individuals (Lemmas 6–7, p. 75) are consistent with individuals remaining the same individuals: "a composite individual can be affected in many ways and yet preserve its nature" (II, 13, Lemma 7, Scholium).[21] For a human being, to be a distinct individual is to have a coherent complex structure of interacting parts that retains patterns of mutual interaction over time and through incidental changes of parts.[22] Because human bodies can remain selfsame individuals while undergoing various changes, "the human mind is capable of perceiving great many things" (II, 14). As the body changes while remaining the same body, the idea of that body changes, and these changes *of* the idea in God are represented *by* that idea itself—the individual mind—as perceptions of (other) things.

This account of the human individual is pivotal for Spinoza's epistemology and philosophy of mind, but what is central here is that while distinct people are not different substances, Spinoza ascribes to each person a distinct essence, which consists of the unique patterns of motion and rest that constitute what is unchanging about *that person's* bodily structure. When Spinoza turns to "the origin and nature of emotions" (III), he extends this concept of individual essences to

---

21 For Spinoza on finite modes, see Martin Lin, "Substance, Attribute, and Mode in Spinoza," *Philosophy Compass* 1 (2006): 144–153 (which includes an overview of other related secondary literature); Nadler, *Spinoza's Ethics*, 98–104; and Alexander Pitts, "Freedom in Spinoza's *Ethics*," honors' thesis, Whitman College, 2017.

22 Cf. Nadler, *Spinoza's Ethics*, 139–42; Amy Schmitter, "Spinoza on the Emotions," *Stanford Encyclopedia of Philosophy*, ed. Edward N. Zalta, 2010, https://plato.stanford.edu/entries/emotions-17th18th/LD5Spinoza.html.

the concept of the "conatus," by which "each thing endeavors to persist in its own being" and which "is nothing but the actual essence of the thing itself" (III, 7). This conatus toward self-preservation is intrinsic to each individual's essence:

> The definition [or essence] of anything affirms, and does not negate, the thing's essence.... So as long as we are attending to the thing itself, and not to external causes, we can find nothing in it which can destroy it.... Each thing... endeavors to persist in its own being. (III, 4 Proof, 5)

Conatus refers to the internal tendency of each thing to persist as the thing that it is. Because composite things change while retaining their essence, Spinoza adds to self-preservation a notion of activity, where to be "active" is to be such that "something takes place ... through our nature" (III, Def 3). Existing as the thing one is is being active, so self-preservation always also aims at increasing one's power of activity. While proportion of motion and rest distinguishes things qualitatively in terms of essential properties, conatus distinguishes them numerically in terms of particular strivings to maintain that essence through activity in a particular space and time.[23]

Once Spinoza develops a robust notion of individual finite things (modes), many of the problems for Descartes's account reappear in Spinoza. Unlike Descartes, who turns at this point to a more practical argument for love, Spinoza rejects the Cartesian parts-of-a-whole model of love and replaces it with an approach to passions in general and love in particular that is more consistent with the egoism implied his conatus theory of individuation. Unfortunately, this approach comes at the cost of giving up on a robust other-directed interpersonal love.

---

23 On quantitative and numerical identity, see Harold Noonan and Ben Curtis, "Identity," in *Stanford Encyclopedia of Philosophy*, ed. Edward N. Zalta, 2014. For application to Spinoza, see Pitts, "Freedom in Spinoza's *Ethics*."

Spinoza orients his account of emotions around self-preservation.[24] His emotion theory's primary postulate is, "The human body can be affected in many ways by which its power of activity is increased or diminished; and also in many other ways which neither increase nor diminish its power of activity" (III, Postulate 1). Emotions are changes in one's state of mind, arising because "whatsoever increases or diminishes . . . the power of activity of our body, the idea of said thing increases or diminishes . . . the power of thought of our mind" (III, 11). "Pleasure" is nothing other than "the passive transition of the mind to a state of greater perfection," where "perfection" refers simply to power of activity (III, 11 Scholium). Emotions are conscious thoughts of these bodily changes that either increase or decrease the body's capacity to remain active in the world. Emotions are thus essentially egoistic in the narrowest sense; one and all, they communicate what is good or bad *for one's own preservation*.

Love, too, is straightforwardly egoist: "Love is merely pleasure accompanied by the idea of an external cause" (III, 13, Scholium). Spinoza rejects Descartes's view that we take direct pleasure from the goods or perfections of what we love. For Spinoza, the object of love is "whatever increases or assists the body's power of activity" (III, 19 Proof; cf. III, 42 Proof). Amelie Rorty aptly explains the implications of this view for interpersonal relationships; one who loves another "will attempt to control [him] so that those aspects of his character that enhance her are strengthened, those that debilitate [her] are weakened."[25] Spinoza's substance-monist metaphysics, which seemed to offer metaphysical backing for a strong Cartesian sort of love, devolves into an egoistic metaphysics of individual finite modes pursuing their own

---

24 Descartes also sees the emotions (or "passions") as serving "to preserve the body or render it more perfect" (XI:429). For Descartes, however, the egoism of the passions is a mere empirical fact about them (or at most a feature of God's goodness in creating us as mind-bodies); for Spinoza, the self-centeredness of emotions literally follows from what it means for a human being to be a distinct particular thing.

25 Rorty, "Spinoza on the Pathos of Idolatrous Love and the Hilarity of True Love," 68.

self-preservation and having "love" only for the means toward that self-centered end.[26] Admittedly, on this account Spinoza does provide a metaphysical basis for what *Spinoza* calls love, but such Spinozist love has nothing of the noninstrumental regard for other persons found in Descartes's example of the lover who "puts their [the beloved's] interests before his own and is not afraid of sacrificing himself in order to save them" (XI:389).

There are two ways that Spinoza might seem to get beyond *mere* egoism and toward a promising metaphysical basis for genuinely other-regarding interpersonal love. Most basically, Spinoza claims that rational knowledge gives rise to the love of God (V, 42 Proof, p. 223) and given that "God" here refers to Reality as such, one might—as Arne Naess did—take this as a concern for the good of the whole universe, over and above one's own narrow interest.[27] Whereas, for Descartes, one who loves God might love the universe that God created and thereby love other persons, for Spinoza, God just *is* the universe, so it seems as though a love of God would imply a consideration of oneself as part of a whole and love of that whole for its own sake. Others might then be loved not merely for how they are conducive to my own power but for the fact that they, too, are modes of God.

For Spinoza, however, love of God is *not* a concern for the well-being of the whole, which would not even make sense since the whole has nothing that could be well- or ill-being. Rather, love of God is pleasure in a specific kind of *personal* well-being. "The mind judges nothing else to be to its advantage except what conduces to understanding" (IV, 26). Now, true understanding involves no individual thing distinct from one's own reason: "The essence of reason is nothing other than our mind insofar as it clearly and distinctly understands" (IV, 26 Proof).

---

26 Cf., too, Jeanette Bicknell, "An Overlooked Aspect of Love in Spinoza's *Ethics*," *Iyyun: The Jerusalem Philosophical Quarterly* 47 (1998): 44–47.

27 Naess, "Spinoza and Ecology"; cf. Rorty, "Spinoza on the Pathos of Idolatrous Love and the Hilarity of True Love."

To understand truths of reason is to be preeminently active and free from influence by external things. But "the highest object that the mind can understand is God," so "the mind's highest good is the knowledge of God" (IV, 28 Proof). When we "love God," we feel pleasure at the expression of self-sufficient agency involved in rationality; our love of God is love of an object of knowledge accessible to us independent of other goods.[28] Spinoza raises the stakes even further in the final sections of *Ethics*, when he argues that "there is necessarily in God an idea which expresses the essence of this or that human body under a form of eternity" and that *this* idea is what is eternal in the human mind (V, 22). As we know God through pure reason, we exercise and identify with that in our mind that does not depend upon durational existence; love of God is really, for Spinoza, a feeling of pleasure in the extent to which our essence is independent of contingent existence; love of God amounts to pleasure in (eternal) self-preservation. As Clare Carlisle explains, "Properly understood, [the love of God] is the affective, experiential expression of the fullest participation in God's nature, which involves a share in God's eternity."[29]

A second place Spinoza might seem to embrace genuinely non-egoist love is when he discusses relations among human beings, suggesting that we can "unite in friendship" with others and insisting that "the good which every man who pursues virtue aims at for himself he will also desire for the rest of humankind" (IV, Appendix 26; Proposition 37). Spinoza develops an account of the value of "living in society" and

---

28 Nadler, *Spinoza's Ethics*; Rorty, "Spinoza on the Pathos of Idolatrous Love and the Hilarity of True Love," 70–79; but cf. Alanen, "Descartes and Spinoza on the Love of God."
29 Carlisle, "The Intellectual Love of God," 441. Carlisle goes on to claim, "The enlightened love in which, through the third kind of knowledge, human self-love becomes inseparable from divine self-love, is nothing like the vacillating, egotistical passion that Spinoza criticizes so forcefully in the *Ethics*. Someone who attains *scientia intuitive* knows that her own power is not in competition with the power of others, nor with the power of God: she understands herself and others as beings-in-God, and thus as channels for the expression of divine power" (447). While I read Spinoza's love as more egoistic than what Carlisle describes here, her account suggests a further route to non-egoistic interpersonal love, one with some affinity to the suggestion I make at the end of the chapter.

being part of a greater social structure of which one is a single part (IV, Appendix 14). As Rorty says,

> The more narrowly defined is an individual's conception of her boundaries, the more readily is she overcome by the vast number of external forces. But the more broadly she identifies herself with other free rational minds, the more actively powerful she becomes: Her nature is not then bounded by, but agrees with others.[30]

Similarly, Bicknell emphasizes that "a constituent part of the self is its need for the society of others" and uses this to support an "expanded self" according to which "the 'self' of self-preservation refers not only to the individual, but also to those with whom... he or she has a relationship."[31] And David Lay Williams emphasizes the important role of "harmony," "love," and "friendship" within Spinoza's political theory, highlighting Spinoza's claim that a central dogma of his "universal faith" is that "the worship of God consists only in justice and charity, or love towards one's neighbor."[32] Connecting the concepts of friendship, charity, and love, Williams argues that "by 'friendship' Spinoza envisions something like the Christian notion of 'charity.' ... What is unique about friends for this purpose is that they share interests in the sense of truly taking the interest of others into account as their own."[33]

Even in these seemingly more altruistic moments in Spinoza, however, the ultimate bases for love, friendship, and cooperation are often presented in egoistic, basically Hobbesian, ways. Society provides for "mutual aid" (IV appendix #28), so "the principle of seeking our own advantage teaches us to be in close relationship with men" (IV, 37,

---

30 Rorty, "Spinoza on the Pathos of Idolatrous Love and the Hilarity of True Love," 78.
31 Bicknell, "An Overlooked Aspect of Love in Spinoza's *Ethics*," 46.
32 Spinoza's *Theologico-Political Treatise*, trans. Samuel Shirley in *Spinoza: Complete Works* (Indianapolis: Indiana University Press, 2002), 186–187; cited in David Lay Williams, "Spinoza and the General Will," *Journal of Politics* 72 (2010): 344.
33 Williams, "Spinoza and the General Will," 344.

Scholium 1) because "if he dwells among individuals who are in harmony with man's nature, by that very fact his power of activity will be assisted and fostered" (IV appendix #7). The exhortation to "act in such a way as serves to strengthen friendship"[34] is so emphatic because "it is before all things useful to men to associate their ways of life" (IV, Appendix #12). Moreover, because other people are subject to emotions that can threaten our well-being, we require a "civil state where good and bad are decided by common agreement and everyone is bound to obey the state" (IV, 37 Scholium 2). The "harmony" created by "fear . . . is untrustworthy," so we do better to ground politics on "filial love."[35] The universal faith itself "does not so much require truth as piety," and the main justification for seeing love of others as constitutive of obedience to God is that such a doctrine is "salutary and necessary . . . for a state, in order that men may live together in peace and concord," where this peaceful state "serves not only for defensive purposes, but is also very useful and, indeed, absolutely necessary," or else "no one would have either the skill or time to provide for his own sustenance and preservation" (TPP 188, 73). Society is necessary for self-preservation given each person's inability to "prepare all that he individually stood in need of" (TPP 73). Because love and friendship are a better foundation for society than fear, we ought to promote love and friendship among one another. Ultimately, however, as even Bicknell acknowledges, this "relationship" by which we expand our sense of self is ultimately one of "mutual benefit."[36]

Despite the widespread invocation of a basically Hobbesian egoistic justification for mutual aid, Spinoza at times seems to argue for a less instrumental and thereby somewhat less egoistic conception of

---

[34] This passage, among others, is cited by Bicknell to support her claim that "friendship . . . is not . . . founded upon self-interest" (Bicknell, "An Overlooked Aspect of Love in Spinoza's *Ethics*," 2), but as I show, the context suggests otherwise.

[35] Williams, "Spinoza and the General Will," 343–344, citing Spinoza, *Ethics* IV 4, Appendix 16 and Appendix 12.

[36] Bicknell, "An Overlooked Aspect of Love in Spinoza's *Ethics*," 46.

the relationship between human beings. Because human reason—that which is most active and eternal in each of us—is a feature of human nature *as such*,

> insofar as men live under the guidance of reason, to that extent... they necessarily do the things which are necessarily good for human nature [as such] and consequently for every single man, that is, which agree with the nature of every single man. (IV, 35 Proof)

Here we might recall a feature of Descartes's proof of the distinctness between mind and body, namely that because we can conceive of mind without body, they are distinct. Spinoza emphatically reiterates the connection between the (epistemic) notion that one thing can be understood without reference to another and the (metaphysical) notion that the things are really distinct (see, e.g., I, Axiom 5, P4). But no individual human being can be understood apart from human nature, and in that way, insofar as I seek to the good of myself, I seek the good of humanity. When Spinoza claims that "insofar as men live by the guidance of reason, they are most *useful* to man" (IV, 37 Proof, p. 173, emphasis added), instead of reading this claim as a contingent Hobbesian claim about the instrumental value of other human beings for myself, we can read it as an essential claim that what is for the good of human reason *as such* is for the good of *my* human reason. When we consider the identification of what is *truly* preserved in my being—my mind under a form of eternity—with my reason, this suggests room for genuine concern about the development of others' reason, not merely as a tool for promoting my reason, but as a shared *form* of reason, something we have in common that I can take pleasure in and with which I can even, in some eternal sense, participate.[37]

---

[37] These and related passages are emphasized by Bicknell, "An Overlooked Aspect of Love in Spinoza's *Ethics*."

Spinoza does not fully develop this aspect of his social and political theory. In *Ethics*, his summary of the "right way of living" treats "other individuals of the same species" and in particular "a man who is guided by reason" as that than which "there is nothing more advantageous to man for preserving his own being," that is, as instrumental goods toward one's self-preservation (IV Appendix #8–9, p. 197). In his *Political Treatise*, too, he relies on his Hobbesian defense of the value of political community and reemphasizes "the universal effort of all men after self-preservation" and the fact that "everything whatever, as far as in it lies, strives to preserve its own existence" (*Political Treatise* [PT], III.18, II.6), and even that "the freer [and more rational] we conceived man to be, the more we should be forced to maintain that he must of necessity preserve his own existence" (PT II.7). We join into communities of mutual self-constraint only because "men are naturally enemies...whom I must...be on my guard against...to which must be added, that without mutual help men can hardly support life and cultivate the mind" (PT II.14–15). In this *Treatise*, Spinoza abandons any *intrinsic* community with others, instead justifying community via individual self-interest. Unlike his appeal to shared human essence, his Hobbesian approach fits well with the important role for his ethical and motivational theory of individual essences, and especially the conatus by which each individual seeks to preserve herself.

However, we might emphasize Spinoza's attention to the shared human nature that is partly constitutive of my essence in order to get a more fundamental way in which we can love other human beings. Just as I rightly love God insofar as God is what is most eternal in my own essence, so too what other rational beings share in common with me by virtue of our shared rationality reflects something eternal about my own essence, and something more particular to me than my shared grounding in God. For Spinoza, even if, with respect to "whatever there is in Nature *external to man*, regard for our own advantage ... teaches us to preserve or destroy it according to its varying usefulness," there is a way in which we can value other human beings that arises from our shared nature and allows for a sort of what we might call love, namely friendship: "Except for mankind, we know of no individual thing in Nature in whose mind we can rejoice, and with which we can unite in friendship or some kind of close tie" (IV, Appendix #26). My human nature—in particular the rationality I share with other human beings—is a lasting feature of my individual essence, and one I can take joy in, whether expressed in my particular mind or in the minds of others who share that nature. I can and should do what is "necessarily good for human nature [as such] and consequently for every single man" (IV, 35 Proof), not merely for the instrumental value of mutual aid for my most particular essence, but also as part of preserving that human nature that partly constitutes my essence. On this view, I have an interpersonal "love" for other persons, not as parts of a whole of which I am also a part, but as fellow instances of a kind of mode of God of which I am also an instance. Insofar as we share an essence with one another, the promotion of what is good for you qua human is a promotion of what is good for humanity, which promotes the good of that humanity in which I partake.

### Conclusion: Beyond Descartes and Spinoza

This chapter focused on two early modern philosophers—Rene Descartes and Baruch Spinoza—who sought to ground accounts of love in metaphysics. Both, in different ways, affirmed the value of interpersonal human love, but both also affirmed egoistic conceptions of individual human persons that posed problems for justifying genuinely altruistic love. In the end, I suggested that Descartes's approach might be salvaged by shifting from a properly metaphysical grounding of love to a more practical one, and that Spinoza has room for a sort of extension of direct regard—friendship—toward others who share our rational human nature. These two philosophers, however, represent only two options within a panoply of early modern philosophers, others of whom—including, for example, Anne Conway (see the chapter on her in this volume)—develop rich accounts of individual persons and the potentially loving relations among them.

CHAPTER 8

# Anne Conway on the Love-Worthiness and Perfectibility of All Things

*Christia Mercer*

Love plays a central role in the radical proposals of the seventeenth-century English philosopher Anne Conway (1631–1679).[1] Because God, as first substance, shares its infectious "vital" love with all creatures, each loves all the others. Love is the primary motivating force and connective glue among the infinity of the world's creatures and so guarantees the world's ultimate perfectibility. An examination of love's role in Conway's metaphysics not only uncovers unnoticed features of her philosophy, it also reveals the unique place her thought occupies in love's history. Her philosophy, as it turns out, is more radical and original than has been previously understood.

---

1 This chapter relies on some previously published work by the author as well as a recent paper by Mercer and Branscum. See Christia Mercer and Olivia Branscum, "Anne Conway," in *The Routledge Handbook of Women and Early Modern European Philosophy*, ed. Karen Detlefsen and Lisa Shapiro (New York: Routledge, 2023), 450–464, and see citations in this chapter to the author's other relevant works.

Because many readers will be unfamiliar with Conway's thought, this chapter includes an overview of her central claims, highlighting their importance in the history of discussions about love. The first section situates Conway's views about love in the history traced in this book, emphasizing points that help illuminate the unusual aspects of her proposals; the next section introduces newcomers to the basics of her philosophy; the third section explicates her account of God's living, loving goodness, and the divinely ordained sympathetic harmony among all creatures that guarantees worldly perfectibility; the fourth section exposes the finer details of the movement of creatures toward goodness through love; and the final section summarizes the chapter's main lessons.

## Past Loves

The goal of *Love: A History* is to present key moments in the evolution of philosophical understandings of love from ancient thought to the twentieth century. In his Introduction, Ryan Hanley distinguishes between the ancient "religious and philosophical concepts of love," which "focus on love's relationship to the transcendent," and more modern approaches, which "focus on love's relationship to the immanent." Whereas ancient authors are keen to examine how lovers "are connected to phenomena that exist in a world beyond the self—phenomena such as the divine, or the good, or the beautiful," Ryan notes that more modern authors tend to be concerned with how lovers "subjectively experience" love "in specific times and places," which "are determined by the conditions of their embodiment and their capacities for sensation" (Introduction, p. 5).

My chapter displays the liminal space that Conway's philosophy occupies between transcendent and intimate kinds of love. By insisting that all creatures bear a loving relation to all others, she models the closeness of creaturely bonds partly on the bond between a lover and her beloved (7.4 [xiv]).[2] On Conway's telling, the loving connection

---

2 Anne Conway, *Principles of the Most Ancient and Modern Philosophy*, ed. and trans. Andrew Arlig, Christia Mercer, and Jasper Reid (New York: Oxford University Press, forthcoming). Roman numerals indicate subsections that have been added to this edition for ease of navigation.

among all creatures will verge on the passionate in its closeness.[3] It is the intimacy of creaturely love, when coupled with universal sympathetic harmony, that guarantees the perfectibility of all creatures. To be clear, although the bond among creatures is in no way erotic, it is (*or inevitably will become*) one of passionate affection and devotion, resulting in an increasingly intimate relation between each creature and its beloved companions.[4] By weaving creaturely love and sympathy into the fabric of her metaphysics, Conway ensures that each of the infinity of created things will eventually acquire a high degree of perfection, its apposite love, and accompanying joy. And in finding such passionate love for its companions, it thereby learns to love their divine source.

One of the things that makes Conway's views about love unusual is her subversive rendering of traditional Christian, Jewish, and Platonist claims about the relation between divine and human love. Hanley notes the historical transition from ancient thinkers' tendency to focus on the object of love as transcendent and the movement among eighteenth- and nineteenth-century thinkers to emphasize the immanent. Conway's position reimagines the relation between the transcendent and the immanent. Her God does not demand that creatures love their divine source first and foremost, but rather that they discover God's perfections among and within themselves. To love God is to cherish all God's creatures. Conway's commitment to the idea that love is an intimate connection between lovers subjectively experienced "in specific times and places" renders her views closer to eighteenth- and nineteenth-century thinkers than to ancient ones. As creatures ascend

---

3 Ryan Hanley, in his Introduction, equates romantic love with "the passionate love of one human being for and by another human being" (p. 5). See the final two sections of this chapter on the intimate and affective bond that every creature will eventually feel for every other.

4 Sharon Krishek, in chapter 11 of this volume, "Kierkegaard's Theistic Conception of Love, Existentially Considered," assigns a similar view to Kierkegaard, writing that "(genuine) romantic love is *essentially* neighborly love, which implies that romantic love should conform to the essential characteristics of neighborly love" (p. 292). In Kierkegaard's words, as quoted in Krishek: "Christianity recognizes really only one kind of love . . . and does not concern itself much with working out in detail the different ways in which this fundamental universal love can manifest itself" (p. 292).

to greater and greater understanding of their world and its perfections, the result is not just a love of what is above or beyond them, but also of what is within them as a community of loving and love-worthy beings, intimately and sympathetically related. In a striking passage, she compares the kind of love that creatures are able to bear one another to the love borne between two human lovers:

> For if two people are markedly in love with one another, they are so greatly unified by this love that no amount of distance in place can separate or divide them. For they are present to one another in spirit, so that a continuous outflowing or emanation of spirits passes between them, whereby they are united and bound together as if by certain cords.... And so, whatever a person loves—whether it be a person, or an animal, or a tree, or silver or gold—when he is united to it, his spirit goes out from him into this thing. (7.4 [xiv])[5]

In order to situate Conway's conception of love more securely in the history of philosophy, it will be helpful to compare her views to earlier conceptions. In chapter 3, "Love in the Christian Tradition," David McPherson emphasizes "the *centrality* of love to the Christian message" (p. 71). The greatest and first commandment is to love God "with all your heart, and with all your soul, and with all your mind," while the second greatest commandment is to "love your neighbor as yourself."

---

5 Like many philosophers in the early modern period, Conway uses 'emanation' to refer both to the "outflowing" of causal power from one creature to another and the importantly different causal relation between God and created things. See Christia Mercer, "Leibniz and Spinoza on Substance and Mode," in *The Rationalists*, ed. Robert M. Adams and Derk Pereboom (Lanham, MD: Rowman and Littlefield, 1999), 283–290; Eileen O'Neill, "Influxus Physicus," in *Causation in Early Modern Philosophy*, ed. Stephen Nadler (University Park: Pennsylvania State University Press, 1993), 27–55; Marcy P. Lascano, *Metaphysics of Cavendish and Conway: Monism, Vitalism, and Self-Motion* (New York: Oxford University Press, 2023), 61–62, 123–127; Eric Schliesser, "Newtonian Emanation, Spinozism, Measurement and the Baconian Origins of the Laws of Nature," *Foundations of Science* 18 (August 2013): 1–19. For more on emanation, see the fourth section of this chapter.

McPherson examines how the second commandment is supposed to follow from the first. One fairly common answer, he explains, is that because human beings are supposed to be made in the image of God (Genesis 1:27), each has a special dignity and worth; and since each has such worth, it is owed a degree of the respect and love that is due God, although to a lesser extent. So, when we fail to show respect and love for our neighbor, we thereby fail to love and respect God.

The most important point for us here is that, for many early Christians, the love we owe other humans is motivated by the love we owe God. So the claim that we are made in the image of God renders every human love-worthy. As McPherson reads the highly influential Augustine, human beings are not to be loved for their own sake, but *because* they are made in the likeness of God (other creatures are not similarly love-worthy because they are not made in God's image). For our purposes, the main point of McPherson's chapter is that for Augustine and for Aquinas, "rightly ordered love" requires "loving the right things in the right ways, specifically in such a way that God is recognized as the highest good, to be loved for Himself, with all else to be loved specifically for His sake" (p. 8). To summarize the point in a manner relevant to Conway's views, for Christians like Augustine and Aquinas, the love-worthiness of human beings is not due to anything intrinsic to their nature, but rather to what is extrinsic.

William Chittick's chapter 4 reveals a striking difference between the core medieval Christian views surveyed by McPherson and prominent medieval Islamic views. The latter suggest that human beings are intrinsically love-worthy. According to the Sufi proposal, for example, the divinity "necessarily loves both human beings and the beauty they manifest." Indeed, love is "God's motive for creating the universe" and so humans "innately love God." The love that all humans innately bear God is "the means whereby human beings can actualize their true humanity." According to Chittick, a core medieval Islamic idea is that "the human soul achieves perfection by way of love" (p. 115). As we will see, Conway agrees that humans are intrinsically love-worthy, though she extends to all creatures both love-worthiness and the capacity to love.

Chapter 5 turns to the fascinating (and understudied) views of prominent medieval contemplatives. The takeaway most relevant to Conway is that, for many medieval contemplatives, love of the divinity can be, in Christina van Dyke's words, "affective and compelling, burning and fierce" (p. 138). The Flemish beguine Hadewijch sounds much like Conway when she writes, "If two things are to become one, nothing may be between them except the glue wherewith they are united together. That bond of glue is Love."[6]

The highly influential Renaissance Platonist (and first translator of Plato's corpus into Latin), Marsilio Ficino, seems to echo the contemplatives' views that an individual's love for God can be a matter of *ardent desire* on the part of the individual lover. As Denis Robichaud shows in chapter 6, by spotlighting the *experience* of desire between lover and beloved, Ficino signals a shift in the Platonist rendering of transcendent love. For the great Florentine Platonist, human beings are *essentially* lovers who intensely seek to be unified with their beloved divinity. According to Robichaud, Ficino "brings us to the intersection of traditional ideas of transcendent being and emerging ideas of the experience of desire, developing a concept of love as a 'third term between lover and beloved.'" Love thereby becomes a metaphysical force that "holds together" the parts of the created world (p. 162).

Conway's metaphysics of love rejects the Augustinian idea that humans' love-worthiness is extrinsic, favoring instead a view similar to medieval Sufi thinkers: human beings are innately love-worthy and actualize the fullness of their humanity through love. Like many medieval contemplatives, she takes love to be an affective and "compelling" power that constitutes a kind of metaphysical glue or binding force that continuously emanates (see p. 207 above) from the lover to the

---

6 Hadewijch, "Letter 16," in *Hadewijch: The Complete Works*, ed. and trans. Mother Columba Hart (Mahwah, NJ: Paulist Press, 1980), 80. Quoted in Van Dyke, X.

beloved. And like her Platonist predecessor, Ficino, she extends love's metaphysical power to all the parts of the world. Conway, however, goes far beyond her predecessors in allocating to all creatures the capacity both to love and to *experience* vividly the love-worthiness of others. Not only is every creature deserving of love, it is itself able to feel *passionately* a loving bond with every other. Her account entails, as we will see, an extreme form of universalism, namely, the idea that each of the infinity of creatures is deserving of—and will eventually acquire—an ever-increasing degree of perfection, its apposite love, and accompanying joy.

### The Basics of Conway's Philosophy

Anne Conway's philosophy is a systematic attempt to solve a wide range of philosophical and theological problems. The full title of her main work, published posthumously in 1690, reveals her broad interests and sources: *Principles of the Most Ancient and Modern Philosophy concerning God, Christ, and Creation, that is, concerning the Nature of Spirit and Matter, thanks to which all the Problems can be resolved which could not be resolved by Scholastic Philosophy nor by Modern Philosophy in general, whether Cartesian, Hobbesian, or Spinozian. A Short Posthumous Work translated from English into Latin, with annotations taken from the ancient philosophy of the Hebrews*. Conway's *Principles* provides an account of reality based on three distinct substances. The first is God, the second is Logos or Christ, and the third is the created world. That is, there are "three classes of Beings" (5.3 [ii]), which "are distinct in substance or essence" (6.4 [i]). She explains:

> God is one and does not have two, three, or more distinct substances in himself, and just as Christ [or Logos][7] is one simple Christ without

---

7 Conway refers to the second substances more frequently as 'Christ' than as 'Logos,' though she does use the latter term. I have chosen to use 'Logos' in order to distinguish clearly between the

further distinct substances in himself... in like manner, creature, or the whole of creation [is] ... one substance or essence, even though it may include many individuals ... that are modally but not substantially or essentially distinct from one another. (6.4 [ii])

There are only three substances, and there could not be more: "the three [substances] just mentioned exhaust all the specific differences in substance that our minds can possibly conceive" (6.4 [i]). Each substance has its own unique level of perfection. God's perfection renders the divine substance "altogether immutable" (5.3 [i]), whereas the two other substances, which are divine products—namely Logos or Christ and Creation—differ in their "kinds of mutability" (5.3 [ii]).[8] Logos as "the most excellent production made outwardly by God, and the ... most perfect image of him" (5.4 [ii]) can change "only from good toward good." Although Creation, like Logos, is "good in its nature," each individual creature "has in it a power to change either toward good or toward bad" (5.3 [ii]). In the end, however, the creatures that God fashions will reach a state of ever-increasing perfection and its attendant joy: "It is the nature of every creature to develop and progress toward ever greater perfection to infinity" (7.2 [vi]).

The history of philosophy is replete with philosophers who insist that the good of the created world follows from the goodness of God. Our collection shows that philosophy's past is packed with thinkers maintaining that God created the world out of love, but that only human beings are love-worthy and love-capable. Conway rejects the idea that current human beings are intrinsically superior to other

---

second substance and the historic Christ, whom I have argued is a mode of third substance. See Christia Mercer, "Anne Conway's Metaphysics of Sympathy," in *Feminist History of Philosophy: The Recovery and Evaluation of Women's Philosophical Thought*, ed. Marcy Lascano and Eileen O'Neill (Cham: Springer Nature Switzerland, 2009), 49–73, especially §4.

8 Conway frequently refers to the third substance as 'creation,' a noun that she sometimes capitalizes. I have chosen to do that here to help newcomers to Conway's thought remember that creatures constitute a single substance, namely, Creation.

creatures. She might be the only thinker to hold that every single one of the infinity of creatures has an innate capacity to love all the others, that each creature is intrinsically love-worthy, and that every created thing will persist through a series of lives, over the course of which it will attain a virtual moral perfection. "God's wisdom," she explains, entails that "every single entity" has the capacity to proceed "along its natural course and order" so that all creatures are "instruments of the divine wisdom, goodness, and power that is at work in them and with them" (9.6 [ii]). Whether the creature is currently a fleck of "vile" dust, horse, or human being, it will eventually approach perfection.[9] Although "individual creatures" are "only finitely good . . . , they are potentially infinite, that is, always capable of further perfection without any end" (6.6 [vii]). The love that each creature bears the others is due to the good of each: "goodness is a great—indeed, the greatest—cause of love, and [so] its proper object" (7.3 [v]). Because each creature is good, it is love-worthy; because each is a living love, it is capable of increasing its goodness and love-worthiness over time. In other words, the created world or "third substance" moves eternally toward perfection, and every creature eventually achieves an ever-increasing perfectibility. Some creatures' expanding capacity for love and goodness will take longer than others to develop. There will be lots of creaturely backsliding. But every single created thing will ultimately become roughly morally commensurate with all the others.

Creatures' innate love for the good drives perfectibility, although it is the sympathetic harmony that God has woven into the fabric of creation that guarantees it. But how?

---

9 There is inadequate space here to display the metaphysical details of Conway's views, but suffice it to say that each creature is a spirit that never dies, but persists through a series of lives. Her view bears striking similarity to both reincarnation and metempsychosis.

## God's Living, Loving Goodness

The *Principles* begins with the assertion that "God is Spirit, light and life, infinitely wise, good, just, mighty, omniscient, omnipresent, and omnipotent" (1.1). Chapters 1 to 3 interrogate these and other divine attributes and unpack their metaphysical and normative implications. Like many of her Platonist-leaning contemporaries (Henry More, Ralph Cudworth, G. W. Leibniz), Conway draws on a variety of Jewish kabbalist and Platonist sources in her account of God, the divine attributes, and God's relation to the world (the latter are "the most ancient" philosophies to which she refers in her book's title). But unlike her contemporaries, she is willing to follow the implications of the divine attributes to (what she considers) their logical conclusion, however unorthodox.

For Conway, God's attributes of goodness and love imbue the created world with moral significance in that they render the world as full of creatures as possible, each of which loves goodness. About divine goodness, she asks, "Did not God create" an [infinity of] creatures to this end: that they be blessed in him and *enjoy* his divine goodness (7.2 [iv]); my emphasis)? About creaturely goodness, she explains that because every creature is inherently good and because goodness is "a magnet of love" (7.4 [iv]), each creature is "drawn to" all the others (7.3 [vii]) from which follows a "universal love in all creatures for one another" (7.3 [ii]).[10]

Conway's notion of perfectibility is grounded in four metaphysical claims: divine perfection, divine emanation, sympathetic enhancement (and the closely related sympathetic harmony), and the package

---

10 On Conway's views about the way love works in the relation between soul and body, see Julia Borcherding, "Loving the Body, Loving the Soul: Conway's Vitalist Critique of Cartesian and Morean Dualism," in *Oxford Studies in Early Modern Philosophy*, ed. Donald Rutherford (Oxford University Press, 2019), 9. © Julia Borcherding. DOI: 10.1093/oso/9780198852452.003.0001. Borcherding emphasizes the importance of similarity between (what I call) the lover and what it loves.

deal.[11] In order to understand these claims, it will be helpful to review two terms, which are much used and debated in the middle decades of the seventeenth century, and well used in the *Principles*.

*Attribute*: In his best-selling philosophical lexicon of 1653, Johann Micraelius explains that a standard sense of *attribute* "is that by which the being" or essence of a thing is understood.[12] Each attribute of God (e.g., wisdom, goodness) is a means by which the essence of God might be comprehended. Conway agrees (see 3.1, 6.6 [i], 6.8 [iv], 7.2 [i]). Protestant thinkers like Micraelius also commonly distinguished, as Conway does, between "communicable" and "incommunicable" attributes. For Conway, love is a communicable attribute of the divinity.[13]

*Mode*: The notion of *modus* has a complicated history in early modern thought.[14] It was common to describe a mode as what *expresses* an essence and to claim that each mode is a different or "determinant" expression of the essence of which it is a mode. According to Conway's well-known contemporary G. W. Leibniz, the essence of the number 6 can be "expressed" as $2 \times 3$, $4 + 2$, or through innumerable other "modes." Each mode expresses the essence in a determinant way, and each "differs from the other."[15] Similarly, Conway maintains that a mode is a unique determination or expression of the substantial essence of which it is a mode (6.4 [ii]), whether the substance is God, Logos, or Creation. Although each mode expresses the essence of its substance, no two modes are alike. As we will see, it follows from the "communicative and multiplicative" nature of God's goodness (2.4)

---

11 Olivia Branscum coined this term. See Mercer and Branscum, "Anne Conway," 459.

12 Johann Micraelius, "Modus," in *Lexicon philosophicum terminorum philosophis usitatorum* (Düsseldorf: Stern-Verlag Janssen, 1966 [1653]), 169–170. About modus, also see Robert Pasnau, *Metaphysical Themes 1274–1671* (Oxford: Oxford University Press, 2011), 145–147.

13 Theological debates about the Trinity, Eucharist, and especially transubstantiation in the early modern period generated lively (and sometimes violent) debates about substance-attribute-mode terminology.

14 See Mercer, "Leibniz and Spinoza on Substance and Mode," for a brief history of mode from Ficino through Descartes to Leibniz.

15 Gottfried Wilhelm Leibniz, *Sämtliche Schriften und Briefe* (Berlin: Akademie-Verlag, 1923), 518–519.

that every mode of third substance (i.e., every creature) must be different from every other.

The next (and penultimate) section elucidates how individual creatures are transformed over millennia to attain near perfection. But first it is important to explicate the four closely related metaphysical claims that ground Conway's account of creaturely perfectibility.

*Divine perfection* entails both that God creates an infinity of creatures and that each is a *unique* mode or expression of God's love. Because the Divinity is (among other things) the most perfectly wise, unified, loving, and powerful entity there is, God *must* create and, in creating, must share the (communicable) divine attributes with everything produced. In Conway's words: "divine goodness and wisdom" constitute "an internal impulse" to create (3.3). Not only is it "an essential attribute of God" to be "a Creator," it is also "an essential attribute of God" that his goodness and love be "communicative" (2.4–5). Because only God can possess the divine attributes perfectly, its products necessarily possess them imperfectly. But in giving "essence to Creatures" (3.3), God shares all the (communicable) divine perfections, from which it follows that *every one* of the infinity of creatures receives from God *all* the (communicable) divine attributes and moreover that each creature is its own unique mode or expression of "living goodness" (7.2 [ii]). Thus, on Conway's reading, divine perfection demands that each of the infinity of creatures is a unique mode of divine love, and like God, each bears a living loving relation with all the others.

*Emanation* is the causal notion employed by most ancient and early modern Platonists (and many Kabbalists) to help explain how the immutable God is able to share the perfect divine attributes with creatures while remaining unchanged. Conway's understanding of *emanative causation* assumes that, for a substance A, that is more perfect than a substance B, A is able to emanate its communicable attributes to B in such a way that B receives those attributes, though B possesses them in a manner inferior to the way they exist in A. So, for example, God— who is perfectly good and loving—emanates those attributes to Logos and to creatures, who then have them in *diminished* ways.[16] Perhaps the most famous example of a communicable attribute occurs in Plato's *Republic*. Examining the relation between the perfect Good itself and the good of individual philosopher-rulers, Socrates and his interlocutors explore the metaphysical and normative assumptions grounding the view that the Good itself causes and explains the goodness of individuals. Good human beings are merely imperfect "off-spring" of "the Good itself." The Good itself is perfectly good; the philosopher-rulers are good in a lesser or diminished manner.[17]

The *package deal* is the claim that every one of the infinity of creatures contains all the (communicable) divine attributes.[18] On Conway's rendering, God emanates all the (communicable) divine perfections to every single one of the infinity of created things, who then possess those attributes, though to a lesser degree than they are contained in God. Because the divine attributes of an individual creature X are proportional (e.g., X's wisdom will be equal in perfection to its generosity and love), an increase in love is matched by the same increase

---

16 The causal notion of emanation is notoriously difficult to articulate. For more on the notion as used in early modern philosophy, see *Plotinus' Legacy: The Transformation of Platonism from the Renaissance to the Modern Era*, ed. Stephen Gersh (Cambridge: Cambridge University Press, 2019). See also Brian Ogren, *The Beginning of the World in Renaissance Jewish Thought: Ma'aseh Bereshit in Italian Jewish Philosophy and Kabbalah, 1492–1535* (Leiden: Brill, 2016), and Christia Mercer, *Leibniz's Metaphysics: Its Origins and Development* (New York: Cambridge University Press, 2001), 178–195. Although emanation is most frequently applied to the relation between God and divine products, the term was also applied to a causal relation between creatures. For recent discussions of the notion as used among Jewish Kabbalists, see Jonathan Garb, *A History of Kabbalah from the Early Modern Period to the Present Day* (Cambridge: Cambridge University Press, 2020), and Ogren, *The Beginning of the World in Renaissance Jewish Thought*. In the seventeenth century, there were a number of different ways of accounting for emanation. For a helpful survey, see Eric Schliesser, "Newtonian Emanation, Spinozism, Measurement and the Baconian Origins of the Laws of Nature," *Foundations of Science* 10, no. 3 (2005): 1–19.

17 See especially 508b–e in Plato, "Republic: Book VI," in *Plato: Complete Works*, ed. John M. Cooper (Indianapolis: Hackett, 1997), 506–510. Although Ficino attributes the causal notion of emanation to Plato, it is arguable as to whether Plato held such a causal theory. As an entrance to this vast topic, see James Wilberding, "The World Soul in the Platonic Tradition," in *World Soul: A History*, ed. James Wilberding (New York: Oxford University Press, 2021), 15–43.

18 I owe the notion of 'package deal' to Olivia Branscum. For more on her views, see Olivia Branscum, "Vitalism and Panpsychism in the Philosophy of Anne Conway," *British Journal of the History of Philosophy* (Forthcoming). https://doi.org/10.1080/09608788.2023.2276719.

in all other attributes. Given our focus on love, it is especially important that every creature contains "spirit, Light, and life," so that "none of these attributes is such that it is not living, or life itself" (7.2 [iii]). Promulgating the close relationship among the attributes of goodness, love, and generosity, Conway writes,

> *God is infinitely good, loving and generous* [*benignus*]; indeed, he is goodness and charity itself, an infinite fountain and Ocean of goodness, charity and generosity. Now, how could this fountain not perpetually flow and release living waters from itself? Would this Ocean not perpetually overflow through its emanation and a certain continuous streaming to produce creatures? *For God's goodness, by his own proper nature, is communicative and multiplicative.* (2.4; my emphasis)

The package deal guarantees both that every creature is love-capable and love-worthy. It is, then, a necessary condition for creaturely perfectibility in that perfectibility depends on the vital, loving goodness of each creature. But it is not sufficient; sympathetic enhancement is also required.

*Sympathetic enhancement* finds its feet in sympathetic harmony, a concept with an ancient pedigree and varied history. The historical roots of the notion extend (at least) to the ancient Stoic idea that all the parts of nature bear an affinity with one another. The collection *Sympathy: A History* offers a nuanced history, including the lively early modern debates about sympathy as a metaphysical, normative, and medical topic.[19] Around the time that Conway was composing

---

19 See Eric Schliesser, ed., *Sympathy: A History* (Oxford: Oxford University Press, 2015). On the history of the notion with special focus on the early period, see Christia Mercer, "Seventeenth-Century Universal Sympathy: Stoicism, Platonism, Leibniz, and Conway," in *Sympathy: A History*, ed. Eric Schliesser (New York: Oxford University Press, 2015), 107–138. Leibniz's doctrine of preestablished harmony is strikingly similar in some ways to Conway's account of universal sympathy. The history of philosophical discussions about sympathy relates significantly to the history of love as discussed in the current volume.

the *Principia*, a young German philosopher, Jacob Heinrich Gangloff, was preparing his university dissertation, *On Sympathy*.[20] The work explores the lively metaphysical and physical debates in the third quarter of the seventeenth century. One of Gangloff's main concerns is to define the term in a way that "unifies" its various senses. He avers that sympathy is "a mutual natural harmony among natural things, arising from a particular hidden affinity on account of which these things, by a friendly affect or *secret love*, are mutually drawn to each other."[21] For Gangloff, it is the "soul of the world" that is the cause of the "gentle sympathy" of all things. In the end, therefore, it is this "spirit of God" that "animates the world" and thereby connects its parts together.[22] For Gangloff and many other early modern thinkers, the affinity of the parts of the world are due to affection and love that the divine spirit has shared with creatures.[23]

Conway's account of sympathetic harmony is more robust than that of her peers. Since God's goodness is "communicative and multiplicative" (2.4) and since the package deal guarantees that all creatures share the attributes of goodness, generosity, and love, her rendering of sympathetic harmony transforms the sympathetic connection among creatures into one of normative enhancement. In emanating the (communicable) divine attributes to all creatures, God guarantees a mutual love among them from which it follows that each will love the others and respond to them sympathetically. Conway magnifies the goodness

---

20 Jacob Heinrich Gangloff, *Disputatio physica de sympathia* (Jena: Samuel Adophus Müller, 1669), A 2r.
21 Gangloff, *Disputatio physica de sympathia*, A 2r–A 2v. My emphasis.
22 Gangloff, *Disputatio physica de sympathia*, §§22–23. For more details on Gangloff and other mid-seventeenth-century thinkers as a background to the use of universal sympathy in Leibniz and Conway, see Mercer, "Seventeenth-Century Universal Sympathy," 108–139.
23 There is insufficient space to discuss the details here, but the point is: God emanates vital love to all creatures, who all accordingly innately love one another. For Gangloff and Conway, the greater the affinity, the greater the love. For more on this point, see Borcherding, "Loving the Body, Loving the Soul."

in the standard sympathetic relations among creatures by insisting that an increase in the goodness of creature X will enhance that of every other creature, a view that I call *sympathetic enhancement*.[24] When two creatures, X and Y, have a *sympathetic enhancement* relation, an increase in the goodness of X will promote an increase in the goodness of Y, although the relation is non-reciprocal (that is, the increase in the goodness of Y will not then promote an increase in X). For Conway, every creature bears such a "multiplicative" relation to every other, guaranteeing the ultimate perfectibility of all creatures.[25]

The metaphysical claims discussed in this section—divine perfection, emanation, the package deal, and sympathetic enhancement—help to expose Conway's highly original philosophy of love. God shares through emanation all the (communicable) divine attributes with every creature. Each creature is a distinctive mode or expression of all the divine attributes, which are proportional in that the level of creature X's wisdom and goodness will be roughly equivalent to its other attributes. For our purposes, the most important attributes are love, generosity, and "living goodness" (7.2 [ii]). Although, as we will see, a creature X can live centuries while remaining unconscious of the relation it bears to all other creatures; X nonetheless loves all the others and harbors generosity toward them. Because divine attributes come as a package deal and because each creature bears a sympathetic enhancement relation to every other, an increase in the wisdom and goodness of X will enhance that of every one of its infinite peers. Given our focus on love, it is especially important that every creature contains "spirit, Light, and life" so that "none of these communicable attributes is such

---

[24] See Christia Mercer, "Anne Conway's Metaphysics of Sympathy," in *Feminist History of Philosophy: The Recovery and Evaluation of Women's Philosophical Thought*, ed. Marcy Lascano and Eileen O'Neill (Cham: Springer International, 2009), 49–73.
[25] Sympathetic harmony does not magnify any kinds of ill or negative feelings, which are themselves a falling away from goodness.

that it is not living, or life itself" (7.2 [iii]). Because each creature is full of living love, it is both love-worthy and love-capable.

An important question remains to be answered: How exactly is a "vile" piece of dust able to be transformed into something angelic?

## Creation's Loving, Living Goodness

Conway may be unique in the metaphysical and normative implications she draws from God's attributes: all creatures are "instruments of the divine wisdom [and] goodness so that God's goodness will be made manifest in "every single entity" (9.6 [ii]). Although individual creatures will struggle, each will ultimately attain an ever-increasing level of perfection, a *joyful love* of the creaturely world it inhabits, and an understanding of God's love.

Recall that, for Conway, there are three distinct substances, each of which possesses a unique essence. The third substance or "Creation" is a single living "substance or entity" that is expressed in an infinite number of determinant modes (7.4 [x]). Because "God is infinitely good and communicates his goodness to all his creatures in an infinity of ways," every creature receives God's "living goodness" and so "has within it life, knowledge, love, and power" (7.2 [ii]). Since all creatures bear a sympathetic enhancement relation to every other, each aids its peers in moving to a state of heightened mutual love, and its attendant joy. Although God looms as the emanative source of the loveworthiness inherent in creatures, each creature develops its loves by responding to the others. God made all creatures "out of one blood, so that all might love one another..., mutually cherish one another," and so bear "a certain universal sympathy and mutual love" (6.4 [iii]). Every creature, then, "is capable of always acquiring greater goodness to infinity" (7.2 [iv]). Each creature's inevitable march toward perfectibility requires perception, affect, and desire, which will "take itself... wherever it desires to be." Although creaturely perception, affect, pain, and desire will lead many creatures astray, each will ultimately be "liberated from this confusion and vanity."[26] The important point for us now is that every creature is full of affective responses to the world around it, which will ultimately lead it to the proper object of love, namely, goodness.

To accommodate both the frequent failures of creatures to love the right things and the inevitability of their ultimate movement toward goodness, Conway builds two unorthodox commitments into the structure of creation. First, boundaries among species (like humans and horses) are permeable. Conway proffers that creatures participate in a kind of regeneration or reincarnation, under which they will either turn into the "nobler" or more morally elevated beings or revert to "lower" ones (6.3 [iii]) in accordance with their moral comportment in a particular life cycle (see 6.7 [i]).[27]

Second, Conway considers suffering "medicinal" in that it is part of God's wise and just plan to improve creatures (6.10 [iii]). God's punishment of creatures comes in two forms: when individual creatures suffer in their current incarnation or when they revert to a "lower" species in their next one. In both cases, the goal is to purify and thereby increase the creature's living love (7.1 [iv]). "God's Justice," she insists, "gloriously shines forth in this transmutation of things from one species into another" (6.7 [i]). In the end, by recognizing the rightness of its punishment, creatures begin to grasp the justice of divine love:

> if an image of a lovable God were better known to humans, such as he truly is, and as he manifests himself in all his dispensations to his creatures; and *if our soul could inwardly feel and taste him, especially*

---

26 This passage is from an unnumbered, introductory paragraph between the Synopsis and §1 of chapter 7, a textual element that other chapters do not have.

27 For more details see Mercer and Branscum, "Anne Conway," which discusses these topics in greater detail. Also, Christia Mercer, "Conway's Response to Cartesianism," in *The Oxford Handbook of Descartes and Cartesianism*, ed. Tad M. Schmaltz, Steven Nadler, and Delphine Antoine-Mahut (New York: Oxford University Press, 49–73, and John Grey, "Species and the Good in Anne Conway's Metaethics," in *Comparative Metaethics: Neglected Perspectives on the Foundations of Morality*, ed. Colin Marshall (New York: Routledge, 2020), 102–118.

*as he just is charity and generosity itself,*... then and not before would people love God above all, and acknowledge that he most of all is lovable, just, merciful, and above all worthy of adoration. (6.9; my emphasis)

We have arrived at a neat answer to the question prompting this section: How exactly is a "vile" piece of dust able to become angelic? Each individual creature X is a distinctive mode of the third substance, and X persists through its reincarnations while maintaining its identity through its recurrent and often radical changes. X might be a piece of "vile" dust now (8.4 [ii]), morph into a horse in several centuries, and then transition to become virtually angelic over the course of time. Regardless of its changes, X remains a distinctive mode or expression of all the (communicable) divine attributes and retains its identity, as X, through them all. Creature X might desire badly and slide into a lower status, but eventually it will be saved by the goodness and love of those around it: sympathetic enhancement guarantees that it will inevitably be lifted by the rising tide of creaturely love, pride in its own accomplishments, and a recognition of God's underlying love.

Conway is clear that X's eventual joy is partly owing to the challenges that it has overcome: "a creature delights in a greater joy, because it owns what it has as the fruit of its own labor" (9.6 [ii]). But X's delight is also due to the progressively close bond it feels with all other creatures, the beauty of which it increasingly recognizes and to which it affectionately responds. Each creature eventually will "feel and taste" (6.9) and delight in "divine goodness" (7.2 [ii]). About the relation between creatures and God, Conway writes,

> But there is yet another cause of love, when beings that love one another are not one substance, but one [substance] gives essence to the other [substance] and is its proper and real cause. And this is the thing that holds between God and creatures. For he allowed everything to be, to live, and to move, and for this reason he esteems them

all, nor can he not esteem them.²⁸ . . . And so, in return, creatures that are not altogether degenerate, and devoid of all sense of God, love him. . . . Indeed, those creatures that progress the closest to *God in similarity love him more.* (7.3 [iv]); my emphasis)

The radical leanings of Conway's thought come into clear focus. She is prepared to pursue to unorthodox conclusions (what she considers) the implications of God's attributes, thereby casting aside assumptions at the heart of orthodox Christianity, Judaism, and Islam. To summarize, she understands attributes like God's goodness, love, and generosity to entail that every one of the infinity of creatures loves all the others and will be morally enhanced by the others. Due to Conway's robust rendering of sympathetic harmony, every creature is able, through a series of incarnations, to increase that love and thereby contribute to the goodness of the whole. Perfectibility is secured because God "works perpetually, and his work is to create or to give essence to Creatures, in accordance with that eternal Idea or wisdom that is in him" (3.7). The divinity's perfection and wisdom demand that divine love extend to all creatures equally, and not just to human beings. Thanks to the love and robust sympathetic bond that each creature X has for the others, X will move through a series of incarnations, which will ultimately result in X's robust love for its creaturely comrades, and for God. In X's eventual state of increasing perfectibility, X will esteem all other creatures, and be esteemed by God. However, because goodness is the strongest "magnet of love" and because God is the "highest good," the divinity will ultimately be loved most (7.3 [v]).

---

28 Conway here refers to Paul, Acts 17:28. She would have used the King James Version of the Bible, which reads, "for in Him we live and move and have our being."

## Conclusion: Conway's Universalist Love

I have claimed that Conway's account of love seems unique in the history of love. Like the ancient approaches to love explored in chapters 1 to 6, she sets divine transcendent love as life's ultimate goal and examines how we human lovers connect to a transcendent good or, in Hanley's words, to the phenomena "beyond the self" (Introduction, p. 5). But, unlike them, she proposes that the means to the transcendent is *through* intimacy and affection: the individual lover seeks (and invariably finds) a sensorily intense pleasure in its beloved. Like the passionate bond between two human lovers explored in chapters 10 to 12 (and related Reflections), every one of the infinity of creatures will "taste" the pleasure of its beloved, which for Conway is *all* other creatures. Such affective love is (to return to Hanley's words) "subjectively experienced by selves that exist in specific times and places, and which are determined by the conditions of their embodiment and their capacities for sensation" (see the first section of this chapter).

The most remarkable feature of Conway's position, however, is its radical universalism. Every one of the infinity of creatures will move through a series of species and (eventually) be humanlike before transitioning to an angelic state in which each will encourage all the others to move constantly toward ever-greater perfection. The road to increasing perfectibility is paved with the pleasures of love. Conway's lovers seek and will eventually attain the transcendent, but first must learn to love and *feel* the pleasure of *loving* all other creatures. Only by recognizing the love-worthiness of all things will we discover the fullness of God's love, a love exemplified in the fact that the world's current dust and debris are bound to become angelic. In the end, her commitment to creaturely love occupies a liminal space within which the transcendent and immanent intermingle.

As a final comment, I would like to make explicit the importance of working on understudied figures like Anne Conway in the history of philosophy and doing so in a way that allows their views to be taken seriously *on their own terms*, and not merely in response to their more famous canonical contemporaries. As I hope to have suggested here, Conway's thought occupies a unique place in philosophy's past, especially in our thinking about the concept of love.

# Reflection

LOVE, SCULPTURE, AND GIAN LORENZO BERNINI

*Ingrid Rowland*

The seventeenth-century Jesuit Athanasius Kircher, a German based in Rome, described his own creative frenzies as "storms of the mind" (*mentis aestus*), great cloudbursts of energy from one of the first people to write extensively about what he called the earth's "athmo-sphaera." Kircher's contemporary and sometime collaborator, the sculptor Gian Lorenzo Bernini, expressed both artistic creation and spiritual ecstasy in more tangible terms: not as celestial winds, but as transports of carnal love. Few artists have shown such relish for the challenge of giving material shape to ethereal ideas, especially in such earthbound materials as stone and clay, but nothing could intimidate Bernini in his pursuit of art. At eighteen, he thrust his own leg into a fire to find out how his patron saint Lawrence must have felt roasting to martyrdom on a grill, holding up a mirror all the while to examine his own anguished face and commemorate the agony in a statue. His painted self-portraits show a skinny youth, and then a gaunt man, looking back at the viewer (himself, of course) with huge, voracious eyes.

# LOVE, SCULPTURE, AND GIAN LORENZO BERNINI

FIGURE 8A.1  Gian Lorenzo Bernini, *Saved Soul*, 1619. Rome, Palazzo di Spagna. Wikimedia Commons.

In 1619, a prodigy of twenty, Bernini carved two life-size marble busts for a Spanish monsignor, Pedro de Foix Montoya (see Figure 8A.1): two souls newly admitted to Heaven and to Hell (see Figure 8A.2). The *Saved Soul* is a graceful young woman with a classical profile and a garland of celestial roses on her head, but the *Damned Soul* is once again Gian Lorenzo making agonized faces in a mirror.

For all her exquisite detail, the *Saved Soul* lacks the personality, and hence the interest, of her doomed companion; Bernini clearly worked best with a real person in front of him. The 1637 portrait

FIGURE 8A.2  Gian Lorenzo Bernini, *Damned Soul*, 1619. Rome, Palazzo di Spagna. Wikimedia Commons.

bust of his mistress Costanza Piccolomini provides a riveting case in point (see Figure 8A.3).

Costanza was twenty-three when he committed her to stone just for the joy of it; only a wealthy sculptor who worked with preternatural swiftness could have afforded such a luxury. With no one but himself to please, he could experiment as radically as he wanted with techniques for conveying color, texture, and temperature; there was no need to plead for artistic license. And so a rasp darkens the marble of Costanza's hair (dark brown in life) by introducing tiny patterns of light and shade onto the stone's roughened surface. The effect rarely appears elsewhere in Bernini's work, perhaps because it looked too "unfinished," but unfinished

FIGURE 8A.3 Gian Lorenzo Bernini, *Portrait of Costanza Piccolomini*, 1636. Florence, Museo del Bargello. Wikimedia Commons.

it is not: the rest of the bust has been polished to a radiant glow by loving hands. Since the time when he carved his unnaturally perfect *Saved Soul*, Bernini had learned that one of the keys to a convincing human figure was irregularity: a half-buttoned button, a stray lock of hair, an unruly beard. Costanza is no exception: her tight braid has worked loose and her blouse is slightly undone, revealing a bosom that is not just "like marble," a poetic cliché as old as the Greeks—it *is* marble, but it still seems to give off heat. She has opened her mouth as if she is about to speak (and so that we can see her teeth, proof positive of her lover's professional virtuosity), and these effortlessly casual details, along with the way she seems to change constantly as we circle around her portrait, bring this worked piece of rock to disconcerting life. It is hard to believe that such a strong, attractive personality really belongs to a disembodied stone head.

With his portrait of Costanza Piccolomini, Bernini has come as close as any sculptor could to Pygmalion's mythical feat of turning a statue into a living person. He clearly loved her, and thanks to the painstaking research of art historian Sarah McPhee, we now know that there was much to love about this exceptionally strong, intelligent woman.[1] Sadly, her affair with Bernini ended just a year later, in 1638, when, at forty, he spied her in the arms of his brother Luigi, a hot-blooded twenty-five and brimming with talent in his own right. Mad with jealousy, Gian Lorenzo chased Luigi across Rome, sword in hand, until their mother finally broke the two apart. As for Costanza, Bernini hired two thugs to slash her face, an injury usually meted out to prostitutes. She survived the attack, as well as a criminal sentence for adultery—she was married to Bernini's assistant Matteo Bonucelli—and eventually became a prominent art dealer in Rome. Gian Lorenzo was swiftly married and fathered fourteen children. Like the Italian painter Giotto, who joked that he painted by day and "sculpted" his large family by night, or Mozart's Don Giovanni, who declared that "there is no more fertile talent than mine," Bernini's creative energy evidently bore a strong erotic charge. Furthermore, he transmitted that charge to his viewers; his success lies not only in his technical virtuosity but also in the fact that many of his sculptures, both male and female, are frankly sexy.

The eros can be playful or serious, or, often, both at once, as in Bernini's *David* of 1622–1624 (see Figure 8A.4).

David's name in Hebrew means "beloved," and the Bible suggests that his libido was as epic as Bernini's own. He was famously heroic

---

[1] Sarah McPhee, *Bernini's Beloved: A Portrait of Costanza Piccolomini* (New Haven, CT: Yale University Press, 2012).

FIGURE 8A.4  Gian Lorenzo Bernini, *David*, 1622–1624. Rome, Galleria Borghese. Wikimedia Commons.

and famously attractive, as well as a splendid poet. Bernini's statue, tellingly, is another self-portrait, at least from the neck up. Unlike Michelangelo's colossal *David*, which Gian Lorenzo must have admired as a child in Florence, his hero is life-size, a mortal face-to-face with mortal danger. This dynamic uncertainty is typical of Baroque art and architecture: rather than a languid victor, we see David's pure tension just before he releases it in a lighting-swift, decisive action. The outcome of his contest with the giant Goliath may be uncertain, but not David's ferocious will—Bernini, looking in a mirror, has seen his own adamant ambition and imprinted it on the luminous Carrara marble. The muscular body is not that of a boy—this David is a grown man, and an extremely well-built man at that. For the time being, a fluttering drapery covers his genitals, but once he finally turns to whip his slingshot through the air, by any law of physics it will have to fall away and leave him majestically naked. As every viewer will quickly realize, the next moment in this stone man's life is going to be extremely interesting.

Bernini's most famously erotic statue is one that portrays divine rather than earthly love: his *Ecstasy of Saint Teresa* (1645–1652), which gives solid form to a vision that this otherwise down-to-earth Spanish nun experienced around 1560 and described in vivid detail. An angel of God appeared to her, and in her plain language she describes what happened next:

He wasn't big, but rather small, his face so alight that he seemed to be one of those very high angels, who seem to be all on fire.... In his hands I saw a long spear of gold and at the tip of the spearhead there seemed to be a bit of fire. This he seemed to put through my heart a few times and it went as deep as my entrails. When he removed it he seemed to take them with it, and he left me entirely afire with a great love of God. The pain was so great that it made me moan, and such is the sweetness that this great pain gives me that there is no desire for it to end, nor is the soul content with anything but God.[2]

Bernini bathes his statue in heavenly light through a hidden window paned in yellow glass shining down on a burst of gilded bronze rods to represent celestial rays; in Rome's Baroque churches, that golden glow was a convention to indicate a source beyond the sun, indeed beyond the edge of the universe (see Figure 8A.5). The young angel's wicked smirk and Teresa's open-mouthed swoon are certainly meant to remind us of ordinary human sex—but not just

---

2  *La Vida de la Santa Madre Teresa de Iesus*, Chapter 29, *Obras de la Gloriosa Madre S. Teresa de Iesus, Fundadora de la Reforma de la Orden de Nuestra Señora del Carmen*, vol. 1 (Madrid: Bernardo de Villa-Diego, 1678), 189–190 (my translation).

FIGURE 8A.5  Gian Lorenzo Bernini, *Ecstasy of St. Teresa*, 1645–1652. Rome, Santa Maria della Vittoria. Wikimedia Commons.

ordinary human sex. Aside from her face, her languid left hand, and her feet (the right relaxed, the left curled around a spur of rock), the physical Teresa does not exist. Bernini conveys her ecstasy not by the motions of her body but by the agitation of her drapery, thereby carving an experience that takes place somewhere in the soul, or the imagination, but definitely not only in the flesh. The surpassing "sweetness of this excessive pain" is *like* the stinging pleasure of eros, but Bernini means for us to see it as infinitely greater, just as Heaven's golden light, at least in a Baroque imagination, is infinitely more intense than the mere clarity of the sun. His Teresa, moreover, is as barefoot as an angel. The real Teresa, and the members of the order she founded, the Discalced ("Shoeless") Carmelites, went around in socks and sandals.

CHAPTER 9

# Love in Kant and the Enlightenment

*Melissa Seymour Fahmy*

*Love* is not a word frequently associated with Immanuel Kant. Terms like "duty" and "respect" are more likely to spring to mind at the mention of his name, especially for those familiar with only his 1785 work, *Groundwork of the Metaphysics of Morals*. But even a less-than-careful reader of Kant's practical philosophy will quickly recognize that Kant takes the subject of love quite seriously. For one thing, Kant recognizes a host of different kinds of love: self-love, love of nature, love of one's neighbor, practical love, duties of love, sexual love, love that wishes well, and love that finds delight in others. Had Kant regarded love as unimportant, he would not have bothered to distinguish so many different kinds.

My aim in this chapter is to articulate the significance of the concept of love in Kant's practical philosophy. I begin in the next section by examining the influence of eighteenth-century sentimentalist thinkers on Kant, as well as his subsequent rejection of sentimentalism. In the third section, I examine three types of love (self-love, love of nature, and love of other human beings) that are pre-moral in the sense that, while they are relevant to the moral life of human beings, they are not matters of duty. In the following section, I consider the types of love that are matters of moral obligation, examining the Kantian notions of practical love, duties of love, and friendship. I also consider Kant's remarks regarding the deliberate cultivation of particular sensible feelings and affective dispositions. In the closing part of the chapter, I endeavor to explain why Kant understood love to be indispensable to the moral life of human beings. Throughout the chapter, I argue that we do Kant a serious disservice if we wrongly assume that he took a hostile attitude toward all sensible feelings. While Kant's moral theory has an exclusively a priori foundation, his normative ethics takes seriously human neediness, vulnerability, and interdependency, and in doing so acknowledges the importance of both love and respect.

## Kant and the Moral Sentimentalists

In the 1760s and 1770s, Kant, like many of his contemporaries in Prussia, read translations of the work of prominent British moral sentimentalists, including Shaftesbury, Hutcheson, Hume, and Smith. A fundamental feature of the sentimental theory of morality is the centrality of moral feeling or moral sense. Speaking broadly, for the sentimentalists, moral motivation and judgment are ultimately grounded in certain kinds of feelings, particularly other-regarding feelings like benevolence and sympathy. During this period, Kant not only read these theorists, he cited them approvingly.[1] The influence of the British sentimentalists is in evidence in Kant's 1764 work *Observations on the*

---

1 See J. B. Schneewind, *The Invention of Autonomy: A History of Modern Moral Philosophy* (Cambridge: Cambridge University Press, 1998), 378; and Manfred Kuehn, *Kant: A Biography* (Cambridge: Cambridge University Press, 2001), 107–108, 132, and 176.

*Feeling of the Beautiful and Sublime.* There Kant makes the following declaration regarding moral principles and the foundation of morality.

> Thus true virtue can only be grafted only upon principles, and it will become the more sublime and noble the more general they are. These principles are not speculative rules, but consciousness of a feeling that lives in every human breast and that extends itself much further than to the special grounds of sympathy and complaisance. I believe that I can bring all this together if I say that it is the **feeling of the beauty and the dignity of human nature**. The first is a ground of universal affection, the second of universal respect. (O 2:217)[2]

The contrast to Kant's mature views on moral principles is striking; however, it is notable that even in this early work we see indications of Kant's view, articulated explicitly in the Doctrine of Virtue, that love and respect are two great moral forces.[3]

While Kant was never entirely uncritical of the British sentimentalists, by the time he published his first major work of ethical theory he had fully rejected sentimentalism. Kant's primary reason for rejecting

---

[2] Citations in the text refer to the following English translations of Immanuel Kant's work. All volume and page numbers refer to the Prussian Academy edition of Kant's *gesammelte Schriften*.

    O    = *Observations on the Feeling of the Beautiful and the Sublime*, trans. Paul Guyer, in *Immanuel Kant: Anthropology, History, and Education*, ed. Günter Zöller and Robert B. Louden (Cambridge: Cambridge University Press, 2007);

    G    = *Groundwork of the Metaphysics of Morals*, trans. Mary Gregor (Cambridge: Cambridge University Press, 1997);

    KpV = *Critique of Practical Reason*, trans. Mary Gregor (Cambridge: Cambridge University Press, 1997);

    KU = *Critique of the Power of Judgment*, trans. Paul Guyer and Eric Matthews (Cambridge: Cambridge University Press, 2001);

    R    = *Religion within the Boundaries of Mere Reason*, trans. Allen Wood and George Di Giovanni (Cambridge: Cambridge University Press, 1998);

    MS = *The Metaphysics of Morals*, trans. Mary Gregor (Cambridge: Cambridge University Press, 1996);

    LE = *Lectures on Ethics*, trans. Peter Heath (Cambridge: Cambridge University Press, 1997);

[3] For an extended discussion of this passage, see Ryan Patrick Hanley, *Love's Enlightenment: Rethinking Charity in Modernity* (Cambridge: Cambridge University Press, 2017), 143–45. I return to the relationship between love and respect later in the chapter.

sentimentalism is rooted in his view that moral principles must have the character of *laws*, that is, they must be universal, necessary, and issue unconditional (categorical) commands. The ground of moral obligation cannot be found in anything empirical, including "the nature of the human being or in the circumstances of the world in which he is placed," because that which is empirical is necessarily contingent (G 4:389).[4] Rather, the ground of obligation must be sought "a priori simply in the concepts of pure reason" (G 4:389). Kant rejects moral sense theory insofar as it provisions morality with an unacceptably empirical foundation. He explains,

> *Empirical principles* are not at all fit to be the ground of moral laws. For, the universality with which these are to hold for all rational beings without distinction—the unconditional practical necessity which is thereby imposed upon them—comes to nothing if their ground is taken from the *special constitution of human nature* or the contingent circumstances in which it is placed. (G 4:442)

By grounding moral judgment and obligation on empirical properties like usefulness and agreeableness, moral sense theories cannot account for moral obligation's *necessary* and *unconditional* nature.

Kant's view appears to be that morality grounded in feeling can obligate us only insofar as we have the appropriate feelings; but whether we have the appropriate feelings is contingent on many factors, some beyond our control. "All rules derived from feelings are contingent, and valid only for beings that have such a feeling" (LE 29:625). However beautiful or noble moral feelings may be, they cannot bind us unconditionally or with absolute necessity. Furthermore, feelings vary from person to person, and from this it follows that if morality were grounded in feeling, we would not be morally bound to the

---

4 See also KpV 5:25–26.

same extent. "If [the prohibition against lying] rested upon the moral feeling, then anyone not possessed of a moral feeling so fine as to produce in him an aversion to lying would be permitted to lie" (LE 27:254).[5] Moral sense theory, like every other empirically based system of morality, is incompatible with Kant's mature understanding of morality as *laws of freedom*.

While Kant unequivocally rejected moral sense theories for the reasons articulated here, he does not abandon the more general notion that certain feelings are morally important. In his mature writings on ethics, Kant acknowledges and affirms at least two types of moral feelings: those produced solely by reason (e.g., moral feeling, respect for the moral law), as well as the more familiar empirically based feelings (e.g., sympathy)—feelings that Kant frequently refers to as "pathological."[6] While morality must seek its foundation in pure reason, Kant is sensitive to the dual nature of human beings. Though we are capable of autonomous behavior, we are merely *finite*, rational beings—that is, rational beings that are sensible and needy. The remainder of this chapter is devoted to explicating the different roles that Kant assigns to various types of love, as well as the closely related feelings of sympathy and gratitude.

## Love That Is Prior to Duty

This section aims to provide an account of three types of love that Kant regards as morally relevant yet not a matter of duty. I have labeled these types of love "prior to duty," although they are not all prior in the same sense. The first is self-love, a form of love that competes with the moral

---

5 See also LE 27:252–253.
6 Kant understands pathological feelings to be empirical in origin (rather than produced solely by reason) and connected with inclination and the feeling of pleasure. See KpV 5:72–80 for a comparison of these two types of feelings.

law for supremacy and must be made subordinate to the moral law if we are to be morally good. The remaining two types of love, love of nature and love of human beings (*Menschenliebe*), prepare human beings to be moral subjects. Kant maintains that love of what is beautiful in nature is "a disposition of sensibility that greatly promotes morality or at least prepares the way for it" (MS 6:443), whereas love of other human beings is one of four natural predispositions of the mind that are the "subjective conditions of receptiveness to the concept of duty" (MS 6:399). As previously noted, Kant recognizes that love can take many forms and can serve as both an impediment and an aid to morally good action and character.

## Self-Love

According to Kant, self-love is likely the first kind of love that human beings experience. Kant refers to the maxim of seeking one's own happiness as the maxim of *self-love*, and throughout his corpus he asserts that all human beings necessarily and unavoidably desire their own happiness.[7] "For us—dependent as we are on objects of the senses—happiness is by *nature* the first that we desire and desire unconditionally" (R 6:47). It is in virtue of our sensible nature that we not only desire happiness but need it as well. The relationship between the maxim of self-love and morality is not a simple one. On the one hand, two of the three predispositions that Kant identifies as predispositions to the *good* in human nature—animality and humanity—involve aspects of self-love. Animality involves mechanical self-love and constitutes a predisposition to the good insofar as it serves the ends of self-preservation, the propagation of the species, and community. Humanity involves a more sophisticated aspect of self-love, one that requires reason and comparison with others, but it too is a predisposition to the good insofar as it

---

[7] See G 4:415; KpV 5:25; MS 6:386–387.

serves the end of self-development.[8] While these forms of self-love give rise to inclinations that can become vices, Kant insists that "these predispositions in the human being are not only (negatively) *good* (they do not resist the moral law) but they are also predispositions *to the good* (they demand compliance with it)" (R 6:28).

At the same time, the claims of self-love present serious temptations to transgress the moral law. While the subjective principle of self-love is not inherently bad (and cannot be eradicated), it is neither a reliable guide to moral action nor a source of moral motivation.[9] The solution to this tension is to subordinate the maxim of self-love to the moral law. The difference between whether the human being is good or evil, Kant tells us, "must not lie in the difference between the incentives that he incorporates into his maxim ... but in their *subordination* (in the form of the maxim): *which of the two he makes the condition of the other*" (R 6:36). We may pursue our own happiness only insofar as it is compatible with the moral law. As Kant explains in the *Critique of Practical Reason*, "Pure practical reason merely *infringes upon* self-love, inasmuch as it only restricts it, as natural and active in us even prior to the moral law, to the condition of agreement with this law, and then it is called *rational self-love*. But it *strikes down* self-conceit altogether" (KpV 5:73).[10] Kant refers to this propensity to reverse this order, to make one's own happiness the condition for complying with morality, as *self-conceit* (KpV 5:74) and *radical evil* (R 6:37).[11] The point I wish to

---

8 For a discussion of Kant's notion of unsocial sociability, see Allen Wood, "The Final Form of Kant's Practical Philosophy," in *Kant's Metaphysics of Morals: Interpretive Essays*, ed. Mark Timmons (Oxford: Clarendon Press, 2002), 1–21.
9 See G 4:442; KpV 5:35.
10 Kant understands self-conceit to be a kind of self-satisfaction or arrogance. His distinction between *rational self-love* and *self-conceit* is likely influenced by Rousseau's concepts of *amour-propre* and *amour de soi*. See Hanley, *Love's Enlightenment*, 147–149.
11 For discussion of Kant's doctrine of radical evil, see Pablo Muchnik, *Kant's Theory of Evil: An Essay on the Dangers of Self-Love and the Aprioricity of History* (Lanham, MD: Lexington Books, 2009); and Sharon Anderson-Gold and Pablo Muchnik, ed., *Kant's Anatomy of Evil* (Cambridge: Cambridge University Press, 2010).

emphasize here is that Kant takes the demands of our sensible nature seriously. This is perhaps seen best in his doctrine of the highest good. Virtue without happiness, Kant argues, cannot be the whole and complete good (KpV 5:110). This is because human beings *need* happiness, and if they are virtuous, they are also *deserving* of happiness. The claims of self-love are legitimate and important, albeit only conditionally so.

## Love of Beautiful Inanimate Nature

In the *Critique of the Power of Judgment*, Kant maintains, "The beautiful prepares us to love something, even nature, without interest" (KU 5:267). He returns to this idea in the Doctrine of Virtue, where he proposes that this form of disinterested love, while not itself a moral feeling, nonetheless serves a moral purpose. There Kant writes,

> A propensity to wanton destruction of what is *beautiful* in inanimate nature (*spiritus destructionis*) is opposed to a human being's duty to himself; for it weakens or uproots that feeling in him which, though not of itself moral, is still a disposition of sensibility that greatly promotes morality or at least prepares the way for it: the disposition, namely, to love something (e.g., beautiful crystal formations, the indescribable beauty of plants) even apart from any intention to use it. (MS 6:443)

Kant's remark here is brief and mysterious. How, one might wonder, does aesthetic appreciation for beautiful inanimate nature prepare human agents for moral life? Though I cannot hope to do justice to the subject in this space, I briefly touch on two important points: first, that the beautiful can serve as a potent symbol of morality, and second, that the sensible feelings that accompany aesthetic appreciation are morally useful and indicative of a virtuous disposition.

First, the beautiful is a symbol of morality insofar as judgments of beauty are independent of our individual interests. In disinterestedly loving the beautiful we prepare ourselves to love the moral law.[12] While love of the moral law is not an attainable goal for human beings, it is nonetheless "the consummate perfection of a disposition devoted to the law" (KpV 5:84). Aesthetic appreciation is frequently accompanied by feelings of pleasure and delight that are notably independent of our sensible inclinations. Given that Kant associates a joyful (*fröhlich*) heart with the temperament of virtue (R 6:23–24), Robert Louden concludes that love of what is beautiful "serves as preparation for morality by properly cultivating the feeling of joyfulness."[13]

## Love of Human Beings

One of the most intriguing and underexplored aspects of Kant's moral psychology is found in section 12 of the "Introduction to the Doctrine of Virtue." This section bears the title "Concepts of What Is Presupposed on the Part of Feeling by the Mind's Receptivity to Concepts of Duty as Such." In this brief but remarkable passage, Kant proclaims that there are four "moral endowments" or "natural predispositions of the mind (*praedispositio*)" that are necessary "for being affected by the concept of duty" (MS 6:399). These endowments are *moral feeling, conscience, love of one's neighbor*, and *self-respect*, which Kant calls the "*subjective* conditions of receptiveness to the concept of duty" (MS 6:399). Kant explains, "To have these predispositions cannot be considered a duty; rather, every human being has them, and it is by virtue of them that he can be put under obligation" (MS 6:399).

This is clear evidence that Kant regards at least one form of love as morally necessary for human beings. What more can we say about this particular moral endowment? Unfortunately, this question is not easily answered. Though Kant devotes a subsection to "Love of Human

---

[12] See Paul Guyer, *Kant and the Experience of Freedom: Essays on Aesthetics and Morality* (Cambridge: Cambridge University Press, 1993), 94–130.
[13] Robert Louden, *Kant's Impure Ethics: From Rational Beings to Human Beings* (Oxford: Oxford University Press, 2010), 112.

Beings" (*Von der Menschenliebe*), in these paragraphs he appears to be more interested in discerning which forms of love can and cannot be duties. Here he tells us that "a duty to love is an absurdity.... To do good to other human beings insofar as we can is a duty, whether one loves them or not.... Benevolence always remains a duty, even toward a misanthropist.... Beneficence is a duty" (MS 6:401–402). These comments will likely strike the reader as frustratingly off topic. We have already been told that there can be no duty to have or acquire any of the four moral endowments; thus we already know that *Menschenliebe*, whatever it may be, cannot be a duty.

Most scholars concur that *Menschenliebe* must be a kind of felt love, for felt love (unlike *practical love*) is the kind of love that cannot be commanded by duty.[14] In the Collins lecture notes, Kant proclaims, "All love is either love that wishes well [*Liebe des Wohlwollens*], or love that likes well [*Liebe des Wohlgefallens*]. Well-wishing love consists in the wish and inclination to promote the happiness of others. The love that likes well is the pleasure we take in showing approval of another's perfections" (LE 27:417). If we can take Kant at his word here, this would appear to leave us with two options: *Menschenliebe* is either a predisposition toward well-wishing love or well-liking love. Elsewhere I have defended the former, arguing that the form of love Kant calls benevolence (*Wohlwollen*) is the seemingly best interpretation of the moral endowment Kant calls *Menschenliebe*.[15] Benevolence, I argue, appears to be related to the duties of love in a manner that is analogous to how self-respect is oriented to duties to oneself. Love that consists

---

14 Notably, *Menschenliebe* is neither practical love nor pathological love—the former because it cannot be commanded as duty, and the latter because "Consciousness of [the moral endowments] is not of empirical origin; it can, instead, only follow from consciousness of a moral law" (MS 6:399). I discuss both types of love in the following section. For a discussion of the distinction between practical love and pathological love in Kant, see also Christoph Horn, "The Concept of Love in Kant's Virtue Ethics," in *Kant's Ethics of Virtue*, ed. Monika Betzler (Berlin: De Gruyter, 2008), 147–173.

15 See Melissa Seymour Fahmy, "Kantian Practical Love," *Pacific Philosophical Quarterly* 91 (2010): 313–331. There I focus on the definition for benevolence that Kant offers at MS 6:452, namely, "satisfaction in the happiness (well-being) of others."

in the wish to promote the happiness of others, as well as a disposition to find satisfaction in others' happiness, primes us to be receptive to the particular obligations of love the way that self-respect primes us to resist temptations to sloth or servility.

While there can be no duty to have this predisposition to love our fellow human beings (*Menschenliebe*), we can nonetheless have a duty to *cultivate* this feeling of love in ourselves. Kant makes this point explicitly in reference to the predisposition he calls *moral feeling*, explaining, "Obligation with regard to moral feeling can be only to *cultivate* it and to strengthen it through wonder at its inscrutable source" (MS 6:399–400).[16] While there are several competing interpretations regarding the kind of felt love *Menschenliebe* is, that Kant regards a predisposition to a certain kind of felt love as morally necessary for human beings is remarkable in itself.[17]

## Love and Ethical Obligation
### One of Two Great Moral Forces

In the Doctrine of Virtue, Kant divides our ethical duties to other human beings into the following categories: duties of love, duties of respect, and duties of friendship. Our duties of love are further divided into duties of beneficence, gratitude, and sympathetic participation. Prior to explicating these particular duties, Kant offers the following comparison:

---

16 It is notable that the paragraph in the lecture notes cited above concludes with, "I am not only obligated to well-doing, but also to loving others with well-wishing, and well-liking, too" (LE 27:418).

17 For commentary on *Menschenliebe*, see Wood, "The Final Form of Kant's Practical Philosophy"; Paul Guyer, "Moral Feelings in the Metaphysics of Morals," in *Kant's Metaphysics of Morals: A Critical Guide*, ed. Lara Denis (Cambridge: Cambridge University Press, 2010), 130–51; Dieter Schönecker, "Kant über Menschenliebe als moralische Gemütsanlage," *Archiv für Geschichte der Philosophie* 92 (2010): 133–175; Christopher Arroyo, "Kant on the Emotion of Love," *European Journal of Philosophy* 24 (2016): 580–606; and Pärttyli Rinne, *Kant on Love* (Berlin: De Gruyter, 2018).

In speaking of laws of duty (not laws of nature) and, among these, of laws for human beings' external relations with one another, we consider ourselves in a moral (intelligible) world where, by analogy with the physical world, *attraction* and *repulsion* bind together rational beings (on earth). The principle of **mutual love** admonishes them constantly to *come closer* to one another; that of the **respect** they owe one another, to keep themselves *at a distance* from one another; and should one of these great moral forces fail, "then nothingness (immorality), with gaping throat, would drink up the whole kingdom of (moral) beings like a drop of water" (if I may use Haller's words, but in a different reference). (MS 6:449)[18]

While this passage is notable for multiple reasons, the feature I wish to emphasize is the fact that Kant explicitly identifies love as a necessary *moral force*. Love is not merely a moral adornment, as Kant suggests elsewhere (MS 6:458); it is a moral force on par with respect. Indeed, the point Kant endeavors to make in this opening passage is that love and respect are both necessary and complementary. Human beings could not do without either; this much is perfectly clear. The analogy Kant makes with the physical laws of attraction and repulsion is more puzzling. The analogy suggests that love and respect pull us in opposite directions, one beckoning us to come closer to our fellow human beings, the other admonishing us to keep our distance. Marcia Baron has argued that the metaphor exaggerates the contrast and opposition between love and respect and does not accurately represent Kant's considered view.[19] Christine Swanton, on the other hand, insists that Kant got things exactly right in portraying love and respect as

---

18 Christine Swanton has described this passage as "arguably one of the most profound passages in normative ethical theory." See Swanton, *Virtue Ethics: A Pluralistic View* (Oxford: Oxford University Press, 2003), 99.
19 Marcia W. Baron, "Love and Respect in the *Doctrine of Virtue*," in *Kant's Metaphysics of Morals: Interpretative Essays*, ed. Mark Timmons (Oxford: Oxford University Press, 2002), 391–407. Baron further argues that the relationship between love and respect is asymmetrical: "Respect does not need love as love needs respect" (397).

opposing forces of approaching and keeping one's distance. The crucial point, according to Swanton, is that love and respect must exist in equilibrium.[20]

## Practical Love

In the passage just quoted, Kant clearly identifies love as a vital moral force. But what sort of love is Kant talking about here? He immediately adds the following qualification:

> In this context, however, **love** is not to be understood as *feeling*, that is, as pleasure in the perfection of others; love is not to be understood as *delight* in them (since others cannot put one under obligation to have feelings). It must rather be thought as the maxim of *benevolence* (practical love), which results in beneficence. (MS 6:449)

The love that Kant identifies as a moral force and a law of duty (principle) is a *maxim* rather than a *feeling*. Kant frequently contrasts what he calls *practical love* with more familiar forms of pathological love, such as "love as an inclination" (G 4:399) and "love that is delight" (MS 6:402, 6:449, 6:450). Practical love is not a feeling or an inclination, and it is the only form of love that can be commanded directly as a duty. But what is practical love? Kant most often describes practical love in terms of benevolence (*Wohlwollen*). Practical love is "the maxim of benevolence" (MS 6:450), "the maxim of benevolence ... which results in beneficence" (MS 6:449), and "active benevolence and so having to do with the maxim of actions" (MS 6:450). It would appear that all that is required to resolve the mystery of practical love is to figure out what Kant means by benevolence.

---

20 Swanton, *Virtue Ethics*, 104–110. See also Swanton, "Kant's Impartial Virtues of Love," in *Perfecting Virtue: New Essays on Kantian Ethics and Virtue Ethics*, ed. Lawrence Jost and Julian Wuerth (Cambridge: Cambridge University Press, 2011), 391–407.

In the Doctrine of Virtue, Kant describes benevolence in dispositional terms. It is an attitude we take toward the well-being of others. Benevolence, Kant tells us, "is satisfaction in the happiness (well-being) of others" (MS 6:452), "taking delight in the well-being of every other" (MS 6:452). Benevolence is something that we can and should extend to all others, and this is partly because it costs us so little to do so. As Kant explains, "Now the benevolence present in love for all human beings is indeed the greatest in its *extent*, but the smallest in its *degree*; and when I say that I take an interest in this human being's well-being only out of my love for all human beings, the interest I take is as slight as can be. I am only not indifferent with regard to him" (MS 6:451).

Accounting for the nature of Kantian practical love is complicated by Kant's use of two similar terms: beneficence (*Wohlthun*; *Wohltätigkeit*) and benevolence (*Wohlwollen*). Sometimes Kant explicitly distinguishes these two concepts: "Benevolence is satisfaction in the happiness (well-being) of others; but beneficence is the maxim of making others' happiness one's end" (MS 6:452). At other times, he appears to define one in terms of the other:

> It is quite obvious that what is meant here is not merely benevolence in *wishes*, which is, strictly speaking, only taking delight in the well-being of every other and does not require me to contribute to it (everyone for himself, God for us all); what is meant is, rather, active, practical benevolence (beneficence), making the well-being and happiness of others my *end*. (MS 6:452)

Where Kant previously defined practical love as *active benevolence* (MS 6:450), he now defines *active, practical benevolence* as *beneficence*. Is practical love beneficence? The key to understanding the relationship between benevolence and beneficence—indeed, the key to understanding duties of love, period—is to acknowledge their relationship to the relevant obligatory end. Kant labels duties of love "duties of virtue" and tells us "Only *an end that is also a duty* can be called a **duty**

**of virtue**" (MS 6:383). The concept of an end that is also a duty is a distinctive feature of Kantian ethics, one that has perhaps not received the attention it is due from nonspecialists.[21] It is not enough that we act in certain ways, nor is it enough that we act in certain ways from the motive of duty. We must make the obligatory ends—one's own perfection and the happiness of others—*our ends*. We make these ends our own by committing ourselves to a lifetime of promoting the ends, but also by working to transform ourselves such that we truly recognize these ends as our own. My own considered view, which I defend elsewhere, is that Kantian practical love, the maxim of benevolence, is a duty of self-transformation. We fulfill this duty by striving to develop the disposition that takes pleasure in the well-being (happiness) of others.[22] What is beyond dispute is that practical love is a matter of *willing*, not *feeling*. But as I hope to make clear now, just because we cannot *will* ourselves to have certain feelings, it does not follow that we have no obligations with regard to other-regarding feelings.

*Duties of Love*

BENEFICENCE

As mentioned earlier, the duties of love are beneficence, gratitude, and sympathetic participation. The duty of beneficence is a duty "to promote according to one's means the happiness of others in need, without hoping for something in return" (MS 6:453). One of the defining features of this duty is that it is wide, meaning that "the duty has in it a latitude for doing more or less, and no specific limits can be assigned to what should be done" (MS 6:393). The fundamental duty of love is the duty to make the obligatory end—others' happiness—*my*

---

[21] Kant specialists have acknowledged the significance of obligatory ends for quite some time. See, for instance, Barbara Herman, *Moral Literacy* (Cambridge, MA: Harvard University Press, 2007).

[22] See Fahmy, "Kantian Practical Love." For an alternative interpretation, see Kate Moran, "Much Obliged: Kantian Gratitude Reconsidered," *Archiv für Geschichte der Philosophie* 98 (2016): 330–363.

end. If others' happiness is my end, then I must be rationally committed to bringing about this end. However, it is impossible to promote everyone's happiness. The latitude permitted by this duty leaves it to the discretion of the agent to determine whose happiness to promote, as well as how and when.[23] Rather than being simply permissive, this discretion calls for a high degree of thoughtfulness and sensitivity. Kant cautions his readers to promote the happiness of others in accordance with *their* conception of happiness, not one's own.[24] Beneficence requires stepping outside of oneself and seeing things from another's perspective. Kant further recognizes that being the recipient of another's beneficence can be humbling if not humiliating, and admonishes his readers to deliver beneficence in a way that minimizes these painful feelings, even practicing beneficence "in complete secrecy" (MS 6:453).

### GRATITUDE

While beneficence is a duty, beneficence is not, strictly speaking, *owed* to others in a manner comparable to respect (MS 6:448–450). Others cannot demand beneficence from us as their due. When we promote the happiness and well-being of others, we put them under an obligation of gratitude. While Kant identifies gratitude as one of our duties of love, gratitude is peculiar among the duties of love in virtue of the features that it shares with respect. Gratitude, Kant tells us, "consists in honoring a person because of a benefit he has rendered us" (MS 6:454). Unlike beneficence, which is *meritorious*, gratitude is *owed* to one's benefactors. Furthermore, Kant explains, "Gratitude is not, strictly speaking, love toward a benefactor on the part of someone he has put under obligation, but rather *respect* for him" (MS 6:458). Why

---

23 See MS 6:390–393. For discussion of the latitude permitted by the wide duty of beneficence, see Thomas E. Hill Jr., *Dignity and Practical Reason* (Ithaca, NY: Cornell University Press, 1992), ch. 8; Marcia Baron, *Kantian Ethics Almost without Apology* (Ithaca, NY: Cornell University Press, 1995), ch. 3; Jens Timmermann, "Good but Not Required?—Assessing the Demands of Kantian Ethics." *Journal of Moral Philosophy* 2 (2005): 9–27; and Melissa Seymour Fahmy, "On Virtues of Love and Wide Ethical Duties," *Kantian Review* 24 (2019): 415–437.

24 MS 6:388, 6:454.

then is gratitude a duty of love? Its status as a duty of love must be explained in terms of its connection to the obligatory end, others' happiness, as well as the other duties of love. Notably, Kant calls gratitude a *sacred* duty in virtue of the fact that failures of gratitude "can destroy the moral incentive to beneficence in its very principle" (MS 6:455). In a recent and exceptionally thoughtful paper, Kate Moran argues that ingratitude threatens the moral incentive to beneficence by engendering misanthropy in human beings and "obscuring facts of human interdependence and neediness."[25] Duties of love are not duties belonging to all rational beings; rather they are obligations belonging to *human beings*—beings that are both rational and sensible. The duties of love are the rational response to human neediness and interdependence, and gratitude in an important aspect of this.

### SYMPATHETIC PARTICIPATION

Kant's duty of sympathetic participation is perhaps the most difficult to explicate, but also where we see the strongest residual influence of the sentimentalist thinkers. Unlike the duty of beneficence, the duty of sympathetic participation is explicitly about one's feelings. The heading above §34 of the Doctrine of Virtue is "Sympathetic Feeling Is Generally a Duty." The duty of sympathetic participation furthermore entails both a direct and indirect component. Kant summarizes the third duty of love in the following sentence:

> But while it is not in itself a duty to share in the sufferings (as well as the joys) of others, it is a duty to sympathize actively in their fate; and to this end it is therefore an indirect duty to cultivate the compassionate natural (aesthetic) feelings in us, and to make use of them as so many means to sympathy based on moral principles and the feelings appropriate to them. (MS 6:457)

---

[25] Moran, "Much Obliged," 354. See also Houston Smit and Mark Timmons, "The Moral Significance of Gratitude in Kant's Ethics," *The Southern Journal of Philosophy* 49 (2011): 295–320.

The indirect component of the duty of sympathetic participation is a duty to employ our natural receptivity to share in the joy and sadness of others in order to cultivate these feelings in ourselves and employ them for moral purposes. But what moral purposes do they serve? Elsewhere I have argued that the primary purpose these feelings serve is the direct duty of sympathetic participation, which is a duty to share actively in the fate of others by communicating our sympathetic feelings to those whose joy or sorrow we share and otherwise engage others with sensitivity and understanding.[26] Other commentators have argued that cultivated sympathetic feelings play a motivational role by prompting us "to perform specific acts of helping others," which, in light of the latitude permitted by wide duties of virtue, are not strictly speaking required.[27] Still others maintain that cultivated sympathetic feelings serve an epistemic function by drawing our attention to morally salient features and providing us with pertinent information.[28]

Kant's *Groundwork* example of the coldhearted benefactor who "tears himself out of [his] deadly insensibility" in order to act beneficently from the motive of duty alone has provoked disapproval and ridicule since its publication.[29] I mention this example in order to highlight the fact that Kant describes the coldhearted benefactor as one who is bereft of "all sympathy with the fate of others." The word he uses in this passage of the *Groundwork*—*Teilnehmung*—is precisely the term he employs to describe the third duty of love in the Doctrine of Virtue. This should be sufficient evidence for rejecting the unfortunately popular view that the coldhearted benefactor is the Kantian

---

26 Fahmy, "Active Sympathetic Participation."
27 Baron, *Kantian Ethics Almost without Apology*, 220. See also Henry Allison, *Kant's Theory of Freedom* (Cambridge: Cambridge University Press, 1990), 166–167.
28 See Nancy Sherman, *Making a Necessity of Virtue: Aristotle and Kant on Virtue* (Cambridge: Cambridge University Press, 1997), 145–146; and Hill, *Dignity and Practical Reason*, 55.
29 The best-known example of this may be Friedrich Schiller's epigram, which begins, "Gladly I serve my friends, but alas I do so with pleasure," though evidence suggests Schiller's intention was to caricature Kant's view.

moral paragon. He clearly is not. He is simply morally *better* than the agent who benefits others from inclination without any thought to duty, which is the only point Kant endeavors to make with the example.

## FRIENDSHIP

The duty of friendship is not exclusively a duty of love. Rather, friendship, according to Kant, "is the union of two persons through equal mutual love and respect" (MS 6:469). The love Kant appears to have in mind here is benevolence (*Wohlwollen*), the love that finds satisfaction in the happiness and well-being of others.[30] Kant, like Aristotle, recognizes that friendship comes in many forms. The type of friendship that is an ethical duty, according to Kant, is "a purely moral one" subject to principles and rules, and not friendship grounded in feeling alone or mutual advantage (MS 6:470–471). The Kantian duty of friendship is like the duty of moral perfection insofar as both oblige agents to strive for a moral ideal that is unachievable by human beings in practice. In his discussion of the duty of friendship, Kant returns to the metaphor of attraction and repulsion: "For love can be regarded as attraction and respect as repulsion, and if the principle of love bids friends to draw closer, the principle of respect requires them to stay at a proper distance from each other" (MS 6:470). Here we see the idea of equilibrium that Swanton suggested.[31] Love needs respect in order to prevent it from becoming overbearing or paternalistic, but there is more to it than that. The union of love and respect is the fertile soil from which trust blooms between friends. As Kant explains it, in true friendship the friend enjoys the freedom of being able to reveal

---

30 See MS 6:469, 6:451–452.
31 We see the idea of equilibrium even more clearly in Kant's remark that "it will be difficult for both to bring love and respect subjectively into that equal balance required for friendship" (MS 6:470). In the case of friendship, love and respect must be balanced within each friend, and each friend's love and respect for the other must be balanced with respect to her friend's love and respect.

himself to another (his thoughts on others, the government, religion, etc.) with confidence that his disclosures will not be used against him, either intentionally or accidentally. The true friend keeps her distance by acknowledging that she is merely a trustee of the secrets disclosed by her friend; they are not hers to share as she pleases. Kant appears to regard trust as the true good of friendship rather than the favors I can count on from my friend when I am in need, and for trust we must have a union of love and respect (MS 6:470–472).

## Love as Feeling

We have seen that Kant held firm to the view that love as a feeling cannot be commanded by duty (G 4:399). A duty *to love*, he tells us, is an absurdity (MS 6:401). We have duties *of love* to other human beings, but these duties fundamentally involve maxims of action rather than feelings. In light of this, one might be tempted to draw the conclusion that Kant endorsed the view that loving feelings have little role to play in the moral life of virtuous human beings (beyond the spark of feeling that is one of the four moral endowments mentioned earlier). Numerous passages in Kant's practical philosophy suggest that this conclusion is mistaken. In the opening section of Part II of the Doctrine of Virtue Kant proclaims, "*Love* and *respect* are the ***feelings*** that accompany the carrying out of these duties" (MS 6:448, emphasis added). A few pages later, in his concluding remarks on the duty of gratitude, Kant explains that gratitude

> involves not regarding a kindness received as a burden one would gladly be rid of . . . but taking even the occasion for gratitude as a moral kindness, that is, as an opportunity given one to unite the virtue of gratitude with love of man, to combine the *cordiality* of a benevolent disposition with *sensitivity* to benevolence (attentiveness to the smallest degree of this disposition in one's thought of duty), and so to cultivate one's love of human beings. (MS 6:456)

While a duty to love may be an absurdity, Kant appears to believe that a duty to *cultivate* love of human beings is not.

In explicating our duties of love to other human beings, it is common for Kant to reference the biblical injunction to "love God above all and your neighbor as yourself."[32] He references this commandment in all three of his major published works on ethics, as well as his lectures on ethics, and associates loving one's neighbor with practical love of human beings.[33] In his discussion of *Menschenliebe* in the introduction to the Doctrine of Virtue, Kant offers the following interpretation:

> So the saying "you ought to *love* your neighbor as yourself" does not mean that you ought immediately (first) to love him and (afterwards) by means of this love do good to him. It means, rather, *do good* to your fellow human beings, and your beneficence will produce love of them in you (as an aptitude) of the inclination to beneficence in general. (MS 6:402)[34]

I am sympathetic to the worry that Kant is being psychologically naïve or excessively optimistic in this passage. One might reasonably wonder about the danger of resentment and misanthropy when our beneficence is met with ingratitude or, depending on the beneficiaries, too little reciprocity. This worry aside, Kant clearly endorses the view that we can and should cultivate love as a feeling (inclination). Indeed, this appears to be his view, at least in part, because he takes the biblical command seriously. Kant offers a similar interpretation in the *Critique of Practical Reason*:

---

[32] This commandment is found in the Gospels of Mark (12:30–31), Matthew (22:38–39), and Luke (10:27). In this context, see also David McPherson's chapter in this volume.
[33] See G 4:399 and MS 6:450.
[34] See also LE 27:417–419.

> *Love God above all, and your neighbor as yourself...* as a commandment it requires respect for a law that *commands love* and does not leave it to one's discretionary choice to make this one's principle. But love for God as inclination (pathological love) is impossible, for he is not an object of the senses. The same thing toward human beings is indeed possible but cannot be commanded, for it is not within the power of any human being to love someone merely on command. It is, therefore, only *practical love* that is understood in that kernel of all laws. To love God means, in this sense, to do what He commands *gladly*; to love one's neighbor means to practice all duties toward him *gladly*. But the command that makes this a rule cannot command us to *have* this disposition in dutiful actions but only to *strive* for it. (KpV 5:83)

Again, the idea is that while love as a feeling cannot be commanded directly, self-cultivation—even *affective* self-cultivation—can be. Here Kant does not recommend any course of action (e.g., beneficence) that might enable us to cultivate a loving disposition toward others, thus avoiding the worry articulated earlier. To be clear, the love we are speaking of here is a universal love of human beings simply because they are human beings. It is not the partial love we have for particular others. This, I take it, is consistent with the doctrine of Christian love and charity that is expressed in the command to love your neighbor as yourself.

### The Significance of Love

It is abundantly clear that Kant regarded love as a feeling, as well as its close cousins, practical love, gratitude, and sympathy, as indispensable to the moral life of human beings. Without a predisposition to love of other human beings, we would not be receptive to the concepts of duty and could not be put under obligation (MS 6:399). Though the moral law cannot command love as a feeling, it can oblige us to cultivate love of our fellow human beings (MS 6:452), the inclination to beneficence (MS 6:402), appreciativeness (MS 6:455), and sympathetic joy and sadness (MS 6:457), so that we may execute our duties to others *gladly* (KpV 5:83). If there is a lingering question, it is *why* Kant believed love to be indispensable to the moral life of human beings.

The answer appears to lie in human finitude. As *finite* rational beings, we necessarily desire our own happiness; indeed, we *need* happiness, but we cannot know for certain what will make us happy, and even if we did, the necessary means to our happiness might lie well beyond our reach.[35] But it is precisely our neediness that puts us in a particular moral relation to other human beings. As Kant describes it, "The maxim of common interest, of beneficence toward those in need, is a universal duty of human beings, just because they are to be considered fellowmen, that is, rational beings with needs, united by nature in one dwelling place so that they can help one another" (MS 6:453). Love—in all its forms, both practical and sensible—draws us closer to one another so that we might satisfy the needs of others and have our own needs met.

Commentators have suggested that cultivated moral feelings play a number of specific roles in Kant's theory. They remove affective obstacles to the performance of morally good or required actions, such as hostility, resentment, and selfishness.[36] Cultivating positive affective dispositions averts the vices of hatred, as well as plays an efficacious role achieving a particular moral end. For instance, I may be more likely to succeed in promoting the happiness of others if I sympathize with them.[37] Kant scholars have also argued that our affective responses express and reveal what we care about and value. To have the right affective responses (e.g., benevolence) is simply to be properly oriented

---

[35] See G 4:417–419; KpV 5:36–37.
[36] See Allison, *Kant's Theory of Freedom*, 167; Guyer, *Kant and the Experience of Freedom*, 379; Hill, *Dignity and Practical Reason*, 55; and Anne Margaret Baxley, *Kant's Theory of Virtue: The Value of Autocracy* (Cambridge: Cambridge University Press, 2010), 166–167.
[37] See Allison, *Kant's Theory of Freedom*, 166–167.

vis-à-vis moral objects.[38] I find all of these suggestions to be plausible and important.

But there is one significant role that Kant denies to sensible moral feelings—even morally cultivated sensible feelings—and that is the role of incentive to morally worthy action. This is one of the places where Kant clearly parts company with the sentimentalists. According to Kant's doctrine of transcendental freedom, we *can* act as morality demands simply because we recognize that this is rationally required of us, and we *only* act in a morally worthy way when we do so.[39] Kant's view remains consistent from the *Groundwork* through the *Metaphysics of Morals*; there is one moral incentive, and it is the motive of duty. As Kant explains in the second *Critique*, "It is very beautiful to do good to human beings from love for them and from sympathetic benevolence, or to be just from love of order; but this is not yet the genuine moral maxim of our conduct, the maxim befitting our position among rational beings as *human beings*" (KpV 5:82). It is our duty to cultivate this moral disposition to duty in ourselves such that "the law being by itself alone the incentive, even without the admixture of aims derived from sensibility" (MS 6:446). In Kant's ethics we find lofty aspirations of moral perfection—indeed, moral *purity*—conjoined with realistic appraisals of human vulnerability. This seems to me precisely as it should be. We should endeavor to become the best that we can be; however, we will surely fail in this endeavor if we ignore or deny our own limitations.[40]

---

38 See Baron, *Kantian Ethics Almost without Apology*, 205; Sherman, *Making a Necessity of Virtue*, 147; Hill, *Dignity and Practical Reason*, 57; and Baxley, *Kant's Theory of Virtue*, 165.
39 See G 4:400–411; KpV 5:81–82.
40 I am grateful to Ryan Hanley for his very helpful suggestions on an earlier version of this chapter.

CHAPTER 10

# Beyond the realms of dream that fleeting shade

ROUSSEAU ON ROMANTIC LOVE

*Eve Grace*

"Love, life of the soul, come sustain mine about to faint away.... Happiness, joys, transports, how sharp are your arrows! Who can bear to be struck by them?" (*J*, 33)[1] So in *Julie ou la Nouvelle Héloïse* does Julie's lover Saint-Preux cry out, in a tone of elation indistinguishable from anguish, as he finally finds out that his beloved is in love with him. There is general agreement that Rousseau did as much as anyone

---

[1] The chapter title is from Percy Bysshe Shelley, "Alastor," 2.205–206.
    With the exception of *Emile*, trans. Allan Bloom (New York: Basic Books, 1979) [*E*], Rousseau's works are cited from *The Collected Writings of Rousseau* [CW]. Titles will be abbreviated with page numbers as follows: *Rousseau, Judge of Jean-Jacques: Dialogues*, CW 1 [*D*]; *Discourse on the Origins of Inequality (Second Discourse)* CW 3 [*SD*]; *The Confessions and Correspondence, including the Letters to Malesherbes*, CW 5 [*C*; *MA*]; *Julie or the New Heloise*, CW 6 [*J*]; *Essay on the Origin of Languages and Writings related to Music*, CW 7 [*EO*]; *The Reveries of the Solitary Walker*, CW 8 [*R*]; *Letter to D'Alembert*, CW 10 [*A*]. Occasional references to the Pléiade edition of Rousseau's works [OC] are cited by volume and page number.

to set fire to the Romantic imagination: his novels[2] enthused throngs of readers and in great measure gave birth to the Romantic sensibility, which governed thought and art long after his death, and from which we still today draw a "romantic" understanding of love. The ideal of romantic love bursts into flame above all in the pages of his indescribably popular epistolary novel *Julie*. The virtuous Julie, after many dark struggles with a love in conflict with the duties prescribed by society and by her own conscience, and even though she finally seemed to have found peace, suddenly dies—or does she commit suicide?—confessing the love of which, try as she might, she cannot cure herself. Perhaps even more than his *Confessions, Julie* shaped a new ethos according to which the life of the heart, and its lifeblood, love, is for a serious human being—in the words of that great disciple of Rousseau, Stendhal—"the greatest of matters or rather the only one."[3] Indeed, few philosophers since Plato have reflected so much, and so comprehensively, on love as did Rousseau.

That Rousseau, the apostle of sentiment, sired Romanticism is so generally acknowledged as to be a threadbare platitude. The extent of his influence in this regard is difficult to exaggerate: like a contagion, Rousseau's words (or at least what they evoked if one had not actually read them) were, so to speak, absorbed into the blood.[4] In his unfinished *Triumph of Life,* the fervent Shelley, who held Rousseau's name "sacred," described Rousseau's thought as a flame from which were lit "a thousand beacons."[5] Rousseau's writings, and in particular the letters in *Julie* that "made an entire epoch weep," spawned what can only be

---

2 In French, *romans.*
3 Stendhal, *La chasse au bonheur* (Paris: E. Sansot, 1913), 67.
4 Gregory Dart, "Rousseau and the Romantic Essayists," in *Jean-Jacques Rousseau and British Romanticism: Gender and Selfhood, Politics and Nation,* ed. Russell Goulbourne and David Higgins (Bedford Square: Bloomsbury Academic, 2017), 211. Cf. W. J. T. Mitchell, "Influence, Autobiography, and Literary History: Rousseau's Confessions and Wordsworth's the Prelude," *ELH* 57 (1990): 648.
5 Percy Bysshe Shelley, "Triumph of Life," ll. 206–207.

called a mania for Rousseau.[6] In the words of George Sand, who baptized herself "son of Jean-Jacques," Rousseau awakened everyone to the "thirst for the ideal."[7] This longing, however, is accompanied as much by doubt as it is by hope.

> Here the self-torturing sophist, wild Rousseau
> The apostle of affliction, he who threw
> Enchantment over passion . . .
> . . . his was not the love of living dame . . .
> But of ideal beauty.[8]

In *Emile*, Rousseau has Emile's tutor say that he will depict love to him "as the supreme happiness of life, because in fact it is" (*E*, 327). Yet this rapturous note is followed by sad tones: "This supreme happiness is a hundred times sweeter to hope for than to obtain. . . . O good Emile . . . Enjoy a long time before possessing. . . . I shall not shorten this happy time of your life. . . . I shall prolong it as much as possible. Alas, it has to end, and end soon" (*E*, 419). The hours of our lives are few, but the hours we can count as happy to have been alive are far fewer. Worse yet, we seem made to be wretched: human beings have "unbounded desires" that hold "eternal deprivation" in store for them (*J*, 73; *E*, 81–82). Human life is a struggle with limitless, nebulous longing; the romantic soul soars like a Gothic spire into an infinite sky. As Chateaubriand expresses the problem in *René*, "I am accused of always giving up on the goal that I could reach: alas, I am only seeking an

---

6 Jean-Louis Bellenot, "Les formes de l'amour dans la 'Nouvelle Héloïse', et la signification symbolique des personnages de Julie et de Saint-Preux," *Annales de la Société Jean-Jacques Rousseau* 33 (1953–1955): 149–150.
7 George Sand, "Quelques réflexions sur Jean-Jacques Rousseau," *Revue des Deux Mondes*, Période initiale, 4ème série, 26 (1841): 711.
8 Lord Byron, *Childe Harold's Pilgrimage*, canto 3, ll. 725–728, 734–740.

unknown good the instinct for which pursues me. Is it my fault if I find limits everywhere, if what is limited has for me no value whatever?"[9]

> We look before and after
> And pine for what is not.[10]

For Rousseau, as for Plato before him, the fact that human beings yearn for a happiness beyond anything they have experienced or can clearly imagine, and that this yearning is inherent to the fullest experience of love, makes love a matter for the most serious reflection (*MA*, 579). Two human beings falling in love do not merely stop for a stirring interlude in the largely pedestrian routine that is otherwise human life. For love casts us out of the everyday and orients us toward what is deepest in us. When one is truly in love, nothing else compares; for love, human beings will joyfully cast aside all that they would ordinarily cling to with all their might—pleasures, interests, life itself. That from the point of view of such sensible concerns there is no madder passion than love is an old, old story.

> Set me as a seal upon your heart,
> as a seal upon your arm;
> for love is strong as death,
> passion fierce as the grave.
> Its flashes are flashes of fire,
> a raging flame....
> If one offered for love
> all the wealth of his house,
> it would be utterly scorned. (Song of Songs 8:6–7)

---

9 François-René de Chateaubriand, *René*, in *Atala, René* (Paris: Librarie de Firmin Didot Frères), 126–127.
10 Percy Bysshe Shelley, "To a Skylark," ll. 86–87.

The Romantics who arose in Rousseau's wake celebrated passion which, without warning, can engulf life and burn it to cinders. The generation of *Sturm und Drang* who read *The Sorrows of Young Werther* and for whom Rousseau was "ancestor and patron" saw in him "the prophet of a new gospel of nature" who dethroned reason and crowned the passions in its place.[11] In *Julie* Rousseau examines the dialectic of love, tracing every subtle shade of the passion as it unfolds, with all of its attendant sentiments, through all of its hopes and trials.[12] Similarly, the final book of what is often considered Rousseau's central work, *Emile or On Education*, a philosophical treatise in the form of a bildungsroman, is crowned by a love match. Emile's love for Sophie is presented not only as the pinnacle of his happiness but as the keystone of his education, for his great passion gives him the strongest reasons to aspire to be truly himself (*E*, 433).

Both novels celebrate the calm joys of marriage and family. The real heart of *Julie*, however, is not the serene domestic bliss of Clarens, but rather the turbulent love affair between Saint-Preux and Julie, for which there is no happily ever after, except in Julie's hope that her virtue will finally be blessed in the afterlife by a reunion with her beloved (*J*, 610). *Emile* seems, unlike *Julie*, to have a cheerful ending: it concludes with a vision of the amorous couple contemplating the vista of their future conjugal happiness. A sequel drafted by Rousseau with the ominous title *Emile and Sophie or, the Solitaries*, however, develops a more melancholic strand of thought in *Emile* according to which the love celebrated by the young newlyweds cannot last. Surely no reader of Romantic novels would be surprised by this, for in them love is troubled, a source of affliction and even ruin. Yet although love can easily drive us to despair, only in its transports are we portrayed as experiencing life most deeply and intensely. For could the domestic scenes that

---

[11] Ernst Cassirer, *Rousseau Kant Goethe*, trans. James Gutmann, Paul Oskar Kristeller, and John Herman Randall Jr. (Princeton, NJ: Princeton University Press, 1947), 13.
[12] Cf. Bellenot, "Les formes de l'amour," 164–169.

are to come, no matter how joyful, be as exhilarating, as absorbing, as the agitation of a heart led on by sweet hope (*J*, 263; *E*, 419, 447)?

For Rousseau, however, love is momentous not only or even principally because it sets the heart in motion. When we fall in love, we are struck by beauty. One's beloved is beautiful, beautiful almost to perfection, and what is perfectly beautiful inspires devotion; there is "no true love without enthusiasm, and no enthusiasm without an object of perfection" (*E*, 391; *J*, 70). One's response to one's own beautiful beloved appears as the first inarticulate intimation of a human nature that longs to lose itself in eternal perfection.[13] Part of this powerful and mysterious human response to beauty is also a kind of self-forgetting, a belief that if we devote ourselves to that beautiful person or cause, we could finally be completely, invulnerably happy (*E*, 287; *J*, 184). As Stendhal puts it, "Beauty is nothing other than the *promise* of happiness."[14] Rousseau repeatedly insists that this "love of the beautiful" is "as natural to the human heart as the love of self" (*A*, 267). For Rousseau, then, as for Plato, falling in love opens us to an immeasurable, heartbreaking longing for something—what?—just beyond reach, that—if we could only touch it—seems to be divine rather than human. And when one's beloved tells you he feels the same, it suddenly does, for a time, seem within reach.

Yet for Rousseau, what reason shows us about nature makes of love nothing but an illusion. His philosophical account of nature, which is given its most radical presentation in the *Second Discourse*, tacitly assumes the truth of the materialist account (or its modern scientific version, modern evolutionary science) that he elsewhere so forcefully attacks. According to that account, human beings are hardly distinguished by "purely spiritual acts about which the laws of mechanics explain nothing"; they are rather to be regarded as "mechanical beings, which act only through impulsion, and whose action [one] could

---

13 Plato, *Symposium* 206a–212a.
14 Stendhal, *De l'amour*, 2 vols. (Paris: Librairie universelle de P. Mongie, 1822), ch. 17 note, 1: 63n1.

calculate only from the laws of motion" (*SD*, 26; *R*, 72). The human animal differs from other animals only in the degree to which its passions and desires are profoundly mutable, transforming themselves under the impact of what it comes to experience as pleasant and useful and to imagine as happiness or perfection (*SD*, 27, 86; *E*, 39). In Rousseau's presentation, however, human or rather animal life has no end or *telos*; there is no good but pleasure (*SD*, 27). Specifically human beings, then, would seem to be animals who by some accident are given to fantasizing and who have become peculiarly clever at enacting their fantasies.

What then is love, in Rousseau's view, according to what reason tells us about nature? It is nothing but delayed or frustrated sexual desire, which—by dint of imagining and reimagining its object, like hunger when it is starved—enhances and magnifies it until it floats almost entirely loose from its moorings in physical desire (*E*, 329). The imaginary object to which we now aspire shapes and fixes desire to such a degree that we can no longer be satisfied by the crude impulse that was its first impetus. Love, in short, is a sublimated sexual drive, the energy of delayed or inhibited sexual desire channeled into belief in a story we have come to tell ourselves about the object of our desire. Desire by nature is sporadic, limited, and content to accommodate itself to the occasion; human animals couple and part with equal ease (*SD*, 39, 89). Once they begin to compare one with another, however, ideas of merit and beauty give birth to preferences, and therefore to a particular passion for *this* human being, such that we cannot imagine ever wanting any other. Burgeoning ideas of merit and beauty seem to reflect nothing, however, but whichever shifting fancies happen to flatter the lover's *amour-propre*. *Amour-propre*—the willful desire to outshine others, from which arises "what is best and worst among men, our virtues and our vices"—drives us to seek one who is more lovable than any other (*SD*, 63, 91–92).

The more difficult we are to please, however, the more difficult it is for us to please others, for others rank us as much as we do them. The awareness that we are dependent on another's preference gives rise to what for Rousseau is the moral element of love. For now, desire subjects us to another's will whether we will or no: we must please, and please more than any other. If the simplest physical desire makes one primp, the wish to be dearest to one's dear can forge one into the being we imagine our beloved imagines of us (*E*, 214–215). It is from this perspective that the stuff of love is largely *amour-propre*, that Rousseau can claim that the "moral element of love" is "an artificial feeling, born of the usage of society" (*SD*, 38–39).

What then in Rousseau's account of love's origins, one might ask, differentiates it from his adversary Voltaire's derisive definition of love in his *Philosophical Dictionary*? Voltaire defines love as follows:

> Here one must have recourse to the physical; it is the fabric of nature that imagination has embroidered. Do you want to have an idea of love? . . . Look at the proud horse [being led] to the quiet mare which awaits him, and which turns her tail to the side in order to receive him, look at his eyes sparkle, hear his neighs . . . but don't be jealous, and think of the advantages of the human species. . . . Since men have received the gift of perfecting everything that nature accords them, they have perfected love. [They have] increased the pleasure of touch . . . made the organs of voluptuousness more sensitive. . . . All the other sentiments then enter into love. . . . *Amour-propre* especially tightens all these bonds. One applauds oneself for one's choice, and a crowd of illusions are the ornaments of this piece of work of which nature has laid the foundations. That is what you have over the animals.[15]

Despite his protestations to the contrary, then, Rousseau's account of human beings and of love seems as relentlessly reductionist as any that he decries. For according to his own *Second Discourse*, a human being

---

15  Translation mine. Voltaire then sardonically adds that one of the ways human beings have "perfected" nature is to become subject to widespread syphilis.

falling in love is not awakened to a deeper longing to find her true nature and destination but seems rather to be merely an ape building castles in Spain.[16]

There seems then, in Rousseau's view, to be a chasm between what reason and what our sentiments tell us love is. If in addition to reasoning scientifically about nature, we also turn our attention to the way in which we experience love, we find that human beings do experience themselves as radically divided between these two different accounts of love. Rousseau is far from denying that as sensual beings we are subject to a very different "passion of love," a carnal furor whose delights need no description. "I know two kinds of love, which are very distinct, very real, and which have almost nothing in common, although they are both very vivid, and both different from tender friendship" (*C*, 23). The two can be felt for the same person, although Rousseau wonders whether one could bear both together at their most passionate (*C*, 183–184). While the perfection of love seems to be to love someone body and soul, the dream that both loves are always ardently felt for the same person does not always come true (*C*, 23). For to fall deeply into what Rousseau sometimes calls "true love" is to be touched by the beauty of the soul, which the face and body only seem to reflect and express (*E*, 214). One can love one's beloved so intensely that one does not want the sexual act, not from any kind of asceticism, but because that is not what one yearns for (e.g., *J*, 41, 115). It is not in the intensity of pleasure that the true lover exalts; there is a splendor about love that no mere physical satisfaction could ever possess. The true lover is nothing like a Monsieur Bovary, "his heart full of the night's joys, his spirit at peace, his flesh content," who ruminates on his happiness "like those who, after dinner, keep masticating the taste of the truffles they are digesting."[17] Love is *moving*—touching, tender—precisely because

---

16 Guillaume de Lorris and Jean de Meun, *Le Roman de la Rose*, ed. Felix Lecoy (Paris: Champion, 1965), l. 2430.
17 Gustave Flaubert, *Madame Bovary*, 1.5 (Paris: Michel Lévy Frères, 1857), 49.

you do not have yourself your beloved, who makes your heart ache, as you might a good meal.

By distinguishing between physical sensation and moral sentiments, Rousseau seems potentially to open the door again to a significant difference between body and soul. Both the sensation of pleasure and the sentiments of joy or happiness, however, are a matter of feeling rather than reason (*SD*, 92). Sentiments are not sensations because they are not simply reducible to the latter; they are not a physical response to sensation, but the inner, felt movements of our passions. The passions, Rousseau argues, are the responses of an "active sensibility" that is different from the passive sensibility of one's body, as can be attested by the fact that they can directly contradict our sensations (*D*, 112).

A notable sign that the "soul" as we experience it is perplexing and difficult to understand simply in materialist terms is that it can enthusiastically cast aside pleasure and even life for something that is emphatically not those things. What we find beautiful above all, Rousseau avers, are noble acts. This love of what is beautiful or noble is the core of devotion to duty, of the capacity of human beings to impose laws on themselves and to sacrifice for justice, not out of calculation, but in the holy name of right. Scorning mere interest, the lover of virtue is inspired by the resplendent image of the noble soul who freely engages in self-sacrifice. We see, then, that self-love seems to carry with it a passionate attachment to qualities of character that go far beyond their usefulness in securing us other goods: for "what is going to one's death for one's interests" (*E*, 289)? This love of the beautiful is, according to Rousseau, the principle of the conscience (*A*, 267; *J*, 183–184; *E*, 287). Sentiments—something for which, according to some of Rousseau's statements, materialists do not account—not sensations, are the real heart of human life.

Self-love, according to Rousseau, the origin and principle of all of our passions, has affection and the desire for affection—not just the desires for security and pleasure—embedded within it. The term "self-love" means that affection for ourselves precedes, and is the motivation for, the desire to preserve ourselves (*E*, 212–213). The first sentiment we feel, then, is pleasure in the sentiment of our own existence, not anxiety or fear (*SD*, 28). In warmer climes, where need is less pressing, the first words spoken by emerging human beings were "aimez-moi" (love me), not "aidez-moi" (help me), as is the case in the harsher regions of the North where necessity governs (*EOL*, 316). If the first sentiment is to love oneself, the second is to seek to have others love us, to feel for us as we feel for ourselves. While we seek what is useful to us, we do not only find those who help us useful; we grow to love those who help us, not because they help us, but because they *want* to help us, apart from any expectation of return. Free gifts are precious because they are given to me for no other reason than because it is I (*E*, 213). The desire to be loved by those who approach us is, in Rousseau's presentation then, inherent to self-love.[18]

The desire to be loved in part fuels the constant comparisons we make among other human beings and, first and most assiduously of all, between them and ourselves. From these comparisons arise ideas of merit and beauty, and from these, the idea of virtue or perfection of self. Rousseau argues repeatedly that human beings are naturally moved by and seek to emulate human beings they find resplendent, and especially those qualities that seem most resplendent. The soul that seems most worthy of love is one that is great in gratitude, generosity, and justice, in the qualities that cannot be had without vigor, those that show panache, and in which therefore one takes pride (*E*, 215, 234, 391, 444). If both love for oneself and love of the beautiful are natural to human beings, then human beings will want to be worthy objects in their own eyes, and to believe that they have some merit and beauty will be crucial to their happiness.

It is when we see ourselves through the eyes of one we love, however, that enthusiasm for virtue reaches its highest pitch, and it is when

---

[18] Speaking of himself, Rousseau says, "To be loved by everyone who approached me was my keenest desire" (*C*, 12).

human beings love the beauty of virtue that love becomes magnificent. For, again, there is "no true love without enthusiasm, and no enthusiasm without an object of perfection" (*E*, 391). The flaws one sees in one's beloved may be more endearing than virtues seen coolly in another; but such flaws can be loved only when they are found along with what seem like shining beauties of character. For "love without esteem never existed in a decent heart because it is only the qualities he values that anyone loves in his beloved" (*E*, 430–431). If there is a lofty joy in raising a throne to virtue in one's own heart, then in raising a throne to one's beloved one joyfully raises it above all to his virtue (*E*, 391). Through love then, we erect the most respectable and the greatest moral authority, the only authority to which we gladly subject ourselves: for to love someone is to respect her judgment, to wish to do as he wills, to glory in her respect and affection. Love is ennobled by inspiring love of the noble, and in turn crowns virtue with its loveliest prize. For in love we win the sweetest of affirmations that we come close to the beauty of character to which we aspire. When one loves, one wants to be loved; one wants to inspire in another the same heady sentiments that the other inspires in one (*E*, 337).

> In love everything is only illusion. I admit it. But what is real are the sentiments for the truly beautiful with which love animates us and which it makes us love. This beauty is not in the object one loves; it is the work of our errors. So, what of it? Does the lover any the less sacrifice all of his low sentiments to this imaginary model? Does he any the less suffuse his heart with the virtues he attributes to what he holds dear? Does he detach himself any the less from the baseness of the human *I*? (*E*, 391)

Love, then, not reason, is the greatest teacher of virtue. The lover, entirely absorbed in her beloved, delights in forgetting herself for her ideal and in emulating the image of herself that she sees in her lover's eyes. "Where is the true lover who is not ready to immolate himself for his beloved, and where is the sensual and coarse passion in a man who is willing to die?" (*E*, 391). The original "romances," such as the *Romance of the Rose*, were tales of chivalry and gallant love; the crowning jewel of these tales was the depiction of devotion unto death to one's beloved. In *Emile*, Rousseau tells a story that illustrates the "noble empire" that love can exercise on the human soul.

> Brantôme says that in the time of Francois I a young girl who had a talkative lover imposed an absolute and unlimited silence on him, which he kept so faithfully for two whole years that it was believed he had become mute as a result of illness. One day in the midst of company, his beloved—who, in those times when love was practiced with mystery, was not known to be such—boasted that she would cure him on the spot and did so with the single word "Speak." Is there not something grand and heroic in that love? What more could the philosophy of Pythagoras—for all its ostentation—have accomplished? (*E*, 393)

One who inspires such love can send "her lovers with a nod to the end of the world, to combat, to glory, to death, to anything else she pleases" (*E*, 393). For Rousseau, such devotion is not simply the picturesque if melodramatic way people used to think of love; it is not incidental but essential to love. Rousseau protests that then, as now, it was common to "make fun of the paladins." "That is because they knew love, and we no longer know anything but debauchery. When these romantic maxims began to become ridiculous, the change was less the work of reason than of bad morals" (*E*, 391). Real passion makes its object its idol and seeks to set it in Heaven (*J*, 11–12).

To aspire to be loved by one's beloved not only inspires one to be a better human being; to be loved is virtually the condition by which we become ourselves. In his very last words in the *Reveries of the Solitary Walker*, Rousseau resurrects himself as a young man, and recalls when he first met the woman by the grace of whose love he could say that he truly lived.

> Today, Palm Sunday, it is precisely fifty years since I met Mme. de Warens.... For a long time yet before possessing her, I only lived in and for her.... No day passes but what I recall with joy and tenderness this unique and brief time of my life when I was myself, fully, without admixture and without obstacle, and when I can genuinely say that I lived. (*R*, 89; cf. *C*, 40)

One sometimes sees someone in love so transformed as to become almost a different person. One might think this is mere pretense, but according to Rousseau that would be a superficial interpretation. The lover is not pretending: his sentiments have genuinely changed as he attempts to embody what his lover sees in him. If the only real mirror in which one can see oneself is another, and the only judgment to which one willingly submits is a loving one, then without one's other, one is only a fragment of what one could be. Rousseau goes so far as to say that if one did not love, one would not really live: without the experience of loving and being loved, one would not develop the habit of sentiments that alone make us truly feel and know one's existence, and the habit of affectionate feelings that make it enjoyable (*C*, 87). Rousseau's encounter with "Maman," then, is the kind of lucky accident we wish to think of as fate, because in it lies the salvation of one's life.[19]

"The first of my needs, the greatest, the strongest, the most inextinguishable, was entirely in my heart: it was the need for an intimate society and as intimate as it could be; it was above all for this that I needed a woman rather than a man, a lover rather than a friend."

---

19 For an account of the explicitly theological language Rousseau uses to describe this encounter in the *Confessions*, see Felicity Baker, "Portrait of the Object of Love in Rousseau's *Confessions*," in *Representations of the Self from the Renaissance to Romanticism*, ed. Patrick Coleman, Jayne Lewis, and Jill Kowalik (Cambridge: Cambridge University Press, 2000), 175–177.

For this even "the closest of union of two bodies could not . . . be enough": "one would need two souls in the same body" (*C*, 348). Rousseau here follows a suggestion Montaigne makes during his account of his unbounded love or friendship for La Boétie: Montaigne describes the pair as joined so closely that between them there was no seam; yet, he adds, if their bodies were joined, they would have been as close in every way as it was possible to be.[20] Yet physical communion, no matter how sweet, would in the end remind one that one can never be as close as one longs to be. This longing to be seamlessly joined is articulated perhaps most famously by Aristophanes in the myth that Plato has him tell in the *Symposium*; the myth speaks to what lovers often say—that they have found their "other halves."[21] In the myth, human beings were originally two souls in one body; sundered by the gods in punishment for their pride, each one of us, now a fragmented, lonely being, spends the rest of existence hoping to heal this wound by finding one's one and only other half in order to be whole again. Aristophanes's myth reveals part of what we seem to long for when we are in love: that one's love be governed by fate, not mere accidents of fortune. His myth also captures the uncanny "sympathy of souls" Rousseau points to, with which from the first word, with the first look, one can care so much for and—correctly—so confidently trust in someone one has barely met (*C*, 43–44).

In Rousseau's view the myth only serves to show how far these hopes are beyond our grasp. The old human dream to be so close that even touch is too distant are vain: we are now forever partial or severed beings; we try so ardently to clasp one another tightly and to join together, but we never can; the moment we seem to fuse is all too soon the moment we must part. Love in Rousseau's depiction is chiefly sorrow: for through love we seek to fulfill longings that are not only

---

20 Michel de Montaigne, *Essais* 1.28. Rousseau therefore corrects Montaigne, who does not seem to think that the love of bodies and of souls can be united in the same person.
21 Plato, *Symposium* 189d5–191d3.

impossible to fulfill, but in tension with one another. We both aspire to what is beautiful and also long for seamless union. Yet were one to achieve such a union, love would die: real intimacy would mean familiarity, and Rousseau is adamant that love *is* enthusiasm for a "chimera, lie, and illusion," for someone seen from a distance.[22] Imagination adorns, magnifies, and gradually transmutes one's beloved into a being so radiant with the promise of happiness that love becomes both the crown and heart of a life beyond compare:

> In the salt mines of Salzburg, a tree branch stripped by winter of its leaves is thrown into the abandoned depths of the mine. Two or three months later, it is taken out, covered with glittering crystals. The smallest [twigs] ... are adorned with an infinite number of shifting, dazzling diamonds. One can no longer recognize the original branch.[23]

Distance intensifies hope of what might be to cast an iridescent veil over what we desire, inflaming longing into love. If we did not see things through this veil and instead saw them as they truly are, Rousseau tells us, "there would be no more love on earth" (*E*, 329). Once we attain the beloved object, the very closeness we yearn for stifles love, for in everything, habit kills the imagination (*E*, 231). One "does not fantasize what one beholds; imagination no longer embellishes anything one possesses" (*J*, 569). We see another as beautiful, then, precisely because we do not see her. When we stop loving we no longer even see the same person, and love often dies as thoroughly as if it had never been, turning to hate, or worse yet, disgust (*J*, 372–373). Once our sentiments change, the "magic veil drops ... love disappears," and with it, the promise of any happiness that lasts (*E*, 329).[24] The dream of perfect

---

22 Hence, in part, Rousseau's insistence on chasteness for both men and women.
23 Stendhal, *De l'amour* 1:8. Translation mine.
24 The French word for veil is *prestige*, which means a magic illusion or spell.

union with the beautiful beloved is therefore a delusion or, to put it more nicely, an unattainable ideal: to be with the one you love is to lose him.

The imaginary transfiguration that gives rise to the deepest romantic love is the product of sublimation, that is, of unsatisfied physical desire. For Rousseau, satisfaction gradually extinguishes desire, for we only long for what we do not have. As such, romantic love necessarily destroys, as it fulfills, itself, for it lasts only as long as absence transforms one's beloved into a shining being who promises a perfect and lasting happiness even beyond one's dreams. The term "hopeless," then, is often added to the term "romantic": a romantic is someone who has longings that reality does not allow her to fulfill, and who cannot accept this impossibility and so still goes on longing.

> But wilt thou accept not
> The worship the heart lifts above
> And the Heavens reject not,—
> The desire of the moth for the star,
> Of the night for the morrow,
> The devotion to something afar
> From the sphere of our sorrow?[25]

The nature of human desire is such that not only does the moth desire from afar; it *must* desire from afar. Paradoxically, it is the obstacles to love that keep it alive: the "apparent obstacle, which seems to keep the object at a distance, is in reality what brings it nearer" (*A*, 313). If real love is love that endures, then the fate of Julie, who dies still so passionately enamored, represents not a tragedy but a triumph. When Saint-Preux must renounce ever seeing Julie again, Julie's friend Claire comforts him by telling him that his renunciation is actually a gain:

---

25 Percy Bysshe Shelley, "One Word Is Too Often Profaned," ll. 10–16.

> Your flame, I confess, has weathered the test of possession, time, absence, and all sorts of woes; it has overcome all the obstacles except the most powerful of all, which is to have no more obstacles to overcome, and feed only on itself. The whole world has never seen a passion weather this test, what right have you to hope that yours would have? Time would have compounded the disaffection of prolonged possession with advancing age and declining beauty.... Be comforted then for the loss of a possession that would have escaped you anyway and would moreover have robbed you of the one you still have. Happiness and love would have vanished at the same time. (*J*, 263; see also 42, 306)

Yet to be in love is to long for happiness, and to want something is to want to hold it; marriage, then, inevitably presents itself as the natural end of romantic love. Even in the best case, however, love subsides into a warm friendship: there is, then, an insurmountable tension between conjugal love and romantic love. In *Emile* the tutor tells Emile and Sophie that human beings would have paradise on earth if only one could "prolong the happiness of love in marriage." That, however, "has never been seen," and he does not hold out much hope for an exception to the rule (*E*, 476). Passion breathes only in freedom, whereas marriage consists of obligation: the act of love is the "sweetest" of all acts precisely and only because it is "the freest ... of all acts" (*E*, 359). But even in perfect freedom, love cannot last: "since the world began a pair of white-haired lovers sighing for each other has never been seen" (*J*, 306). Nothing endures in the human heart.

> Everything connected with man feels the effects of his transitoriness. Everything is finite and everything is fleeting in human life, and if the state which makes us happy lasted endlessly, the habit of enjoying it would take away our taste for it. If nothing changes from without, the heart changes. Happiness leaves us, or we leave it. (*E*, 447; cf. *J*, 71; *R*, 46)

Love blossoms only in a state of novelty or suspense, and therefore, while we want love to last at its most intense, intensity and duration cannot both be had.[26] "Do you believe, dear Emile," his tutor asks him, "that a man ... can be happier than you have been for these past three months? If you believe it, disabuse yourself. Before tasting the pleasures of life" (that is, before his marriage), "you have exhausted its happiness" (*E*, 447). Painfully aware as she is of this fact, Julie hopes to keep her own love alive in a state of sweet, yearning tranquility for as long as possible by deferring its consummation. But this yearning is painful as well as sweet. Hence Saint-Preux for his part declares that he cannot "prefer tranquility to supreme felicity." He is willing, for a quarter hour of bliss, to face the inevitable and painful loss of intensity to follow (*J*, 41–43). Is this not Hobson's choice?

Because human beings are all too painfully aware of how transitory love is, they all too soon see that love is a form of delusion (e.g., *J*, 68, 105, 229). Rousseau may therefore encourage us to see love as the kind of short-lived delirium that it is, to revel in it as the momentary stuff of our fragile happiness. Moreover, if it is our chimera we truly love, then we should realize that it is the sweet and radiant image of our beloved, not "the object to which we apply it," that we love. Our true love, then, is not our beloved, but love itself (*E*, 329). At the end of this road, we see a Rousseau who dreams at his ease, creating an ideal world "peopled with beings according to my heart"—while, he indicates, using various physical "supplements" to mimic the physical contact that cannot entirely be imagined (*MA*, 577–579; *E*, 333–334; *C*, 91, 278). Such autoeroticism could strike one as essentially ugly, and indeed pitiable. Yet since, in Rousseau's view, no actual object can or will ever live up to our imagination of it, such a deliberate embrace of fantasy might paradoxically acknowledge what most of us refuse to admit: my beloved is not as I see him; nor does he love me, but rather a figment of his mind.

---

26 Cf. Bellenot, "Les formes de l'amour," 182.

One may well ask, then: why move forward into willful delirium rather than retreat to the sober ground seemingly dictated by reason? Rousseau himself argues that human wisdom consists in directing our imagination so that it does not so inflame our passions as to put us at odds with the real world, for "all the pains which make us truly unhappy" arise from the conflict between our hopes and necessity (*E*, 219). Indeed, he cautions that "enthusiasm for the decent and fine" can soar to such a pitch that it can catastrophically make one reject reality altogether (*E*, 405).

Yet at the same time, in his view, human beings cannot *help* having illusions, for imagination, our most powerful faculty, shapes our passions and therefore entangles itself in everything we think and do; so powerful is it that it mixes something "moral" even in what seems to us to be only sensation (*E*, 81, 152, 333). More than our other needs or desires, the object of love, whether "real or imaginary," always exists in the imagination: the "existence of finite beings is so poor and so limited that when we see only what is, we are never moved" (*E*, 391, 158). And as much as one tries to be reasonable, when one falls in love, "Health, gaiety, well-being, contentment of mind are no longer anything but visions" by comparison to the smile one did not receive, or the letter one did (*E*, 83). Indeed, the happiness of love lies not in the actual possession of a good, but only in the anticipation of it; precisely insofar as we possess it, it ceases to be a good (*E*, 476). The contentment, order, and gaiety of the conjugal life portrayed in *Julie*, and that is the life promised to Emile and Sophie at the end of *Emile*, is not the happiness of life. Paradoxically it is not the possession of one's happiness, but, as Jane Austen puts it, the "sanguine expectation of happiness that *is* happiness itself."[27] Austen's novels, therefore, like *Emile*, stop at the point when the vista of a golden future in which the protagonists live happily ever after is now assured but still in the offing. It is golden

---

27 Jane Austen, *Sense and Sensibility*, 3 vols. (Whitehall: T. Egerton, 1811), 2:14, emphasis added.

because it has not yet been fully tasted; love seems therefore doomed to inevitable disappointment.

> The land of illusions is on this earth the only one worth living in, and such is the void of things human that, with the exception of the Being who exists in himself, the only beauty to be found is in things that are not. (*J*, 569)

It is not for lack of courage, however, that Rousseau urges us to cherish our idylls. For in his view it is only under the spell of illusion, paradoxically, that nature comes to fruition. At the heart of human happiness, for Rousseau, at the core of a life truly lived, is intensity of existence. "The man who has lived the most is not he who has counted the most years but he who has most felt life. Men have been buried at one hundred who died at their birth. They would have gained from dying young; at least they would have lived up to that time" (*E*, 42, 80; *Fragments*, *OC* 2:1325). A great ideal, an intense love affair, that makes one devote oneself to it body and soul concentrates our energies like sunlight focused through a magnifying glass, intensifying the energy of our existence and enlivening life.[28] The implicit willingness to risk "dying young"—that is, the force of passion that risks life, that is willing to suffer and even die for the sake of love—makes us most "feel life."

The chimera of love, of exhilarating beauty, then, is no mere empty illusion. Yes, this beauty "is not in the object one loves; it is the work of our errors. So, what of it?" (*E*, 391). Does it not produce real effects, in uplifting us to the happiness and perfection we long for, and thereby making us feel our short lives as intensely as we can? For Rousseau, the nature of human existence is such that we cannot escape falling into illusion, because to be human is to be subject to unlimited and

---

28 Eve Grace, "The Restlessness of 'Being': Rousseau's Protean *Sentiment of Existence*," *History of European Ideas* 27 (2001): 133–151.

indefinite—hence illusory—desire (*J*, 483n). Nature is not teleological: desire has no definite object as its predetermined goal; rather, our desires insist that the objects we happen across actually fit the images that gave birth to them. Our dreams, however, will always be more attractive than the finite beings we see. Imagination "extends for us the measure of the possible ... and nourishes the desires by the hope of satisfying them. ... No longer seeing the country we have already crossed, we count it for nothing; what remains to cross ceaselessly grows and extends" (*E*, 81). The dream, then, is the thing. For what else but a love beyond compare could possibly satisfy the exhaustingly inexhaustible longing that drives us on?

> If all my dreams had been turned into realities they would not have been enough for me; I would have imagined, dreamed, desired again. I found an inexplicable void in myself that nothing could fill. (*MA*, 579)

The question remains, however, whether the illusions that give love life and that make life lovable can be maintained in the face of the desire to possess, to experience, to hold onto one's happiness. Rousseau seems to argue that we can be happy only in hope or in imagination. Even he has to admit, however, that the "nothingness" of his dreams sometimes constricted his heart and even cast him into despair (*MA*, 579). Once Rousseau has torn aside the "magic veil," then, and one is enlightened to the true nature of love, one wonders whether it would be possible to feel love without some irony, to say the least. There is, after all, nothing really lovable about two lunatic animals coincidentally being driven by the same chemical reactions and the same kind of delusions.

Living with one eye open and one eye shut, as it were, the Romanticism that followed Rousseau fosters what can be called a kind of "exalted melancholy," for one cannot overcome the longings of a heart at odds with itself, nor can one escape the relentlessness of time.[29]

---

29 Simon May, *Love: A History* (New Haven, CT: Yale University Press, 2011), 153.

One of Rousseau's letters to Malesherbes captures this mood well. In it, he describes with what almost unendurable intensity he longed for a happiness that he could not attain. His yearning itself "was enjoyment, since from it I was penetrated by a very lively feeling and an attractive sadness that I would not have wanted not to have" (*MA*, 579). It is preferable, Rousseau seems to say, to feel the exaltation and the pain of longing than to be contented with the meager attempts at satisfaction one actually can experience.

Yet fully to grasp that love is an illusion is also to live in the light of the difficult truth that nothing lasts, that everyone can be replaced. One wonders, then, whether one could live in light of this truth without suffering a kind of motion sickness.[30] At any rate, in his final words to us, Rousseau describes—twice, in case we fail to pay it due attention—the greatest happiness he ever experienced as a state in which he was neither able, nor wanted, to love anything; poor little human beings feel a rapturous calm only in a semiconscious or almost vegetative state, which is to be preferred to all the fleeting joys of love, no matter how blissful (*R*, 12, 46). Perhaps the only way to escape this melancholic consequence would be, as it were, to travel back to Plato and to examine whether this self-critique of love truly shows us that "there is nothing beautiful except that which is not" (*E*, 447).

---

30 Lucretius, *De rerum natura* 1.1–29, 2.1048–1075.

# Reflection

LOVE IN JANE AUSTEN'S NOVELS

*Albert J. Rivero*

Jane Austen wrote courtship novels. Courtship novels end in marriage. Marriage happens when two people, finding each other "charming," as Emma Woodhouse says in *Emma* (1816), fall in love.[1] In *Sense and Sensibility* (1811), Austen's first published novel, Marianne Dashwood slips and falls. The dashing Willoughby, hunting in the neighborhood, sees Marianne's fall, rushes to her rescue, picks her up in his arms, and hurries her into the rented cottage where she lives with her mother and two sisters. Admiring the "rapidity of thought" evident "in his carrying her into the house with so little previous formality," she falls in love with him.[2] He seems to fall in love with her. They do not marry. As happens in Austen's other novels, *Sense and Sensibility* distinguishes between first and second attachments. A first attachment is often the result of love at first sight or blush, as one body, without apparent premeditation or judgment, reacts to or is affected by another. A second attachment is the result of a more rational process, when

---

[1] Jane Austen, *Emma*, ed. Richard Cronin and Dorothy McMillan (Cambridge: Cambridge University Press, 2005), 90. Emma is answering a question about her not being married: "I have none of the inducements of women to marry. Were I to fall in love, indeed, it would be a different thing!"

[2] Jane Austen, *Sense and Sensibility*, ed. Edward Copeland (Cambridge: Cambridge University Press, 2006), 51.

a first love turns out to be less than promised. For Austen, reason should ideally be in control of the passions, though she sympathizes with and entertains the Humean alternative. As she writes near the end of the novel, Marianne "was born to an extraordinary fate." She survives her first, passionate love for Willoughby and marries Colonel Brandon, "a man who had suffered no less than herself under the event of a former attachment." Friends and relatives agree that Marianne is Brandon's "reward" for his suffering. Marianne's "whole heart," the narrator asserts, will become "in time, as much devoted to her husband, as it had once been to Willoughby."[3]

As usual with Austen, the happy ending here raises questions about the nature of romantic love. Austen seems to distrust the heart when unregulated by the mind, but the heart must and will have its way. Marianne and Brandon get compensation for their losses in love. In Marianne's case, however, her first attachment remains a haunting, exacting memory. Brandon will succeed only when he measures up to the Willoughby standard. The passage of time can indeed work wonders, but it cannot erase the past. For instance, at the end of *Mansfield Park* (1814), we are assured that Edmund Bertram eventually transfers his affections from the alluring Mary Crawford to his quiet cousin, Fanny Price, in whom by his kindness he has engendered a love more conjugal than fraternal, when he learns to "prefer soft light eyes to sparkling dark ones."[4] The joke merely underscores the difficulty of governing the visceral demands of love. But governed they must be. It is a duty we owe to ourselves as well as to others. Marianne is wrong to think that her sister Elinor can govern her feelings for Edward Ferrars because her feeble emotions are easily subdued. As readers given

---

[3] Austen, *Sense and Sensibility*, 429–430.
[4] Jane Austen, *Mansfield Park*, ed. John Wiltshire (Cambridge: Cambridge University Press, 2005), 544.

access to her thoughts, we know that Elinor is just as passionate as Marianne, but she has learned to restrain her emotions for the sake of others. As Harriet Byron avers in Samuel Richardson's *Sir Charles Grandison* (1753–1754), one of Austen's favorite novels, romantic love focused on one person can paradoxically become "a narrower of the heart" and an impediment to sympathetic engagement with our fellow human beings.[5] For Austen, the disciplined exercise of reason is the crucial step to advance from self-love to love of community.

The marriages in Austen with the best prospects of enduring success—the happily-ever-after her readers desire for characters whom they have grown to love while reading her novels—are those in which love does not narrow the heart but leads the lovers to embrace a world of social responsibilities. Elizabeth and Darcy in *Pride and Prejudice* (1813) fall in hate at first sight, after he insults her looks at the dance where they first meet. Elizabeth's looks improve after she works up a sweat walking on dirty roads to visit her ailing sister at Netherfield, to the exquisite delight of Darcy as he admires "the brilliancy which exercise had given to her complexion."[6] He tries to resist her sexual attraction but, as he confesses at the beginning of his marriage proposal, "in vain."[7] Flattering a woman with the effort it has taken for the proposing man to overcome his disdain for her low family connections is usually a recipe for disaster. Elizabeth angrily rejects the insulting proposal, her continued hatred fueled by her suspicion that Darcy has played a major role in alienating Bingley's affections from her sister Jane. Elizabeth begins to change her mind about Darcy

---

[5] Samuel Richardson, *The History of Sir Charles Grandison*, ed. Jocelyn Harris (Oxford: Oxford University Press, 1986), 3:131.

[6] Jane Austen, *Pride and Prejudice*, ed. Pat Rogers (Cambridge: Cambridge University Press, 2006), 36.

[7] Austen, *Pride and Prejudice*, 211.

after she rereads a letter he puts in her hand the morning after the proposal. A subsequent tourist visit to Darcy's ancient family seat with her aunt and uncle, lowborn but with impeccably genteel manners, makes Elizabeth feel that "to be mistress of Pemberley might be something!"[8] Growing out of gratitude for persisting in his love for her even after Lydia's scandalous elopement with Wickham, Elizabeth's love for Darcy includes her acceptance of the social duties she will be expected to discharge as his wife.[9]

Another, more radical version of romantic love leading to the occupation of a place in the world at large occurs in *Persuasion* (1818), Austen's last completed novel, published posthumously. Anne Elliot, the second daughter of a vain and useless baronet, has lost her chance at happiness when, at the age of nineteen, she is persuaded not to marry Frederick Wentworth, an ambitious, impulsive, and handsome sailor. Eight years later, Captain Wentworth returns into Anne's neighborhood, successful, wealthy, and still handsome, searching for a wife. Tortured by the memory of her failed first attachment, Anne is no longer, at twenty-seven, the "extremely pretty girl" she had once been.[10] Her "bloom and spirits" lost, Wentworth is reported to have said, after seeing her, that she was "so altered he should not have known [her] again."[11] While on a visit to Lyme, a "fine" coastal wind revives Anne's "bloom and freshness of youth." Her glowing "complexion" is admired by a passing gentleman, later revealed to be Mr. William

---

8 Austen, *Pride and Prejudice*, 271.
9 For Austen, gratitude is a component of love, as she declares with mock self-deprecation at the end of *Northanger Abbey*: "I must confess that [Henry Tilney's] affection originated in nothing better than gratitude.... It is a new circumstance in romance, I acknowledge, and dreadfully derogatory of an heroine's dignity" (*Northanger Abbey*, ed. Barbara M. Benedict and Deirdre Le Faye [Cambridge: Cambridge University Press, 2006], 252–253).
10 Jane Austen, *Persuasion*, ed. Janet Todd and Antje Blank (Cambridge: Cambridge University Press, 2006), 28.
11 Austen, *Persuasion*, 30, 65.

Elliot, heir to Anne's father. Noticing the stranger's admiration, Wentworth gives Anne "a glance of brightness, which seemed to say, 'That man is struck with you,—and even I, at this moment, see something like Anne Elliot again.'"[12] Though they must still travel a painful road to their final destination as a married couple, as Austen asks at the beginning of the novel's last chapter, "Who can be in doubt of what followed?"[13] Anne and Frederick, Austen's oldest and wisest lovers, are thus restored to their first attachments the second time around. The "dread of a future war all that could dim her sunshine," Anne glories "in being a sailor's wife, but she must pay the tax of quick alarm for belonging to that profession which is, if possible, more distinguished in its domestic virtues than in its national importance."[14] In marrying Captain Wentworth, Anne repudiates the world of idleness and stagnation into which she was born and joins a community of the self-made, a citizen of a nation on the brink of an exciting but uncertain future. In *Persuasion*, romantic love and love of country are inextricably bound in creating a new world.

---

12  Austen, *Persuasion*, 112.
13  Austen, *Persuasion*, 270.
14  Austen, *Persuasion*, 275.

CHAPTER 11

# Kierkegaard's Theistic Conception of Love, Existentially Considered

*Sharon Krishek*

### INTRODUCTION: RELIGIOUS LOVE AND ROMANTIC LOVE

Søren Kierkegaard, the nineteenth-century Danish philosopher, is an interesting case in the philosophical writing about love. On the one hand, he is in line with Christian tradition in his acclamation of neighborly love.[1] In this sense, his focus on this kind of love in the context of *Works of Love*—the 1847 essay that presents his only explicit analysis of love—is typical of Christian treatment of the matter.[2] On the other

---

1 The kind of love that is based on the commandment "You shall love your neighbor as yourself" (Matthew 22:39). On the Christian tradition's understanding of love, see David McPherson's chapter in this volume.

2 Accordingly, with respect to Kierkegaard's conception of love, it is quite common for scholars to consider him as a straightforward adherent to the Christian view, which takes genuine love to posit as its ultimate object (apart from God) the "neighbor." See, for example, M. Jamie Ferreira, *Love's Grateful Striving: A Commentary on Kierkegaard's Works of Love* (Oxford: Oxford University Press, 2001); Amy Laura Hall, *Kierkegaard and the Treachery of Love* (Cambridge: Cambridge

hand, however, Kierkegaard is atypical in allowing for an unapologetic, even if only implicit, endorsement of romantic (i.e., erotic) love.[3] Nevertheless, focusing on *Works of Love*, it might seem to demonstrate, rather to the contrary, an attack on preferential (and hence also romantic) love. And indeed, there were more than a few readers who thought that Kierkegaard in fact *denounces* this kind of love, deeming it essentially different from the neighborly kind. However, as careful exegetical efforts of recent years have demonstrated, a more attentive reading of *Works of Love* proves that Kierkegaard's analysis permits the affirmation of spontaneous[4] love (including the romantic kind).[5]

Notwithstanding the importance of this correction to the reading of *Works of Love*, I nevertheless think that limiting Kierkegaard's understanding of love to his analysis in this text alone does injustice to his unique approach to the topic.[6] Accordingly, in this chapter I show that it is rather Kierkegaard's *existentialism*—namely, his philosophical inquiry into that which is specific to humans as conscious *temporal* creatures—that allows for a real harmonization between neighborly love and romantic love. Bear in mind that Kierkegaard is motivated in his philosophical explorations not only by religious devotion but also by more general existential concerns. He is interested, therefore, not only in the value of the human being's existence before God but also in

---

University Press, 2002); C. Stephen Evans, *Kierkegaard's Ethic of Love: Divine Commands and Moral Obligations* (Oxford: Oxford University Press, 2004); Sylvia Walsh, *Kierkegaard: Thinking Christianly in an Existential Mode* (Oxford: Oxford University Press, 2009), ch. 6; Terence Irwin, *The Development of Ethics: A Historical and Critical Study* (Oxford: Oxford University Press, 2009), vol. 3, ch. 77; and Murray Rae, *Kierkegaard and Theology* (London: Bloomsbury, 2010), ch. 7.

[3] See my *Lovers in Essence: A Kierkegaardian Defense of Romantic Love* (New York: Oxford University Press, 2022), where I use Kierkegaard's ideas to develop an independent theory of romantic love.

[4] Namely, the kind of love that comes naturally to a person (and not by commandment).

[5] See, in particular, Ferreira, *Love's Grateful Striving*; Evans's *Kierkegaard's Ethic of Love*; and John Lippitt, *Kierkegaard and the Problem of Self-Love* (Cambridge: Cambridge University Press, 2013).

[6] In this respect I am in disagreement with other recent readers of *Works of Love*. See Sharon Krishek, "Kierkegaard on Impartiality and Love," *European Journal of Philosophy* 25 (2017): 109–128, for more details.

the value of her existence *in the world*: the value, that is, of her earthly, temporal existence.

In *Works of Love*, however, Kierkegaard's existentialism comes less to the fore. In this text (as we will shortly see), he distinguishes between the equality of eternity ('eternity' meaning that which is explicitly God-related), and the dissimilarities—namely, inequality—of temporality (i.e., of earthly life). When loving in a neighborly way, we love a person by virtue of her being a person, a neighbor. We love her for her personhood (which is common to all people), and in this sense our love is equal (because it is directed, at least potentially, at every person).[7] Hence, in loving the neighbor, Kierkegaard claims, we are like God, and accordingly he considers this kind of love to be "eternal." When loving romantically, however, we love a person by virtue of her particular qualities, which distinguish her from everybody else. Our love, then, is grounded not in her "eternal equality"—that is, in her being a "neighbor"—but rather in her "temporal dissimilarities."

Now, my claim is that for an unreserved endorsement of romantic love, we need an unreserved affirmation of temporality. This is because romantic love (more conspicuously than neighborly love) is essentially a part of temporality. First, as we have just noted, romantic love is grounded in the beloved's "temporal dissimilarities": namely, in that which *distinguishes* the beloved from others rather than in that which makes her *the same* as others. Second, being thus grounded, romantic love reflects a different involvement of the lover in the act (or work) of love: that of self-affirmation. In what way? The attraction of the romantic lover to her beloved on the basis of the latter's particular

---

[7] My assumption is that love—neighborly and romantic alike—is grounded (at least partly) in the value of the beloved. I elaborate on this assumption elsewhere. (See, e.g., Sharon Krishek, "Kierkegaard's Notion of a Divine Name and the Feasibility of Universal Love," *Southern Journal of Philosophy* 57 (2019): 539–560; and Sharon Krishek, *Lovers in Essence: A Kierkegaardian Defense of Romantic Love* (New York: Oxford University Press, 2022), chs. 2 and 7.)

qualities implies attention not only to the *beloved's* interests and concerns but also to that of the *lover*. After all, if love is grounded in the value of the beloved, then loving (romantically) X and not Y attests to the lover being guided by that which makes X valuable in *her* eyes. It is therefore guided (among other things) by her interests, concerns, inclinations, desires. Hence, romantic love implies (more manifestly than neighborly love) self-affirmation.

And self-affirmation of this kind indicates, again, how crucial the positive valuation of temporality is for romantic love. This is because it indicates that romantic love, by virtue of being grounded in the "temporal dissimilarities" of the beloved, is indirectly grounded also in the "temporal dissimilarities" of the *lover* (who is attracted to the particular beloved also by virtue of *her own* particularity: her inclinations, desires, temperament, etc.). Thus, to give romantic love its due, a genuine affirmation of temporality is required. Such an affirmation, I claim, is to be found in two of Kierkegaard's more existentially oriented works, *Fear and Trembling* (1843) and *The Sickness unto Death* (1849).[8] As I attempt to show here, Kierkegaard's analysis of human nature (in the latter) allows for an unequivocal affirmation of "temporal dissimilarities," while his analysis of faith (in the former) allows for an unequivocal self-affirmation.

It is therefore the conflation of these two aspects of Kierkegaard's thought—the religious and the existential—that captures the spirit of Kierkegaard's singular conception of love. Only by taking *both* into consideration can we see that he offers us a religiously grounded understanding of love that not only tolerates the romantic but allows for a reclaiming of its value.

---

8 Many of Kierkegaard's writings were published under pseudonyms, including these two. The reason for this is a matter for scholarly debate, which I avoid here. In spite of Kierkegaard's choice not to sign these essays in his name, I refer to the ideas he expresses in them as his own. For a justification of this move, see Sharon Krishek, *Kierkegaard on Faith and Love* (Cambridge: Cambridge University Press, 2009), 138–141.

## *Works of Love*'s Conception of Love: Loving the Neighbor

Kierkegaard's aim in this essay is to present what he takes to be the real nature of love, and he firmly claims that for this purpose we must turn to Christianity and not—as one might be mistakenly inclined—to poetry. The difference between the kind of love praised by the former (neighborly love) and the kind of love praised by the latter (romantic love) is rather evident—the former is rooted in duty, the latter in spontaneous inclination—and Kierkegaard formulates it in this way:

> The issue between the poet and Christianity can be defined very precisely as follows: *Erotic love and friendship are preferential love [Forkjerlighed] and the passion of preferential love*; Christian love [*Kjerlighed*] is self-denial's love, for which this *shall* vouches.... preferential love's most passionate boundlessness in excluding means to love only one single person; self-denial's boundlessness in giving itself means not to exclude a single one.[9]

Romantic love, Kierkegaard justly observes, is passionate and emphatically exclusive, while neighborly love is based on self-denial and emphatically *not* exclusive. The tension between them, then, seems to be irreconcilable. However, Kierkegaard is criticizing not romantic love *in itself* but rather the poet's conception of it. Hence, despite its dissimilarity with what Kierkegaard posits as the ideal (i.e., neighborly love), romantic love is not judged by him as *essentially* wrong. The commandment of love, he says, will "teach erotic love and friendship genuine love: ... in erotic love and friendship, preserve love for the neighbor."[10]

Thus, as is now widely agreed by Kierkegaard scholars, the issue is not so much a *rejection* of romantic love but rather a *renewed understanding*

---

9 Søren Kierkegaard, *Works of Love*, trans. Howard V. Hong and Edna H. Hong (Princeton, NJ: Princeton University Press, 1995), 52, emphases in the original.
10 Kierkegaard, *Works of Love*, 62.

of it in light of the model of neighborly love. Kierkegaard's concern, in other words, is not to forbid his readers to love romantically but to teach them how to love *correctly*. Accordingly, the question is how romantic love should relate to neighborly love. Since Kierkegaard asserts that "Christianity . . . recognizes really only one kind of love" (i.e., neighborly love), and given his claim that it is not preoccupied with "working out in detail the different ways in which *this fundamental universal love can manifest itself*,"[11] he seems to understand the relation between neighborly and romantic kinds of love as follows.

If we understand love to be a general phenomenon that has distinct manifestations (such as romantic love, friendship, parental love, familial love, etc.), then the above quote indicates that, for Kierkegaard, neighborly love is the general phenomenon and romantic love is one of its various manifestations. This means that (genuine) romantic love is *essentially* neighborly love, which implies that romantic love should conform to the essential characteristics of neighborly love. What are these characteristics?

For Kierkegaard, the quintessential characteristic of neighborly love is its being an attitude of self-denial. "To love the neighbor," he says, "is self-denial's love."[12] What does he mean by "self-denial"? The prayer that opens Kierkegaard's discussion of love reads,

> How could one speak properly about love if you were forgotten, you God of love . . . who spared nothing but in love *gave everything* . . . How could one speak properly about love if you were forgotten, you who revealed what love is, you our Savior and Redeemer, who *gave yourself* in order to save all. How could one speak properly of love if you were forgotten, you Spirit of love, *who take nothing of your own* but remind us of that *self-sacrifice*.[13]

---

11 Kierkegaard, *Works of Love*, 143, my emphasis.
12 Kierkegaard, *Works of Love*, 55.
13 Kierkegaard, *Works of Love*, 3, my emphases.

Based on this description, we see that in Kierkegaard's view, genuine love is an act of selfless giving. Namely, it is an act driven by the lover's *concern* for the beloved: qua lover, it is *this* that motivates her. To love, in other words, is to will that which is good for the beloved—and as this is the essence of love, it is apt to characterize it in terms of self-denial. By this, Kierkegaard emphasizes that the "self" who loves is not the focus of love—but rather the beloved. The "denial," then, attests to the lover being concentrated on her beloved; she does not seek "her own" but rather pursues what is best for the beloved.

Kierkegaard's conception of love as primarily based on self-denial explains his deep reservation with regard to preferentiality. Still referring to the poet's understanding of love and the need to rectify it, Kierkegaard takes preferentiality to be a form of selfishness: "[O]*nly when one loves the neighbor . . . is the selfishness in preferential love rooted out.*"[14] What is it about preferentiality that Kierkegaard deems selfish?

Kierkegaard observes that "[e]ven if passionate preference had no other selfishness in it, it would still have this, that . . . there is self-willfulness in it."[15] He explicitly connects selfishness and self-willfulness, then, and takes preference to be an instance of the latter (and hence selfish): "When the lover or friend is able to love only this one single person in the whole world . . . there is an enormous self-willfulness in this enormous devotion."[16] To act in self-willfulness is to be guided only (or primarily) by one's will: it is to act principally in accordance with what one wishes or fancies. Hence, it is fairly clear why Kierkegaard considers it the opposite of self-denial, and thus, from his point of view, selfish.[17] But why does he take preferentiality to be an instance of self-willfulness?

---

14 Kierkegaard, *Works of Love*, 44, emphasis in the original.
15 Kierkegaard, *Works of Love*, 55.
16 Kierkegaard, *Works of Love*, 55.
17 Kierkegaard's implicit identification between self-willfulness and selfishness—which coheres with his ambivalence toward preferential love in this essay (and might well explain it)—is not justified. While, indeed, any act of selfishness includes self-willfulness, not every act of self-willfulness is

To answer this question, we should note that Kierkegaard distinguishes between "temporal dissimilarities" and "eternal equality."[18] In being a neighbor—that is, a person—everybody is "the same" (and in this sense "equal"), but every person also bears particularities that make him different and distinct from other persons. However, "preference," as Kierkegaard rightly claims, "is always related to dissimilarities."[19] The romantic lover, for example, cannot (and should not) love romantically every person; she loves a particular person who has particular (as opposed to universal and equal) qualities that attract her. In this sense, we may say that when one loves preferentially, one is guided in her love by her desires: she responds to the qualities of the beloved that appeal to her and conjure her will. She loves the beloved in (and due to) his particularity—his distinctiveness—that captures her attention by appealing to her interests, that is, to her will. Hence, preferentiality reflects self-willfulness.

Further, it is in light of Kierkegaard's conception of love as rooted in self-denial that his characterization of love as *equal* should be understood. Kierkegaard asserts, as we saw, that "*only when one loves the neighbor, only then is the selfishness in preferential love rooted out and the equality of the eternal preserved.*"[20] But in what sense can love be equal?

To begin with, the demand for equality refers to the *object* of one's love. Neighborly love is equal in the sense that it applies to all: every person deserves to be loved in this way. Hence, if one is a neighborly lover, she should love *every* person by virtue of his being a person, a neighbor. The demand for equality, then, renders love an attitude that should be equally directed to every given person, regardless of that

---

necessarily selfish. One can be genuinely concerned with the interests and good of another while at the same time also being concerned with one's own desires and wellbeing. Such a simultaneous concern for self *and* other, I claim later, is precisely what structuring love in the model of the double movement of faith allows.

18 See, e.g., Kierkegaard, *Works of Love*, 72.
19 Kierkegaard, *Works of Love*, 62.
20 Kierkegaard, *Works of Love*, 44, emphasis in the original.

person being one's friend or one's enemy, one's romantic beloved or a complete stranger. What kind of attitude can meet this demand?

As his opening prayer indicates, Kierkegaard characterizes love as an attitude of concern.[21] Concern for X means to will the good for X, to wish X's flourishing. It is an attitude of benediction and benevolence. Now, I think that when Kierkegaard demands of the genuine lover to care for every single (relevant)[22] person, he does not mean by this that the lover should care for everyone in the same way or with the same degree of intensity (say, to care for a stranger as much as one cares for one's husband or child). If he would demand equality *in this sense*, then it is not clear how he could have affirmed natural relationships (such as romantic or parental), which essentially involve an intensity of concern (and commitment) that cannot be equally practiced with regard to *every* person.

I therefore think that Kierkegaard demands equality with respect to the very act of caring—its mere occurrence—while he allows that its intensity and extent (as well as any practical actions taken) depend on who the beloved is (one's spouse or a stranger) and, more generally, on the relevant circumstances.[23] "To love the neighbor is, while remaining in the earthly dissimilarity allotted to one, essentially to will to exist equally for unconditionally every human being."[24] The point, then, is to care genuinely for every person, genuinely will good for him—even if there is not much that we can do on a practical basis in order to advance his good.

---

21 Which is also reflected in the Danish word that he uses for love—*Kjerlighed*—which means "caring" (see Ferreira, *Love's Grateful Striving*, 43).

22 Namely, the persons she actually encounters, those who take some (even minimal) part in her reality.

23 See, in this regard, Evans, *Kierkegaard's Ethic of Love*, 200: "Suppose that I see a homeless person ... holding a sign that says 'Hungry. Will work for food.' What should I do? The principle of neighbor-love does not by itself generate an answer to that question. Perhaps I should stop and give the man some money. Perhaps I should stop and refer him to a social agency ... [or] talk with him about helping him to get a job. Perhaps I must pass him by because I have a responsibility to another neighbor that I would violate by stopping to help."

24 Kierkegaard, *Works of Love*, 83–84.

The ideal of such an equal caring (in the sense just explained) is obviously not easy to achieve. Here, the characterization of love as based on self-denial becomes evident. One needs intentionally to set aside one's immediate and natural interests—including one's tendencies for self-defense and one's disposition to put oneself at the center—so that one can care for the relevant person who needs one's caring. (This, naturally, becomes more difficult the less close the relevant neighbor is.)

However, as demanding and admirable an ideal as this is, it is not enough, I claim, to count as love.[25] In other words, if this is *all* the ideal amounts to, then how is it any different from a clear-cut moral ideal, and if so, why call it love? I therefore contend that the kind of concern that Kierkegaard takes to be love must be accompanied by emotion. But is there any emotion that can meet the demand for equality? Is there any emotion that can be equally felt regardless of who the beloved is?

I suggest that compassion is such an emotion. Compassion, or "suffering with," is the feeling of sorrow and sadness that arises in response to the suffering of another. The suffering in question does not have to be of a grand scale. It would suffice for *some* suffering to be present, in order for the person witnessing it to feel compassion. And suffering, I claim, is *always* present: it is intrinsic to being human. The kind of suffering that is always present can be termed "existential suffering." This is the suffering entailed in one's life simply by virtue of being human. Finite, mortal, experiencing the constant loss of time (and everything in it), limited and hence susceptible to frustration and pain: humans are doomed to suffer—if not for anything else, then at least by virtue of their vulnerability.

Every encounter with *any* neighbor (assuming that one is truly open to it; an openness that can only be secured through self-denial), then,

---

25 Here I diverge from Evans and Lippitt (and also Ferreira, in a way), who consider only (or mostly) the moral dimension of neighborly love. For a detailed discussion of their positions, see Krishek, "Kierkegaard on Impartiality and Love."

should involve a sensitivity to the neighbor's actual suffering—at least in the minimal sense of existential suffering. And if so, compassion will naturally follow. It is therefore more than plausible to assume that Kierkegaard takes love to be a compassionate[26] caring, which is based on self-denial and is equal in the sense that it should be directed at, and felt toward, any given person.

But how does romantic love fit with this ideal?

> Take away the distinction of preferential love so that you can love the neighbor. But you are not to cease loving the beloved because of it—far from it. If in order to love the neighbor you would have to begin by giving up loving those for whom you have preference, the word "neighbor" would be the greatest deception ever contrived.... it is only the preferential love that should be taken away.[27]

We already saw that Kierkegaard rejects preferentiality because he associates it with selfishness. He can therefore hold, as he does here, that the neighborly lover should keep her love for, say, her romantic beloved while only "taking away" the preferentiality—that is, the selfishness that prevents her from loving others as well—from her love. Thus, Kierkegaard indeed affirms the legitimacy of spontaneous kinds of love (such as romantic), which is rather plausible. After all, the romantic beloved is also a neighbor, and (as we demonstrated) there is no reason to assume that Kierkegaard is committed to the claim that every neighbor should be treated with the same (degree and intensity of) caring.

However, Kierkegaard *is* committed to the claim that romantic love is *essentially* neighborly love. Recall his assertion that "Christianity

---

26 Indeed, Kierkegaard does not explicitly discuss compassion, but he does refer to the parable of the Good Samaritan in a way that seems to equate the Samaritan's *love* for the wounded stranger with his mercy—i.e., compassion—for him (see *Works of Love*, 22). There may be a case to claim that for Kierkegaard love *is* compassion, but developing this suggestion further is beyond the scope of this project.

27 Kierkegaard, *Works of Love*, 61.

recognizes really only one kind of love ... and does not concern itself much with working out in detail the different ways in which this fundamental universal love can manifest itself."[28] While this claim does not suggest that romantic love is to be ruled out, it does suggest that that which renders it *love* is its essence as neighborly love, that is, as compassionate caring.

To demonstrate this point, let us think about a classic paradigm of romantic love: Jane Eyre's passionate love for Edward Rochester.[29] According to Kierkegaard's understanding of love, Jane is allowed to love Edward romantically, and she can well be a genuine (i.e., neighborly) lover in doing so. However, if we accept Kierkegaard's analysis, then we are obliged to say that that which turns her passionate romantic love into genuine *love* is her compassionate concern for him. Accordingly, this means that the aspects of her love that make her romantic love *romantic*—say, her eros, her thrill, her longing—are taken as inessential to her love (qua love).

This, of course, is completely in line with Kierkegaard's attitude toward romantic love in *Works of Love*. In the spirit of Christianity (as he himself indicates), he is not interested in "working out in detail" the *distinction* between different forms of love.[30] However, for the romantic lover, this may well sound offensive, or at least an inadequate way to account for her love. In its rendering inessential to her love precisely that which makes it what it is—namely, passionate *romantic* love—the model of *Works of Love* fails to capture the unique nature of *this kind* of love.[31] Ironically enough, this "offended" lover may well be

---

28 Kierkegaard, *Works of Love*, 143.
29 Charlotte Brontë, *Jane Eyre* (Oxford: Oxford University Press, 1969 [1847]).
30 See also his claim that "the wife and the friend are not loved in the same way, nor the friend and the neighbor, but this is not an essential dissimilarity, because the fundamental similarity is implicit in the category 'neighbor'" (*Works of Love*, 141).
31 The challenge to find a unitary model of love that accounts for that which is *common* to all kinds of love, while maintaining that which *distinguishes* them as essential, goes beyond Kierkegaard's specific model. This is a substantial challenge regarding the nature of love. For an expanded discussion on this topic, see my *Lovers in Essence*, ch. 3.

Kierkegaard himself. In *Fear and Trembling*, he posits a romantic lover as an exemplar of faith, and his repeated references to this kind of love betray a deeper valuing of its singular quality.

Can the gap between the "two Kierkegaards" be bridged? Romantic love is most evidently the kind of love that *essentially* responds to that which is unique to the beloved, that which distinguishes him from anybody else (Jane loves Edward *in particular*). Moreover, it is most evidently guided by that which is unique to the *lover*—her inclinations, desires, and aspirations (Jane loves Edward and not John because, for example, Edward's warmth, passion, and wit are good *for her*). Hence, to give romantic love its due, "temporal dissimilarities"—that which make people *different* from one another—should not only be respected (as they are in *Works of Love*) but more positively *endorsed*. Furthermore, self-affirmation—which would make the lover's interests a legitimate part of the work of love—should also be considered as positive.

Does Kierkegaard allow for such a positive endorsement of "temporal dissimilarities" and "self-affirmation" in *Works of Love*? I think not, and in the next two sections I explain why. Accordingly, I demonstrate how turning to *The Sickness unto Death* and to *Fear and Trembling*, respectively, provides the endorsement of "temporal dissimilarities" and "self-affirmation," respectively—hence preparing the ground for a positive valuation of romantic love.

## The Existential Twist of *The Sickness unto Death*: The Value of "Temporal Dissimilarities"

In *Works of Love*, Kierkegaard posits the neighbor—the person in his personhood—as the ultimate object of love. The "neighbor" is the common ground between the king and the beggar, the rich and the poor, the friend and the enemy. Whether the lover is naturally attracted to a person X, or is indifferent to a person Y, does not make a real difference from the point of view of the neighborly lover. They are both her "neighbor," and as such should be loved. Hence, Kierkegaard stresses the "eternal equality" of the neighbor—the equality, that is, of all humans, which is rooted in their being created by God and in God's image: "on the basis of dissimilarity he is not your neighbor . . . He is your neighbor on the basis of equality with you before God."[32]

Given Kierkegaard's subject in this essay—that is, neighborly love—it may not be surprising that he expresses little interest in that which distinguishes one person from another: "Christianity . . . allows all the dissimilarities to stand but teaches the equality of eternity."[33] However, Kierkegaard seems not only uninterested in dissimilarities, but somewhat dismissive about them: "Dissimilarity is temporality's method of confusing that marks every human being differently, but the neighbor is eternity's mark—on every human being."[34] On the one side there is temporality, with its "confusing" dissimilarities; on the other side there is eternity, where truth abides.[35] The conclusion is unavoidable: temporality takes us away from the truth.

Kierkegaard is in fact quite explicit in his positing of temporality as inferior to eternity. From the point of view of what counts as the true essence of any given person, it is clear that temporality is only secondary: "the dissimilarity of earthly life is just like an actor's costume,"[36] he says. Namely, it is inessential to who one *really* is:

> When at death the curtain falls on the stage of actuality . . . then they [the king, the beggar, etc.] . . . are all one, they are human beings. All of them are what they essentially were, what you did not see because of the dissimilarity that you saw—they are all human beings.[37]

---

32  Kierkegaard, *Works of Love*, 60.
33  Kierkegaard, *Works of Love*, 72.
34  Kierkegaard, *Works of Love*, 89.
35  Kierkegaard clearly identifies eternity with truth. See, for example, *Works of Love*, 87.
36  Kierkegaard, *Works of Love*, 87.
37  Kierkegaard, *Works of Love*, 87.

Even if we assume that Kierkegaard's move here is mainly rhetorical, aiming at correcting the common view that tends to put more emphasis on temporality and its dissimilarities; and even if it is true that later in this essay he speaks of dissimilarities more positively,[38] we might well be left with the uneasy impression that he takes temporality to be essentially lesser (in value, in importance, in truth) than eternity.

But then comes *The Sickness unto Death*. Published two years after *Works of Love*, this essay expresses what Kierkegaard (by his own admission) takes to be the ideal of the religious life.[39] It is therefore significant that he presents in this essay an analysis of human nature that posits temporality to be not only important but rather *essential* to being human. Temporality is no longer conceived as only a "garment" that "hides" one's true nature. Rather, it is now conceived as an essential part of that nature: "A human being is a synthesis of the infinite and the finite, of the temporal and the eternal, of freedom and necessity."[40] Accordingly, as we will see, a human being's "essence" amounts not only to her personhood (her God-like—i.e., eternal—qualities) but also to her being a *particular* person (distinguished from others by her particular qualities, i.e., "temporal dissimilarities").

Kierkegaard's claim is that to describe adequately the nature of a human being, we need the six categories detailed here. A human being *is* finite and infinite, temporal and eternal, subject to necessity and free. But what does it mean to belong in *all* of these categories? Commentators agree that the three sets of syntheses convey different aspects of one fundamental characteristic of humans: their being both limited (in this sense they are "temporal, finite, and subject to

---

38 See Ferreira, *Love's Grateful Striving*, 99–116.
39 He did not publish it under his own name—but rather under the name of Anti-Climacus—because he did not want his readers to assume that he himself accomplished the ideal he portrays in this book. See the translators' introduction in Kierkegaard, *The Sickness unto Death*, trans. Howard V. Hong and Edna H. Hong (Princeton, NJ: Princeton University Press, 1980), xxiii.
40 Kierkegaard, *Sickness unto Death*, 13. As a matter of fact, Kierkegaard's main interest in this essay is in the nature of a human being who is a *self*. However, for the purpose of this article, I leave aside this further layer.

necessity") and capable of transcending their limitations (in this sense they are "eternal, infinite, and free").[41] I think that this basic observation is correct, but a further explanation is required in order to understand the richness of the picture that Kierkegaard depicts by using these different categories. For this, I suggest that we distinguish between two (compatible) senses of "being limited"—and hence also of the capability of "transcending" (the relevant limitations).

First, a human being is limited by virtue of being situated in time and space, namely, in "the world." Being born in a certain place, at a certain time, and to a certain family, for example, are facts that are independent of the person's will and action, and in this sense limit her. Transcending *this* kind of limitation is rooted in the person's various qualities and abilities. For example, she can move to a different place, live in accordance with ideals belonging to a different time, rebel against the expectations of her family.

However, there is another important sense in which a human being is limited. She is limited in having *particular* qualities. She has certain talents, a certain temperament, certain inclinations. These are also 'facts' about her, and they limit her in the sense that they allow her to do some things but not others. *This* kind of limitation can be transcended by means of the person's *universal* qualities, those she has by virtue of being a person (for example, her rationality).

Returning to Kierkegaard's opposing of "temporal dissimilarities" with the "equality of eternity" in *Works of Love*, it is clear that "temporal dissimilarities" include both limitations in the first sense (being a king or a beggar, say) and limitations in the second sense (say, being a woman or a man, looking in a way X rather than in a way Y, having these and those talents and inclinations and not others). Accordingly,

---

41 See, for example, John Davenport, "Selfhood and 'Spirit,'" in *The Oxford Handbook of Kierkegaard*, ed. John Lippitt and George Pattison (Oxford: Oxford University Press, 2013), 235; Anthony Rudd, *Self, Value, and Narrative: A Kierkegaardian Approach* (Oxford: Oxford University Press, 2012), 41; and Patrick Stokes, *Kierkegaard's Mirrors: Interest, Self, and Moral Vision* (London: Palgrave, 2010), 64.

the "equality of eternity" attests to two things. First, it attests to being a person (a "neighbor") who is created in God's image and as such is "the same" as everybody else. Second, referring specifically to her *qualities*, the "equality of eternity" attests to her having some qualities that are universal, that is, shared by *all* humans by virtue of their being created in God's image.

In *Works of Love* Kierkegaard seems to appraise "the eternal" as more valuable and significant than the temporal:

> But God is love and therefore we can be like God only in loving . . . Insofar as you love the beloved, you are not like God . . . Insofar as you love your friend, you are not like God . . . But when you love the neighbor, then you are like God.[42]

In as much as to be "like God" relates to the "eternal" in human nature, the implication is that "the eternal" is higher than "the temporal." After all, it is only when the lover appeals to the "eternal" in others—to their being God-created (as neighbors)—that she loves like God, and it is only when she loves like God that she herself is "eternal," that is, acts in accordance with her likeness to God. In *Works of Love*, then, Kierkegaard posits the eternal as more significant to being human.

In *The Sickness unto Death*, however, the eternal and the temporal are *on par with each other*. According to Kierkegaard's analysis here, *both* the eternal and the temporal are essential to being human. Thus, unlike his analysis in *Works of Love*, here he does not take humans to be essentially only *eternal* (in their being God-created and God-related) while considering their temporal "embodiment" as merely a contingent "garment" that "hides" their true nature. No, temporality is no less essential than eternality to being a human being. Accordingly, it should be no

---

[42] Kierkegaard, *Works of Love*, 62–63.

less essential to the grounding of our love for humans, which is particularly significant when it comes to romantic love.

## Self-Denial Coupled with Self-Affirmation: Love as Modeled in the Structure of Faith

A positive endorsement of temporal dissimilarities is crucial for romantic love because this kind of love responds to the beloved in his "dissimilarity" from others (rather than to his "sameness" with them). Furthermore, it is not only the beloved's "dissimilarity" that plays a central role in this kind of love but also that of the lover. Edward is the beloved of *Jane in particular*. A different woman, one with different inclinations, desires, and longings, may well have remained indifferent to him. Jane's romantic love for Edward, in other words, is telling not only in respect to who, in particular, Edward is but also in respect to who, in particular, *she* is. Recall, however, that to be guided by such an attentiveness to oneself—to one's inclinations, desires, and so forth—is ruled out in *Works of Love* as "self-willfulness." In this text, as we saw, Kierkegaard identifies the correct way of loving with self-denial: for love to be genuine, it should be motivated by a pure concern for the other. But is it necessary for such a concern to exclude a concern also for oneself, namely, to exclude an affirmation of one's interests, desires, and so on? Cannot one be motivated *both* by seeking the good for the other and affirming that which is good for oneself?

Kierkegaard's condemnation of "self-willfulness" implies that he thinks that self-denial necessarily excludes self-affirmation: if one is motivated (as one should be) by seeking the good for another, one cannot at the same time be motivated by seeking the good for oneself. Kierkegaard is right that it is natural for humans to experience a clash between these two motivating forces, which often lead to their mutual exclusion. But this does not mean that these two motivating forces are *essentially* exclusive. As long as one's self-affirmation does not distract one from a genuine concern for another, there is nothing problematic or offensive in such an affirmation. There is nothing wrong in self-affirmation per se, then: the problem is its potential to prevent a genuine concern for another. For this reason, self-denial is needed. On *this* stands the distinction between (morally neutral) self-affirmation and (morally wrong) selfishness. Self-denial safeguards the former from becoming the latter.

The correct attitude of love, then, is to affirm (when relevant) one's interests, desires and longings—while being entirely motivated (qua lover) by the concern for the beloved. It is, in other words, to "return" to oneself while denying oneself—to perform self-denial and self-affirmation at one and the same time. To understand the correct attitude of love in terms of this kind of doubleness, one indeed needs to go beyond what Kierkegaard presents in *Works of Love*. However, we can nevertheless learn about this attitude from Kierkegaard's own words and ideas. Such an attitude is implicitly a part of faith, which is presented in *Fear and Trembling* as a *double* attitude to the world.[43]

Published pseudonymously in 1843, *Fear and Trembling* is probably Kierkegaard's best-known work. Focusing on the faith of the biblical Abraham at the moment of the Binding, he defines faith (in general) as a double movement of resignation and faith—meaning by this that resignation is a necessary condition for faith, and an integral part of it. But what does Kierkegaard mean by resignation? Addressing not only one's relationship with God but also, crucially, the so-called human condition, I suggest that the context for understanding Kierkegaard's concept of faith (and hence of resignation) is no less existential than it is theological. Accordingly, as we will see, it is again Kierkegaard's existentialism that paves the way for endorsing that which is necessary for the existence of romantic love (in this case, self-affirmation).

Being temporal, we—as well as everything that we value and care about—are finite. Thus, since finitude entails loss, we may say that

---

[43] For a more elaborated and textually grounded discussion of the analysis of faith than I present here, see Krishek, *Kierkegaard on Faith and Love*, chs. 2 and 3.

loss is a constant component of human life. And loss, indeed, is a central (though implicit) theme in *Fear and Trembling*. Focusing on the Binding of Isaac as paradigmatic of Abraham's faith, the horrifying impending loss of his beloved son naturally takes a crucial part in Abraham's act of faith. Less dramatically (but no less crucially), the potential loss of a beloved princess and the actual loss of time play a significant role in the faith of two other exemplars.

Thus, the existential point of departure for Kierkegaard's conception of faith is this painful aspect of human life: everything (by virtue of its finitude) is *essentially* lost to every human being. By "essentially" I mean that Isaac (for example) is in a fundamental way lost to Abraham even if he is alive (and lives as long as Abraham does). This is because, due to his finitude, Isaac is liable to being lost—and this liability is essential (namely, it is necessary for Isaac to have this liability). So even though Isaac is not necessarily *actually* lost to Abraham, his *essential* liability to being lost necessarily affects the nature of Abraham's relationship with him.

Thus, seeing any X as essentially lost does not mean seeing it as necessarily gone. Rather, while X is *present*, one sees the possibility of its *absence* in the most vivid way possible; the possibility of its loss becomes a steadfast accompaniment to its existence. Now, one way to define the loss of X is that we cease to possess it. Accordingly, since everything is finite (thus essentially lost), we do not genuinely possess anything. The nature of things and our relation to them—our control over them and our ability to secure our hold over them—is such that we do not possess them, and *cannot ever* possess them.

I therefore suggest that (Kierkegaardian) resignation amounts to fully acknowledging the fact that everything in our life is essentially lost. Renouncing X means acknowledging that I cannot *secure its presence* in my life. I therefore do not, and cannot, possess X. Such an acknowledgment changes one's attitude toward X in a way that is highly relevant to love (as Kierkegaard understands it) because it precludes *selfishness*.

Broadly speaking, selfishness toward X occurs whenever one (implicitly or explicitly, intentionally or not) regards X as a pathway that leads, eventually, to oneself. It is to regard X, while actually being concerned about oneself. Such an attitude, obviously, fails to appreciate X for what it is, as X is conceived through the veil of one's preoccupation with oneself. However, if one renounces X, there is necessarily a shift of focus. The gaze of selfishness is inconsistent with the gaze of resignation (as it were) because such gazes result in diametrically opposed conceptions of X. While the former is directed at X but actually sees Y (oneself), the latter, by conceiving X as (essentially) lost—with all the pain that the conceiving of something valuable as lost entails—cannot but see, and be focused on, X.

And if resignation precludes selfishness, then it necessarily includes self-denial (as the latter is the opposite of selfishness). In this sense, resignation is at the very least akin to self-denial. Now, recall that in *Works of Love* Kierkegaard claims that self-denial is the ultimate attitude toward the beloved. However, in *Fear and Trembling* he claims that as far as faith is concerned, resignation is *not* enough. A further "movement"—which for the sake of simplicity I shall term "affirmation"—is required.[44] The best way to appreciate the meaning and significance of *this* movement is to consider, with Kierkegaard, the faith of Abraham.[45]

According to my interpretation, God's demand that Abraham sacrifice Isaac reflects the status of Isaac as essentially lost. Abraham, in

---

44 Kierkegaard does not use this term. However, since he speaks of the second movement of faith in terms of "getting" or "receiving" (the resigned thing) back, I think "affirmation" captures the idea he wishes to convey. See, for example, Kierkegaard, *Fear and Trembling*, trans. Howard V. Hong and Edna H. Hong (Princeton, NJ: Princeton University Press, 1983), 36, 40, 49–50.

45 Kierkegaard's reading of this biblical story (as well as the story itself) is controversial, and there are many scholarly debates regarding its proper interpretation. Here, I present in a nutshell my own interpretation of Kierkegaard's use of the story, but space constraints prevent me from justifying it. For such a justification, see Krishek, *Kierkegaard on Faith and Love*, ch. 3; and Sharon Krishek, "The Existential Dimension of Faith," in *Kierkegaard's Fear and Trembling: A Critical Guide*, ed. Daniel Conway (Cambridge: Cambridge University Press, 2015), 106–121.

the most dramatic way possible, has to acknowledge that he does not possess Isaac, and never will. Being a "knight of faith" (as Kierkegaard calls it), Abraham first of all *renounces* Isaac. His willingness to sacrifice his son demonstrates that he wholeheartedly accepts the loss of Isaac (both the essential one and the actual, impending one).

But the story does not end here, of course. While Abraham's willingness to sacrifice Isaac exemplifies his resignation, Abraham's *faith* exemplifies his trust that Isaac, despite all evidence to the contrary, will nevertheless be *returned* to him, that is, will *live* along with him in this *earthly, temporal* world: "He did not have faith that he would be blessed in a future life but that he would be blessed here in the world."[46] Moreover, Kierkegaard emphasizes Abraham's ability to take joy in his son (who might well be demanded again) when they descend from the mountain.[47] Thus, faith, as construed here, is tested in the ability to live *joyfully* in this world. After all, from a natural point of view, taking unreserved joy in X is dependent on "holding" it and hence is incompatible with considering X as essentially lost—namely, as resisting one's secure hold. However, faith is precisely the ability to *regain* security, which is based on the believer's trust in God.

Positing the joyful "return" to earthly life—its *affirmation*—as the locus for faith implies *self*-affirmation in two ways. First, "joy" is a self-affirming attitude. Second, attention to one's own concerns and desires is an integral part of earthly existence (being, as it is, bodily, affective, and passionate). This is best reflected in the two other exemplars of faith that Kierkegaard presents in *Fear and Trembling*. One is a person who looks like a "tax collector," fully immersed in the little pleasures

---

46 Kierkegaard, *Fear and Trembling*, 36. It should be stressed that Abraham's trust in this specific case is grounded in God's promise to him that Isaac will live, so that the point is *not* that a person of faith is entitled to believe that a dead son will be restored to life (Abraham is unique in receiving such a promise). Rather, what the story demonstrates is the ability to trust God under the most horrifying circumstances.

47 See Kierkegaard, *Fear and Trembling*, 35, 37.

and concerns of daily life while being a knight of faith through and through.[48] The other is a knight of faith who is a *romantic* lover:

> And yet it must be wonderful to get the princess, and the knight of faith is the only happy man, the heir to the finite ... To get the princess this way, to live happily with her day after day ... to live happily every moment this way ... every moment to see the sword hanging over the beloved's head, and yet not to find rest in the pain of resignation but to find joy by virtue of the absurd—this is wonderful.[49]

To come full circle, the return to the world—expressing as it does a positive valuation of temporality—accords with the affirmation of "earthly dissimilarities" that we find in *The Sickness unto Death*. Earthly dissimilarities, we said, are crucial for romantic love, as this kind of love responds to that which is *unique* to the beloved, and is motivated by that which is *unique* to the lover. It must be the *particular* princess—no other girl, no other "neighbor," will do—and this is so for a *particular* lover, with particular inclinations, desires, and longings.

It is therefore the existential ground on which Kierkegaard's theology develops that allows romantic love to be crowned again (after having been dethroned in *Works of Love*) as an arena for genuine religiosity. This inauguration does not compromise any of the demands that Kierkegaard posits in *Works of Love*. It only extends the conception of love to include not only self (and world) *denial* but also self (and world) *affirmation*.

## Conclusion

Being a religious philosopher, Kierkegaard is faithful to the central dogmas of Christianity, including the importance of neighborly love.

---

48 See Kierkegaard, *Fear and Trembling*, 38–41.
49 Kierkegaard, *Fear and Trembling*, 50.

Yet what is special in Kierkegaard's approach is his nondogmatic affirmation of these dogmas. As such, Kierkegaard's philosophy takes as its point of departure not such dogmas (which, indeed, he often seeks to defend), but rather existential (and hence universal) concerns. This is particularly evident in his analysis of love. As I have argued here, both his demand to love the neighbor and his affirmation of the glory of romantic love can be defended and justified by an appeal to existential sensibilities.

And it is this existential aspect of Kierkegaard's philosophy that allows us to grant romantic love its due: it allows us to affirm this love in the passionate way that corresponds with its centrality to human life. Kierkegaard's existentialism, then, colors his conception of love with its specific hue. And so the melding of his romantic passion, existential sensibility, and religious devotion yields an unparalleled concept of love, which makes a singular contribution to the understanding of love's nature.

# Reflection

THE CONCEPT OF LOVE IN MODERN PSYCHOLOGY

Robert J. Sternberg

Almost all of us experience love in our lives, but what exactly is it? In my field of psychological science, love has been viewed in numerous ways. Sigmund Freud famously defined love as a seeking of complementarity by finding someone who represents one's ideal self.[1] In Freud's wake, later psychologists have variously defined it as a form of attachment, a form of addiction, an evolutionary adaptation, a cultural adaptation, and an expansion of the self, among others.[2]

The work of Phillip Shaver and Cynthia Hazan on attachment theory builds on Freud, as well as on the work of John Bowlby. Shaver and Hazan, like Freud and Bowlby, suggested that infant attachment can have major effects on the kind of romantic love one is likely to experience as an adult. Thus, although romantic

---

[1] See Sigmund Freud, *Three Essays on the Theory of Sexuality*, in *The Standard Edition of the Complete Psychological Works of Sigmund Freud*, ed. J. Strachy and A. Freud (London: Hogarth Press, 1905), 7:136–243; see also Martin S. Bergmann, "Freud's Three Theories of Love in the Light of Later Developments," *Journal of the American Psychoanalytic Association* 36 (1988): 653–672.

[2] For these definitions, see the essays collected in Robert J. Sternberg and Karin Sternberg, *The New Psychology of Love*, 2nd ed. (New York: Cambridge University Press, 2019).

love is typically experienced in adulthood, its origins can be traced to experiences very early in life. The notion of an expansion of self-proposed by Arthur Aron most closely follows upon Freud's notion. In Aron's theory, one's partner helps one expand oneself beyond one's present boundaries toward an ideal self. This theory thus builds on Freud's notion of seeking an ideal self. In my own work with Michael Barnes, I have found that ideal images of oneself and of a partner actually play a greater role in relationship satisfaction than does one's perception of one's actual self and of one's actual partner. I have proposed that love can be understood in terms of two elements: a series of triangles and a set of stories.

## The Triangle of Love

In particular, I have suggested that love comprises three elements: intimacy, passion, and commitment.[3] Intimacy involves feelings of warmth, trust, care, compassion, and communication. High levels of intimacy constitute essentially a good friendship. Whereas intimacy is largely emotional, passion is more motivational. High levels of passion involve an urgent desire to be with someone, a feeling that one's life could not go on without that someone, a feeling of intense need for that someone, and the sense that the loved one is like a dream come true. Commitment, in contrast to intimacy and passion, is more cognitive. High levels of commitment involve the belief that one is in a relationship for keeps, no matter what happens, and that one ideally would like to spend one's whole life with a person.

---

[3] Robert J. Sternberg, "A Triangular Theory of Love," *Psychological Review* 93 (1986): 119–135; and Sternberg, *Cupid's Arrow: The Course of Love through Time* (New York: Cambridge University Press, 1998).

Different combinations of the elements of love yield different kinds of love. In particular, intimacy by itself constitutes liking of the kind found in a close friendship; passion by itself is infatuation or infatuated love; commitment by itself is empty love; intimacy plus passion yield romantic love; intimacy plus commitment yield companionate love; passion plus commitment equals fatuous or foolish love; and intimacy, passion, and commitment combined yield consummate or complete love.

Love relationships change over time as levels and balances of the components change. For example, what starts off as consummate love can become companionate love if the passion goes away. Or what starts off as romantic love can trail off into a friendship if the passion dissipates.

Each individual in a relationship has a real and an "ideal" triangle. The real triangle represents the way the individual feels toward the loved one. The ideal triangle represents the way one ideally would like to feel. The more those two triangles correspond, in general, the happier one will be in a relationship. Furthermore, our research has revealed that one is happier to the extent one's real and ideal triangles match those of one's partner. In other words, success in a relationship depends in large part upon matching of triangles. It further depends on sheer amounts of intimacy, passion, and commitment. If one simply does not have enough of these elements, it becomes harder to make a relationships work. Our research further shows that a particularly powerful predictor of success in a love relationship is the difference between what one hopes for from the other person, and what one feels one is getting in terms of the triangle of love. There is only a modest correlation between what one thinks one is getting and what the partner believes he or she is giving.

## Love as a Story

How do triangles of love form? This question is addressed by a second theory, called the theory of love as a story.[4] According to this theory, literally from the time we are born, we are exposed to stories about love—our parents', those of our parents' friends, in movies, on television, or wherever. This theory builds on Freud's views, in that love is seen as developing out of childhood experiences. As an interaction between our personality and the stories to which we are exposed, we start to form our own set of stories about what we believe love should be. These stories are hierarchically arranged—that is, some are more preferred and others less preferred. Each story has two roles, and a love relationship between two people involves one person filling each of the two roles.

What are some examples of stories? One story is a fairy-tale story, with a prince and a princess. Another is a travel story, with two travelers through time trying to stay on the same path. And yet another story is a business story, involving two business partners. Some stories are less prosocial. A horror story, for example, involves a terrorizer and a victim, and a police story involves a police officer keeping careful track of a suspected criminal. An art story involves one seeing the other as a work of art (and hence is very dependent on the maintenance of physical attractiveness), whereas a collector story involves one's collecting of partners to meet different needs.

## The Duplex Theory

The two theories together—of triangles and stories—form a duplex theory.[5] In the duplex theory, stories generate triangles. For

---

[4] Robert J. Sternberg, *Love Is a Story* (New York: Oxford University Press, 1998).
[5] Robert J. Sternberg, "A Duplex Theory of Love," in *The New Psychology of Love*, ed. Robert J. Sternberg and Karin Sternberg, 2nd ed. (Cambridge: Cambridge University Press, 2018), 280–299.

example, those with a business story generally will have lower levels of passion than those with fairy-tale stories. Someone with a horror story may have a high level of passion, but the lack of intimacy quickly can harm the relationship.

Questionnaires are available for people to assess their triangles and stories. By better understanding what they are seeking, people potentially can find relationships that will help them optimize their happiness and long-term satisfaction.

CHAPTER 12

# Love and Desire in Nietzsche and Levinas

*Fiona Ellis*

PRELIMINARIES

It is a truth universally acknowledged that Friedrich Nietzsche stands opposed to otherworldly philosophy and to religion, that he criticizes Arthur Schopenhauer (the "European Buddhist"), Buddhism, Christianity, and theism more generally in this context, and that his aim is to defend a framework that is resolutely this-worldly and life-affirming—all the better to provide a solution to the problem of nihilism, we are to suppose. What is less clear is how this earthly descent is to be understood, and what the implications are for an understanding of love and desire. Martha Nussbaum talks of Nietzsche's commitment to "an art of this-worldly love," the love in question involving the transfiguring power and magic of *eros*.[1] Robert Pippin

---

1 Martha Nussbaum, "Nietzsche, Schopenhauer, and Dionysus," in *The Cambridge Companion to Schopenhauer*, ed. Christopher Janaway (Cambridge: Cambridge University Press, 1999), 369.

Fiona Ellis, *Love and Desire in Nietzsche and Levinas* In: *Love*. Edited by: Ryan Patrick Hanley, Oxford University Press. © Oxford University Press 2024. DOI: 10.1093/oso/9780197536476.003.0018

claims that the problem of nihilism is a problem of desire, and that the possibility of sustaining a kind of unrequited love is one of the best images for the question Nietzsche wants to ask about nihilism.[2] Others take him to be embracing an unrelenting egoism, the implication being that genuine love has been squeezed from the picture in favor of an egoistic will to power.[3] The complaint makes sense on the assumption that Nietzsche's love is erotic, and that erotic love is irredeemably selfish—that it is 'egocentric' and 'acquisitive,' as the theologian Anders Nygren so familiarly and influentially put it.[4] Some of what Nietzsche says suggests a commitment to this picture.[5] However, this conception of *eros* as selfish can be disputed, and we shall see that Nietzsche's will to power admits of an interpretation that narrows the gap between his own approach and the religious position he is seeking to upstage. As Georg Simmel puts it in the context of questioning Nietzsche's attack on Christianity, "He was unaware that in great measure his own values and those of Christianity could be subsumed under the same standard."[6] There will be a question here—central to the dispute between Nietzsche and Emmanuel Levinas—of whether

---

2 Robert Pippin, "The Erotic Nietzsche: Philosophers without Philosophy," in *Erotikon: Essays on Eros, Ancient and Modern*, ed. Shadi Bartsch and Thomas Bartscherer (Chicago: University of Chicago Press, 2005), 187. Pippin's position is also spelled out in his "Morality as Psychology, Psychology as Morality: Nietzsche, Eros, and Clumsy Lovers," in *Idealism as Modernism: Hegelian Variations* (Cambridge: Cambridge University Press, 1997), 351–374; and Pippin, "Love and Death in Nietzsche," in *Religion after Metaphysics* (Cambridge: Cambridge University Press, 2003), 7–28.

3 Bertrand Russell compares Nietzsche to Machiavelli, claiming that "both have an ethic which aims at power and is deliberately anti-Christian." He claims also that "it does not occur to Nietzsche as possible that a man should genuinely feel universal love, obviously because he himself feels almost universal hatred and fear.... His 'noble' man—who is in daydreams—is a being wholly devoid of sympathy, ruthless, cunning, concerned only with his own power." See Russell, *History of Western Philosophy* (London: Routledge, 2005), 680.

4 Anders Nygren, *Agape and Eros: The Christian Idea of Love*, trans. Philip S. Watson (Philadelphia: Westminster Press, 1953), 175. On Nygren, see also chapter 3 in this volume.

5 See, e.g., Friedrich Nietzsche, *The Gay Science*, ed. Bernard Williams, trans. Josefine Nauckhoff (Cambridge: Cambridge University Press, 2001), book 1, §14: "The Things People Call Love."

6 Georg Simmel, *Schopenhauer and Nietzsche*, trans. Helmut Loiskandl, Deena Weinstein, and Michael Weinstein (Urbana: University of Illinois Press, 1991), 140.

desire's transfigurative power can be accommodated in the absence of God, and what the implications are for its relation to love.

Erotic love is to be distinguished from Christian love or *agape* according to Nygren. As he puts it, they belong to two entirely separate spiritual worlds—selfish *eros* pertaining to the grasping and needy human, and selfless *agape* to the Divine: "God loves because it is His nature to love, and His love consists, not in getting, but in doing good."[7] A similar effusive movement is enacted when we partake in this love by doing good, and Nygren talks in this context of the desire that God's will should be done, distinguishing it from the erotic desire at issue when we are striving for something that we lack and need.[8] On this framework, then, erotic desire is to be distinguished from love, as the latter involves giving rather than taking. It is granted, however, that there is a nongrasping desire at the heart of love, and we are to suppose that (nonacquisitive) desire and love are perfectly united in God.[9]

Nietzsche associates Christian love with the life-denying attitude it is his purpose to transcend, objecting that its underlying values—compassion, self-denial, and self-sacrifice—are that on the basis of which one says 'no' to self and life.[10] He claims further that Christianity *poisoned* eros[11]—turning to bitterness the most precious thing in life, as Pope Benedict XVI sums up the complaint.[12] So it is denied that Christian love has the power to transfigure in any positive sense, and Nietzsche associates it rather with a kind of stagnation and

---

7 Nygren, *Agape and Eros*, ix.
8 Nygren, *Agape and Eros*, ix.
9 As Pope Benedict XVI puts it in his Encyclical *Deus Caritas Est*, God's love is wholly *eros* and wholly *agape*.
10 Friedrich Nietzsche, *On the Genealogy of Morality*, ed. Keith Ansell-Pearson, trans. Carol Diethe (Cambridge: Cambridge University Press, 2017), Preface, §5.
11 "Christianity gave Eros poison to drink:—he did not die from it, but degenerated into a vice" (Friedrich Nietzsche, *Beyond Good and Evil*, eds. Rolf-Peter Hortsmann and Judith Norman, trans. Judith Norman [Cambridge: Cambridge University Press, 2002], part 4, 168).
12 See his Encyclical *Deus Caritas Est*.

apathy—the kind of apathy that is going to be central to an understanding of the supposed *problem* of desire.

Desire is likewise fundamental to Levinas's scheme of things. He agrees with Nygren that erotic love has its origin in the grasping and needy human being, even while granting that its trajectory exceeds this selfish perspective to move, albeit equivocally, in a transcendent direction.[13] He agrees also that *agape*, or as he puts it, "love of one's neighbour; love without Eros, charity,"[14] has its source in God, arguing that it is expressed in the responsibility we have toward others,[15] and that it must be cultivated if we are to realize our true humanity and make the world a better place. This would seem on its face a perfect counterblast to Nietzsche given Nietzsche's antipathy to religion and religious morality. But things are rather more complex, and we shall see that their seemingly disparate conceptions of love and desire have more in common than one might suppose. First, Levinas agrees that our focus must be *this* world, for neighborly love, as he understands it, involves taking responsibility for other human beings, and he denies in any case that there is any "world behind our world,"[16] referring with relief to "the death of a certain god inhabiting the world behind the scenes."[17] Second, this neighborly love is a desire-involving love, albeit a nonerotic desire that has a transformative power of its own insofar as it motivates us to be moral. Third,

---

[13] Emmanuel Levinas describes the erotic encounter as "the very contrary of the social relation.... It is complacent, it is pleasure and dual egoism" (*Totality and Infinity*, trans. Alphonso Lingis [Pittsburgh: Duquesne University Press, 1969], 265–266). He grants that the trajectory of *eros* exceeds this selfish perspective, and that there is a kind of "movement unto the invisible" (258), but this movement is "broken and satisfied as the most egoist and cruellest of needs" (254).

[14] Emmanuel Levinas, "Philosophy, Justice, and Love," in *Entre Nous*, trans. Michael B. Smith and Barbara Harshav (London: Continuum, 2006), 88.

[15] See Levinas, "Philosophy, Justice, and Love," 88. For some doubts about the extent of Levinas's commitment to Christian *agape*, see Claire Catz, "Levinas between Agape and Eros," *Symposium* 11 (2007): 333–350.

[16] Emmanuel Levinas, "Meaning and Sense," in *Basic Philosophical Writings*, ed. Adriann T. Peperzak, Simon Critchley, and Robert Bernasconi (Bloomington: Indiana University Press, 1996), 60.

[17] Emmanuel Levinas, *Otherwise Than Being or Beyond Essence*, trans. Alphonso Lingis (Dordrecht: Kluwer, 1991), 185.

Levinas's characterization of this "love without eros" suggests a commitment to the very inflammatory ingredients one might have supposed to be exclusive to *eros*.[18] Finally, Levinas describes this desire as insatiable, claiming that it nourishes itself not with food but with hunger.[19] This would seem to be a clear case of what it could mean for desire to be self-sustaining, although it remains to be seen whether the image of an unrequited lover is appropriate, and where this leaves the aforementioned problem of desire.

## Two Conceptions of Desire

Nietzsche's work abounds with erotic images and motifs, all of which testify to his preoccupation with the affective dimension of human existence.[20] One such motif—familiar from Plato—is that of the philosopher as erotic lover, although Nietzsche adds a flourish that pits him against Plato (and philosophy more generally), and which suggests that the typical philosophical lover has deviated from his true path. As he puts it, the philosopher's approach has involved a "grotesque seriousness"; his advances have been "clumsy" and "unsuitable."[21] Nietzsche's main bone of contention is the assumption that what we really want is something beyond this world—something untainted by "human flesh and colour and a mass of perishable rubbish,"

---

18 Stella Sanford offers a helpful discussion of this ambivalence in her *The Metaphysics of Love* (London: Athlone Press, 2000), ch. 5.
19 Levinas, *Totality and Infinity*, 34.
20 See, for example, *On the Genealogy of Morality*, Preface, §1: "'Where your treasure is, there will your heart be also'; *our* treasure is where the hives of our knowledge are, As born winged-insects and intellectual honey gatherers we are constantly making for them, concerned at heart with only one thing—to 'bring something home.'" See also the opening of *Thus Spoke Zarathustra*, ed. Adrian Del Caro and Robert Pippin (Cambridge: Cambridge University Press, 2006), 3: "I am weary of my wisdom, like a bee that has gathered too much honey.... I want to bestow and distribute.... Bless the cup that wants to flow over, such that water flows golden from it and everything carries the reflection of your bliss."
21 Nietzsche, *Beyond Good and Evil*, 3. It is in the light of this criticism that we can appreciate this work's opening: "Suppose that truth is a woman and why not?"

as Diotima puts it in her famous speech,[22] and which, alone, can afford genuine fulfillment.

We have here the kind of stance that Nietzsche diagnoses and deplores in his 'otherworldly' opponents, and I have noted already his supposed commitment to an art of this-worldly love. Pippin sees in his positive approach some important implications for an understanding of philosophical desire and desire more generally. In short, he wants to claim on Nietzsche's behalf that (1) there is a desire or "longing" at our core that is "at a level deeper than everyday dissatisfactions and desires,"[23] and "categorically different" from them;[24] (2) this desire cannot be comprehended in the terms presupposed by Plato and theism; (3) a more fruitful alternative involves seeing us as unrequited lovers; and (4) the possibility of sustaining an unrequited love is central to Nietzsche's solution to the problem of nihilism.[25]

The idea that there is a longing at the core of our being is familiar from Plato and from Christian developments of his position as found, for example, in Augustine's claim that our hearts are restless until they rest in God.[26] The further claim that this longing exists at our *core* suggests that it is essential to what we are, and it is made clear that what is at stake here is our humanity: it is "indispensable in a life being human," as Pippin puts it.[27] What little we have said on Nietzsche's behalf suggests that he takes issue with the Platonist and theistic conception of

---

22 Plato, *Symposium*, trans. Walter Hamilton (London: Penguin, 1951), 211e. See also chapter 2 in this volume.
23 Pippin, "The Erotic Nietzsche," 182.
24 Pippin, "The Erotic Nietzsche," 181.
25 Pippin, "The Erotic Nietzsche," 187.
26 Augustine, *Confessions* 1.1.
27 Pippin, "The Erotic Nietzsche," 183. Nietzsche is operating here at the level of meaning rather than biology, and Pippin suggests that this is part of what he means when he tells us that love (eros) must be learned: "Even he who loves himself will have learned it this way—there is no other way. Love, too, must be learned" (*The Gay Science*, book 4, §334: "One Must Learn to Love"). David McPherson offers a gripping account of the relation between deep desires and the space of meaning in his "Deep Desires," *Religious Studies* 55 (2019): 389–403.

this longing. Pippin spells out the envisaged difficulty as follows, gesturing on his behalf toward a possible alternative position:

> We want a picture of striving without the illusion of a determinate, natural lack that we can fill. To anyone with an intellectual conscience, it will have to feel as though there just can be no human whole, not as proposed by Plato or Aristotle or Christianity or Schiller or Hegel, and so forth, and yet it can't just "not matter" that there can be no such harmony or completion, because all of the ways we have come to think about such desire start out from these assumptions about caused needs or an incompleteness that we strive to complete.[28]

It is not invariably an illusion to suppose that striving involves reference to a determinate, natural lack that we can fill, for the picture appropriately fits at least some of our desires—for example, the appetitive desires at issue when we feel hunger and thirst. Levinas describes such desires in precisely these terms, classifies them as "needs," and claims that they stem from a lack in the subject that is filled by consuming or "assimilating" an object that satisfies the desire.[29] As he puts it, "I can 'feed' on these realities and to a very great extent satisfy myself, as though I had simply been lacking them."[30] Levinas is going to distinguish these "needs" from a different kind of desire, which, he insists, is fundamental to our proper humanity.

Let us grant that there could be a picture of striving without the illusion of a determinate, natural lack that we can fill, but how are its details to be understood? Pippin associates the position to be avoided with Plato and theism, claiming that it involves a commitment to the idea that there is an incompleteness that we strive to complete, and that

---

28 Pippin, "The Erotic Nietzsche," 187.
29 Levinas, *Totality and Infinity*, 117.
30 Levinas, *Totality and Infinity*, 34.

*can* be completed because there exists the requisite "human whole" or "harmony" or "completion." Presumably this harmony is to be found when we "rest in God" (Augustine), or alternatively, when we "contemplate[] absolute beauty with the appropriate faculty and [are] in constant union with it" (Plato).[31]

We have been encouraged to suppose that there is a serious problem with this picture, and I have suggested that the point had better not be that the "lack" model of desire is unacceptable across the board. Rather, it must be that it is inappropriately applied in the context in which Plato and Augustine are operating. It is inappropriately applied because it encourages us to suppose that our deepest longings are voids within us that demand to be filled, that their satisfaction brings elimination, and that they can be satisfied only by something beyond this world. Assuming that these longings are essential to what we are *qua* human beings, then it is an implication of this model that we ought not to be. It suggests also that the world is fundamentally deficient, and that real life is elsewhere. Add to this that it is an illusion to suppose that real life thus understood exists, and we have a further damning charge against the offending model of desire. The objections are spelled out—or spat out—by Nietzsche as follows:

> God having degenerated into a *contradiction of life* instead of its transfiguration and eternal *yes*! God as declared aversion to life, to nature, to the will to life! God as the formula for every slander against "the here and now," for every lie about the "beyond"! God as the deification of nothingness, the canonization of the will to nothingness![32]

---

31 Plato, *Symposium* 212c.
32 Nietzsche, *The AntiChrist*, §18, in *The Anti-Christ, Ecce Homo, Twilight of the Idols*, ed. Aaron Ridley and Judith Norman, trans. Judith Norman (Cambridge: Cambridge University Press, 2005), 15–16.

They are repeated more recently by Gilles Deleuze, who spells out in the clearest terms the implications for an understanding of desire:

> Desire: who except priests would want to call it "lack"?... Those who link desire to lack, the long column of crooners of castration, clearly indicate a long resentment, like an interminable bad conscience.[33]

So desire is not invariably linked to lack, and according to the alternative proposed model, it is to be comprehended in terms of a creative giving or abundance. What could this mean? Pippin introduces the relevant shift in the context of a discussion of the death of God and Nietzsche's remark that Brahms "does not create out of an abundance; he *languishes* for abundance."[34] This is what he says:

> This distinction between desire as a lack—and the death of God as a new lack—and desire as abundance, excess—and so the death of God as freeing such generosity—will emerge frequently in what follows.[35]

We are familiar with the idea of desire as lack—it is associated with the theistic picture to be rejected, and involves seeing the desiring subject as striving toward a completion or perfection that she lacks. The suggestion now is that one who is wedded to this conception of the desiring subject will take God's absence to be a further expression of the relevant lack, or a new occasion for languishing in it. By contrast, there is an alternative conception of desire that liberates us from this tragic conception of humanity, and that becomes available *only* when

---

[33] Gilles Deleuze and Claire Parnet, *Dialogues*, trans. Hugh Tomlinson and Barbara Habberjam (New York: Columbia University Press, 1987), 91.
[34] Pippin, "Love and Death in Nietzsche," 9. The quote from Nietzsche comes from his *The Case of Wagner*, in *Basic Writings of Nietzsche*, trans. Walter Kaufmann (New York: The Modern Library, 1968), 643.
[35] Pippin, "Love and Death in Nietzsche," 9.

God is out of the picture. According to this alternative conception, desire is to be understood as abundance, excess, and generosity, and it is expressed in Nietzsche's talk of an "overflow" of "outpouring forces," and his use of the image of the beehive overloaded with honey to describe the striving soul. The implication here is that we have desire in abundance. But where does it come from? What keeps it going? And what, if anything, does it have to do with the effusive movement that theologians associate with the love of God?

## Unrequited Love

These questions are central to Pippin's concerns, for he associates nihilism with desire's *failure*—the "flickering out of some erotic flame," as he puts it[36]— and takes Nietzsche to be engaged with the problem of how it is to be reignited. There is a concession here to Plato and Augustine in the sense that the desire at issue is *erotic*, but Nietzsche's position supposedly parts company with this framework by conceiving of desire as an overflow of outpouring forces rather than a lack to be filled. I have challenged the assumption that this conceptual shift is the prerogative of the atheist by noting that Levinas is similarly dismissive of the "lack" model as it applies to our properly human desires. We can note also that an analogous conceptual shift is enacted by Diotima in Plato's *Symposium*,[37] and that the notion of an effusive or outpouring force is fundamental to the theist's description of the love of God— this "infinite overflow of love" in which we participate when we reach out to others. The description comes from Max Scheler, who talks also of an "abundance of vital power,"[38] quoting Matthew's claim that "[a] good man out of the good treasure of his heart, bringeth forth good

---

36 Pippin, "The Erotic Nietzsche," 177.
37 See *Symposium* 206c, where Plato takes us from a conception of desire as lack to desire as "creating out of abundance"' or "giving birth in beauty."
38 Max Scheler, *Ressentiment*, trans. Lewis B. Coser and William W. Holdheim (Milwaukee: Marquette University Press, 2003), 64.

things."[39] Scheler is responding here to Nietzsche's complaint that Christian love involves an aversion to life and nature, insisting that what we have rather is an "organic and experienced bond between 'the kingdom of God' and the visible realm." Scheler distinguishes such a picture from one in which the "kingdom of God" is relegated to the "other world" to "stand[] mechanically beside 'this world.'"[40]

Nietzsche likewise uses Matthew's image of the heart's treasure, citing with approval his "[w]here your treasure is, there will your heart be also." Assuming, however, that theism has been rejected, then the heart's treasure in this context cannot have its source in the infinite overflow of God's love, and cannot be understood to be oriented in this direction. It is in the context of tackling the question of how its source and trajectory are to be understood that we can appreciate Pippin's use of Nietzsche's image of the unrequited lover: not one who hankers after an inaccessible object (the lack model), but one who loves her unrequited love, and which she would "at no price relinquish for a state of indifference."[41] Hence:

> The possibility of such an unrequited love, especially the possibility of sustaining it, turns out to be one of the best images for the question Nietzsche wants to ask about nihilism and our response.[42]

The aim here is to accommodate desire's effusive power, and to do so without reference to an external source and object (God's infinite loving desire). The image of the unrequited lover offers a model of how such desire could be sustained, but only if the object of love is the

---

39 Matthew 12.34. Scheler, *Ressentiment*, 67.
40 Scheler, *Ressentiment*, 59.
41 Pippin, "The Erotic Nietzsche," 187. This is the passage in full from Nietzsche: "Restless discovering and divining has such an attraction for us, and has grown as indispensable to us as is to the lover his unrequited love, which he would at no price relinquish for a state of indifference perhaps, indeed, we too are *unrequited* lovers!" (Nietzsche, *Daybreak*, ed. Maudemarie Clark and Brian Leiter; trans. R. J. Hollingdale [Cambridge: Cambridge University Press, 1997], 429).
42 Pippin, "The Erotic Nietzsche," 187.

unrequited love itself rather than some inaccessible object. The terms "desire" and "love" seem to be interchangeable in this account of the dialectic, and we can note that the idea of desire somehow feeding off itself is to be found also in Levinas. As he puts it, "It nourishes itself... with its hunger."[43]

Levinas has moved beyond the "illusion of a lack to be filled" in his conception of desire, and he distinguishes it from everyday dissatisfactions and satisfactions. Hence: it is "not an appeal to food,"[44] and has nothing to do with wanting completion: it "desires beyond everything that can simply complete it."[45] So Levinasian desire fits much of the Nietzschean bill. The difference, however, is that it has its source in something beyond the desirer—something that "animates" the desire, and by virtue of which it is to be distinguished from desires that "proceed[] from the subject."[46] This something—its "object"—is referred to as "the Desirable,"[47] "the Other,"[48] "the Most High,"[49] "the Invisible,"[50] "the Transcendent,"[51] and "Infinity,"[52] and desire thus understood is described as "Revelation."[53] We are left in no doubt about its theistic significance.

How can desire be self-nourishing if it also has an external source? There is no conflict here for Levinas, for the desire in question is not a mere impulse within the subject to be related to its source as effect to cause. Rather, its revelatory status is intrinsic to its nature, the point of describing its object and source as "external" being to capture the sense

---

43 Levinas, *Totality and Infinity*, 34.
44 Levinas, *Totality and Infinity*, 63.
45 Levinas, *Totality and Infinity*, 33.
46 Levinas, *Totality and Infinity*, 62.
47 Levinas, *Totality and Infinity*, 35.
48 Levinas, *Totality and Infinity*, 35.
49 Levinas, *Totality and Infinity*, 35.
50 Levinas, *Totality and Infinity*, 35.
51 Levinas, *Totality and Infinity*, 78.
52 Levinas, *Totality and Infinity*, 78.
53 Levinas, *Totality and Infinity*, 62.

in which it relates the desiring subject to something beyond herself. Desire thus understood is a mode of cognition,[54] but this "thinking" is irreducible to the contemplation of some object, for God cannot be grasped in this way, and the "thinking" at issue here has an irreducibly affective dimension. It is in this latter respect that it counts equally as a mode of desire.[55] How then is the relation between desiring subject and desired object to be understood if not in terms of a "bringing together" or a "disappearance of distance" (the lack model)? This relationship, we are told, is one "whose positivity comes from remoteness, from separation," and Levinas goes so far as to describe the Desired as "invisible." It is "invisible" not just in the sense that it eludes comprehension, but in the sense that it is not given to the subject as an object.

Levinas is talking about God in this context, and he is trying to capture the sense in which we relate to God not as represented object to subject, but rather by partaking in the desire-involving movement that has its source in God and that motivates our (moral) love for others. The desire at issue here is loving desire, and because we have moved beyond the "lack" model thereof, there is no longer any implication that God's role is to fill this lack, and in this way to bring the desire to an end. From Levinas's point of view this would be to terminate all relations with God, for relating authentically to God requires that we desire in the relevant way. This is what he is getting at when he tells us that "the true Desire is that which the Desired does not satisfy, but hollows out."[56] It is in this sense that desire is insatiable, where this means not that it fails to attain what it really wants (the lack model again) but

---

[54] Emmanuel Levinas, "Philosophy and the Idea of the Infinite," in *To the Other: An Introduction to the Philosophy of Emmanuel Levinas* (West Lafayette, IN: Purdue University Press, 1993), 112.

[55] Hence: "The infinite is not object of a contemplation, that is, is not proportionate to the thought that thinks it. The idea of the infinite is a thought which at every moment *thinks more than it thinks*. A thought that thinks more than it thinks is Desire. Desire 'measures' the infinity of the infinite" ("Philosophy and the Idea of the Infinite," 113. Levinas is committed to rejecting the Neo-Humean assumption that desire stands opposed to cognition. See my "Religious Experience and Desire," *Religious Studies* 55, no. 3 (2019): 355–373 for an examination of this alternative approach to the question of religious desire.

[56] Levinas, "Philosophy and the Idea of the Infinite," 114.

that it is incessantly nourished or renewed. It is at this level of interaction that we are said to "express" the infinite.[57]

We have what Scheler would describe as an "organic and experienced bond" between God and man, but Levinas makes clear that this loving desire is not easy, and he talks in this context of a "difficult adoration."[58] It is difficult because God is out of the picture in one clear enough sense, demanding "the superhuman of man" as we face the "excessive" requirements of morality. He insists that man "will love Him in spite of all God's attempts to discourage such love."[59] Difficult and discouraged adoration returns us to the theme of unrequited love, albeit a love that has seemingly been purged of any erotic dimension—understandably so, if eros involves an irreducibly selfish moment which forestalls its "movement unto the invisible."

The Nietzschean will object that this God is declared aversion to life, to nature, to the will to life, and that such an unrequited love cannot sustain the "erotic flame" that it is *her* purpose to accommodate. It would be like trying to light a fire with a watering hose. Add to this that theism must be rejected (belief in God has become unbelievable),[60] and the question is not simply why we should value such desire, but how it could be sustained in the first place. We can agree that there is a question of why we should cling to a dehumanizing form of desire, and there are familiar Nietzschean answers. However, it has not been shown that desire for God *is* dehumanizing. Indeed, Levinas himself describes this "love without eros" as involving a "dazzling, where the eye takes more than it can hold, an igniting of the skin which touches

---

57 Hence: "The infinite is not 'in front of me'; it is I who express it, but I do so precisely in giving a sign of the giving of signs, of the 'for the other' in which I am disinterested: here I am [*me voici*]" (Emmanuel Levinas, "God and Philosophy," in *Of God Who Comes to Mind*, trans. Bettina Bergo [Stanford, CA: Stanford University Press, 1998], 75).
58 Emmanuel Levinas, "Loving the Torah More Than God," in *Difficult Freedom: Essays on Judaism*, trans. Sean Hand (Baltimore: Johns Hopkins University Press, 1990), 144–145.
59 Levinas, "Loving the Torah More Than God," 144–145.
60 This is how Nietzsche sums up the idea of the death of God (*The Gay Science*, book 5, §343).

and does not touch what is beyond the graspable, and burns."[61] The image of an erotic flame suddenly seems entirely appropriate, and we are forced to question yet again the assumption that eros and agape are to be disjunctively opposed.

As for the complaint that theism must be rejected, Nietzsche has not provided a convincing argument to establish this conclusion; nor has it been shown that "there just can be no human whole, not as proposed by Plato or Aristotle or Christianity or Schiller or Hegel, and so forth." The "and so forth" is telling, particularly in the light of our current Levinasian interests, for Levinas forces us to rethink not just what it could mean for God to be present, but what the implications might be for an understanding of human wholeness or completion. I shall return to these issues later. First, though, we must tackle the question of the nature and source of Nietzschean desire.

## Nietzschean Desire

We want a picture of striving without the illusion of a lack to be filled. This condition is met by a Levinasian conception of desire, but Levinasian desire has its source in God, and Nietzsche must presumably reject this feature. Second, the desire in question is intended to involve a transfiguring power. Such power is characteristic of Levinasian desire insofar as its subject becomes a morally responsible, loving human being, but Nietzsche takes issue with theistic morality, and we have been encouraged to suppose that the transfigurative power with which *he* is concerned has its origin in *eros* rather than *agape*.

Assuming that *eros* and *agape* are to be dualistically opposed à la Nygren, then it makes sense to say of Nietzschean desire that it has its origin in the subject, that it is egocentric and acquisitive, and that the allegedly transformative power it involves has more in common with

---

61 Levinas, "God and Philosophy," 163.

Schopenhauer's relentlessly hungry will than with anything pertaining to morality, spirituality, and God. This interpretation fits some of what Nietzsche says of the will to power, for this vital power—which is supposedly key to our motivational makeup—is said to be "essentially a process of appropriating, injuring, overpowering the alien and the weaker, oppressing, being harsh, imposing your own form, incorporating, and at least, the very least, exploiting." Exploitation, he continues, "does not belong to a corrupted or imperfect, primitive society: it belongs to the *essence* of being alive as a fundamental organic function; it is a result of genuine will to power."[62] He claims elsewhere that love involves the same instinct as greed, making clear that this goes for *agape* as well as *eros*.[63]

The idea that *eros* is a selfish love returns us to Levinas, and it will be remembered that he grants an ambiguity in its trajectory—one that compromises the idea that it is the same instinct as greed, and that testifies to its (obscure) transcendent dimension. An equal ambiguity is to be found in Nietzsche's conception of *eros* and in this case too there is a move away from an exclusively selfish paradigm. The emphasis now is upon the perfecting of a kind of spiritual power—one that seems to have more in common with the effusive and dynamic force of *agape* than a mean-spirited and static egoism. The general idea is familiar from what has been said about the trajectory of Nietzschean desire, and Nietzsche talks in this context of "the feeling of fullness, of power that wants to overflow, the happiness associated with a high state of tension, the consciousness of a wealth that wants to make gifts and give away."[64] He describes one who possesses such wealth as a "noble person," claiming that such a person "helps the unfortunate too, although not (or hardly ever) out of pity, but rather more out of

---

62  Nietzsche, *Beyond Good and Evil*, §259.
63  Most explicitly in book 1, §14 of *The Gay Science* ("The Things People Call Love").
64  Nietzsche, *Beyond Good and Evil*, §260, p. 154. *Beyond Good and Evil*, ed. Rolf-Peter Hortsmann and Judith Norman, trans. Judith Norman (Cambridge: Cambridge University Press, 2002).

an impulse generated by the overabundance of power." There is surely something more going on here than unreconstituted egoism.[65]

Jacob Golomb agrees that the notion of spiritual power and growth is fundamental to Nietzsche's mature philosophy, and argues that we should see his concept of the will to power in this light.[66] Power thus understood has nothing to do with coercion or force— for which latter the term *Kraft* rather than *Wille* is more appropriate.[67] Rather, it involves a "triumph over blind nature and basic instincts,"[68] a "dynamic growth,"[69] a "spiritualization of power"[70] as one strives to "become an autonomous person capable of devising and effectuating values," overcoming "whatever elements are alien to the inner organic personality and its creativity and freedom."[71] The further crucial claim is that will to power is insatiable: it is "a perpetual movement of the whole person in relation to everything it encounters. . . . By nature this activity is incessant, for its range of operation is infinite and in principle inexhaustible."[72] Nietzsche is said to be aspiring to the Socratic value of encouraging only the good life, and to be recommending "a 'healthy' egoistic morality which springs

---

65 We should bear in mind that the German word for which "pity" is the translation is *Mitleid*, and that *Mitleid* also means "compassion." The word "pity" carries negative connotations that help to make sense of Nietzsche's attitude to a morality based on this idea. Scheler distinguishes between two forms of sacrifice, the first of which "is a beautiful and natural overflow of one's forces," and which corresponds to Nietzsche's conception of effusive power or healthy egoism. The second is "inspired by self-hatred, by hatred of one's own weakness and misery . . . love for the 'small', the 'poor', the 'weak', and the 'oppressed' is really disguised hatred" (*Ressentiment*, 64–65). Scheler himself takes the first conception of sacrifice to be fundamental to Christian love properly so called, acknowledging that there are deficient forms thereof that fall foul of Nietzsche's objections.
66 Jacob Golomb, "Will to Power: Does It Lead to the 'Coldest of All Cold Monsters'?," in *The Oxford Handbook of Nietzsche*, ed. John Richardson and Ken Gemes (Oxford: Oxford University Press, 2013), 526.
67 Golomb, "Will to Power," 527.
68 Golomb, "Will to Power," 528.
69 Golomb, "Will to Power," 529.
70 Golomb, "Will to Power," 531.
71 Golomb, "Will to Power," 526.
72 Golomb, "Will to Power," 536–537.

out of a kind of power which fosters vitality and strength rather than fear and weakness."[73] Hence,

> Persons who love and esteem themselves are in psychologically better position to express unconditionally their love to others without being afraid that by this act they might weaken their own power and selfhood. Similarly, genuine gifts generally come from persons who experience their own selves as gifts while the genuinely altruistic acts are performed by egoists endowed with a strong sense of positive power. Their inherent and abundant richness overflows and is offered gratis to others.[74]

This could almost be Scheler on Christian love. Golomb insists, however, that, for Nietzsche, there is no escape from the "nihilism" of the age, and that we can go forward only by "honestly facing the stark truth about the sheer immanency of our universe (GS 108–11), i.e., that there is no absolute truth, no transcendent goal, no value or meaning in itself."[75]

## Picking Up the Pieces

We have returned full circle to the nihilistic themes with which we began, and are in a position now to adjudicate the relevant disputes surrounding the notions of love and desire, including their bearing upon the supposed problem of nihilism. First, and most significantly, Nietzsche has not offered a convincing debunking of theism. Contemporary Nietzschean scholarship tends to be premised on the assumption that he has, but this assumption is contestable, and with it Nietzsche's insistence that belief in God is unbelievable. So there *is*

---

[73] Golomb, "Will to Power," 538.
[74] Golomb, "Will to Power," 538–539.
[75] Golomb, "Will to Power," 543.

a possible escape from the "nihilism" of the age, although the crucial questions are what it means for God to be part of the equation, and where this leaves the so-called problem of desire. This is where the case of Levinas becomes significant, for Levinas agrees with Nietzsche that we must reject the God behind the scenes who says "no" to all things human; and his conception of God's presence in the world—the only world there is—concedes in large measure to the atheist's outlook. There are important implications here for what it means to talk of the universe's sheer immanency.

It is fundamental to Levinas's picture that desire is oriented toward God, and we can say that it has a transcendent goal in this respect provided that this is not taken to mean that desire's trajectory is mapped out in advance,[76] or that it is aimed at its own extinction.[77] On the contrary, the focus is upon desire's ever-growing depth and the moral and spiritual journey this involves. Nietzsche is concerned equally with desire's incessant life and its significance for our humanity, objecting that this life is compromised on a theistic framework. The worry here is that, on such a framework, there is nothing intrinsically valuable about desire and humanity, and the goal that serves to compromise these things—union with God—cannot be taken seriously in any case. This latter complaint has been disputed. As for the worry that theism fails to accommodate the value of (human) life and desire, these things are inextricably tied and valued as far as Levinas is concerned, although

---

[76] Hence: "This remoteness [of the Desirable] is radical only if desire is not the possibility of anticipating the desirable, if it does not think it beforehand, if it goes toward it aimlessly" (Levinas, *Totality and Infinity*, 34).

[77] Levinas takes as his focus desire as it plays out in the human realm, and is not interested in speculating about its possible posthuman life. Among those theologians who do engage in such speculation, Gregory of Nyssa is not untypical: "Every desire for the Good which is attracted to that ascent constantly expands as one progresses in pressing on to the Good.... This truly is the vision of God: never to be satisfied in the desire to see him.... No limit would interrupt growth in the ascent to God, since no limit to the Good can be found nor is the increasing of desire for the Good brought to an end because it is satisfied" (Gregory of Nyssa, *The Life of Moses*, trans. Abraham J. Malherbe and Everett Ferguson [New York: Paulist Press, 1978], §238–239). See Talbot Brewer's *The Retrieval of Ethics* (Oxford: Oxford University Press, 2009), 56–65, for further notable examples in the theological tradition.

his agapeic framework seems to be in danger at times of undermining the significance of a properly human self-concern. The concessions he makes in the direction of *eros* help to deflect the force of this worry,[78] and his insistence that the desire at issue is to be understood as an effusive and insatiable power puts him in the company of Nietzsche.

Nietzsche's task is to accommodate the possibility of this insatiable power without reference to God. The desire in question is erotic, and seemingly a world apart from that with which Levinas is concerned, assuming that *eros* and *agape* are to be dualistically opposed. Some of the evidence lends justice to this opposition. Equally, however, and more in line with Nietzsche's concern for the future development of humanity, we find a picture that begins to resemble the Levinasian approach, even to the extent that the vitality and power at issue have an irreducibly moral dimension. If this is a healthy *egoism*, then it is an egoism that has more in common with the rightful self-concern of the properly human being than the appropriative attitude of one who seeks only self to please.

The gap has been narrowed between these putatively distinct kinds of desire, and we are returned again to the question of whether such desire can sustain itself in the absence of God. It seems easy enough to imagine a purely self-generated desire that has nothing to do with God—think of Schopenhauer's relentlessly hungry will. Yet we have moved beyond a merely animal urge to accommodate desires that are tied up with our humanity, including those that are operative in the context of morality. Could these desires be purely self-generated? The question becomes more complex once it is acknowledged that they are irreducible to urges, and Nietzsche himself concedes something to the

---

78 See Hilary Putnam, "Levinas and Judaism," in *The Cambridge Companion to Levinas*, ed. Simon Critchley and Robert Bernasconi (Cambridge: Cambridge University Press, 2002), 33–62, for some Aristotelian worries about Levinas's position. Michael Morgan responds to these worries on Levinas's behalf in his *Discovering Levinas* (Cambridge: Cambridge University Press, 2007), 289–299.

cognitive model that it is Levinas's purpose to defend.[79] It is unclear what it could mean for desire in this sense to be self-generated, except insofar as we are granting the (innocuous) truth that the relevant desires belong to subjects, although the Nietzschean could predictably extend the creative act to desire's object (God and morality as human inventions).

There is no resolving the matter conclusively, and I want to end by reflecting briefly on a beautiful passage from Nietzsche's late notebooks, which has a bearing upon the issue. The specific focus is whether the transfigurative power of love involves creation or discovery:

> Is the most astonishing proof wanted of how far the transfigurative force of intoxication can go? 'Love' is that proof, what's called love in all the languages and mutenesses of the world. Intoxication here gets the better of reality in such a way that, in the consciousness of the lover, the cause seems obliterated and something else located in its place [ . . . ] but love, and even love of God, the saintly love of "saved souls," at root remains one thing: a fever that has reasons to transfigure itself, an intoxication that does well to lie about itself... And anyway, when one loves one is a good liar, to oneself and about oneself: one strikes oneself as transfigured, stronger, richer, more perfect, one *is* more perfect [ . . . ] But it would be a mistake to stop at love's power to lie: it does more than just imagine, and actually alters the ranking of values. And not only does it change the feeling of values.... The lover is more valuable, is stronger[ . . . ]The lover becomes a spendthrift: he's rich enough for it. He now dares, becomes an adventurer, becomes a donkey of generosity and innocence; he believes in God again, he believes in virtue because he

---

79 Hence: "The mistaking of passion and *reason*, as if the latter were an entity of its own rather than a state of relations between different passions and desires; and as if every passion did not have within itself its quantum of reason" (Nietzsche, *Writings from the Late Notebooks*, ed. Rüdiger Bittner, trans. Kate Sturge [Cambridge: Cambridge University Press, 2003], Notebook 11, November 1887 and March 1888, 310).

believes in love. On the other hand this idiot of happiness grows wings and new capacities, and even the doors of art open up to him.[80]

Nussbaum sees in this an allusion to Plato's *Phaedrus*—both with respect to its reference to the lover growing wings and in its insistence on love's generosity. The further crucial idea is that love's transformative power involves both creation and discovery: it is illusion in the sense that it corresponds to no preexisting reality; "And yet it is its own this-worldly reality, and its fiction-making makes fictions that are gloriously there."[81] Nietzsche's way of expressing the point is to say that love "actually alters the ranking of values[ ... ] The lover is more valuable."

The lover's growing wings in the *Phaedrus* are nourished by the soul's vision of the good.[82] In this respect there is a parallel with Levinas, although Levinas insists that this vision is "without image." As for the idea that love's transformative power corresponds to no preexisting reality, this could just be a way of lending emphasis to its *transformative* power, and there need be no implication that what comes forth has the status of a fiction. Indeed, even Levinas must concede that we "create value" in this sense, not least because it is fundamental to his picture that God has hidden his face so as to demand the superhuman of man. Love alters the ranking of values in *this* respect, but what of the transformative power of *eros*? Is this not more appropriately aligned with illusion? It certainly *can* involve illusion, given the human potential for fantasy and self-deception—it "has the power to lie" in this respect. However, we know from Nietzsche that such a threat is not peculiar to *eros*, and it is compatible with this potential failing in the subject that love can bring a kind of truth. Isn't this possibility belied by Nietzsche's talk of intoxication? Certainly so, if intoxication spells illusion, and Levinas stresses how important it is to distinguish desire's

---

80 **Nietzsche**, *Writings from the Late Notebooks*, Notebook 14, spring 1888, 14[120], 255.
81 Nussbaum, "Nietzsche, Schopenhauer, and Dionysus," 371.
82 Plato, *Phaedrus*, trans. Christopher Rowe (London: Penguin, 2005), 246a–249d.

insatiable life from the "romantic dream" at issue when one is getting off on a beautiful feeling.[83] A further possible paradigm for the figure of the unrequited lover, and it makes perfect sense to suppose that such a feeling could be preferred not only to a state of indifference but to a real-life loving relationship. Evidence suggests that Nietzsche is not a romantic dreamer in *this* sense, and that his talk of "intoxication" is testimony to the significance he accords to the transformative power of eros—a power that has an irreducibly effusive dimension. He is in the company of many notable theologians in this latter respect, all of whom grant not merely that *eros* and *agape* are productively and perhaps even inextricably intertwined, but that this goes also for divine desire and love.[84] This latter concession would be a step too far for both Nietzsche and Levinas—Nietzsche because he objects to theism, and Levinas because he thinks that genuine love is nonerotic. I hope to have shown that these seemingly massive differences become considerably less significant upon analysis. Perhaps even Nietzsche "believes in God again," and perhaps he does so "because he believes in love."[85]

---

[83] Levinas, *Totality and Infinity*, 179.
[84] See Sarah Coakley's *God, Sexuality, and the Self* (Cambridge: Cambridge University Press, 2013) for an illustration and defense of this approach as it plays out in the theological tradition.
[85] I thank Ryan Hanley, Sarah Coakley, and John Cottingham for helpful discussion of these issues.

# Reflection

## LOVE AS SOCIAL FORCE: MARTIN LUTHER KING JR.

### *Andre C. Willis*

A particular understanding of love was central to the life and thought of Martin Luther King Jr. His brilliant speeches and writings broadly deployed love as both a "means" and an "end," a present practice and a timeless ethic, a Christian virtue as well as a secular norm. More specifically, it is fair to say that King thought of love as a social force, "the supreme unifying principle of life."[1] His powerful political vision was grounded in the idea that this social force could inspire political movement, and his courageous commitment to expanding American democracy via this love-as-action—grounded in prophetic Black Christianity—manifested itself in different ways.

King jettisoned sentimental appeals to love and deemphasized its romantic qualities. He highlighted a love that, when enacted, could generate public connection and motivate social action. His most simple expressions of this affective, social love—say, how it

---

[1] "When I speak of love I am not speaking of some sentimental and weak response. I am speaking of that force which all of the great religions have seen as the supreme unifying principle of life. Love is somehow the key that unlocks the door which leads to ultimate reality" (Martin Luther King Jr., "Beyond Vietnam: A Time to Break Silence" [delivered April 4, 1967]) in *A Call to Conscience: The Landmark Speeches of Dr. Martin Luther King Jr.*, ed. Clayborne Carson and Kris Shepard (New York: Warner Books, 2001), 161.

Andre C. Willis, *Reflection* In: *Love.* Edited by: Ryan Patrick Hanley, Oxford University Press.
© Oxford University Press 2024. DOI: 10.1093/oso/9780197536476.003.0019

manifested in his exchanges with children—may very well have been his most potent. For example, his description of love to junior high students in Cleveland, Ohio, in 1964—"Love is the greatest power in the world, for it is love that makes the world turn around.... The highest good is love"[2]—is as compelling as the tears he cried when he encountered starving students in Head Start in Marks, Mississippi, in 1966.[3] King's creative acts of love—in word and deed—can be thought of as exemplifying distinctive forms of Afro-Protestant compassion.

King thus worked out of a tradition of love forged by a people whose communities had been destroyed. It is perhaps this legacy, and its persistent aim to rebuild communities, that informed his linking of love as a social force to the ideals of justice and equality. Weaving together numerous insights on love from Augustine, Howard Thurman, Gandhi, and Paul Tillich (among others), King both preached and practiced this social love via nonviolent speech and peaceful resistance. His rhetorical use of love in his spellbinding speeches and writings, and his commitment to the practice of love via his nonviolent love-ethic of resistance, were central in the movement to expand American democracy. What is most striking to me, however, and what I want to focus on in the remainder of this reflection, is his less celebrated practices of loving poor and working-class people. These compassionate acts constituted everyday, commonplace exchanges. Yet these simple acts of love powerfully contributed to community-building.

At the time he was assassinated, King was fighting alongside sanitation workers, forging a cross-racial campaign for poor people, and highlighting the injustices built in to late modern capitalism.

---

[2] Martin Luther King Jr, Address delivered at Addison Junior High 11/03/1964. http://www.thekingcenter.org/archive/document/mlks-address-addison-junior-high (accessed April 20, 2018).

[3] Ralph Abernathy, *And the Walls Came Tumbling Down* (New York: Harper and Row, 1989), 412–413.

Poverty and economic inequality—along with the Vietnam War (with its own class elements)—were his core interests. Of course, class injustice is marked by race, so his focus on poverty and economic inequality included a racial dimension.[4]

In addition to his reasoning regarding the factors behind the social problems of poverty and class inequality, and his commitment to organizing the Poor People's Campaign, I find King's personal choice to live among the poor in Chicago in 1965 (with his wife and four children) to fittingly illuminate this duty to love. Neither simply a reflection of his supporting the theological preferential option for the poor, nor merely a strategic episode to draw attention to the plight of the vulnerable, I take this move as an attempt to actualize the force of love at the individual level by placing himself in proximity—in a daily, personal way—to a particular form of suffering: the despair of the "disinherited." This type of suffering was deeply rooted in African American heritage, as was its antidote.[5] In the face of systematic harm, King's task was to love those suffering in broken communities shaped by conditions of poverty in ways that would allow them to create "beloved communities" influenced by restorative love.

King's move into Chicago's "slum of Lawndale," which he described as an "island of poverty in the midst of an ocean of plenty,"[6] afforded him daily engagement with those who carried the stigma of worthlessness. How did King love people—at the level of everyday, casual, and face-to-face encounters—who had been taught that they were unworthy? He connected with them—or,

---

[4] One wonders how he might have woven gender inequality into his analysis of poverty had he not been murdered, and how his language of social love regarding issues central to women would have worked.

[5] For more on this point, see Howard Thurman, *Jesus and the Disinherited* (Boston: Beacon Press, 1949).

[6] The *Autobiography of Martin Luther King Jr.*, ed. Clayborn Carson (New York: Warner Books, 2001), 300.

in his description of the children in his building, he "saw the light of intelligence glowing in their beautiful dark eyes" and "realized their overwhelming joy because someone had simply stopped to say hello."[7] King loved poor people enough to walk, eat, and rest among them.

We might think about King's intentional choice to live with poor people as a form of democratic friendship or even a type of civic love. To me, however, it feels more like a vital expression of a particular kind of *tenderness*, a fundamental teaching of the Black Church. Thinking about the Kings living in a dilapidated housing project, extending warm smiles and enacting unique forms of fellowship that assuage Black despair, reminds me that small acts of love—not overarching theories or sparkling rhetoric—are important. They improve quality of life and create the solidarity required to transform oppressive sociopolitical conditions.

King's encounters in a Chicago ghetto demonstrate how being present and paying openhearted attention to one's neighbors is a way to begin forging "communities of love and justice." Physically nesting with those who are most at risk, regardless of how wounded their communities might be, was, for King, an act of social love that could "make the world go around" (that is, generate social motion). It led to the mass mobilizations in Chicago in 1965–1966.

Thoughtful consideration of King's speeches and writings on the idea of social love should not overlook the smaller acts of tenderness that marked his daily engagement. Enhancing our connections with the most vulnerable among us remains crucial in a moment of widening class disparity and deepening divisions in our citizenry. Of course, small acts are not enough to tackle the cruel realities of systemic poverty. Yet they are vital for considering how we might begin to create social motion.

---

7 *Autobiography of Martin Luther King Jr.*, 300.

# General Bibliography

### *Works before 1900*

Alighieri, Dante. *Commedia*, trans. Allen Mandelbaum, Digital Dante, Columbia University Libraries, New York, 2018. https://digitaldante.columbia.edu/dante/divine-comedy/inferno/inferno-2/.
Anonymous. *The Cloud of Unknowing: With the Book of Privy Counselling*, trans. Carmen Acevedo Butcher. Boulder, CO: Shambhala, 2009.
Aquinas, Thomas. *Summa Theologica*. 5 vols., trans. Fathers of the English Dominican Province. Notre Dame, IN: Ave Maria Press, 1948.
Aristotle. *Nicomachean Ethics*, ed. and trans. Roger Crisp. Cambridge: Cambridge University Press, 2000.
Aristotle. *Nicomachean Ethics*, trans. Terence Irwin. Indianapolis: Hackett, 1999.
Aristotle. *Nicomachean Ethics Books VIII and IX*, trans. Michael Pakuluk. Cambridge: Cambridge University Press, 1998.
Augustine. *On Christian Teaching*, trans. R. P. H. Green. New York: Oxford University Press, 1997.
Augustine. *The City of God*, trans. Henry Bettenson. New York: Penguin, 2003.
Augustine. *Confessions*, trans. Henry Chadwick. Oxford: Oxford University Press, 1991.
Augustine. *On the Trinity*. In *Augustine: Later Works*, trans. John Burnaby. Philadelphia: Westminster Press, 1955.
Austen, Jane. *Emma*, ed. Richard Cronin and Dorothy McMillan. Cambridge: Cambridge University Press, 2005.
Austen, Jane. *Mansfield Park*, ed. John Wiltshire. Cambridge: Cambridge University Press, 2005.

Austen, Jane. *Northanger Abbey*, ed. Barbara M. Benedict and Deirdre Le Faye. Cambridge: Cambridge University Press, 2006.

Austen, Jane. *Persuasion*, ed. Janet Todd and Antje Blank. Cambridge: Cambridge University Press, 2006.

Austen, Jane. *Pride and Prejudice*, ed. Pat Rogers. Cambridge: Cambridge University Press, 2006.

Austen, Jane. *Sense and Sensibility*. 3 vols. Whitehall: T. Egerton, 1811.

Austen, Jane. *Sense and Sensibility*, ed. Edward Copeland. Cambridge: Cambridge University Press, 2006.

Avicenna. *See* Ibn Sīnā.

Boccaccio, Giovanni. *The Decameron*, trans. G. H. McWilliam. New York: Penguin, 2003.

Bonaventure. *Brevilioquium*, Part Four: *On the Incarnation of the Word*. In *S. Bonaventurae Opera Theologica Selecta*, vol. 5. Firenze: Quaracchi, 1964.

Bonaventure. *Works of Bonaventure: Journey of the Mind into God—The Triple Way, or Love Enkindled—The Tree of Life—The Mystical Vine—On the Perfection of Life, Addressed to Sisters,* trans. José DeVinck. Mansfield Centre, CT: Martino Publishing, 2016.

Brontë, Charlotte. *Jane Eyre*. Oxford: Oxford University Press, 1969.

Catherine of Siena. *Catherine of Siena: The Dialogue*, trans. Suzanne Noffke. Mahwah, NJ: Paulist Press, 1980.

Chateaubriand, François-René de. *Atala, René*. Paris: Librairie de Firmin Didot Frères, 1871.

Chrétien de Troyes. *The Complete Romances of Chrétien de Troyes*, trans. David Staines. Bloomington: Indiana University Press, 1990.

Conway, Anne. *Principles of the Most Ancient and Modern Philosophy*, ed. and trans. Andrew Arlig, Christia Mercer, and Jasper Reid. Oxford: Oxford University Press, forthcoming.

*Corpus Dionysiacum*. Vol. 1. *De divinis nominibus*, ed. Beate Regina Suchla. Berlin: Walter de Gruyter & Co., 1990.

Daylamī, Abu'l-Ḥasan al-. *Kitāb ʿaṭf al-alif al-maʾlūf ʿalāʾl-lām al-maʿṭūf*, trans. Joseph Norment Bell and Hasan Mahmood Abdul Latif Al Shafie as *A Treatise on Mystical Love*. Edinburgh: Edinburgh University Press, 2006.

Descartes, René. *Lettres sur l'amour*, ed. Pierre Chanut. Paris: Editions Mille et une nuits, 2013.

Descartes, René. *Oeuvres de Descartes*, ed. Ch. Adam and P. Tannery. Rev. ed. Paris: Vrin/C.N.R.S., 1964–1976.

Fārābī, Abū Naṣr al-. *Mabādiʾ ārāʾ ahl al-madīnat al-fāḍila / On the Perfect State*, ed. and trans. Richard Walzer. Chicago: Kazi, 1998.

Ficino, Marsilio. *Commentaire sur le Banquet de Platon*, ed. Raymond Marcel. Paris: Les Belles Lettres, 1956.

Ficino, Marsilio. *Commentaire sur le Banquet de Platon, De l'Amour. Commentarium in convivium platonis, De amore*, ed. Pierre Laurens. Paris: Les Belles Lettres, 2002.

Ficino, Marsilio. *Commentaires sur le Traité de l'amour ou le Festin de Platon*, ed. Sylvain Matton. Paris: SÉHA, 2001.

Ficino, Marsilio. *Dionysii Areopagitae. De mystica theologia, De divinis nominibus, interprete Marsilio Ficino*, ed. Pietro Podolak. Napoli: M. D'Auria Editore, 2011.

Ficino, Marsilio. *On Dionysius the Areopagite*, ed. and trans. Michael J. B. Allen. 2 vols. Cambridge, MA: Harvard University Press, 2015.

Ficino, Marsilio. *Epistola ad Fratres Vulgaris*, ed. Paul O. Kristeller. In *Supplementum ficinianum*, 2 vols., 2:109–128. Florence: Olschki, 1937–1945.

Ficino, Marsilio. *Excerpta Marsilii Ficini ex graecis procli commentariis in Alcibiadem Platonis primum*. Venice: Aldus Manutius, 1497.

Ficino, Marsilio. *Lettere*, ed. Sebastiano Gentile. 2 vols. Florence: Olschki, 1990–2010.

Ficino, Marsilio. *The Letters of Marsilio Ficino*, vol. 1, trans. Members of the Language Department of the School of Economic Science, London. London: Shepheard-Walwyn, 1975.

Ficino, Marsilio. *Marsilio Ficino, El Libro dell'Amore*, trans. Sandra Niccoli. Florence: Olschki, 1987.

Gangloff, Jacob Heinrich. *Disputatio physica de sympathia*. Jena: Samuel Adophus Müller, 1669.

Ghazālī, Muḥammad al-. *Iḥyā' 'ulūm al-dīn*. 4 vols. Beirut: Dār al-Hādī, 1993.

Ghazālī, Muḥammad al-. *Love, Longing, Intimacy and Contentment. Kitāb al-maḥabba wa'l-shawq wa'l-uns wa'l-riḍā. Book XXXVI of The Revival of the Religious Sciences*, trans. with an introduction by Eric Ormsby. Cambridge: Islamic Texts Society, 2011.

Gregory of Nyssa. *The Life of Moses*, trans. Abraham J. Malherbe and Everett Ferguson. New York: Paulist Press, 1978.

Hadewijch. *Hadewijch: The Complete Works*, ed. and trans. Mother Columba Hart. Mahwah, NJ: Paulist Press, 1980.

Hirtenstein, Stephen, trans. *The Alchemy of Human Happiness. Chapter 167 of Ibn 'Arabi's Meccan Illuminations*. Oxford: Anqa, 2017.

Horace. *Carmen Saeculare*, ed. and trans. Niall Rudd. Cambridge, MA: Harvard University Press, 2004.

Ibn al-'Arabī, Muḥyī al-Dīn. *al-Futūḥāt al-makkiyya*. 4 vols. Cairo: Bulaq Press, 1911.

Ibn al-ʿArabī, Muḥyī al-Dīn. *Traité de l'amour*. Abbreviated trans. Maurice Gloton. Paris: Albin Michel, 1986.

Ibn al-Farid. *The Wine of Love and Life: Ibn al-Farid's al-Khamriyah and al-Qaysari's Quest for Meaning*, ed. and trans. Emil Homerin. Middle East Documentation Center on Behalf of the Center for Middle Eastern Studies, University of Chicago, 2005.

Ibn Sīnā. *al-Ilāhiyyāt min al-shifāʾ / The Metaphysics of The Healing*. Text and trans. Michael E. Marmura. Provo, UT: Brigham Young University Press, 2005.

Ibn Sīnā. *al-Ishārāt waʾl-tanbīhāt*, ed. Sulaymān Dunyā. Cairo: Muṣṭafā al-Bābī al-Ḥalabī, 1947. Trans. Shams Inati as *Ibn Sīnā and Mysticism: Remarks and Admonitions: Part Four*. London: Kegan Paul International, 1996.

Ibn Sīnā. *al-Mabdaʾ waʾl-maʿād*, ed. ʿAbdullāh Nūrānī. Tehran: McGill Institute of Islamic Studies, 1984.

Ibn Sīnā. *al-Najāt*, ed. Mājid Fakhrī. Beirut: Dār al-Āfāq al-Jadīda, 1982.

Ibn Sīnā. *Risāla fīʾl-ʿishq*, ed. Ḥusayn al-Ṣiddīq and Rāwiyya Jāmūs. Damascus: Dār al-Fikr, 2005. Translated by Emil L. Fackenheim as "A Treatise on Love by Ibn Sina." *Medieval Studies* 7 (1945): 208–228.

Ibn Sīnā. *Sharḥ kitāb Uthūlūjiyya*. In ʿAbd al-Raḥmān Badawī, *Arisṭū ʿind al-ʿarab*, 35–74. Kuwait: Wikālat al-Maṭbūʿāt, 1978.

Ibn Sīnā. *al-Taʿlīqāt*, ed. ʿAbd al-Raḥmān Badawī. Cairo: al-Hayʾat al-Miṣriyya al-ʿĀmma liʾl-Kitāb, 1973.

Ibn Ṭufayl. *Ḥayy ibn Yaqẓan: A Philosophical Tale*, trans. Lenn E. Goodman. Chicago: University of Chicago Press, 2009.

Ikhwān al-Ṣafāʾ. *Rasāʾil Ikhwān al-Ṣafāʾ*. 4 vols. Beirut: Dār Ṣādir, 1957.

John de Caulibus (?). *Meditationes Vitae Christi*, ed. Mary Stallings-Taney. *Corpus Christianorum Continuatio Mediaevalis* (CCCM 153). Turnhout: Brepols, 1997.

John de Caulibus (?). *Meditations on the Life of Christ*, trans. F. X. Taney, Anne Miller, and C. Mary Stallings-Taney. Asheville, NC: Pegasus Press, 2000.

Kant, Immanuel. *Critique of the Power of Judgment*, trans. Paul Guyer and Eric Matthews. Cambridge: Cambridge University Press, 2001.

Kant, Immanuel. *Critique of Practical Reason*, trans. Mary Gregor. Cambridge: Cambridge University Press, 1997.

Kant, Immanuel. *Grounding for the Metaphysics of Morals*, trans. James W. Ellington. 3rd ed. Indianapolis: Hackett, 1993.

Kant, Immanuel. *Groundwork of the Metaphysics of Morals*, trans. Mary Gregor. Cambridge: Cambridge University Press, 1997.

Kant, Immanuel. *Lectures on Ethics*, trans. Peter Heath. Cambridge: Cambridge University Press, 1997.

Kant, Immanuel. *The Metaphysics of Morals*, trans. Mary Gregor. Cambridge: Cambridge University Press, 1996.

Kant, Immanuel. *Observations on the Feeling of the Beautiful and the Sublime*, trans. Paul Guyer. In *Immanuel Kant: Anthropology, History, and Education*, ed. Günter Zöller and Robert B. Louden, 18–62. Cambridge: Cambridge University Press, 2007.

Kant, Immanuel. *Religion within the Boundaries of Mere Reason*, trans. Allen Wood and George Di Giovanni. Cambridge: Cambridge University Press, 1998.

Kierkegaard, Søren. *Fear and Trembling*, in *Fear and Trembling and Repetition*, trans. Howard V. Hong and Edna H. Hong, 1–123. Princeton, NJ: Princeton University Press, 1983.

Kierkegaard, Søren. *The Sickness unto Death*, trans. Howard V. Hong and Edna H. Hong. Princeton, NJ: Princeton University Press, 1980.

Kierkegaard, Søren. *Works of Love*, trans. Howard V. Hong and Edna H. Hong. Princeton, NJ: Princeton University Press, 1995.

*La Vida de la Santa Madre Teresa de Iesus*. In *Obras de la Gloriosa Madre S. Teresa de Iesus, Fundadora de la Reforma de la Orden de Nuestra Señora del Carmen*, vol. 1. Madrid: Bernardo de Villa-Diego, 1678.

Leibniz, Gottfried Wilhelm. *Sämtliche Schriften und Briefe*. Berlin: Akademie-Verlag, 1923.

Lorris, Guillaume de, and Jean de Meun. *Le Roman de la Rose*, ed. Felix Lecoy. Paris: Champion, 1965.

Maimonides, Moses. *Dalālatu 'l-Hā'irīn*, trans. and ed. Salomon Munk. Paris: 1856–1866; reprinted Osnabrück: Zeller, 1964.

Maimonides, Moses. *Hakdamot ha-Rambam la-Mishnah*, ed. Isaac Shailat. Jerusalem: Ma'aliyot, 1995.

Maimonides, Moses. *Mishneh Torah (The Book of Knowledge)*, trans. and ed. Moses Hyamson. New York: Feldheim, 1974.

Maimonides, Moses. *The Guide to the Perplexed*, trans. Lenn Goodman and Phillip Lieberman. Stanford, CA: Stanford University Press, 2024.

Marguerite d'Oingt. *Page of Meditations*. In *Oeuvres de Marguerite D'Oyngt Prieure de Poleteins*, ed. Edouard Philipon, 1–33. Lyon: N. Sheuring, 1877.

Mechthild of Magdeburg. *Mechthild of Magdeburg, The Flowing Light of the Godhead*, trans. Frank Tobin. Mahwah, NJ: Paulist Press, 1998.

Micraelius, Johann. "Modus." In *Lexicon philosophicum terminorum philosophis usitatorum*, 169–170. Düsseldorf: Stern-Verlag Janssen, 1966 [1653].

Mullā Ṣadrā. *al-Ḥikmat al-muta'āliya fi'l-asfār al-'aqliyyat al-arba'a*. 9 vols. Beirut: Dār Iḥyā' al-Turāth al-'Arabī, 1990.

Mullā Ṣadrā. *al-Mabda' wa'l-ma'ād*, ed. Muḥammad Dhabīḥī and Ja'far Shāh-Naẓarī. 2 vols. Tehran: Bunyād-i Ḥikmat-i Islāmī-yi Ṣadrā, 1381/2002.

*The New Oxford Annotated Bible: New Revised Standard Version with the Apocrypha*, 3rd ed. Oxford: Oxford University Press, 2001.

Nietzsche, Friedrich. *The Anti-Christ*, in *The Anti-Christ, Ecce Homo, Twilight of the Idols*, ed. Aaron Ridley and Judith Norman, trans. Judith Norman. Cambridge: Cambridge University Press, 2005.

Nietzsche, Friedrich. *Beyond Good and Evil*, ed. Rolf-Peter Hortsmann and Judith Norman, trans. Judith Norman. Cambridge: Cambridge University Press, 2002.

Nietzsche, Friedrich. *The Case of Wagner*. In *Basic Writings of Nietzsche*, trans. Walter Kaufmann, 601–654. New York: Modern Library, 1968.

Nietzsche, Friedrich. *Daybreak: Thoughts on the Prejudices of Morality*, ed. Maudemarie Clark and Brian Leiter, trans. R. J. Hollingdale. Cambridge: Cambridge University Press, 1997.

Nietzsche, Friedrich. *The Gay Science*, ed. Bernard Williams, trans. Josefine Nauckhoff. Cambridge: Cambridge University Press, 2001.

Nietzsche, Friedrich. *On the Genealogy of Morality*, ed. Keith Ansell-Pearson, trans. Carol Diethe. Cambridge: Cambridge University Press, 2017.

Nietzsche, Friedrich. *Thus Spoke Zarathustra*, ed. Adrian Del Caro and Robert Pippin. Cambridge: Cambridge University Press, 2006.

Nietzsche, Friedrich. *Writings from the Late Notebooks*, ed. Rüdiger Bittner, trans. Kate Sturge. Cambridge: Cambridge University Press, 2003.

*Novum Testamentum Graece*, ed. Fridericus Branscheid. Freiburg: Herder, 1901.

Petrarch, Francesco. *Petrarch's Lyric Poems: The Rime Sparse and Other Lyrics*, ed. and trans. Robert M. Durling. Cambridge, MA: Harvard University Press, 1999.

Pico della Mirandola, Giovanni. *Commento*, trans. Stéphane Toussaint. Lausanne: Éditions l'Age d'Homme, 1989.

Plato. *Phaedrus*, ed. and trans. Harold North Fowler. Cambridge, MA: Harvard University Press, 2005.

Plato. *Phaedrus*, trans. Christopher Rowe. London: Penguin, 2005.

Plato. *Phaedrus*. In *Plato on Love: Lysis, Symposium, Phaedrus, Alcibiades, with Selections from Republic, [and] Laws*, ed. C. D. C. Reeve. Indianapolis: Hackett, 2006.

Plato. *Plato's Lysis*, ed. and trans. Terry Penner and Christopher J. Rowe. Cambridge: Cambridge University Press, 2005.

Plato. *Republic*, trans. G. M. A. Grube, rev. trans. C. D. C. Reeve. In *Plato: Complete Works*, ed. John M. Cooper, 971–1223. Indianapolis: Hackett, 1997.

Plato. *Symposium*, trans. Harold North Fowler. Cambridge, MA: Harvard University Press, 1925.

Plato. *Symposium*, trans. Walter Hamilton. London: Penguin, 1951.
Plotinus. *Enneads*. 7 vols., trans. A. H. Armstrong. Cambridge, MA: Harvard University Press, 1969–1988.
Plotinus. *Traité*, ed. and trans. Pierre Hadot. Paris: Éditions du Cerf, 1990.
Porete, Marguerite. *The Mirror of Simple Souls*, trans. E. L. Babinsky. Mahwah, NJ: Paulist Press, 1993.
Pseudo-Dionysius. *Corpus Dionysiacum*, vol. 1, *De divinis nominibus*, ed. Beate Regina Suchla. Berlin: Walter de Gruyter, 1990.
Pseudo-Dionysius. *Dionysiaca. Recueil donnant l'ensemble des traductions latines des ouvrages attribués au Denys de l'Aréopage*, ed. Philippe Chevalier, 2 vols. Bruges: Desclée de Brouwer, 1937–1950.
Proclus. *In Alcibiadem*, ed. Alain-Philippe Segonds, 2 vols. Paris: Les Belles Lettres, 2003.
Proclus. *Excerpta Marsilii Ficini ex graecis procli commentariis in Alcibiadem Platonis primum*. Venice: Aldus Manutius, 1497.
Proclus. *Sur le Premier Alcibiade de Platon*. ed. Alain-Philippe Segonds. 2 vols. Paris: Les Belles Lettres, 2003.
Richardson, Samuel. *The History of Sir Charles Grandison*, ed. Jocelyn Harris. Oxford: Oxford University Press, 1986.
Rousseau, Jean-Jacques. *Collected Writings of Rousseau*, ed. Christopher Kelly and Roger D. Masters. 14 vols. Lebanon, NH: University Press of New England, 1990–2007.
Rousseau, Jean-Jacques. *Emile*, trans. Allan Bloom. New York: Basic Books, 1979.
Rousseau, Jean-Jacques. *Œuvres complètes*, ed. Bernard Gagnebin and Marcel Raymond. 5 vols. Paris: Gallimard, 1959–1995.
Rūmī, Jalāl al-Dīn. *Kulliyyāt-i Shams yā dīwān-i kabīr*, ed. B. Furūzānfar. 10 vols. Tehran: Dānishgāh, 1336–1346 / 1957–1967.
Rūmī, Jalāl al-Dīn. *The Mathnawī*, ed. R. A. Nicholson. 8 vols. London: Luzac, 1925–1940.
Sappho. *If Not, Winter: Fragments of Sappho*, trans. Anne Carson. New York: Vintage, 2002.
Shapiro, Lisa, ed. *The Correspondence between Princess Elizabeth of Bohemia and René Descartes*. Chicago: University of Chicago Press, 2007.
Spinoza, Baruch. *Ethics*, trans. Samuel Shirley. In *Ethics: with Treatise on the Emandation of the Intellect and Selected Letters*, ed. Seymour Feldman. Indianapolis: Hackett, 1992.
Spinoza, Baruch. *Theologico-Political Treatise*, trans. Samuel Shirley. In *Spinoza: Complete Works*. Indianapolis: Indiana University Press, 2002.
Stendhal. *De l'amour*. 2 vols. Paris: Librairie universelle de P. Mongie, 1822.

Stendhal. *La chasse au bonheur*. Paris: E. Sansot, 1913.
Suhrawardī, Shihāb al-Dīn. *Fī ḥaqīqat al-'ishq / On the Reality of Love*, text and trans. Wheeler Thackston. In *The Philosophical Allegories and Mystical Treatises*, 58–76. Costa Mesa, CA: Mazda, 1999.
Windeatt, Barry, ed. *English Mystics of the Middle Ages*. New York: Cambridge University Press, 1994.
Wolf, A., trans. *Spinoza's Short Treatise on God, Man, and His Well-Being*. London: Adam and Charles Black, 1910.

## *Works after 1900*

Abernathy, Ralph. *And the Walls Came Tumbling Down*. New York: Harper and Row, 1989.
Abrahamov, Binyamin. *Divine Love in Islamic Mysticism: The Teachings of Al-Ghazālī and Al-Dabbāgh*. London: Routledge, 2003.
Alanen, Lilli. "Descartes and Spinoza on the Love of God." In *DE NATURA RERUM: Scripta in honorem professoris Olli Koistinen sexagesimum annum complentis*, ed. Hemmo Laiho and Arto Repo, 74–97. Turku: University of Turku, 2016.
Allen, Michael J. B. *The Platonism of Marsilio Ficino: A Study of His Phaedrus Commentary, Its Sources and Genesis*. Berkeley: University of California Press, 1984.
Allison, Henry. *Kant's Theory of Freedom*. Cambridge: Cambridge University Press, 1990.
Alpern, Kenneth D. "Aristotle on the Friendships of Utility and Pleasure." *Journal of the History of Philosophy* 21 (1983): 303–315.
Anderson-Gold, Sharon, and Pablo Muchnik, eds. *Kant's Anatomy of Evil*. Cambridge: Cambridge University Press, 2010.
Andrei, Filippo. *Boccaccio the Philosopher: An Epistemology of the* Decameron. Cham: Palgrave Macmillan, 2017.
Annas, Julia. *The Morality of Happiness*. Oxford: Oxford University Press, 1993.
Armstrong, Arthur H. "Platonic *Eros* and Christian *Agape*." *Downside Review* 79 (1961): 105–121.
Arroyo, Christopher. "Kant on the Emotion of Love." *European Journal of Philosophy* 24 (2016): 580–606.
Baker, Felicity. "Portrait of the Object of Love in Rousseau's *Confessions*." In *Representations of the Self from the Renaissance to Romanticism*, ed. Patrick Coleman, Jayne Lewis, and Jill Kowalik, 171–199. Cambridge: Cambridge University Press, 2000.

Barney, Rachel. "Note on Plato on the *Kalon* and the Good." *Classical Philology* 105 (2010): 363–377.
Barolini, Teodolinda. "A Philosophy of Desire." In *Dante and the Origins of Italian Literary Culture*, 23–102. New York: Fordham University Press, 2006.
Baron, Marcia. *Kantian Ethics Almost without Apology*. Ithaca, NY: Cornell University Press, 1995.
Baron, Marcia. "Love and Respect in the *Doctrine of Virtue*." In *Kant's Metaphysics of Morals: Interpretative Essays*, ed. Mark Timmons, 391–407. Oxford: Oxford University Press, 2002.
Bashier, Salman. *Ibn al-'Arabī's Barzakh: The Concept of the Limit and the Relationship between God and the World*. Albany: State University of New York Press, 2004.
Baxley, Anne Margaret. *Kant's Theory of Virtue: The Value of Autocracy*. Cambridge: Cambridge University Press, 2010.
Beierwaltes, Werner. "The Love of Beauty and the Love of God." In *Classical Mediterranean Spirituality: Egyptian, Greek, Roman*, ed. Arthur Armstrong, 189–205. London: Routledge, 1986.
Belfiore, Elizabeth. *Socrates' Daimonic Art: Love for Wisdom in Four Platonic Dialogues*. Cambridge: Cambridge University Press, 2012.
Bell, Joseph Norment. *Love Theory in Later Hanbalite Islam*. Albany: State University of New York Press, 1979.
Bellenot, Jean-Louis. "Les formes de l'amour dans la 'Nouvelle Héloïse', et la signification symbolique des personnages de Julie et de Saint-Preux." *Annales de la Société Jean-Jacques Rousseau* 33 (1953–1955): 149–207.
Benedict XVI. *God Is Love: Deus Caritas Est*. San Francisco: Ignatius Press, 2006.
Bergmann, Martin S. "Freud's Three Theories of Love in the Light of Later Developments." *Journal of the American Psychoanalytic Association* 36 (1988): 653–672.
Bicknell, Jeanette. "An Overlooked Aspect of Love in Spinoza's *Ethics*." *Iyyun: The Jerusalem Philosophical Quarterly* 47 (1998): 41–55.
Blankert, Albert. "Heraclitus en Democritus bij Marsilio Ficino." *Simiolus: Netherlands Quarterly for the History of Art* 1, no. 3 (1966–1967): 128–135.
Blum, Paul Richard. "Human and Divine Love in Marsilio Ficino." In *Platonic Love from Antiquity to the Renaissance*, ed. Carl Séan O'Brien and John Dillon, 201–210. Cambridge: Cambridge University Press, 2022.
Borcherding, Julia. "Loving the Body, Loving the Soul: Conway's Vitalist Critique of Cartesian and Morean Dualism." *Oxford Studies in Early Modern Philosophy*, vol. 9, ed. Donald Ruthersford, 1–36. Oxford: Oxford University Press, 2019.

Branscum, Olivia. "Vitalism and Panpsychism in the Philosophy of Anne Conway." *British Journal of the History of Philosophy*, 2024.

Brewer, Talbot. *The Retrieval of Ethics*. Oxford: Oxford University Press, 2009.

Brink, David. "Rational Egoism, Self and Others." In *Identity, Character, Morality*, ed. Owen Flanagan and Amelie Rorty, 339–378. Cambridge, MA: MIT Press, 1990.

Brogaard, Berit. *On Romantic Love: Simple Truths about a Complex Emotion*. New York: Oxford University Press, 2015.

Burnaby, John. *Amor Dei: A Study of the Religion of St. Augustine*. London: Canterbury Press, 1938.

Burnyeat, Myles F. "*De anima* II 5." *Phronesis* 47 (2002): 28–90.

Carlisle, Clare. "The Intellectual Love of God." In *A Companion to Spinoza*, ed. Yitzhak Melamed, 440–448. Oxford: Blackwell, 2021.

Carson, Anne. *Eros the Bittersweet: An Essay*. Princeton, NJ: Princeton University Press, 1989.

Cassirer, Ernst. *Rousseau Kant Goethe*, trans. James Gutmann, Paul Oskar Kristeller, and John Herman Randall Jr. Princeton, NJ: Princeton University Press, 1947.

Catz, Claire. "Levinas between Agape and Eros." *Symposium* 11 (2007): 333–350.

Celenza, Christopher. *The Intellectual World of the Italian Renaissance: Language, Philosophy, and the Search for Meaning*. New York: Cambridge University Press, 2018.

Chastel, André. *Art et humanisme à Florence au temps de Laurent le Magnifique*, 3rd ed. Paris: PUF, 1982.

Chevalier, Philippe. *Dionysiaca. Recueil donnant l'ensemble des traductions latines des ouvrages attribués au Denys de l'Aréopage*. 2 vols. Bruges: Desclée de Brouwer, 1937–1950.

Chittick, William C. *Divine Love: Islamic Literature and the Path to God*. New Haven, CT: Yale University Press, 2013.

Chittick, William C. *Ibn 'Arabi: Heir to the Prophets*. Oxford: Oneworld, 2005.

Chittick, William C. "The Religion of Love Revisited." *Journal of the Muhyiddin ibn 'Arabi Society* 54 (2013): 37–59.

Chittick, William C. *The Self-Disclosure of God: Principles of Ibn al-'Arabī's Cosmology*. Albany: State University of New York Press, 1998.

Chittick, William C. *The Sufi Path of Knowledge: Ibn al-'Arabī's Metaphysics of Imagination*. Albany: State University of New York Press, 1989.

Chittick, William C. *The Sufi Path of Love: The Spiritual Teachings of Rumi*. Albany: State University of New York Press, 1983.

Comacchi, Maria Vittoria. "Yehudah Abarbanel's Astromythology: In the Footsteps of Marsilio Ficino's Prisca theologia." *Bruniana & Campanelliana* 26 (2021): 437–452.

Coughlin, Rebecca. "Uniting with Divine Wisdom: Theurgic Prayer and Religious Practice in Dionysius and Marsilio Ficino." *Dionysus* 36 (2018): 142–155.

Christ, Matthew R. *The Limits of Altruism in Democratic Athens.* Cambridge: Cambridge *University Press*, 2012.

Coakley, Sarah. *God, Sexuality, and the Self: An Essay "On the Trinity."* Cambridge: Cambridge University Press, 2013.

Cooper, John M. "Aristotle on the Forms of Friendship." *Review of Metaphysics* 30 (1977): 619–648.

Cottingham, John. "Impartiality and Ethical Formation." In *Partiality and Impartiality: Morality, Special Relationships and the Wider World*, ed. Brian Feltham and John Cottingham, 65–83. Oxford: Oxford University Press, 2010.

Cottingham, John. "Love and Religion." In *The Oxford Handbook of Philosophy of Love*, ed. Christopher Grau and Aaron Smuts, 559–574. Oxford: Oxford University Press, 2024.

D'Arcy, Martin C., SJ. *The Mind and Heart of Love*. New York: Meridian Books, 1947.

Dart, Gregory. "Rousseau and the Romantic Essayists." In *Jean-Jacques Rousseau and British Romanticism: Gender and Selfhood, Politics and Nation*, ed. Russell Goulbourne and David Higgins, 209–230. Bedford Square: Bloomsbury Academic, 2017.

Davenport, John. "Selfhood and 'Spirit.'" In *The Oxford Handbook of Kierkegaard*, ed. John Lippitt and George Pattison, 230–251. Oxford: Oxford University Press, 2013.

Deleuze, Gilles, and Claire Parnet. *Dialogues*, trans. Hugh Tomlinson and Barbara Habberjam. New York: Columbia University Press, 1987.

della Torre, Arnaldo. *Storia dell'Accademia Platonica di Firenze*. Florence: Tipografia G. Carnescchi e Figli, 1902.

Detlefsen, Karen. "Cavendish and Conway on the Individual Human Mind." In *Philosophy of Mind in the Early Modern and Modern Ages*, ed. Rebecca Copenhaver, 134–156. New York: Routledge, 2018.

Dillon, John, and Andrei Timotin, eds. *Platonic Theories of Prayer*. Leiden: Brill, 2016.

Ellis, Fiona. "Religious Experience and Desire." *Religious Studies* 55 (2019): 355–373.

El Murr, Dimitri. "*Philia* in Plato." In *Ancient and Modern Conceptions of Friendship*, ed. S. Stern Gillet and G. M. Gurtler, 3–34. Albany, NY: SUNY Press, 2014.

Evans, C. Stephen. *Kierkegaard's Ethic of Love: Divine Commands and Moral Obligations*. Oxford: Oxford University Press, 2006.

Fahmy, Melissa Seymour. "Active Sympathetic Participation: Reconsidering Kant's Duty of Sympathy." *Kantian Review* 14 (2009): 31–52.

Fahmy, Melissa Seymour. "Kantian Practical Love." *Pacific Philosophical Quarterly* 91 (2010): 313–331.

Fahmy, Melissa Seymour. "On Virtues of Love and Wide Ethical Duties." *Kantian Review* 24 (2019): 415–437.

Ferrari, Giovanni. "Platonic Love." In *The Cambridge Companion to Plato*, ed. Richard Kraut, 248–277. Cambridge: Cambridge University Press, 1992.

Ferreira, M. Jamie. *Love's Grateful Striving: A Commentary on Kierkegaard's Works of Love*. Oxford: Oxford University Press, 2001.

Ferry, Luc. *On Love: A Philosophy for the Twenty-First Century*, trans. Andrew Brown. London: Polity, 2013.

Field, Arthur. *The Origins of the Platonic Academy of Florence*. Princeton, NJ: Princeton University Press, 1998.

Field, Arthur. "The Platonic Academy of Florence." In *Marsilio Ficino: His Theology, His Philosophy, His Legacy*, ed. Michael J. B. Allen and Valery Rees, 359–376. Leiden: Brill, 2002.

Flora, Holly. *The Devout Belief of the Imagination: The Paris Meditationes Vitae Christi and Female Franciscan Spirituality in Trecento Italy*. Disciplina Monastica 6. Turnhout: Brepols, 2009.

Frankfurt, Harry. *The Reasons of Love*. Princeton, NJ: Princeton University Press, 2004.

Freud, Sigmund. *Three Essays on the Theory of Sexuality*. In *The Standard Edition of the Complete Psychological Works of Sigmund Freud*, ed. J. Strachy and A. Freud, 7 vols. London: Hogarth Press, 1905.

Freyhan, R. "The Evolution of the Caritas Figure in the Thirteenth and Fourteenth Centuries." *Journal of the Warburg and Courtauld Institutes* 11, no. 1 (1948): 68–86.

Frierson, Patrick. "Learning to Love: From Egoism to Generosity in Descartes." *Journal of the History of Philosophy* 40 (2002): 313–338.

Frigo, Alberto. "A Very Obscure Definition: Descartes's Account of Love in the *Passions of the Soul* and Its Scholastic Background." *British Journal for the History of Philosophy* 24 (2016): 1097–1116.

Gaita, Raimond. "Goodness beyond Virtue." In *A Common Humanity: Thinking about Love and Truth and Justice*, 12–28. New York: Routledge, 1998.

Garb, Jonathan. *A History of Kabbalah from the Early Modern Period to the Present Day*. Cambridge: Cambridge University Press, 2020.

Gentile, Sebastiano. "In margine all'epistola 'De divino furore' di Marsilio Ficino." *Rinascimento* 23 (1983): 33–77.

Gentile, Sebastiano. "Il manoscritto della Theologia Platonica di Proclo appartenuto al Ficino." In *Marsilio Ficino e il ritorno di Ermete Trismegisto*, ed. Sebastiano Gentile and Carlos Gilly, 76–80. Florence: Centro Di, 2000.

Gentile, Sebastiano. "Per la Storia del testo del *Commentarium in Convivium* di Marsilio Ficino." *Rinascimento* 21 (1981): 3–27.

Gersh, Stephen. *Marsilio Ficino as Reader of Plotinus: The 'Enneads' Commentary*. Leiden: Brill, forthcoming.

Gersh, Stephen, ed. *Plotinus' Legacy: The Transformation of Platonism from the Renaissance to the Modern Era*. Cambridge: Cambridge University Press, 2019.

Giffen, Lois Anita. *Theory of Profane Love among the Arabs: The Development of the Genre*. New York: New York University Press, 1971.

Golomb, Jacob. "Will to Power: Does It Lead to the 'Coldest of All Cold Monsters'?" In *The Oxford Handbook of Nietzsche*, ed. John Richardson and Ken Gemes, 525–550. Oxford: Oxford University Press, 2013.

Gombrich, Ernst H. "Botticelli's Mythologies." *Journal of the Warburg and Courtauld Institutes* 8 (1947): 7–60.

Goodman, Lenn E. *The Book of Theodicy: Translation and Commentary on the Book of Job*. New Haven, CT: Yale University Press, 1988.

Goodman, Lenn E. *The Holy One of Israel*. New York: Oxford University Press, 2019.

Goodman, Lenn E. "Is Maimonides a Moral Relativist?" In *Jewish Religious and Philosophical Ethics*, ed. Curtis Hutt et al., 87–106. New York: Routledge, 2018.

Goodman, Lenn E. *Judaism: A Contemporary Philosophical Investigation*. New York: Routledge, 2017.

Goodman, Lenn E. "Judaism and the Problem of Evil." In *The Cambridge Companion to the Problem of Evil*, ed. Chad Meister and Paul Moser, 193–209. Cambridge: Cambridge University Press, 2017.

Goodman, Lenn E. *Love Thy Neighbor as Thyself*. New York: Oxford University Press, 2008.

Gordon-Roth, Jessica. "What Kind of Monist Is Anne Finch Conway?" *Journal of the American Philosophical Association* 4 (2018): 280–297.

Grace, Eve. "The Restlessness of 'Being': Rousseau's Protean Sentiment of Existence." *History of European Ideas* 27 (2001): 133–151.

Greene, Ellen, ed. *Reading Sappho: Contemporary Approaches*. Berkeley: University of California Press, 1996.

Grey, John. "Conway's Ontological Objection to Cartesian Dualism." *Philosophers' Imprint* 17, no. 13 (2017): 1–9.

Grey, John. "Species and the Good in Anne Conway's Metaethics." In *Comparative Metaethics: Neglected Perspectives on the Foundations of Morality*, ed. Colin Marshall, 102–118. New York: Routledge, 2020.

Guyer, Paul. *Kant and the Experience of Freedom: Essays on Aesthetics and Morality*. Cambridge: Cambridge University Press, 1993.

Guyer, Paul. "Moral Feelings in the Metaphysics of Morals." In *Kant's Metaphysics of Morals: A Critical Guide*, ed. Lara Denis, 130–151. Cambridge: Cambridge University Press, 2010.

Hadot, Pierre. "'L'amour magicien.' Aux origines de la notion de *magia naturalis*: Platon, Plotin, Marsile Ficin." In Marsile Ficin, *Commentaires sur le Traité de l'amour ou le Festin de Platon*, ed. Sylvain Matton, 69–81. Paris: SÉHA, 2001.

Hall, Amy Laura. *Kierkegaard and the Treachery of Love*. Cambridge: Cambridge University Press, 2002.

Halperin, David M. "Plato and Erotic Reciprocity." *Classical Antiquity* 5 (1986): 60–80.

Hankins, James. "Cosimo de' Medici and the 'Platonic Academy.'" *Journal of the Warburg and Courtauld Institutes* 53 (1990): 144–162.

Hankins, James. "Humanist Academies and the 'Platonic Academy of Florence.'" In *On Renaissance Academies: Proceedings of the International Conference "From the Roman Academy to the Danish Academy in Rome," October 11–13, 2006*, ed. Marianne Pade, 31–46. Rome: Edizioni Quasar, 2011.

Hankins, James. "The Invention of the Platonic Academy of Florence." *Rinascimento* 42 (2002): 1–39.

Hankins, James. "The Myth of the Platonic Academy of Florence." *Renaissance Quarterly* 44 (1991): 429–475.

Hankins, James. "The Platonic Academy of Florence and Renaissance Historiography." In *Forme del neoplatonismo: Dalla eredità ficiniana al platonismo di Cambridge, atti del convegno Firenze, 25–27 ottobre 2001*, ed. Luisa Simonetti, 75–96. Florence: Olschki, 2007.

Hanley, Ryan Patrick. *Love's Enlightenment: Rethinking Charity in Modernity*. Cambridge: Cambridge University Press, 2017.

Harris, Nigel. *The Thirteenth-Century Animal Turn: Medieval and Twenty-First-Century Perspectives*. Cham: Palgrave Macmillan, 2020.

Hebron, Malcolm. *The Medieval Siege: Theme and Image in Middle English Romance*. Oxford: Oxford University Press, 1997.

Helm, Bennett W. *Love, Friendship and the Self*. Oxford: Oxford University Press, 2010.

Herman, Barbara. *Moral Literacy*. Cambridge, MA: Harvard University Press, 2007.

Hill, Thomas E., Jr. *Dignity and Practical Reason*. Ithaca, NY: Cornell University Press, 1992.

Hill, Thomas E., Jr. "Kantian Virtue and Virtue Ethics." In *Kant's Ethics of Virtue*, ed. Monika Betzler, 29–59. Berlin: De Gruyter, 2008.

Hitz, Zena. "Aristotle on Self-Knowledge and Friendship." *Philosophers' Imprint* 11 (2011): 1–28.
Hollywood, Amy, and Patricia Z. Beckman, eds. *Cambridge Companion to Christian Mysticism*. Cambridge: Cambridge University Press, 2012.
Horn, Christoph. "The Concept of Love in Kant's Virtue Ethics." In *Kant's Ethics of Virtue*, ed. Monika Betzler, 147–173. Berlin: De Gruyter, 2008.
Hughes, Aaron. *Texture of the Divine: Imagination in Medieval Islamic and Jewish Thought*. Bloomington: Indiana University Press, 2003.
Irwin, Terence. *The Development of Ethics: A Historical and Critical Study*. Oxford: Oxford University Press, 2009.
Irwin, Terence. *Plato's Ethics*. Oxford: Oxford University Press, 1995.
Jenkins, Carrie. *What Love Is: And What It Could Be*. New York: Basic Books, 2017.
Kahn, Charles. *Plato and the Socratic Dialogue: The Philosophical Use of a Literary Form*. Cambridge: Cambridge University Press, 1996.
Kambouchner, Denis. "Spinoza and the Cartesian Definition of Love." In *Mind, Nature and Morality, A Volume Honoring Lilli Alanen*, ed. F. Svensson and M. Reuter, 226–238. Abingdon: Routledge, 2019.
Karnes, Michelle. *Imagination, Meditation, and Cognition in the Middle Ages*. Chicago: University of Chicago Press, 2011.
Kiang, Dawson. "Bramante's 'Heraclitus and Democritus': The Frieze." *Zeitschrift für Kunstgeschichte* 51, no. 2 (1988): 262–268.
King, Martin Luther, Jr. *The Autobiography of Martin Luther King, Jr.*, ed. Clayborn Carson. New York: Warner Books, 2001.
King, Martin Luther, Jr. *A Call to Conscience: The Landmark Speeches of Dr. Martin Luther King, Jr.*, ed. Clayborne Carson and Kris Shepard. New York: Warner Books, 2001.
Kiosoglou, Sokratis-Athanasios. "Notes on the Presence of the *Elements of Theology* in Ficino's Commentary on the *Philebus*." In *Reading Proclus and the Book of Causes*, vol. 2, ed. Dragos Calma, 391–403. Leiden: Brill, 2021.
Kocher, Suzanne. *Allegories of Love in Marguerite Porete's Mirror of Simple Souls*. Medieval Women: Texts and Contexts. Turnhout: Brepols, 2009.
Konstan, David. *Beauty: The Fortunes of an Ancient Greek Idea*. Oxford: Oxford University Press, 2014.
Konstan, David. *Friendship in the Classical World*. Cambridge: Cambridge University Press, 1997.
Kosman, Aryeh. "Beauty and the Good: Situating the *Kalon*." *Classical Philology* 105 (2010): 341–357.
Kosman, Aryeh. "Platonic Love." In *The Virtues of Thought*, 27–42. Cambridge, MA: Harvard University Press, 2014.

Krishek, Sharon. "The Existential Dimension of Faith." In *Kierkegaard's Fear and Trembling: A Critical Guide*, ed. Daniel Conway, 106–121. Cambridge: Cambridge University Press, 2015.

Krishek, Sharon. *Kierkegaard on Faith and Love*. Cambridge: Cambridge University Press, 2009.

Krishek, Sharon. "Kierkegaard on Impartiality and Love." *European Journal of Philosophy* 25 (2017): 109–128.

Krishek, Sharon. "Kierkegaard's Notion of a Divine Name and the Feasibility of Universal Love." *The Southern Journal of Philosophy* 57 (2019): 539–560.

Krishek, Sharon. *Lovers in Essence: A Kierkegaardian Defense of Romantic Love*. New York: Oxford University Press, 2022.

Kristeller, Paul O. *Il Pensiero filosofico di Marsilio Ficino*. Firenze: Le Lettere, 2005.

Kristeller, Paul O. "Marsilio Ficino and His Work after Five Hundred Years." In *Marsilio Ficino e il ritorno di Platone: Studi e documenti*. 2 vols, ed. Gian Carlo Garfagnini, 15–196. Florence: Olschki, 1986.

Kristeller, Paul O. "Marsilio Ficino as a Man of Letters and the Glosses Attributed to Him in the Caetani Codex of Dante." *Renaissance Quarterly* 36, no. 1 (1983): 1–47.

Kuehn, Manfred. *Kant: A Biography*. Cambridge: Cambridge University Press, 2001.

Lascano, Marcy. "Anne Conway: Bodies in the Spiritual World." *Philosophy Compass* 8 (2013): 327–336.

Lascano, Marcy. *The Metaphysics of Margaret Cavendish and Anne Conway: Monism, Vitalism, and Self-Motion*. Oxford: Oxford University Press, 2023.

Lear, Gabriel Richardson. *Happy Lives and the Highest Good: An Essay in Aristotle's Nicomachean Ethics*. Princeton, NJ: Princeton University Press, 2004.

Le Brun, Jacques. *Le pur amour. De Platon à Lacan*. Paris: Seuil, 2002.

Leitgeb, Maria-Christine. *Amore e Magia: La Nascita di Eros e il De amore di Ficino*, trans. Nicola Gragnani and Sebastiano Panteghini. Revised by Paola Megna and Stéphane Toussaint. Lucca: Cahiers Accademia, 2006.

Leitgeb, Maria-Christine. *Liebe und Magie. Die Geburt des Eros und Ficinos De amore*. Maria Enzersdorf: Roesner, 2004.

Levinas, Emmanuel. "God and Philosophy." In *Of God Who Comes to Mind*, trans. Bettina Bergo, 55–78. Stanford, CA: Stanford University Press, 1998.

Levinas, Emmanuel. "Loving the Torah More Than God." In *Difficult Freedom: Essays on Judaism*, trans. Sean Hand, 142–145. Baltimore: Johns Hopkins University Press, 1990.

Levinas, Emmanuel. "Meaning and Sense." In *Basic Philosophical Writings*, ed. Adriann T. Peperzak, Simon Critchley, and Robert Bernasconi, 33–64. Bloomington: Indiana University Press, 1996.

Levinas, Emmanuel. *Otherwise Than Being or Beyond Essence*, trans. Alphonso Lingis. Dordrecht: Kluwer, 1991.

Emmanuel Levinas, "Philosophy and the Idea of the Infinite." In *To the Other: An Introduction to the Philosophy of Emmanuel Levinas*. West Lafayette, IN: Purdue University Press, 1993.

Levinas, Emmanuel. "Philosophy, Justice, and Love." In *Entre Nous*, trans. Michael B. Smith and Barbara Harshav, 88–104. London: Continuum, 2006.

Levinas, Emmanuel. *Totality and Infinity*, trans. Alphonso Lingis. Pittsburgh: Duquesne University Press, 1969.

Lewis, C. S. *The Four Loves*. Orlando, FL: Harcourt, 1960.

Lin, Martin. "Substance, Attribute, and Mode in Spinoza." *Philosophy Compass* 1 (2006): 144–153.

Lippitt, John. *Kierkegaard and the Problem of Self-Love*. Cambridge: Cambridge University Press, 2013.

Long, Anthony A. "*Eudaimonism*, Divinity and Rationality in Greek Ethics." *Proceedings of the Boston Area Colloquium in Ancient Philosophy* 19 (2004): 123–143.

Louden, Robert. *Kant's Impure Ethics: From Rational Beings to Human Beings*. Oxford: Oxford University Press, 2000.

Ludwig, Paul. *Eros and Polis: Desire and Community in Greek Political Theory*. Cambridge: Cambridge University Press, 2002.

Lutz, Cora. "Democritus and Heraclitus." *The Classical Journal* 49, no. 7 (1954): 309–314.

Marcel, Raymond. *Marsile Ficin (1433–1499)*. Paris: Les Belles Lettres, 1958.

Mariano, Patricia. *Philosophy of Sex and Love: An Opinionated Introduction*. London: Routledge, 2019.

May, Simon. *Love: A History*. New Haven, CT: Yale University Press, 2011.

McNamer, Sarah. *Affective Meditation and the Invention of Medieval Compassion*. Philadelphia: University of Pennsylvania Press, 2009.

McPhee, Sarah. *Bernini's Beloved: A Portrait of Costanza Piccolomini*. New Haven, CT: Yale University Press, 2012.

McPherson. David. "Deep Desires." *Religious Studies* 55 (2019): 389–403.

McPherson. David. *Virtue and Meaning: A Neo-Aristotelian Perspective*. Cambridge: Cambridge University Press, 2020.

McPherson. David. *The Virtues of Limits*. Oxford: Oxford University Press, 2022.

Melamed, Yitzhak. "The Enigma of Spinoza's Amor Dei Intellectualis." In *Freedom, Action and Motivation in Spinoza's Ethics*, ed. N. Naaman-Zauderer and N. Naaman, 222–238. London: Routledge, 2019.

Mercer, Christia. "Anne Conway's Metaphysics of Sympathy." In *Feminist History of Philosophy: The Recovery and Evaluation of Women's Philosophical Thought*, ed. Marcy Lascano and Eileen O'Neill, 49–73. Cham: Springer International, 2009.

Mercer, Christia. "Anne Conway's Response to Cartesianism." In *The Oxford Handbook of Descartes and Cartesianism*, ed. Tad M. Schmaltz, Steven Nadler, and Delphine Antoine-Mahut, 707–720. New York: Oxford University Press, 2019.

Mercer, Christia. *Leibniz's Metaphysics: Its Origins and Development*. New York: Cambridge University Press, 2001.

Mercer, Christia. "Leibniz and Spinoza on Substance and Mode." In *The Rationalists*, ed. Robert M. Adams and Derk Pereboom, 283–290. Lanham, MD: Rowman and Littlefield, 1999.

Mercer, Christia. "Seventeenth-Century Universal Sympathy: Stoicism, Platonism, Leibniz, and Conway." In *Sympathy: A History*, ed. Eric Schliesser, 108–139. New York: Oxford University Press, 2015.

Mercer, Christia, and Olivia Branscum. "Anne Conway." In *The Routledge Handbook of Women and Early Modern European Philosophy*, ed. Karen Detlefsen and Lisa Shapiro, 450–464. New York: Routledge, 2023.

Miller, Mitchell. "Reading the Laws as a Whole: Horizon, Vision, and Structure." In *Plato's Laws: Force and Truth in Politics*, ed. Gregory Recco and Eric Sanday, 11–30. Bloomington: Indiana University Press, 2013.

Minnis, A., and R. Voaden, eds. *Medieval Holy Women in the Christian Tradition c. 1100–c. 1500*. Turnhout: Brepols, 2010.

Monfasani, John. "Two Fifteenth-Century 'Platonic Academies': Bessarion's and Ficino's." In *On Renaissance Academies: Proceedings of the International Conference "From the Roman Academy to the Danish Academy in Rome," October 11–13, 2006*, ed. Marianne Pade, 61–76. Rome: Edizioni Quasar, 2011.

Moore, Kenneth Royce. "*Eros, Hybris* and Mania: Love and Desire in Plato's *Laws* and Beyond." *Polis* 24 (2007): 112–133.

Moran, Kate. "Much Obliged: Kantian Gratitude Reconsidered." *Archiv für Geschichte der Philosophie* 98 (2016): 330–363.

Morgan, Michael. *Discovering Levinas*. Cambridge: Cambridge University Press, 2007.

Muchnik, Pablo. *Kant's Theory of Evil: An Essay on the Dangers of Self-Love and the Aprioricity of History*. Lanham, MD: Lexington Books, 2009.
Munn, Mark. "Ερως and the Laws in Historical Context." In *Plato's Laws: Force and Truth in Politics*, ed. Gregory Recco and Eric Sanday, 31–47. Bloomington: Indiana University Press, 2013.
Murata, Kazuyo. *Beauty in Sufism: The Teachings of Rūzbihān Baqlī*. Albany: State University of New York Press, 2017.
Murata, Sachiko. *The Tao of Islam: A Sourcebook on Gender Relationships in Islamic Thought*. Albany: State University of New York Press, 1992.
Murray, Oswyn. *Sympotika: A Symposium on the Symposion*. Oxford: Clarendon Press, 1995.
Nadler, Steven. *Spinoza's Ethics: An Introduction*. Cambridge: Cambridge University Press, 2002.
Naess, Arne. "Spinoza and Ecology." *Philosophia* 7 (1977): 45–54.
Newman, Barbara. *Medieval Crossover: Reading the Secular against the Sacred*. Conway Lectures in Medieval Studies. Notre Dame: University of Notre Dame Press, 2013.
Newman, Barbara. *Virile Woman to WomanChrist: Studies in Medieval Religion and Literature*. Philadelphia: University of Pennsylvania Press, 1995.
Noonan, Harold, and Ben Curtis. "Identity." *Stanford Encyclopedia of Philosophy*, ed. Edward N. Zalta and Uri Nodelman. 2014. https://plato.stanford.edu/archives/fall2022/entries/identity/.
Nussbaum, Martha. "Nietzsche, Schopenhauer, and Dionysus." In *The Cambridge Companion to Schopenhauer*, ed. Christopher Janaway, 344–374. Cambridge: Cambridge University Press, 1999.
Nussbaum, Martha. *Upheavals of Thought: The Intelligence of Emotions*. New York: Cambridge University Press, 2001.
Nygren, Anders. *Agape and Eros*, trans. Philip S. Watson. Philadelphia: Westminster Press, 1953; and Chicago: University of Chicago Press, 1982.
Obdrzalek, Suzanne. "Why *Eros*?" In *The Cambridge Companion to Plato*, ed. David Ebrey and Richard Kraut, 2nd ed., 202–233. Cambridge: Cambridge University Press, 2022.
O'Brien, Carl Séan, and John Dillon, ed. *Platonic Love from Antiquity to the Renaissance*. Cambridge: Cambridge University Press, 2022.
O'Connor, David K. "Two Ideals of Friendship." *History of Philosophy Quarterly* 7 (1990): 109–122.
Oderberg, David. "Self-Love, Love of Neighbour, and Impartiality." In *The Moral Life: Essays in Honour of John Cottingham*, ed. Nafsika Athanassoulis and Samantha Vice, 58–84. New York: Palgrave Macmillan, 2008.

Ogren, Brian. *The Beginning of the World in Renaissance Jewish Thought: Ma'aseh Bereshit in Italian Jewish Philosophy and Kabbalah, 1492–1535*. Leiden: Brill, 2016.

O'Neill, Eileen. "Influxus Physicus." In *Causation in Early Modern Philosophy*, ed. Stephen Nadler, 27–55. University Park: Pennsylvania State University Press, 1993.

Pasnau, Robert. *Metaphysical Themes 1274–1671*. Oxford: Oxford University Press, 2011.

Piana, Marco, and Matteo Soranzo. "The Way Philosophers Pray: Hymns as Experiential Knowledge in Early Modern Europe." *Mediterranea: International Journal on the Transfer of Knowledge* 5 (2020): 51–89.

Pieper, Josef. *Faith, Hope, Love*. San Francisco: Ignatius Press, 1997.

Pippin, Robert. "The Erotic Nietzsche: Philosophers without Philosophy." In *Erotikon: Essays on Eros, Ancient and Modern*, ed. Shadi Bartsch and Thomas Bartscherer, 172–191. Chicago: University of Chicago Press, 2005.

Pippin, Robert. "Love and Death in Nietzsche." In *Religion after Metaphysics*, ed. Mark A. Wrathall, 7–28. Cambridge: Cambridge University Press, 2003.

Pippin, Robert. "Morality as Psychology, Psychology as Morality: Nietzsche, Eros, and Clumsy Lovers." In *Idealism as Modernism: Hegelian Variations*, 351–374. Cambridge: Cambridge University Press, 1997.

Pitts, A. "Freedom in Spinoza's *Ethics*." Honors thesis. Whitman College, 2017.

Podolak, Pietro. "Le commentaire de Marsile Ficin au ps. Denys l'Aréopagite entre Renaissance et philosophie médiévale." In *Le Pseudo-Denys à la renaissance: actes du colloque Tours, 27–29 mai 2010*, ed. Stéphane Toussaint and Christian Trottmann, 143–159. Paris: Honoré Champion, 2014.

Poncet, Christophe. "Ficino's Little Academy of Careggi." *Bruniana & Campanelliana* 19, no. 1 (2013): 67–76.

Pope, Stephen J. *The Evolution of Altruism and the Ordering of Love*. Washington, DC: Georgetown University Press, 1994.

Pope, Stephen J. "The Order of Love and Recent Catholic Ethics: A Constructive Proposal." *Theological Studies* 52 (1991): 255–288.

Prauscello, Lucia. *Performing Citizenship in Plato's Laws*. New York: Cambridge University Press, 2014.

Price, Anthony. "Emotions in Plato and Aristotle." In *The Oxford Handbook of Philosophy of Emotion*, ed. Peter Goldie, 122–141. Oxford: Oxford University Press, 2009.

Price, Anthony. *Love and Friendship in Plato and Aristotle*. Oxford: Clarendon Press, 1989.

Pugliese, Nastassja. "Monism and Individuation in Anne Conway as a Critique of Spinoza." *British Journal for the History of Philosophy* 27 (2019): 771–785.

Putnam, Hilary. "Levinas and Judaism." In *The Cambridge Companion to Levinas*, ed. Simon Critchley and Robert Bernasconi, 33–62. Cambridge: Cambridge University Press, 2002.

Quispel, Gilles. "God Is Eros." In *Early Christian Literature and the Classical Tradition: In Honorem Robert M. Grant*, ed. W. R. Schoedel and R. L. Wilken, 189–205. Paris: Beauchesne, 1979.

Rae, Murray. *Kierkegaard and Theology*. London: Bloomsbury, 2010.

Rees, Valery. "'A bono in bonum omnia diriguntur': Optimusm as a Dominant Strain in the Correspondence of Marsilio Ficino." *Accademia: revue de la société Marsile Ficin* 10 (2008): 7–28.

Rinne, Pärttyli. *Kant on Love*. Berlin: De Gruyter, 2018.

Robichaud, Denis J.-J. "The Afterlife of Chaldean Angels in Iamblichus, Proclus, Psellos, Pletho, and Ficino." *Travaux et Mémoires* of the Centre d'études sur l'Histoire et la Civilisation de Byzance of the Collège de France, Paris, special issue: *Inventer les anges de l'Antiquité à Byzance* 25, no. 2 (2022): 763–808.

Robichaud, Denis J.-J. "Cardinal Bessarion and the *Corpus Dionysiacum*: Platonic Love between East and West." In *Byzantine Platonists (284–1453)*, ed. Frederick Lauritzen and Sarah Klitenic Wear, 231–253. Steubenville, OH: Franciscan University Press, 2021.

Robichaud, Denis J.-J. "Ficino and the *Nodus Divinus*: Timaean and Iamblichean Mean Terms and the Soul in *Platonic Theology* 1–4." *Bruniana & Campanelliana* 26, no. 2 (2020): 379–401.

Robichaud, Denis J.-J. *Plato's Persona: Marsilio Ficino, Renaissance Humanism, and Platonic Traditions*. Philadelphia: University of Pennsylvania Press, 2018.

Robichaud, Denis J.-J. "The Twelve Gods of Plato's *Phaedrus*: Mathematical Theology, Polytheistic Myths, and Divine Names in Marsilio Ficino." In *Plato's Phaedrus: Proceedings of the 5th Platonic Summer Seminar / Letnie Seminarium Platońskie, Instytut Filozofii i socjologii, Uniwersytet Pedagogiczny im. KEN w. Krakowie and KRONOS: metafizyka, kultura, religia, Lanckorona, Poland*, ed. Andrzej Serafin. Leiden: Brill, forthcoming.

Robichaud, Denis J.-J., and Matteo Soranzo. "Philosophical or Religious Conversion? Marsilio Ficino, Plotinus's *Enneads* and Neoplatonic *epistrophe*." In *Simple Twists of Faith: Changing Beliefs, Changing Faiths: People and Places*, ed. Simona Marchesini and James Nelson Nova, 135–166. Verona: Alteritas, 2017.

Robinson, Jennifer. *Deeper Than Reason: Emotion and Its Role in Literature, Music, and Art*. Oxford: Oxford University Press, 2005.

Robinson, Joanne. *Nobility and Annihilation in Marguerite Porete's Mirror of Simple Souls*. Albany: State University of New York Press, 2001.
Rorty, Amélie. "Descartes on Thinking with the Body." In *The Cambridge Companion to Descartes*, ed. John Cottingham, 371–392. Cambridge University Press, 1992.
Rorty, Amélie. "The Functional Logic of Cartesian Passions." In *Emotional Minds: The Passions and the Limits of Pure Inquiry in Early Modern Philosophy*, ed. S. Ebbersmeyer, 3–17. Berlin: de Gruyter, 2012.
Rorty, Amélie. "Spinoza on the Pathos of Idolatrous Love and the Hilarity of True Love." In *Feminist Interpretations of Baruch Spinoza*, ed. M. Gatens, 204–224. University Park: Pennsylvania State University Press, 2009.
Rudd, Anthony. *Self, Value, and Narrative: A Kierkegaardian Approach*. Oxford: Oxford University Press, 2012.
Russell, Bertrand. *History of Western Philosophy*. London: Routledge, 2005 [1946].
Rutherford, Donald. "Descartes's Ethics." *Stanford Encyclopedia of Philosophy*, Edward N. Zalta ed. 2013 edition, accessed June 4, 2018. http://plato.stanford.edu/archives/spr2013/entries/descartes-ethics/.
Saffrey, Henri Dominique. *L'Héritage des anciens au moyen âge et à la renaissance*. Paris: Vrin, 2002.
Saffrey, Henri Dominique. "Notes platoniciennes de Marsile Ficin dans un manuscrit de Proclus." *Bibliothèque d'Humanisme et Renaissance* 21 (1959): 161–184.
Sand, George. "Quelques réflexions sur Jean-Jacques Rousseau." *Revue des Deux Mondes*. Période initiale, 4ème série, 26 (1841): 703–716.
Sanford, Stella. *The Metaphysics of Love*. London: Athlone Press, 2000.
Sanzotta, Valerio. "Some Unpublished Notes by Marsilio Ficino on Plato's *Parmenides* in MS. Laur. 89 Sup. 71." *Journal of the Warburg and Courtauld Institutes* 77, no. 1 (2014): 211–224.
Scheler, Max. *Ressentiment*, trans. Lewis B. Coser and William W. Holdheim. Milwaukee: Marquette University Press, 2003.
Schliesser, Eric. "Newtonian Emanation, Spinozism, Measurement and the Baconian Origins of the Laws of Nature." *Foundations of Science* 10, no. 3 (2005): 1–19.
Schliesser, Eric, ed. *Sympathy: A History*. Oxford: Oxford University Press, 2015.
Schmitter, Amy. "Spinoza on the Emotions." In *Stanford Encyclopedia of Philosophy*, Edward N. Zalta ed.2010 edition. https://plato.stanford.edu/entries/emotions-17th18th/LD5Spinoza.html.
Schneewind, J. B. *The Invention of Autonomy: A History of Modern Moral Philosophy*. Cambridge: Cambridge University Press, 1998.

Schofield, Malcom. "Friendship and Justice in the *Laws*." In *The Platonic Art of Philosophy*, ed. George Boys-Stones, Dimitri El Murr, and Christopher Gill, 283–297. Cambridge: Cambridge University Press, 2016.

Schönecker, Dieter. "Kant über Menschenliebe als moralische Gemütsanlange." *Archiv für Geschichte der Philosophie* 92 (2010): 133–175.

Shapiro, Lisa. "Cartesian Generosity." In *Norms and Modes of Thinking in Descartes*, ed. Tuomo Aho and Mikko Yrjönsuuri. *Acta Philosophica Fennica* 64 (1999): 249–275.

Shapiro, Lisa. "Descartes on Human Nature and the Human Good." In *The Rationalists*, ed. J. Smith and C. Fraenkel, 13–26. New York: Springer, 2011.

Shapiro, Lisa. "Descartes's Ethics." In *Blackwell Companion to Descartes*, ed. Janet Broughton and John Carriero, 445–463. Oxford: Blackwell, 2007.

Sheffield, F. C. C. "Beyond *Eros*: Friendship in the *Phaedrus*." *Proceedings of the Aristotelian Society* 111 (2011): 251–273.

Sheffield, F. C. C. "*Eros* and the Pursuit of Form." In *Cambridge Critical Guides: The Symposium*, ed. Pierre Destrée and Zina Giannopoulou, 125–141. Cambridge: Cambridge University Press, 2017.

Sheffield, F. C. C. "Love and the City: *Eros* and *Philia* in Plato's Laws." In *Emotions in Plato*, ed. L. Candiotto and O. Renaut, 330–372. Leiden: Brill, 2020.

Sheffield, F. C. C. "Moral Motivation in Plato's *Republic*? *Philia* and Return to the Cave." *Oxford Studies in Ancient Philosophy* 69 (2021): 79–131.

Sheffield, F. C. C. *Plato's Symposium: The Ethics of Desire*. Oxford: Oxford University Press, 2006.

Sheffield, F. C. C. "The *Symposium* and Platonic Ethics: Plato, Vlastos and a Misguided Debate." *Phronesis* 57, no. 2 (2012): 117–141.

Sherman, Nancy. *Making a Necessity of Virtue: Aristotle and Kant on Virtue*. Cambridge: Cambridge University Press, 1997.

Simmel, Georg. *Schopenhauer and Nietzsche*, trans. Helmut Loiskandl, Deena Weinstein, and Michael Weinstein. Urbana: University of Illinois Press, 1991.

Singer, Irving. *The Nature of Love*. Chicago: University of Chicago Press, 1966.

Smart, J. J. C., and Bernard Williams. *Utilitarianism: For and Against*. Cambridge: Cambridge University Press, 1973.

Smit, Houston, and Mark Timmons. "The Moral Significance of Gratitude in Kant's Ethics." *The Southern Journal of Philosophy* 49 (2011): 295–320.

Steel, Carlos. "Ficino and Proclus: Arguments for the Platonic Doctrine of the Ideas." In *The Rebirth of Platonic Theology*, ed. James Hankins and Fabrizio Meroi, 63–118. Florence: Olschki, 2013.

Sternberg, Robert J. *Cupid's Arrow: The Course of Love through Time*. New York: Cambridge University Press, 1998.

Sternberg, Robert J. "A Duplex Theory of Love." In *The New Psychology of Love*, ed. Robert J. Sternberg and Karin Sternberg, 2nd ed., 280–299. Cambridge: Cambridge University Press, 2018.

Sternberg, Robert J. *Love Is a Story*. New York: Oxford University Press, 1998.

Sternberg, Robert J. "A Triangular Theory of Love." *Psychological Review* 93 (1986): 119–135.

Sternberg, Robert J., and Karin Sternberg. *The New Psychology of Love*, 2nd ed. New York: Cambridge University Press, 2019.

Stokes, Patrick. *Kierkegaard's Mirrors: Interest, Self, and Moral Vision*. London: Palgrave, 2010.

Stump, Eleonore. *Wandering in Darkness: Narrative and the Problem of Suffering*. Oxford: Oxford University Press, 2010.

Svensson, Frans. "Non-Eudaimonism, the Sufficiency of Virtue for Happiness, and Two Senses of the Highest Good in Descartes's Ethics." *British Journal of the History of Philosophy* 23 (2015): 277–296.

Svensson, Frans. "The Role of Virtue in Descartes' Ethical Theory, Or, Was Descartes a Virtue Ethicist?" *History of Philosophy Quarterly* 27 (2010): 215–236.

Swanton, Christine. "Kant's Impartial Virtues of Love." In *Perfecting Virtue: New Essays on Kantian Ethics and Virtue Ethics*, ed. Lawrence Jost and Julian Wuerth, 241–259. Cambridge: Cambridge University Press, 2011.

Swanton, Christine. *Virtue Ethics: A Pluralistic View*. Oxford: Oxford University Press, 2003.

Tanturli, Giuliano. "Marsilio Ficino e il volgare." In *Marsilio Ficino: fonti, testi, fortuna*, ed. Sebastiano Gentile and Stéphane Toussaint, 183–213. Rome: Edizioni di Storia e Letteratura, 2006.

Taylor, Charles. *Sources of the Self: The Making of the Modern Identity*. Cambridge, MA: Harvard University Press, 1989.

Thomas, Emily. "Anne Conway on the Identity of Creatures over Time." In *Early Modern Women on Metaphysics*, ed. Emily Thomas, 131–149. Cambridge: Cambridge University Press, 2018.

Thomas, Emily. "Anne Conway as a Priority Monist: A Reply to Gordon-Roth." *Journal of the American Philosophical Association* 6 (2020): 275–284.

Thurman, Howard. *Jesus and the Disinherited*. Boston: Beacon Press, 1949.

Timmermann, Jens. "Good but Not Required?: Assessing the Demands of Kantian Ethics." *Journal of Moral Philosophy* 2 (2005): 9–27.

Toner, Jules. *Love and Friendship*. Milwaukee: Marquette University Press, 2003.

Toussaint, Stéphane. "Les formes de l'invisible." In Giovanni Pico della Mirandola. *Commento*, trans. Stéphane Toussaint, 9–69. Lausanne: Éditions l'Age d'Homme, 1989.

Toussaint, Stéphane. "L'Influence de Ficin à Paris et le Pseudo-Denys des humanistes: Traversari, Cusain, Lefèvre d'Étaples. Suivi d'un passage inédit de Marsile Ficin." *Bruniana & Campanelliana* 5, no. 2 (1999): 381–414.

Unterman, Jeremiah. *Justice for All: How the Jewish Bible Revolutionized Ethics.* Lincoln: Jewish Publication Society and University of Nebraska Press, 2017.

van den Doel, Marieke J. E. *Ficino and Fantasy: Imagination in Renaissance Art and Theory from Botticelli to Michelangelo.* Leiden: Brill, 2022.

Van Dyke, Christina. *A Hidden Wisdom: Medieval Contemplatives on Self-Knowledge, Reason, Love, Persons, and Immortality.* Oxford: Oxford University Press, 2022.

Van Dyke, Christina. "From Meditation to Contemplation: Broadening the Boundaries of Philosophy in the Thirteenth to Fifteenth Centuries." In *Pluralizing Philosophy's Past: New Reflections in the History of Philosophy,* ed. A. Griffioen and M. Backmann. Palgrave Macmillan, forthcoming.

Vlastos, Gregory. "The Individual as Object of Love in Plato." In *Plato II: Ethics, Religion and the Soul,* ed. Gail Fine, 137–163. Oxford: Oxford University Press, 1999.

Vlastos, Gregory. "Justice and Equality." In *Social Justice,* ed. Richard Brandt, 31–72. Englewood Cliffs, NJ: Prentice Hall, 1962.

Walker, Daniel Pickering. *Spiritual and Demonic Magic: From Ficino to Campanella.* London: Warburg Institute, 1958.

Walsh, Sylvia. *Kierkegaard: Thinking Christianly in an Existential Mode.* Oxford: Oxford University Press, 2009.

Walzer, Richard. "Platonism in Islamic Philosophy." In *Greek into Arabic: Essays on Islamic Philosophy,* 236–252. Oxford: Bruno Cassirer, 1962.

Waterlow, Sarah. "The Good of Others in Plato's *Republic.*" *Proceedings of the Aristotelian Society* 73 (1972): 19–36.

Wear, Sarah Klitenic. "Ficino's Hymns and the Renaissance Platonic Academy." In *Laus Platonici Philosophi: Marsilio Ficino and His Influence,* ed. Stephen Clucas, Peter J. Forshaw, and Valery Rees, 133–148. Leiden: Brill, 2011.

Webb, Heather. "Catherine of Siena's Heart." *Speculum* 80, no. 3 (2005): 802–817.

Wee (Lim), Cecelia. "Self, Other and Community in Cartesian Ethics." *History of Philosophy Quarterly* 19 (2002): 255–273.

Whiting, Jennifer E. "Impersonal Friends." *Monist* 74 (1991): 3–29.

Whiting, Jennifer E. "The Nicomachean Account of *Philia.*" In *The Blackwell Guide to Aristotle's Nicomachean Ethics,* ed. Richard Kraut, 276–304. London: Blackwell, 2006.

Wilberding, James. "The World Soul in the Platonic Tradition." In *World Soul: A History,* ed. James Wilberding, 15–43. New York: Oxford University Press, 2021.

Williams, Bernard. "Persons, Character and Morality." In *Moral Luck: Philosophical Papers, 1973–1980*, 1–19. Cambridge: Cambridge University Press, 1981.

Williams, David Lay. "Spinoza and the General Will." *Journal of Politics* 72 (2010): 341–356.

Winch, Peter. *Trying to Make Sense*. Oxford: Blackwell, 1987.

Wood, Allen. "The Final Form of Kant's Practical Philosophy." In *Kant's Metaphysics of Morals: Interpretative Essays*, ed. Mark Timmons, 1–21. Oxford: Clarendon Press, 2002.

Zargar, Cyrus Ali. *The Polished Mirror: Storytelling and the Pursuit of Virtue in Islamic Philosophy and Sufism*. London: Oneworld, 2017.

Zargar, Cyrus Ali. *Sufi Aesthetics: Beauty, Love, and the Human Form in the Writings of Ibn 'Arabi and 'Iraqi*. Columbia: University of South Carolina Press, 2012.

# Index

*For the benefit of digital users, indexed terms that span two pages (e.g., 52–53) may, on occasion, appear on only one of those pages.*

Tables, figures, and boxes are indicated by an italic *t*, *f* and *b* following the page number.

Abi'l-Khayr, Abū Sa'īd, 108
Abraham, 6–7, 19–20, 30, 31, 35–36, 39–40, 119–20, 305–6
Adam and Eve, 6–7, 17–19
addiction, 311
affective appraisal, 43–44, 44n.5
*agape*, 5, 70–71, 85–93, 138–39, 167–68, 318, 319–20, 330–32
*Agape and Eros* (Nygren), 8, 85–93, 316–18, 330–31
Alexander the Great, 143–44, 145–46
Al-Fārābī, 106
*Allegory of Good and Bad Government* (Lorenzetti), 133–37
All-Merciful Breath, 124–25
*al-tashabbuh bi'l-ilāh*, similarity to God, 102
*amor*, 126–27, 137–47
*Amores* (Ovid), 68–69
*amour-propre*, 265–66
Aphrodite, 164–67
Aquinas, Thomas, 8, 70–71, 77, 78–85, 91, 208
Aristophanes, 272–73
Aristotle, 7–8, 38, 42–43, 143–44, 172–73, 253–54, 322, 330
  *eros*, 52–55
  love of God, 35
  *philia*, 60–65
Aron, Arthur, 311–12
Augustine, 8, 77, 85–87, 141–43, 162–63, 208, 322–23, 325–26, 340
  order of love, 70–71, 78–85
Austen, Jane, 12–13, 278–79, 282–83
Avicenna, 8–9, 10–11, 95, 97–98, 99–100, 101–6, 107–8, 110–12, 114, 118, 122, 123–24

Babylonian Talmud, 29–30
Barnes, Michael, 311–12
beauty, Greek notion of, 45–47, 45n.8
beneficence, duty of love, 249–50
benevolence, practical love, 247–49
Bernini, Gian Lorenzo, 226–34
  assistant Matteo Bonucelli, 230
  *Damned Soul* sculpture, 227, 228*f*
  *David* sculpture, 230–32, 231*f*
  *Ecstasy of St. Teresa* (sculpture), 232–34, 233*f*
  Portrait of Costanza Piccolomini sculpture, 227–30, 229*f*
  *Saved Soul* sculpture, 227*f*, 227–30
Bicknell, Jeanette, 198

Boccaccio, Giovanni, 10–11, 155–56, 158
body and soul, Rousseau on, 268
Bonaventure, 129–30, 130n.6
Bonucelli, Matteo, Bernini's assistant, 230
*Book of Privy Counseling* (anonymous), 137–38, 141–43
Bowlby, John, 311–12
Breath of the All-Merciful, 124–25
Brethren of Purity, 95, 100, 101
Buddhism, 316–18

Carità (Piero del Pollaiolo) 142*f*
*caritas*, 8, 78, 79–80, 92, 126–27, 137–47
Carlisle, Clare, 196–97
Casket with Scenes of Romances, Paris, 143*f*
Catherine of Siena, 140–43
  offering her heart to Christ, 146–47, 147n.42, 148*f*
Chittick, William, 8–9, 94–125, 208–9
Christianity, 54–55, 70–71, 316–18, 322, 330
  *agape* and *eros*, 85–93
  centrality of love in, 72–73, 207–8
  love in New Testament, 71–77
  Nietzsche and, 13–14, 316–18
  order of love (Augustine and Aquinas), 78–85
*Cloud of Unknowing* (anonymous), 137–38, 141–43
Coffret (Minnekästechen), German, Upper Rhineland, 147*f*
*Commentary on the First Alcibiades* (Proclus), 171–72
concubinage, 19–20
*Confessions* (Augustine), 78–79
*Confessions* (Rousseau), 259–60
contemplative prayer, meditation, 128–29
Conway, Anne, 10–11, 202–3, 204–5
  Creation's goodness, 220–23
  God's goodness, 213–20
  metaphysics and love, 204–5, 209–10
  philosophy, 205–6, 210–12
  three substances of God, Christ (Logos) and Creation, 210–11
  universalist love, 224–25

*Corpus Dionysiacum*, 162–63, 167–68, 171–72, 175–76, 177
Cottingham, John, 71–72
covetousness, 79–80
creation
  Conway on, 210–11, 214–15, 220–23
  God's love in, 16
  joyful love of, 220
creatures, God's love for, 204, 206–7
*Critique of Practical Reason* (Kant), 241–42, 255
*Critique of the Power of Judgment* (Kant), 242
Cudworth, Ralph, 213

*Damned Soul* (sculpture), Bernini, 227, 228*f*
Dante Alighieri, 155–58
David (Bible), 22–24
*David* (sculpture)
  Bernini, 230, 231*f*
  Michelangelo, 230–32
*De amore* (Ficino), 159–61, 162–63, 167–68, 171–72, 175–76, 178
*De anima* (Aristotle), 172–73
Deborah, 21
*Decameron* (Boccaccio), 158
*De divinis nominibus* (Ficino), 167–70, 172–73, 175–76, 177
Deleuze, Gilles, 324
Descartes, René, 10–11, 179–80
  on love for others, 184–85, 187–88, 191–92
  on metaphysical basis for love, 181–90
  Spinoza and, 180–81, 191–93, 202–3
desire, 5–8, 13–14, 45–47, 51–52, 54–55, 79–80, 91–92, 109–10, 153, 159–64, 176, 220–21, 240–41, 264–66, 275, 279–80, 289–90, 316–25, 330–33
de Troyes, Chrétien, 143–44
Dionysius the Areopagite, 167–68, 169
*Discourse on the Method* (Descartes), 187–88
*Divine Comedy* (Dante), 156, 157–58
divine perfection, Conway on, 215
*Doctrine of Virtue*, Kant, 237, 242, 243, 245, 248, 251, 252–53, 254, 255
d'Oingt, Marguerite, 130–31, 141–43, 150

duplex theory of love, 314–15
duties of love
  beneficence, 249–50
  friendship, 253–54
  gratitude, 250–51
  Kant on, 249–54
  sympathetic participation, 251–53
duty of virtue, Kant on, 248–49

ecstasy, 10–11, 91, 137–38, 232–34
*Ecstasy of Saint Teresa* (sculpture), Bernini, 232–34, 233*f*
egoism, 7–8, 335
*Elements of Theology* (Proclus), 175–76
Ellis, Fiona, 13–14, 316–38
emanation, 187–88, 207, 215–16, 219–20
*Emile* (Rousseau), 261–62, 263–64, 270–71, 276, 277, 278–79
*Emile and Sophie or, the Solitairies* (Rousseau), 263–64
*Emma* (Austen), 282–83
enlightenment, 35–36, 37
*Enneads* (Plotinus), 175–76
enthusiasm, 12–13, 264, 269–70, 278
eros
  Aristotle, 52–55
  Bernini, 230
  Christianity, 70–71, 85–93
  Ficino, 159–78
  Nietzsche, 316–18
  Plato, 42–43, 44–52
  Torah, 24–25
*Eroticus* (Laertius), 52
*Ethics* (Spinoza), 180–81, 190, 196–97, 201
*eudaimonia*, 7–8, 43, 47–50, 53–54, 62–63
*eunoia*, 56–57, 60–61
existentialism, Kierkegaard, 288–89, 310

Fahmy, Melissa, 11–12, 235–58
*falsafa*, 95
*Fear and Trembling* (Kierkegaard), 13, 290, 298–99, 305–6, 307, 308–9
Ficino, Marsilio, 10, 209
  Christianization of Plato, 162–63

*Corpus Dionysiacum*, 162–63, 167–68, 171–72, 175–76, 177
*De amore*, 159–61, 162–63, 167–68, 171–72, 175–76, 178
*De divinis nominibus*, 167–70, 172–73, 175–76, 177
Good, 161–62, 166–67, 174–76, 178
Plato's philosophy of love, 172–73, 177–78
principles of being, life, and intellect, 165–66
Pseudo-Dionysius and, 169–72
theory of two loves, 164–65
*Fī ḥaqīqat al-ʿishq* (Suhrawardī), 112
filial love, 198–99
fin 'amor, 9–10, 126–27, 137–47, 144n.32
*First Alcibiades* (Plato), 171–72
First Letter of John, centrality of love in, 73
*Flowing Light of the Godhead* (Mechthild of Magdeburg), 152
*Form of Living, The* (Rolle), 141–43
*Four Loves, The* (Lewis), 138–39
Frederick II, 155–56
Freud, Sigmund, 13–14, 40–41, 311–12
friendship, 6–7, 22–24, 42–43, 55–65, 78, 81–82, 91, 140–41, 190, 198–99, 201–3, 253–54, 267–68, 272–73, 275, 291, 313, 342
Frierson, Patrick, 10–11, 179–203
*Futūḥāt al-makkiyya* (Ibn Arabi), 124

Gangloff, Jacob Heinrich, 217–18
Genesis, 17–19, 79–80
Gandhi, 340
al-Ghazālī, 108, 109
Giotto (Italian painter), 230
Giovanni, Don, 230
Giovanni di Turino, Madonna of the Magnificat, 135*f*
God
  command to love, 5–7, 8, 13, 16, 29, 71–72, 73–75, 110–11, 140–41, 207–8, 255–56
  Conway on, 210–23
  Kirkegaard on, 302–3
  Levinas on, 327–29
  Nietzsche on, 323–25, 333–38

Golomb, Jacob, 332–33
Goodman, Lenn, 6–7, 16–41
Good Samaritan
   Jesus' parable of, 76–77
   reflections on parable of, 84–85
Gospel of John, 74–75
Gospel of Luke, 75, 76–77
Gospel of Matthew, 71–72, 75–76
Grace, Eve, 12–13, 259–81
gratitude, 250–51, 254, 269
Gray, Erik, 7–8, 66–69
*Groundwork of the Metaphysics of Morals* (Kant), 11–12, 235, 252–53, 258
*Guide to the Perplexed, The* (Maimonides), 37
Guigio II, 127–28, 128n.2, 129

Hadewijch, 139–40, 146–47, 149–51, 209
Hanley, Ryan, 1–16, 205
harmony, 198–99, 217–19, 322–23
*Ḥayy ibn Yaqẓān* (Ibn Ṭufayl), 119–20
Hazan, Cynthia, 311–12
Hegel, G. W. F., 330
ḥesed, 6–7, 27–28, 29–31, 32–33, 37
Hesiod, 161–62
Homer, 69
homonoia, 64–65
ḥubb (term) 95–96, 106
Hughes, Aaron, 118
human beings
   love of, 243–45
   loving for God's sake, 81–82
   self-love, 240–45
*humanitas* (term), 31
ḥusn (term), 96, 112
*Hymn to Love* (Eros) (Pseudo-Hierotheus), 169–70

Iamblichus, 172–73, 175–76
Ibn ʿArabī, 95, 102, 113, 119–22, 123–25
Ibn Ṭufayl, 118–20
*Iḥyāʾ ʿulūm al-dīn* (al-Ghazālī), 108
imaginative meditation, 128–29
Imitatio Dei, 31–32

ʿināya (term), 97
*In Calumniatorem platonis* (Bessarion), 171–72
individuation, conatus theory of, 193–94
Isaac, 20, 305–6
ʿishq, term, 95–96
Islamic philosophy
   all-pervading mercy, 118–25
   early philosophy, 100–5
   God's love for Himself, 106–10
   perfection of human soul by love, 208–9
   universal love for God, 110–17
Israel, 22–23, 27, 31

jamāl (term), 96, 112
Jeremiah, 38–39, 40
Jesus, 119–20, 129–30, 210–11, 214–15
Jewish law
   laws of love, 27–29
   living and learning, 29–32
   love concept, 206–7
   ve-shinantam, 29–30
Julian of Norwich, 141–43
*Julie ou la Nouvelle Héloïse* (Rousseau), 259–60, 263–64, 275–76, 278–79
jurisprudence (*fiqh*), 94–95

kalon, 45–47, 46n.12
Kant, Immanuel, 74–75, 235–36
   beneficence, 249–50
   conception of duty, 75–76
   duties of love, 249–54
   friendship, 253–54
   gratitude, 250–51
   laws of freedom, 238–39
   love and ethical obligations, 245–56
   love as feeling, 254–56
   love of human beings, 243–45
   love "prior to duty," 239–40
   moral principles, 236–37, 237n.2
   moral sense theory, 237–39
   moral sentimentalists and, 236–39
   mutual love and respect, 245–47
   practical love, 247–49

self-love, 240–45
significance of love, 256–58
sympathetic participation, 251–53
*khayal*, 118, 120–21
Kierkegaard, Søren, 13
 "equality of eternity," 302–3
 existentialism, 288–89, 310
 existential suffering, 296
 *Fear and Trembling*, 290, 298–99, 305–6, 307, 308–9
 romantic love, 297, 298–99
 *The Sickness unto Death*, 290, 299–304, 309
 "temporal dissimilarities" and "eternal equality," 294, 299–304
 *Works of Love*, 287–89, 291–99, 301, 302–4, 305, 307, 309
King, Martin Luther, Jr., 14–15, 339–42
Kircher, Athanasius, 226–27
*Kraft* (term), 332–33
Krishek, Sharon, 13, 287–310
Kumar, Akash, 10–11, 155–58

ladder of love, 49–50
Laertius, Diogenes, 52
*Lamentation over the Dead Christ* (Lorenzetti), 136f
*Laws* (Plato), 42–43, 51–52, 56–57, 58–61
*lectio divina*, meditation exercise, 128–29
*Legenda major* (Raymond of Capua), 146–47
Leibniz, G. W., 213, 214–15
Levinas, Emmanuel, 13–14, 337–38
 desire, 322, 326–29, 333–35, 334n.77
 erotic encounter, 319n.13
 Nietzsche and, 316–18
Lewis, C. S., 89–90, 138–39
Lorenzetti, Ambrogio
 *Allegory of Good and Bad Government*, 133–37
 *Lamentation over the Dead Christ*, 136f
Louden, Robert, 242–43
love
 Austen's novels, 282–86

concept in modern psychology, 311–15
duplex theory, 314–15
as social force, 339–42
as a story, 314
triangle of, 312–13
unrequited, 325–30
Voltaire defining, 266
*Love: A History* (Hanley), goal of, 205
*Lysis* (Plato), 42–43, 55–56, 61

*Mabādi' ārā' ahl al-madīnat al-fāḍila* (Al-Fārābī), 106–7
McPhee, Sarah, 230
McPherson, David, 8, 70–93, 207–8
Madonna and Child Enthroned (unknown), sculpture, 134f
Madonna of the Magnificat (Giovanni di Turino), 135f
Maimonides, 6–7
 acts of God, 33–34
 bodily needs, 35–36
 enlightenment, 35
 God's ḥesed, 31–32
 God's rule, 32
 on Jeremiah, 40
 moral virtues, 34, 37
 on wisdom, 34
*Mansfield Park* (Austen), 283–84
*Mathnawī* (Rūmī), 117
Mechthild of Magdeburg, 146–47, 152
medieval Christian tradition
 debate over intellect vs. will, 126–27
 first-person experiences of transcendent love, 147–53
 nature of love (*caritas*, *amor* and *fin'amor*), 137–47
 practice of love, 127–37
 supremacy of love, 153–54
 See also Christian tradition
meditation, 128–29, 153
*Meditations* (Descartes), 187–88
*Meditations on the Life of Christ* (John of Caulibus), 129, 129n.5, 131–37, 141–43

*Menschenliebe* (love of human beings), Kant, 239–40, 243–45
Mercer, Christia, 10–11, 204–25
mercy, 33–34, 96–97, 110, 118–25, 140–41
metanoia, 74–75
*Metaphysics* (Avicenna), 107–8
*Metaphysics* (Aristotle), 54–55
*Metaphysics of Morals* (Kant), 235, 258
Michelangelo, 230–32
Micraelius, Johann, 214
*Mirror of Simple Souls* (Porete), 141–43, 145–46
Mishnah, 29–30, 31
*mishpat*, 39
*mitzvot*, 28, 31–32
Montoya, Pedro de Foix, 227
moral feeling, 236–37, 238–39, 243, 245, 257–58
moral force, 11–12, 245–47
moral sense theory, 237–39
moral virtues, 35–36, 37
Moran, Kate, 250–51
More, Henry, 213
Moses, 32, 35–36, 119–20
mutual love, 220–21, 246, 253–54
*Mystical Vine, The* (Bonaventure), 129–30

Naess, Arne, 192, 196
Necessary Existence, 97, 104, 107–8, 109, 110, 114–15, 118, 121, 122, 123–24
neighbor(s)
  creations of God, 82
  Jesus' concept of, 76–77
  loving for God's sake, 81–82
  *Works of Love* conception of neighborly love, 291–99
New Testament, 8, 70–77
*Nicomachean Ethics* (Aristotle), 42–43, 52–53, 60–61, 64–65
Nietzsche, Friedrich, 13–14, 316–38
  Christianity and, 316–18
  conceptions of desire, 320–25, 330–33
  Levinas and, 319–20
nihilism, 316–18, 333
Nussbaum, Martha, 316–18

Nygren, Anders, 8, 85–90, 91–92, 316–18, 330–31

*Observations on the Feeling of the Beautiful and Sublime* (Kant), 236–37, 237n.2
*Odyssey* (Homer), 69
*On Christian Teaching* (Augustine), 78, 82–83
*On Sympathy* (Gangloff), 217–18
*On the Trinity* (Augustine), 79–80
*Origin and Return* (Avicenna), 97–98, 101–2
*Origin and Return* (Sadrā), 97–98, 109–10
Ovid, 66–69

*Page of Meditations* (d'Oingt), 130–31, 141–43
Parmenides, 7–8, 42–43
passion, 24–27, 35–36, 267–68
*Passions of the Soul* (Descartes), 182, 183, 184, 189
perfectibility, Conway's notion of, 213–14
Peripatetics, 98
*Persuasion* (Austen), 285–86
Petrarch, 10–11, 155–56, 157–58
*Phaedrus* (Plato), 42–43, 51–52, 56–57, 60–61, 67–68, 167–68, 337–38
*philanthropous*, lovers of humankind, 64–65
philia
  Aristotle, 7–8, 53–54, 60–65
  Plato, 42–43, 45–47, 55–60
  semantic range, 55n.32
Philo, 26–27
*Philosophical Dictionary* (Voltaire), 266
Piccolomini, Costanza, Bernini's portrait of, 227–30, 229f
Pieper, Josef, 89–93
*pietas* (term) 31
Pippin, Robert, 316–18, 321–23, 324, 326
Plato, 7–8, 10–11, 127–28, 167–68, 259–60, 262, 272–73, 320–21, 322–23, 325–26, 330
  eros, 42–43, 44–52
  Ficino's supposed Christianization of, 162–63
  philia, 42–43, 55–60

# INDEX

philosophy of love, 69
*Republic*, 35
Rousseau and, 264
*Symposium*, 7–8, 10, 35
platonic love poetry, 66–69
Platonism, 38, 54–55, 206–7, 209
Plotinus, 54–55, 164, 165–66, 172–73
*Political Treatise* (Spinoza), 190, 201
*Politics* (Aristotle), 42–43, 64–65
polygamy, 19–20, 21
Poor People's Campaign, 341
Porete, Marguerite, 141–43, 145–47
Porphyry, 172–73
practical love, Kant, 247–49
*Pride and Prejudice* (Austen), 284–85
Prime Mover, heavenly bodies as object of love, 54–55, 54n.28
Prime Reality, Maimonides, 34
*Principia Philosophia* (Spinoza), 190
*Principles of Philosophy* (Descartes), 187–88
*Principles of the Most Ancient and Modern Philosophy* (Conway), 210, 213–14, 217–18
Proclus, 54–55, 164, 171–72, 175–76
profane love, genre, 94–95
Proverbs, 21
Pseudo-Dionysius, 162–63, 167–68, 169–72

Qur'an, 94–95, 96–97, 99

radical evil, 241–42
*raḥma* (term) 97
rational self-love, 241–42
*René* (Chateaubriand), 261–62
*Republic* (Plato), 35, 42–43, 58–60, 59n.41, 215–16
*Rerum vulgarium fragmenta* (Petrarch), 157
respect, principle of, 246
*Reveries of the Solitary Walker* (Rousseau), 271–72
Richardson, Samuel, 283–84
Rivero, Albert J., 12–13, 282–86
Robichaud, Denis, 10, 159–78, 209
Rolle, Richard, 141–43
*Romance of the Rose*, 270–71

romanticism, 2–3, 54–55, 259–61, 280–81
romantic love, 5, 12–13
  Kierkegaard, 289–90, 297, 298–99
  Rousseau, 259–81
Rorty, Amelie, 191–92, 195–96, 197–98
Rousseau, Jean-Jacques, 12–13
  *amour-propre*, 265–66
  *Confessions*, 259–60
  *Emile*, 261–62, 263–64, 270–71, 276, 277, 278–79
  falling in love, 264–65
  illusions, 278–80, 281
  imaginary transfiguration of love, 272–75
  *Julie*, 259–60, 263–64, 275–76, 278–79
  longing for happiness, 276–77, 278–79
  nature of human desire, 275–76
  passions, 278–79
  *Reveries of the Solitary Walker*, 271–72
  self-love, 268–69
  view of love, 265
Rowland, Ingrid, 10–11, 226–34
Rūmī, 113, 116–17, 121–22, 123

Saadiah, 31–32
Sabbath, 29–30, 79–80
Ṣadrā, Mullā, 8–9, 95, 97–98, 109, 110, 114, 115, 118
Sand, George, 260–61
Sappho, 66–69
*Saved Soul* (sculpture), Bernini, 227–30, 227f
*scala amoris*, Plato, 45
Scheler, Max, 325–26, 329, 333
Schiller, Friedrich, 322, 330
Schopenhauer, Arthur, 316–18, 330–31, 335–36
*Second Discourse* (Rousseau), 264–65, 266–67
self-affirmation, 304–9
self-disclosure (*tajallī*), term, 110–11
self-love
  Kant, 240–45
  Rousseau, 268–69
self-transcendence, 8
self-willfulness, Kierkegaard's condemnation of, 304–5

*Sense and Sensibility* (Austen), 282–83
Shaver, Phillip, 311–12
Sheffield, Frisbee, 7–8, 42–65
*Short Treatise on God, Man, and His Well-Being* (Spinoza), 190
*Showings* (Julian of Norwich), 141–43
*Sickness unto Death, The* (Kierkegaard), 290, 299–304, 309
Singer, Irving, 3–4
*Sir Charles Grandison* (Richardson), 283–84
Socrates, 7–8, 12–13, 43–44, 52–53, 67–68
Sodom, 27
solitude, 110
Song of Songs, 6–7
   celebrating love, 25–26
   erotic passion, 34
   symbolism in, 40–41
*Sorrows of Young Werther, The* (Goethe), 263
Spinoza, Baruch, 10–11, 179–80
   conatus, 193–94
   emotions around self-preservation, 195
   epistemology and philosophy of mind, 193–94
   friendship, charity and love, 198
   monism, individuation, love, 190–202
*Statesman* (Plato), 42–43, 58–60
Station of No Station, 118, 119–20
Sternberg, Robert, 13–14, 311–15
*storge* (term), 138–39
story, loves as a, 314
Sufism, 8–9, 101–2
Suhrawardī, 95, 112, 121–22
Supreme Lover, 123–24
Swanton, Christine, 246–47, 253–54
sympathetic enhancement, 218–19, 248
sympathetic participation, 251–53
*Sympathy: A History* (Schliesser), 217–18
*Symposium* (Plato), 7–8, 10, 35, 42–43, 44, 47–50, 52–53, 159–60, 161–62, 164, 167–68, 272–73, 325–26

*ta'alluh*, deiformity, 102
Ten Commandments, 72

Thurman, Howard, 340
Tillich, Paul, 340
Torah
   bonds of fellowship, 28
   commandments, 28, 30–31, 71–72
   first love in, 17–19
   intellectual love, 32–41
   kindness, 30
   Lamech, 18–19
   love and friendship, 22–24
   marriage, 19–21
   transcendence, 5–11, 14–15, 29, 91, 95, 103–4, 121, 126–54, 205, 206–7, 209, 224, 319–20, 333–35
*Treatise on Love* (Avicenna), 101–2, 103–4, 107, 110–11
triangle of love, 312–13
*Triumph of Life* (Shelley), 260–61
true love, Rousseau on, 264, 267–68
*tzedakah*
   derivation of, 39–40
   idea of, 6–7
   righteousness, 39–40

unification, 100, 111
union of affection, 91
Universal Intellect, 101–2
universalist love, Conway's, 224–25
Universal Soul, 101, 124
University of Paris, 129–30
unrequited love, 143–44, 325–30

Van Dyke, Christina, 9–10, 126–54, 209
*ve-shinantam*, "teach them diligently," 29–30
Vietnam War, 340–41
*Vita Nuova* (Dante), 158
Voltaire, 266

Wee, Carole, 186–87, 188
Williams, David Lay, 198
Willis, Andre C., 14–15, 339–42
Winch, Peter, 84–85
*Works of Love* (Kierkegaard), 13, 287–89, 291–99, 301, 302–4, 305, 307, 309
*wujūd*, concept of, 118

The manufacturer's authorised representative in the EU for product safety is Oxford
University Press España S.A. of El Parque Empresarial San Fernando de Henares,
Avenida de Castilla, 2 – 28830 Madrid (www.oup.es/en or product.safety@oup.com).
OUP España S.A. also acts as importer into Spain of products made by the manufacturer.

Printed in the USA/Agawam, MA
July 25, 2025

891003.001